MUSTANG SALLY'S GUIDE
TO
WORLD BICYCLE TOURING

MUSTANG SALLY'S GUIDE

TO

WORLD BICYCLE TOURING

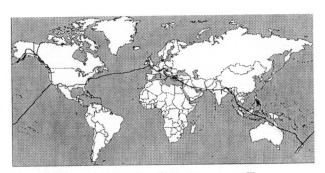

World Wander
1995 - 1996

Sally Martin

To order additional copies of this book, contact:
Xlibris Corporation
1-888-795-4274
www.Xlibris.com
Orders@Xlibris.com
25066

CONTENTS

PART 3: MUSTANG SALLY'S GUIDE TO ASIA

PART 4: NEW ZEALAND AND THE ISLANDS

PART 5: THE WEST COAST, THE DEMPSTER HIGHWAY, AND ALASKA

DEDICATION

To my beloved husband, Charles, who not only gave me steadfast support, he did all that stuff I hate like answering mail and paying bills for a whole year and one half. Also Bank-by-Phone who paid the rest of the bills. Automatic deposit by the teacher's pension and Social Security kept the necessary greenbacks flowing into the ATM which produced lots of funny money out of a slot in the wall in foreign countries. Couldn't have done this trip without them. Who will do those nitty gritty things when you travel?

This is my first and probably only book and I am trying to do the right thing, hence, the

Introduction

You must be thinking of taking a trip around the world by bicycle. Well, how silly. Or perhaps you have a lot of time to read. Or you may be somehow associated with Mustang Sally and feel, therefore, obligated to read this in case I expect YOU to remember MY bicycle trip around the world.

Questions in italics are the questions most asked during my scintillating slide show presentations. I haven't a clue to people who haven't a clue so sometimes questions and answers don't match too well. Also being old, I have a tendency to ramble off in strange directions when somebody asks something interesting. Example:

"You must have dreamed of that trip for years."

Apres retirement . . . well, most of my dreams had been of traveling about the world to compete in Cross Country ski events. Traveling would be very expensive. It is tough to save money by bicycling and camping in the winter, besides there are all those skis, poles, boots, and waxes to carry. So, to make more money, I made distracted efforts at several professions that require long hours for success. I was, unfortunately, not willing to do the long hours, nor give up any invitation, real or imagined, to travel. I ended up, finally, as a landlady with fifteen units. This was not bad for an increasing interest in sports oriented travel. Travel is complicated, expensive, and may be broadening in the weight gaining sense and if stuff is rented, lots of money is available. Please understand that I don't have to travel. I like being where ever I am. I only jump at the chance to take off over some new horizon whenever it arises. It is, after all, a new horizon.

I look at the pounds of travel brochures that arrive by mail, and try to think which ones are do-able. I have a mental list of places Iwould like to see and places I wouldn't like to see. Age is also a factor. How far can you get from life support systems at 65?

"How far can you get from life support systems at 65?"

One of my favorite travel companions was Franz Rodine, 87, from Seattle.

"What is in the Mustang Sally name?"

It came from my pals in Kathmandu. We went to a bar where *Mustang Sally*, the song, came on and my pals decided that the song was right for my trail name. After all, we had just trekked back from the Mustang Province of Nepal. The song says something about "Ride, Sally, ride" I believe the ride was on a horse, but that's pretty close. I never could understand all the words. Is it clean?

"What was the most difficult?"

I guess I can be a grumpy old rebel. Getting along with other bicyclists is always the most challenging problem. I have learned to carefully tend my store of strength and not go up unnecessary hills when riding a loaded touring bicycle. When I am tired, I must rest. When push comes to shove, I would rather go it alone than force myself beyond my ability.

"When are you going tell about your trip?"

PART 1

SHAKE-DOWN RIDE:
ACROSS THE USA,
SOUTHERN TIER

Chapter I

THE CALIFORNIA DESERT

. . . and more

"As relentless as a Texas hailstorm: there is no escape, no place to hide, and it won't quit."

Lyndon Johnson

I never liked intersections much and considered cloverleaf intersections to be one of the most dangerous places for the touring bicycle. The graceful loops that shunted I-20 from I-10 in West Texas were a climb from the valley floor into the blackening sky and increasing headwinds, but thankfully, little traffic. Decision time. If I went up I-20 I might be able to meet up with Helen and the group in Pecos. Pecos and Hanging Judge Roy Bean and the group sounded like fun but what I could see of it was up-hill. I-10 looked better on the map and what I could see I-10 was down-hill. With any luck, it would be downhill all the way to Austin where I planned to meet my husband. On the map, there were two small towns not far away on I-10. It looked like a long way to Pecos in the fearsome Texas desert with not many ice cream stops. As I straddled the bicycle and studied the map indecisively, a great blast of wind wrestled Spot, the Wonderbike, loaded with panniers, from my grasp and threw her against the safety rail. That did hurt a bit. I cowered beside the bike waiting for the sudden storm front to pass. Wind whipped the desert sand to bullets that beat my back and legs. It was suddenly cold and hailstones pounded on my head as I dug into the pack for the plastic poncho. It was an effort just to put the billowing poncho on and then it flapped like an angry rooster against my legs. Then the rain came. It was a downward force that squashed me further down toward the road. The few cars and trucks on the road had turned on their lights and pulled off the pavement to let the madness of the storm front pass.

I figured that this was a sign that I was to forget the erstwhile companions and Pecos and head down I-10 for Brogado. When the winds eased a bit I climbed back on the bike. It is not a good thing to bike in such wind, but with the poncho frantically flapping, I biked down I-10. Brogado turned out to be just a small collection of dreary trailers like many West Texas towns. The next town to try was Balmorhea which was off I-10 by a couple of miles. The side road went down and then turned so that finally I wouldn't be going directly into the gale. Each pedal was an agony. I pushed the bike through the wall of wind into an area of cultivated fields which sloped downward to a distant oasis where a group of tall trees were twisting wildly in the wind. The road led to a pair of roads on either side of a raging stream that lead past a few scattered, ramshackle, adobe houses with flowers, lawns, and tired cars around them. In despair, rainwater running into my eyes, I would have paid any price for glasses with windshield wipers, I cruised both sides of the stream and finally came to a restaurant and across the street, a stout, charming, two-story, adobe, Spanish-style inn.

The inn had traditional balconies and beautiful grilled windows. It advertised rooms for rent. After trying several doors, I found the owner. He was trying to control a flooded area of his office and was very sympathetic. A cozy ground floor room was available. He didn't seem to mind the wretched condition of either the bike, with its soggy packs, or the chilled and miserable bicyclist. I was led to a guest room in the back of the building that had its own little patio that overlooking therampaging stream. When the owner left, I peeled off my wet clothing, wringing each piece in the sink. The bathroom had a comfortable tub which was soon filled with steaming water into which I sank with a thankful sigh of contentment. Later, I dressed in the only dry clothing I had and picked my way across the still flooded street to an old adobe ranch house which over the years had grown into a spacious restaurant. The main feature of the restaurant was its huge fireplace which held a warming fire. Friendly Texans chatted with me about my trip and bought me a local favorite drink. I feasted on a fine steak and slept a peaceful night.

There. Done. Adventure travel books must start out with some perilous adventure which leaves the reader waiting, breathless, for the series of incidents which leave the hero/heroine clinging by the fingernails to the highest cliff or on the brink of death by starvation or trussed up in a large stewpot with the natives looking around for matches. I try to have some dignity. It is not easy when on a loaded bicycle. Think of camping, crawling out of a tiny tent on hands and knees. Anyhow, traveling the roads with ten ton trucks is adventure enough and does not need the extra challenge of biking through Borneo or over the Andes. (The Pecos group had a miserable night with tents blowing down, etc.)

Mustang Sally's Trip Preparation Tips:

Surely you have a list from the last time you went camping. Get that out. (If you haven't been camping, try it this weekend.) Make a list.

Draw a line through anything on the list that you didn't use and don't carry it anymore. Chances are that no matter how Spartan your packing, you will be mailing lots of stuff home later.

Underline everything that will keep things dry in a deluge and take those things.

You are going to camp:
Tent, the lightest, for 1 person . . . 3 ½ lbs.;
Mattress, the lightest 1 lb.;

Sleeping bag, the lightest 3 ½ Lbs.;
Ground cloth, 4 oz.;
Flashlight, 4 oz.,
for a total of 8 lbs.

Do take all this. There are so many places where there is no motel. B&Bs, bless them, are expensive and may not be thrilled to have a grubby biker in rooms filled with chintz and antiques.

Clothing: wind jacket, rain jacket, sweater or fleece jacket, undies, shorts, slacks or bike tights, shirts, both long and short sleeved and no sleeve running top. Fifteen lbs. I like plastic clothing like polypropylene for cold weather and cotton for hot. However, cotton takes a long time to dry and food dribbles last forever.

Tools: Swiss Army Knife, two tire tubes, tube repair kit, tire, tire tools, wrenches, vice grips, chain tool. Five lbs. Tape spare spokes to the frame. I like bike shops. They can take care of the tough stuff.

You now have 30 lbs. of gear.

Books: *Youth Hostelling International Guidebook. Lonely Planet Guide.* 2 Lbs. Total:32 lbs. That's it. If you are a little old lady who writes: Sharp's Zaurus 5000; who draws: sketching pencils, 1 pen, cheap watercolors in pan; who takes photos: small auto focus with zoom lens, film and mailers; other stuff: total @37 lbs.

(Send finished memoirs and artzy stuff home before it gets rainsoaked or lost. Never pass a Post Office without donating something.)

The bicycle panniers carry all this gear and are very important. Good panniers are expensive but will make it around the world several times. A backpack is bad because wearing it puts the center of balance dangerously high. Also, with a backpack, each little movement requires a lot of correcting which will exhaust the back and shoulders. Carry the weight on the bike and as low as possible and distribute it evenly front to back of the bike as much as possible. I watched ladies on this very tour lay their bikes down which jostled the panniers off the racks. They just pulled the bikes up and rode off into serious crashes when the dislodged panniers went into their wheels. They composed outraged letters of complaint to the manufacturers of the same packs that I was using with no problems. The moral is: try to lean the loaded bike rather than lay it down. If there is nothing to lean on, at least check to make sure everything is firm when you get back on, before you crash. A kick stand is useless. The loaded bike curls up around it and drops to the ground like an exhausted cat. Besides, it marks you as a hopeless novice with a cheap bike. Take it off.

The bike weighs 23 lbs. Your goal total is the 60 pounds permitted as baggage by the airlines. Bikes are free on overseas travel but must not exceed the weight limit. One nifty help to me was a big, very gaudy, cheap, but tough plastic bag which I picked up in Greece. That bag is big enough to hold all four or five panniers so they are not so beaten up in air travel and are easier to find in the baggage claim area. If you are using a bike box or bike bag to travel, the plastic bag is still helpful because you are allowed two bags and the bike is one of those two; the panniers are in the other. I have a small, simple daypack that went around the world once before. It rides on top of the back panniers and is very handy when doing city day tours or just shopping after putting up the tent. It fits under the seat in the plane.

Save all the bills for anything you have to buy. Stuff is covered by your homeowners policy but you will need the receipts to claim lost or swiped items. If you buy stuff during the trip, mail the receipts home so they don't get soaked by the scattered showers and turned into paper mache.

There, now. The mechanical things have been expedited. I figured the total of my bike and gear to be worth $2600. For some of our Wanderers, the bike alone cost $5000.

Mental Planning

No matter how annoying it may be, write out a little essay about why you are biking around the world and what you hope to gain.

Sample essay: "Why I Want to Bicycle Around The World"

I'm writing this because Ole, organizer of the World Wander Bicycle Tour, suggested it. I feel put upon doing it. Is this a busy work assignment? I don't write much about myself or about anything else. However, I suppose that the organization of thinking required by writing should help to clarify goals and at the end, I shall be able to see if goals were accomplished.

1. How to answer the people who say, "Are you nuts?" Right now that question is coming from the mirror.

My biggest problem is that I have so much to give up: my most beloved husband, the only really fun person in the whole entire world; my slothful, exciting, travelful life as a world class competitor in swimming, triathlon, X-Country skiing; My kids and grandkids who will be one whole year and 1/2 years older when I get back. My comfy bed. It is the world's most comfortable bed. My tub. The world's most comfortable tub. My dog. She loves me but she is a real tramp and loves just everybody.

2. Survival. At sixty-five, I will be the oldest person in the group. I have done my time on the rock pile as a public school teacher for twenty-seven years. I raised three married, college graduates of my own. I have my comfy pension and, being almost 65, my adorable Social Security, so finances should not be a problem.

My real focal point in this is the leader, Ole. He travels on a mountain bike and carries one hundred twenty pounds. He should be someone that I can keep up with. Keeping up is important to me, I don't want to be a drag. I can usually keep up with fellow Pittsburgher, Helen, who is about 10 years younger and who has done a lot of bicycling. She also carries a small mountain of stuff which makes her bicycle slow and cumbersome.

3. Learn More about the World. The most excellent prospectus that Ole put together outlines a trip across the US, Europe, India, Nepal, Thailand, Malaysia, Australia New Zealand, and ends up with Alaska to San Diego. Ole has done a lot of touring and seems to have the tour planned very well. Helen and I went to check him out in Nantucket where he was the award winning manager of an American Youth Hostel. He has long hair and a beard but swears that he does not do drugs. We also met his pal Ric. Ric worked on Nantucket as a bartender and lifeguard. The original idea of the around the world bike trip was his. He was quite charming and attractive. Regina was in Nantucket then also and her friend Jim. Everyone seemed interesting and pleasant to me. But what do I know? After being a landlady for seven years I have lost faith in my ability to judge character.

4. Health. I expect to replace about ten pounds of winter fat with an equal amount of bicycle muscles after we are out a while. X-Country skiing should keep me in generally good shape until March when we start then it will be a matter of bum bunions for a while. If I carry too much weight on the bike my arthritic old knees will give out. One out of every five days is to be a rest day and Ibuprophen should handle any other problem. Older people don't recover as quickly as young people.

5. Travel in comfort. 18 months is a long time to be miserable. I'm centering on Ole because I white-line as badly as anyone else. White Line Disease refers to the white line on the side of the road: One stares at that white line hour after hour: if 60 miles is a comfortable day . . . why not do 70 miles . . . if one survives 70, why not do 80 . . . if 80, why not do 90, etc., etc. until the stress runs into a wall of fatigue and severe depression and loneliness set in. That is "White Lining". Ole suggests 200 miles every five days.

I've done a lot of bike touring myself. I'm hoping that Ole is the tiny pocket of sanity in the mad, mad world of bicycling that will prevent this from becoming the usual ride-until-you-drop syndrome. When I did Bikecentennial '76 ride across America, there was a girl whose goal each day was to find a public swimming pool in which to float about. It took me years to respect the reasonableness of such white-line disease prevention instead of my own stress-laden 80-100 mile days. Having to cook meals and tenting on this tour may make a large difference.

Travel styles may be a problem. I am up at the crack of dawn and have some distance in before the traffic gets bad then I take a late breakfast break. It is best if someone in a pleasant cafe does the cooking. Then I survive on munchies until 5:00 in the afternoon.

The routine of bicycle touring will set in: the automatic lifting of the body from the sleeping bag. Socks seem to fly to the feet and shoelaces tie themselves. The rising and slow stretching that herald a day of enjoyment of the body being required to do the kind of work a body can do. The observation of dewdrops and "rosy-fingered Dawn." The automatic packing of dew-dampened tent and gear; the tingle of fear at setting out another day into the unknown. Shoving hands into stiffened gloves and buckling on that helmet. On to the bike with a grunt of pain when the rear and seat meet. Then off into the sunrise with dew or fog collecting on glasses and eyelashes, a nip of cold biting through the jacket, and telling oneself to enjoy the coolness because it will be a scorcher later. And humming down the byway one muses that this is the best of all possible places, and the only thing to be doing.

My bicycling family is always off the road by 5 PM because that is when the whoopee's start cruising, looking for something to hassle. (Do I want this? Do I need this?) I checked with Ole to see if he would mind if I motel it sometimes and he says fine, do it.

But to get back to the subject. Why I want to ride my bicycle, etc., etc. Helen suggested it. I met Helen when I was on a search for friends. I seem to have parted company with the neighbor-type friends who were raising kids at the same time I was raising kids. They are still there in the neighborhood and they are holding up well, in good shape and healthy, enjoying life. They go to the beach once a year and sit around for a week or so. I bike to North

Carolina to get to the beach. They walk a couple of miles a day. I aim to swim a couple of miles a day (before biking or running). I'm a freak. But I don't like to feel like a freak all the time. Well, so is Helen. She is a great hiker and biker. Then there is Alma with whom I hiked across England. She is interested in doing part of the trip.

They are both younger and stronger than I but have tolerated my slowness. So does this seem like the way to enjoy friendship? Extreme effort and traveling together? Perhaps it does seem right. The way to go. We all work and make money, we all are ready to travel at a small suggestion. I have sold my landlady business and Helen and Regina have given up their jobs for the trip. We all have kids and grandkids to brag and worry about. We will know each other very well before the end of this trip and I hope it will be the lasting friendships. One is alone most of the day when bicycling. I hope for people to converse with over dinner and breaks, the amiable camaraderie of the road. And anyhow, I am leaving my best pal behind.

Bicycle touring is intense. If it works out, it works out. If not, hopefully the trained leaders like Helen and Ole will be able to do skilled leading. My observation of failed ventures is that they collapsed internally. Power struggles. Most of the people planning the trip whose resumes I have read have done most of their bicycle touring alone. The World Wander will be a crowd of individualists.

I am ready for the physical and emotional challenge. I'll be there the first day. I'll be there for the first month, the first continent, the first world. I'm ready. Let's start tomorrow." End of essay.

1. Everything I gave up to go was waiting for me when I got back: husband, kids, grandkids, and I have a lot of great photos and can give travel lectures about the trip. Silly twits say, "Write a book!" From now on. I'll say: "You, first!"

2. I survived. The leadership chose to clear out the trash and that was me! But I survived.

3. Friends. Oops. Alma and I are barely speaking. Helen and I are not making big plans to travel together. My best buddy is still my beloved husband. We are closer than ever.

21

According to my doctor I have the bones and heart of a 20 year old!!! (but I'm going to WeightWatchers.)

I'm still tired.

I'm still a freak.

"So, start already!"

FEBRUARY 27, 1995

Salt Lake City Airport: Just parted from my husband of forty-four years. We were both very sad and wondering if this expedition, bicycling around the world, isn't incredibly stupid. We like each other a lot and have a mutual dependency. I hate for him to go off without me. I hate to leave him and go. On the other hand, it is nice to be free for awhile. The breaks from each other add spice to our reencounters when we go through a reacquainting. I had decided to never go anywhere without him because I miss him so much. He is just more fun than anyone.

Then along comes Helen saying,

"How about taking a bicycle trip around the world?"

Imagine how flattering!

There was Ole with a well-prepared twenty-one page synopsis who was looking for companions.

I said, "Sure. Why not?"

Salt Lake is in a beautiful area but like so many places in the U.S., it looks as though all of the arable land is being taken up by housing and shopping centers. The urban sprawl just seems so wrong.

In the time when the Roman armies conquered most of Europe, they would set up a camp each night. With the great organization that typified the civilization that the Romans brought to the savages of Europe, they laid out the camp surrounded by four walls and gates in the center of each wall. Two roads intersected in the center of the compound and in this area were the commanders. Each soldier knew where his sleeping area should be and he built his section of the wall before he worked on his own housing each night.

There were requirements for water and fuel for the six thousand men as well as being sited in an easily protected area. The walls traditionally had a ditch in front. To get this they dug down six feet and this dirt used to construct a six foot wall on which they put a six foot palisade fence. All this effort, made and then abandoned as the legions moved on, was not scorned by the local nomads.

Like most other humans, the locals copied the conqueror's technology in order to be able to conquer or not be enslaved or "ethnically cleansed". And so, they moved into these easily fortified areas when the Romans left and put up permanent walls and built cities. Throughout the Middle Ages it was much better to live in a walled city which could protect you from wandering bands of hoodlums. Bad guys were banished from cities and ended up in gangs that wandered the country side, sort of like our Old West So, cities were small, tight areas and when you left them you were in the country side which was farmed by people from the city. Thus the farmland of Europe has been spared the sort of encroachment and urban sprawl for which the United States is famous. In our West, you had to assert your claim to land by living on it, no matter how lonely. Thanks to the government, it was impossible for farmers to live in town as had Europeans. All this means that Europe is great for bicycling. Is it too late for the U.S. to save green land around our urban sprawl and stop the spread of the poisoned lawns? Actually, Roman poet Horace used to worry about the sprawl of the cities back in ancient times.

San Diego FEBRUARY 28, 1995

I joined the groups recommended for US travel but was too scatterbrained to use them. Most require writing ahead so I won't recommend them. Too much planning. If you can't just phone ahead, forget it. Better to travel with the Christmas list and visit old friends and relatives. The first visit was to San Diego Mary, my Penn State pal. My first peek outside of Mary's guest room in San Diego was a shock—Wow! snow! Actually it was the white gravel that Mary has for grass. The back yard of her house is a golf course, so they don't have to mow that either. That is planning.

Meanwhile, at the San Diego Hostel, Ole had arrived and departed with a person that he had known eight years before. With my Spartan spirit, the sumptuousness of his loaded bike being one hundred twenty pounds was mind boggling. There is also 39 year old, tiny female whose bike load is one hundred sixty pounds. These people wear blue jeans!! Blue jeans are heavy, stiff, slow drying. They will rasp the skin right off your body. My clothing is all plastic. Nylon and gortex and lycra are light, shed rain and dry quickly when washed, rained on, or just sweated up. Lycra is just a bunch of little bitsy rubber bands that glue themselves to every middle-aged bulge and so, OK, so I look ridiculous. But my bike weight with bike, tent, clothing, sleeping bag, and eating gear, is a carefully calculated 60 pounds. Both Ole and the young thing of 39 have chunky little mountain bikes while Spot's chrome-moly steel on 1 1/2" tires looks positively sylph-like. Spot is about fifteen years old and one of the last true touring bikes produced by Panasonic, a Japanese company. I used the Panasonic because it was almost a twin to Helen's Schwinn. In a pinch we could interchange parts. Actually it hadn't been used much in the last six years because I had converted a mountain bike for touring duty. If the Panasonic dies, I will drop back to Green, the Diamond Back mountain bike. It hadn't occurred to me to question whether the Panasonic would make the proposed 25,000 miles until people started asking such things as:

"How many bikes will you need for the trip?"

Bike shop people, with whom I discussed this, thought that the Panasonic would last very well. It would need new cables, chains, cogs, and, of course, tires and tubes. This is just maintenance. They reminded me of a Cannondale that local racer, Danny Chew had used for five years as a measure of how much punishment bikes can take. Danny is a big fellow who pounds out 3000 miles a month and has won RAAM, the Race Across AMerica. My husband Chuck has used his Swiss made Allegro, Big Red, for 25 years. Every once and a while he gets it stripped down and painted. It shows no sign of deterioration. It isn't a touring bike, just an all purpose road bike and, oh dear, may not have sufficient braze-ons to carry the stuff needed when he joins me on the tour. It doesn't hurt the longevity that his Allegro is fully Campagnolo, and therefore the Ferrari of bicycling.

The Panasonic, "Spot", arrived by way of UPS at a bike shop in San Diego and was mostly assembled when I arrived. UPS is cheaper and safer than plane transport for a bike inside the US. But, I had to take her back to the bike shop to get the front wheel tuned and the cogs retightened (first bike shop) and decided to replace Spot's saddle with a new Georgina Terry seat made especially for women. We were acquainted with Georgina when she lived in Pittsburgh. She has gone big time since moving to Rochester, New York.

I had debated about calling Spot "Old Paint" in honor of her Rustoleum touchups. Spot is a female because she will turn on you for no clear reason and do injury. A lot of mechanical things get names in our family. They are probably all descendants of my mother's car, Dynamight. Dyna might work or might not work.

Mary took me to lunch in the grand old hotel where "Some Like It Hot" was filmed. Pictures of Jack Lemon, Tony Curtis, and Marilyn decorated the walls. Later Mary and husband Bob, a retired Navy Commander, treated me to a delightful dinner in a restaurant that overlooked the bay where the carrier Enterprise was resting. A Pacific sunset over the water was background when one of the Americas Cup yachts sailed by. The yachts nest here. We wandered down there and peeped at the women's yacht.

The next day, Ole and I opened the box of T-shirts that I had ordered my daughter Kitty, the artist, to design. The design was a map of the world with a little biker making a dotted line tour. Red and black on yellow tee shirts. We ooohed-and-ahhed and a friend of a Wanderer wanted to buy one—SUCCESS!! I had the map put on the back because I find it so very annoying when people use a finger to trace the course over the boobs if the map is on the front.

THURSDAY, MARCH 2, 1995

First person to greet me is wearing the T-shirt. This is shirt day. The T-shirt guy was right. I am the only person, in the world who likes medium tee shirts. No, Regina likes mediums also. She took two, I took two, and we gave away two to Jody, the pretty young thing who is a white-water rafter from Maine and her girl friend, Chris. I gave the rest to Ole, suggesting that he sell them to make money for an emergency pot. The smallest girl (about 90 pounds) with 140 pounds of bicycle gear—wanted an extra large to sleep in! So I held off the women until the guys got their shirts. It must have worked out because there are none left.

Last night's dinner cost $1.00 each. At the meeting, nineteen of us gathered and planned to try group cooking. (Helen is opposed to group cooking.) We will meet for newspapers and TV at 9:00 A.M. and we will leave at 9:30 and push because we are going from sea level to the twn of Ramona at 2000 feet. Two of the group riders decided to join the group so late that they didn't have tents. The first evening there were some group activities like talking about yourself and making bets on how many get to New York (attrition: one of three) and how many get to San Diego again (attrition: of 40%). Thank goodness we didn't have to read"Why I want to ride my bike around the world." (As it turned out, all but one made it across the US. Eight women started and twelve men. Four men finished the entire trip and **all eight women.**)

Ole's announcement that he did not wish to be the leader of such a large group was a shocker. He got us together and figures that is enough. He is done! This is not inconsistent with his stated position that six to eight traveling companions would be best. Did I say that he did all he did for free?

Chas and I were in Canmore, Alberta, Canada for the World Masters Championship Cross Country Ski meet just before I came to San Diego. The most exciting thing that happened to me there was meeting up with Dick Hunt, the U.S. Coach, at the Parade of the Athletes, who said,

"Mavis Jones is looking for you".

"I don't know Mavis," I said. Why is she looking for me?"

"If you do the relay there is a sure medal and she thinks you can beat the Canadians and get a first place."

I'm not medal hungry. Much. My chances of getting an individual medal at the world championships are non-existent. So I was trying to explain this to Chas and also figure out how I could be getting a medal at the Championship and the same day, be starting a bicycle trip around the world in San Diego, when a young man standing nearby said,

"Are you starting March first from San Diego"?

"Yes, and our leader is Ole Ohleson."

"So are my Dad and Cynthia."

The young man was from Anchorage, Alaska and was at therace to be a guide for Barbara Lewis, a blind skier from Connecticut. The blind skier is also black so she stands out in a crowd of cross-country skiers. In the small world category, she got her masters degree from the University of Pittsburgh. Anyway, to make a large world really small, the young man's parents, John and Cynthia, showed up at San Diego. If they sounded like superior people, that turned out to be very true.

20 World Wanderers leaving San Diego. March 1, 1995.

March 2, 1995. Day 1 was an all day cruise of bicycle friendly San Diego's charming harbor bike paths and lanes to a canyon which then went up and up. Helen and I were off and pushing the bikes through Ramona to a state park where we cooked and ate spaghetti in the dark. There is an unfortunate lack of daylight hours in March. Then it started to drizzle (it never rains in California). The mouth of my bivvy, (a Gore-Tex Bag that goes over a sleeping bag) couldn't be open to catch the breezes. Claustrophobic I became. I was using the bivvy because it is lighter than a tent. When the bright green bivvy is open it looks like the alligator that chases Captain Hook. There is just enough room for one tired biker inside. I climbed in the bivvy and faded out. At 1:40 A.M. I awoke in a flood. All the goodies I had piled by the mouth of the bivvy to keep them away from varmints were soaked. I grabbed the whole mess and slogged to the ladies room in the downpour. I was quite comfy there for the rest of the night.

Day 2 was enough to keep anyone from envying our adventure. Helen and I pushed the bikes up hills that were obscured by the chilling downpour (it never rains in California).

It was so cold that Helen and I opted for a motel for the night. Regina joined us and we dried gear and listened to the tale of the mountain lions: Helen and Regina had come out to California from Pittsburgh two weeks early to get in shape and so Regina could practice camping.

At the first campground they heard about the mountain lion that had died of bubonic plague. Disturbed, they bought body and bike alarms to frighten wild animals. At the second campground they heard about a 51 year old lady jogger who had been killed by a mountain lion. We don't dwell on the really abominable but the rangers killed the lion and found pieces of the woman inside!

At the third campground the passage of a small animal set off the bike alarm at 3 A.M. and made our bicyclers most unpopular.

Day 3. Today was our day off and it started in Julian at 32 degrees on the top of a mountain. We went down-hill through a heavy, cold, rain and bitter wind chill. I had to stop to warm my aching hands. Down and down we flew, to the valley floor and

Anza-Borrego Desert where it was warm. Ole and the guys did pushups. The women watched, thrilled. At Borrego Springs we had a half-day to wander around the desert oasis's unusual palm trees and worry about tomorrow and how much water we will need to get to the next stop. Farmers were selling fresh asparagus which I like raw.

MARCH 5, 1995. After gazing at the stars until I drifted off, I was awakened by the patter of raindrops on my bivvy around 1:00 A.M. Desert. California. Never rains . . . Groggily giving some thought about this as being a problem, I grabbed the bivvy and headed for the ladies room. A bivvy is portable and can easily be slung over the shoulder to continue the night's rest, broken by rainfall, in the ladies room. One of my fellow campers (is using fellow sexist when the fellow is female?) said,

"I wouldn't sleep in that thing if you paid me!"

Actually the worst is that I keep leaving the ground cloth behind and having to buy new ones. The other bicyclers are perhaps more mentally prepared to spend 19 months outdoors because they have a tents that are palatial. A tent is a tiny island of privacy.

I was now in the ladies shower with light, paper, pencil and time to perfect my writing craft. I was so happy. Truly. The euphoria of biking hits me at night and I am too happy to sleep.

It is so hard to write and keep notes in this camping mode. No table. No light. I had offered to produce something in writing by March 10th for the Health and Fitness Magazine, with the deadline on the 18th. I plan to mail it home and Chas will get a friend in an office to type it up and then send it, with all the mistakes, to the magazine. Everything concerned with the writing is wrapped three times in plastic bags.

The third day was when Jody and Chris split. See, it isn't just grouchy old ladies that can't get along. We camped wild in the desert where someone saw a rattlesnake. Now, the bivvy was great because I could watch the stars. The fourth day started with a nice easy ride to I-10. As Helen and I started up the ramp over the interstate, the wind came howling down the valley with such force that we got off our bikes and started walking them up the interstate ramp. Liz, the short but tough rider of the 160 lbs. pack was ahead of us. She fell flat on the pavement, and though she up quickly, try as she might, she couldn't get her scrambled bike back up. A RV with an elderly couple arrived and couldn't go around Liz and we all watched with horror while she grappled with her recalcitrant bike. Finally, John, a large and gentle biker from Seattle arrived and helped her get the bike off the heavy road. He also helped her rearrange the load. Helen and I finally arrived at this scene in time to see tough Liz take off biking up the next hill which climbed a couple of thousand feet into the Joshua Tree Monument. Helen and I pushed our bikes up the mountain to the top. The Joshua Tree only grows over 3500 feet of altitude. The Joshua Tree looks like a yucca with a skateboarders haircut.

I had two different children on my Golden Age Passport, Helen and Kevin. Golden Agers are free in National Parks plus everyone else in the vehicle. Perhaps Uncle Sam feels that anyone kind enough to travel with old folks (remembering Pampers) deserves a gift in return.

MARCH 8, 1995 A busy day in 29 Palms. I stayed behind the group to rest and write my article for Western Pennsylvania Health & Fitness. The monthly magazine plans to carry a series of my essays about the trip. The Pittsburgh Post Gazette also plans to carry a series of articles about the aging, old crone who is biking around the world. Walking around town to locate the library and FAX gave the first injury: blisters from walking.

The article for Health and Fitness:

"Nineteen bicyclists gathered in the American Youth Hostel in San Diego, California on March 1, 1995 to begin a trip around the world.

There were seventeen of the twenty-three who had said they would be there plus two who decided to come at the last minute. There was one from California, the leader Ole Ohleson, a couple in their 20's, two girls from Warren, Pa., a bicycle racer (from Montana), a big, tall, red-haired fellow from South Carolina, a computer guy from Seattle, two from Texas, the couple from Anchorage, one very young man speaks native Spanish because his parents were with the United Nations and lived in different countries. He left a three year bride at home. Michael, a former lawyer, left a 15 year bride at home and there am I with a husband to call when there is a phone.

There are one each recently divorced male and female, a seven-year-separated female, one survivor of four divorces, and I guess the rest are neverevers. Bicycle tours tend to not be intensely romantic because lack of privacy and not a whole lot of romantic discretion. We ladies are at our most awful as we crawl out of our tents grumbling about whatever body part has gone bad. Guys tend to be weirdos and gear heads endlessly debating frames, derailleurs, and tire tread. They also worry about numbness of the personal bottom bracket. Nevertheless, we'll be out there a long time. Jody and Chris are cute girls and Louise is incredibly sweet and obliging. Regina has a good friend who traveled with us for several days, in his car. Liz is a ruggedly independent person.

The group was assembled from ads in American Youth Hostels and League of American Bicyclist publications. In response to inquiries Ole sent out 140 copies of his excellent prospectus. The prospectus outlined the general time and place of the trip and detailed the first couple of weeks. It suggested proper gear and expenditures. He expects to spend $12 per day and that includes housing, camping wild, and cooking vegetarian meals. I checked with Ole before we started and he said it was OK if I hostelled or motelled and ate in restaurants. I brought all the cooking gear anyhow, but I hate the cooking stuff.

Ole, Louise, and Helen have all left American Youth Hostels jobs for the tour and three of the guys are computer persons. Regina worked at PlantScape in Pittsburgh. Kevin sold everything he owned and is suddenly an abused person with his riding companion being loud, ex-Air Force, Gene who can embarrass us all with his entertaining but ear-splitting comments.

Most have a riding companion. Helen and I have been riding together for years now. Jim bikes with us a lot because he is just a little faster than we are but likes our company. We also bike at about the same pace as the John and Cynthia from Alaska and with their help, I may be able to convince Helen that drafting is a viable option for headwindy days. Liz, with her heavy load brings up the rear. Regina rides with us off and on but she is younger and packed lighter than Helen and goes faster than we do. She is usually with Ole, John, and Louise.

We broke up into four groups to cook. Each day one group figures the menu, buys the food, cooks and cleans up. The evening meal cooking has been very uneven with a couple of hungry guys wolfing down most of the food, so we also had to dish the food up. One night when I helped cook, I made a nice salsa of what I thought was quite a few fresh tomatoes and peppers. The first guy picked up the bowl and poured the whole thing on his food and ate it all. Another night everything was so spicy that I could eat only bread with two slices being allowed. Whatever the problems, paying one or two dollars for dinner is a good deal and it should get better as we get better at estimating how much to buy. However, the death of ambience has to be cooking by flashlight and eating in the rain.

The first split among the bikers was the youngest. Jody and Chris, friends all their lives in Warren, PA, split because Jody got mad at Chris. Jody was riding alone near Mecca, Ca. Mecca is a very Mexican town on the north end of the Salton Sea. She was riding alone through groves of oranges and grapefruit when a truck load of young Mexicans boxed her off and the guys piled out to offer comments and whistles. Jody is a classic babe, with long blonde hair and a great face and figure. She wears flashy bike clothes. She looks good even on a bike. She's not just a pretty face. She let loose with a string of invective that cleared a path through the men. Later, she got mad at Chris because she wasn't there, riding with her, to be another person in case of trouble. They didn't ride together much after that.

There have been a lot of flat tires, the majority suffered by the Alaska couple and their brand new bikes. One guy's rear cog disintegrated. In both caes passing vans were flagged down and pressed into service to carry the offending bikes and parts to distant bike shops.

New equipment is the chanciest stuff. Regina's bike is a $5000 hand built to order by Tom Kellog and Jim's is a $5000 titanium touring bike. The rest are various stages of ageing down to Ole's which is, like my Spot, touched-up by Rustoleum. Ole's dad painted "Bruce's Bike" on the frame. Ole's and mine will be the last to be stolen." End of article.

Last night, here in 29 Palms, I had a dream that ex-President Eisenhower and Mamie were biking with us. Ike looked great and all I could think of was that the Republicans could really use him. He smiled a lot and didn't say no when I suggested it. Wow! Later we were in a Greek Village and I was trying to remember how to do the line dance and couldn't but the Greeks couldn't remember either. There wasn't enough to eat because no one expected all the reporters that showed up. After I woke up I was still trying to call Chas to tell him about riding with Ike and Mamie. When I finally remembered that Ike was long dead and the Republicans will have to do with out him, I wondered what the "Father of the Interstate Highway System" would have done had he been touring on a bicycle instead doing Europe in a Jeep. We'd have had ICETEA earlier and lots of rail-trail conversions completed.

My tiny, bitty home town hates the very idea of the rail-trail we could have had there. They hate me, too, for being a part of Rail-Trail. Such a thing. It always reminds me of the plaintive Beetles song about not understanding how people can hate people who only want to sing love songs.

MARCH 9, 1995. The desert from way more than twenty-nine, 29 Palms to the Colorado River was a two day effort with the group turning north ten miles on the California side of the river to camp in a Bureau of Land Management site.

There were group discussions on my rest day absence and the possibility of splitting the group into young/strong Vs old/weak came up—possibly precipitated by my wimping. No one responded and the motion died, but one offshoot was Gene coming around with a list and telling me that I could send home both of the fuel bottles and the stove I am carrying. Hallelujah! Great! At the last mail point I mistakenly sent home my second pair of bicycle tights and all of my socks. I hate the stove and survived 150 miles of the Appalachian Trail without it. It starts the burning period with a flame that shoots about 20 feet high, plus a puddle of flame that flows over the picnic table and has everybody running to put the fire out before the woods or whatever goes up in expensive smoke. If you set a forest on fire these days you have to pay for the people who come to put it out as well as the lumber damage. Not to mention the helicopters with flame retardant. I would have to go back and teach another twenty-seven years to pay it off.

The food was better tonight, rice and lentil beans with salad. Seven of the now 20 are vegetarians so the decision was for the carnivores to get their meat from the non-group meals.

Chapter II

ARIZONA . . . from arid (dry) zona (zone?)

We enter into Mountain Time as we cross the Colorado today. Ole suggests canoeing on the Colorado for our day in Lake Havasu City. The river is placid here, dammed at Parker and rimmed by thousands of mobile homes and RV parks.

MARCH 11, 1995—LAKE HAVASU CITY (2:30 AM)

I'm back in ladies room, being driven out of the campground by noise and winds. I'm encased in a shower that is big enough for my gear and me stretched out on the mattress. I thought I would be able to write some but feel better sliding back into the bivvy where I have been since 8:00 PM.

The Colorado River here is attractive to the Snow Birds from Seattle and Canada and lined with trees and RV Parks. And it rained and rained.

Ole fell for a scam he says. Lake Havasu City is the phoniest resort place going. Lake Havasu's claim-to-fame, other than being a cut above the trailer towns of portable aluminum along the River, is the London Bridge. The bridge, of "London Bridge is falling down" fame is still in London. This bridge is one built after WW II. The Brits decided it wasn't what they needed and were going to replace it with another. A scam developer named McCullock bought it for scrap and shipped it over here. He had an island built on the Colorado so it had water to bridge and there it is: a pumice-stone, Roman-style bridge. Nothing special and we came 100 miles out of our way to see it!!! On bikes!!!!

Regina has begun to suffer severely from what was probably Helen's cold. Ole has it also and I have a raw throat. Regina had to go to hospital to get a piece of stuff removed from her eye. Her bike attacked her while she was cleaning it. (This was a warning, it fell apart in Athens.)

Bikes have a personality. My bike, Spot, has developed terminal cancer of the nipple. I wasn't happy with the front wheel and had it checked in Pittsburgh. The wheel didn't come with Spot but was a replacement for the one I had leaned against the van in a parking lot while I loaded the bike in the van. I drove off without the wheel putting the wheel in also, and when I went back to look for it, some inconsiderate person had walked off with it. The Ambridge bike shop, back home, said they had just what I needed and practically gave me a wheel they had sitting around. This was many years ago. Anyway, the wheel was checked in Pittsburgh. I was still nervous about it and had it checked in San Diego. It continued to sound like it was falling apart with groaning, grinding spokes. The bike shop guy here said the nipples were too rusted to tighten, just since San Diego. Well, why not? We've had eight of eleven days raining plus sand which is the worst of bicycling in the desert. So Spot will grind and groan to Phoenix, where with luck we'll find the bike shop that can give me a new front wheel and perhaps a new back wheel.

Tonight should be interesting. I've been invited to an Alcoholics Anonymous meeting. Seems three of the guys are AA. One of them has been sober for sixteen years and still has a messianic fervor. He says that there will be AA groups all over the world and also that he is as happy as he can ever remember, being on the bicycle tour. Bike touring can indeed be euphoric.

Jody, the young and pretty, will leave us in Phoenix to go back to her old job for two months. She is a white water guide in Maine and this is probably the most exciting time to work and make money. She is somewhat bored with us old folks but she enlivens our drab lives with tales of having smuggled jewels out of Kathmandu.

The AA meeting was moving. Anything that happens there is confidential. I felt honored that they asked me to go. The four (of nineteen) who are AA were at first, pretty leery about discussing their problem with the rest of us. Me, I always figure that all but the very young have some sort of monkey on the back and that they have come out bicycle touring to wrestle with the problem. With one of the ladies it is a family who died young of diabetes, heart disease and stroke. Those aren't exactly immune system disorders but throw in a really stupid social relationship that needed to be forgotten. Tomorrow we head out toward Phoenix. What makes me run and ride? In my mother's family the women all died of cancer before they were fifty. I believe deeply that bicycle touring has kept me alive and well for 15 years of borrowed time already.

Helen, Spy, John, and Ole, offering advice.

MARCH 12, 1995 410+65 = 475 MILES SO FAR!! I'm writing this from an almost abandoned house trailer. What ever works as a place to write, use it. We held up after 65 miles from Lake Havasu in Bouse, Arizona. We planned to collect and then go five miles into the desert to camp. The restaurant where we stopped had excellent food and the owner offered her back lot area, grassed, and a double-wide trailer for restroom, and for free. After going to bed at 7:30, I woke up at 4:30, chilled and wet with dew and retreated to the trailer to thaw out and dry out. It was a clear night and crisp and the bivvy was soaked by heavy dew for the first time.

Yesterday four of the strongest young men took off from the group to go adventuring on the dirt roads. We will meet with them in Phoenix on Thursday where we will take a free day to give another group time to rent a car and drive north to see the Grand Canyon.

MARCH 13, 1995 Chris, the pretty young thing of 27, is the first to be sporting a knee wrap. Knees can go bad from bicycling.

Mustang Sally's Back and Knee Rule: If the knees go bad, raise the seat; if the back goes bad, lower the seat.

The bad knee fear keeps me wanting to avoid mountains. My knees are eroded from arthritis. When they are bad, a ropy thing in the front of the knee cap flops back and forth in front of the cap until it swells up a lot then it quits doing that and just hurts, for miles. For days. A year and a half. Chris has been riding alone. Her friend Jody is now riding with Kevin who is always accompanied by comedian Gene. Gene rubs every wound raw at the top of his voice. You laugh through your tears and shame.

We rode back to Parker from Lake Havasu City back down the Colorado which is placid and lined with RV's and mobile homes. It is a meeting place for snow birds who will soon head north, leaving the desert to fry in the summer heat. Some have already left. The AARP is the most active group in Bouse, AZ.

The ride was easy with little or no wind, and the 65 miles accomplished by 3:00 PM. There is a 60 mile or 80 mile option today and it will depend on wind direction and velocity which I will do because I need to get to Phoenix with my bad wheels. Ole broke a spoke. It was on the back, cluster side, of course, in his $600 wheels. He is most annoyed at having to go through the tedium of removing the back cluster to replace the spoke. We met a pair of young bicyclers in Parker yesterday who had broken spokes in a back wheel (cluster side, of course) and had lost two days biking already. They had no spare spokes, no chain wheel whip, no vice grips, or spoke wrench for the dark side of the wheel. Actually I don't carry all that stuff either. As we chatted with them a police car drove up and the policeman had information about a local bicycle weirdo who might be able to help.

Leaving the Colorado we headed for Phoenix. I was alone, aiming for a bike shop when the back tire picked up a huge staple that went in the bottom, hit the rim and popped out the side allowing the green slime inside to come spurting out. I got a taxi to take Spot and me to a bike shop. The bike shop needed time for all this and I taxied again to a very expensive motel in the city.

The next day, after another taxi ride to recover Spot, I arrived late at the designated meeting place at the A.Y.H. Hostel in Phoenix. The female manager wandered about with a beer in hand and a fairly slack attitude, but hostels are deluxe after camping out. I ended up singing old camp songs with her while she played guitar in her quarters. Some of the group camped instead of staying at the hostel because camping is cheaper yet. Ole was so grouchy that I got all upset and, sniveling, inquired if he wanted me to leave. He said no.

The young guys returned, distressed, from their tour of the dirt roads. The roads were so eroded that, after much pain, they were forced to turn around and come back the way they went in. The young, fast, strong group was wanting to move on and annoyed at having to hang around waiting for the Grand Canyon group to collect. The Canyon group never got to the canyon. Hey. It is March and the Canyon has altitude. The Grand Canyon has snow.

Mustang Sally's List of No-Nos For Touring Groups: In Phoenix truly strange decision was made: no one has to show up at the appointed place at the appointed time. Anyone could just go off in whatever direction for whatever reason. I, personally, found that to be very disagreeable. I don't mind (prefer) traveling alone but I like being able to count on place and time to meet. We travel at such different speeds. Not only that, but, if you are not in the place where decisions are being made, too bad! Why would anyone bother to inform you? My advice: Don't skip meetings no matter how tired or inconsequential you are. (I'm too tired to finish the no-nos.) Anyhow, however stupid the decisions, you must, slavishly, brainlessly, agree. Nod your head and smile. A lot. Michael tried to set up a phone system that you could call if missing or lost. I never figured the phone system out. My darling husband became the info center.

The biggest worry: Every national park has a strong pull on our non-leader. He seems determined to see them all. Fine idea if you have a RV. My problem is that every mountain is knee pain. My case of "climb every mountainitis" was cured years ago. I'm becoming depressed at even the thought of my precious knees on a fully loaded bike when it is still freezing cold in the higher altitudes.

MARCH 19, 1995 Tucson, Arizona. I'm again doing the bike shop scene. Spot, the Wonderbike, was having those wheel problems and then the chain started going "clunk" and slipping. So, I went back to the "absolutely last bike shop in Tucson". Now the main pack is sitting around at Saguaro (pronounced Sue-air-o) National Monument (East) waiting for the group to collect—or not collect. They will have until around 3:00 PM to look for a state park campground which may or may not exist and I guess I will miss this exodus and perhaps never see them again. We have Michael's telephone answering system code to call if lost beyond hope. If anyone remembers to use it.

The Tucson bike shop is having a problem with Spot because she is, like me, such an old fossil that they don't have replacement parts. The problem this time is the back hub. At first they thought the axle was broken but have now decided that this axle is fine but the sealed bearings are frozen up from lack of attention. Can I blame the rains of California and the sands of Arizona? The guy in the shop picked up a hammer and started toward Spot. He must have heard me gasp because he stopped, and with great sensitivity, suggested that I take a break and get something to eat. How thoughtful to throw me out while he loosened up my rusted darling.

The bike shop guys respect Spot and always assure me that a touring bike is great for touring, much better than a mountain bike, they say. I think they would replace all kinds of parts on the poor old thing if they just had them. I'm beginning to compile a list of things to be requested every time we get near a bike shop. Chunky mountain bikes are usually the only things for sale in the bike shops nowadays. Spot has a recurring dream of rolling into a REAL bicycle shop where, in a display case, against a backdrop of red velvet, the royal blue cases display an endless variety of Campanolo grupos sparkling as though they were Rolexes or Liz Taylor's diamonds. Spot finds the just right grupo and has it installed and rolls proudly out the door again.

Our Liz says you can get all this stuff by catalogue. Once you have it you have to locate the bike shop that has the tools to install the equipment. I wouldn't have the crust to do that. I would let the bike shop order and install parts. The bike shop in Tucson could do nothing about checking my back hub or bottom bracket because they didn't have the tools. So Spot and I move on.

Mustang Sally's Guide to Heat Stroke. The next day was hot again and I was feeling waves of nausea and a pounding headache. I left Helen and Jim and pushed hard to finish the miles on the Pima Pioneer Highway and get out of the heat. When you are prone to heat stroke and know that one of the early symptoms is "clouded thinking", you can't figure out whether going faster to get there sooner is smart or just another example of "stupid think"!! It is important to lower the temperature of the body core.

This time, going faster to get out of the heat worked: I left Helen and Jim, who had decided to rest in the boiling sun, and really cranked and caught up with the main group, exhausted, to sit around and recover in an air-conditioned restaurant. I was entertained with tales of the group politicking. Ole has admitted to having an "unfriendly" attitude much of the time (was anyone else in tears?) He had laid out the first three weeks of the trip in careful detail in the brochure, and we are doing that. He knows the area and he usually makes all the decisions, but when asked for instance what decision has been made while one was sleeping, responds with an answer like, "You have to make up your own mind".

Well, honestly, this is bothersome. What mind? I don't know anything about anything. We are a long way from home and I feel like going home to sulk. Somehow he may have confused all the psychology courses he took with the leadership courses. An enigma. I have done a lot of my bike touring alone as has Ole. As have many of the others.

I took many hours of "touchy/feely" stuff, sponsored by the school district. The hours spent boosted me on the pay scale. The one thing that stuck was "Winners have alternatives." So, the upshot of all this distress was that I called Chas and asked him to order Adventure Cycling's maps of the Southern Tier from Austin area to the Atlantic. What intense delight! I am on such a high! He plans to meet me in Austin and will bike for 10 days.

Phoenix was before Tucson and then came Casa Grande.

I was really fried by the time I got to Casa Grande; 65 miles in 90 degree heat. I forgot to put sunscreen on my legs!!! The skin had turned shiny and transparent like red celophane.

Mustang Sally's Guide to Social Life. People will give you the addresses of family and friends. Keep these in a dry place. These are pure gold. See all these people. This is how you get into homes to see how people live. And, there is a free lunch. At Casa Grande Monument Janice Hadley Leary, who grew up in Bradfordwoods, picked me up and took Spot and me to her house. Janice was a pert, pretty contrast to our sunburned, bedraggled band of gypsies. With her gorgeous auburn hair, lime-colored blouse and crisp white shorts, she was like a breath of fresh air. Spot left a grease imprint on the white shorts as she was loaded into Jannie's van. It is great to see people's homes. Jannie's lawn like Mary's lawn in San Diego, was pebbles. We walked the dog down her suburban street and out to the desert where she takes the children to ride their bikes around the dirt tracks. The dog ran until exhausted. Her husband, Jim flies planes for a world-class sky diving drop zone near by. Jannie teaches music in an elementary school.

Anyhow, if I miss connections with the group, I know that they will eventually arrive in the town of Wilcox on I-10. Coming this far south we have avoided a lot of the Rockies but as we get into New Mexico we will be doing some 8000 foot passes and perhaps encountering snow. Nevertheless it has been fun and great biking so far in Arizona: long, flat stretches of fascinating cactus against a back drop of jagged peaks. There are lots of people like Janice and Jimmy here who just love living in the desert.

(The group never went to Wilcox)

MARCH 20, 1995 The group is having huge discussions! The upshot is that the young and strong are restive and impatient with the old and puddled. Also, the young and some of us creaky types would like to take only three months to cross the States in order to spend more time in Europe. I have missed all the discussions because I go to bed so early.

Noon and Ole was off on one of his weird tangents, extolling the virtues of 100 mile days. We had already done about 35 miles and were having lunch in a Pizza Shop in Benson, Arizona. Most of the miles had been on the shoulder of I-10 with huge trucks roaring by. This not the bicycler's dream. Ahead was a 12 mile, 2000 foot climb to the top of a pass to be followed by 12 more miles of paved then ten miles of dirt road for Jim and the rest to get to another National Park.

Helen and I had already decided not to test our skills and equipment on the dirt road to the Chiracaua Monument. We and Jim are a riding group that constitutes not the slowest, but the oldest ones on the tour. We carefully tend our strength and ability but Ole had hooked Jim into the hilly dirt road trip to Chirichua Monument by telling him he wouldn't be able to be in the rest of the tour if he didn't take the dirt road tour! This making no concessions to Jim's physical limitations that come from being in his 60's and having a slow form of cancer. Well, guess where this puts an even older female who is not going to do gravel or hills?

Mustang Sally's Guide to Competitive Touring: If you can't win fair, CHEAT! The Pizza Shop was small and not at all busy. The owner was a bicycler and had recently sponsored a mountain bike race. He offered, for a fee, the use of his delivery guy who had a big pickup truck, to the top of the big mountain. So we took a ride—past the group of about ten which was already struggling up the 12 mile mountain. Helen said it was the best $7 she has spent so far on the trip. Giggling like little kids, we unloaded the three bikes at the top and cruised nine miles down to the point where Jim got his first flat, a staple. While we were fixing the flat and chatting with a farm family, Ric, the strongest rider, came up, amazed that we had slipped by him!! So we had another laugh as he breezed off on his way. They have to have seen the bikes in the back of the pickup, right?

Well, no. On the shoulder of an Interstate you try to pretend that traffic isn't there. As Helen and I pulled into a Motel 6 in Wilcox at 5:00 the Cateye read 69 miles—our longest day so far.

Ric, the fastest rider, was Ole's buddy from Nantucket. Ric was a bartender and lifeguard and Ole was the manager of the AYH Hostel there. Ric thought up the idea for the around the world tour and Ole did the brochure. By this time they were on the outs and barely speaking. Ric had money problems. He got mad at me one day when I said I was receiving Social Security. He didn't think I should take it. I said I paid for it, ergo it was mine. He said I was getting more than I deserved. So I said that when the government quit doling out SSI, that is, giving Social Security money to people who had never earned it, I would consider it. He was mad at me about that. I was trying to not talk religion, politics, or education. Sometimes I forget.

The delight with which we snagged a ride is probably a measure of frustration, we feel with our leader. We should have switched our World Wander T-Shirts for the old "Old Age and Chicanery Will Beat Youth and Talent". When Ole, our leader, extols mountains and how much he loves them I respond,

"Me, too. In the summer I grab a back pack and hike them. In the winter I cross-country ski them. I own a condo in a ski resort. With a loaded touring bike I avoid them!"

Mustang Sally's CARE FOR TENDER PARTS

Perhaps some day the nether parts may be tough enough to ride a bike day after day wearing gym shorts like Ole instead of padded lycra bike shorts. I wear the preferred bike shorts every day because the other two pairs give me trouble. When the temperature rises even the favorite shorts, the Schnaubelt ones with carefully contoured for women padding, become like sandpaper, abrading the delicate flesh of one's personal bottom bracket. A trip to the ladies' room is the reality of pouring acid over raw membranes. At that point, Vaseline, baby powder and my favorite, baby wipes, become the order of the day. At night discrete baggy shorts allow the affected area an air bath. Given even a day's rest from the bike seat, the condition will improve.

MARCH 21, 1995 Wilcox, Arizona. Today should be an easy day, only 24 miles to Bowie, AZ, Jim Bowie?, Bowie knife? Alamo? We are on I-10 and at 5000 feet and climbing, so it should be relatively cool. When son Mac was competing big time in bicycle racing, he wanted to live in this area, in Bisbee. I can see why: the roads are bicycle friendly with well spaced facilities and it has altitude. Helen and I took a half day off in Wilcox, intending to stop at Bowie. There was nothing in Bowie but a trailer camp where the lady shooed us off so we continued on to Road Forks, doing 67 miles in five hours. A strong tail wind blew us right up the magnificent orange, poppy covered hills. California poppies are everywhere because there has been so much rain this year. Right after an admonishment to keep a journal comes this four day gap. Do as I say, not as I do.

March 25 Lordsburg. New Mexico. The next day we arrived in Lordsburg early and, leaving the bikes in a KOA, rented a car to sightsee the dirt roads of the Chiricahua National Monument. It all seemed much too civilized for bicyclers.

The dirt road went up Apache Pass and climbed again to reach the area dedicated to Cochise and the Chiricahua Apaches. The view from the top was of a fascinating array of strangely shaped rock formations that stood like well-disciplined soldiers on jagged terrain. Cochise was a diplomat who found himself in a ten year war with the US after a foolish young Army lieutenant tried to arrest him. (Info board stuff.)

We met Ole biking up the switchbacks without his gear. He was cheerful and friendly. I am sure he was happy to have found THE macho citadel after a big, masculine-only effort, and where little old ladies on bicycles won't show up.

We found the group's campsite at the monument and chatted with them a bit. Helen was tense and anxious to be politically correct. Frankly, my dear, I didn't give a darn what they thought of me or if I got bounced from the group.

Chapter III

New Mexico

March 26.1995 Silver City, New Mexico.

March 27, 1995 To arrive in Silver City at all is an accomplishment! Helen and I chugged up and over the Continental Divide with no stops, no pushi

That brings me to my great poetry effort. I started this poem in England in 1994 while Chas and I were walking the heather covered moors. As we climbed the mountain to the Continental Divide, the cactus and scrub were, like heather, no more than knee high. This can be a problem for discreet, middle-aged ladies. The poem is based on the British thing of calling a toilet a "loo".

NO PLACE TO GO

What do you do in lieu of loo,
When as far as the eye can see,
There's not a bush, nor fence, nor tree?
What do you do in lieu of loo?

What do you do in lieu of loo,
When nature calls you to account for
Three cups of tea and the water fount?
What do you do in lieu of loo?

What do you do in lieu of loo?
If I were queen of some great nation,
I'd trade it all for a gas station.
O what do you do in lieu of loo?

47

The AYH Hostel in Silver City New Mexico was one of the nicest in the US. It is in a big old house next to the court house in the very pleasant, old section of town. The architecture here is low: adobe or mud-brick look. The fruit trees are in bloom. It is an oasis in this desert area. A small university here seems to attract a wild collection of young folks who patronize the thrift shops for their clothing and hairdos. Restaurants are a wide range from pure Mexican to gourmet and decorated with original art. Billy The Kid is the local claim to fame. There is a nice bike shop and all in all this is the most enjoyable place that we have stopped. Friday evening there was the local version of the Mexican "paseo" with cars cruising the main street.

Bicycles are usually not permitted on interstate highways but we did quite a few miles on I-10 in Arizona. Here in New Mexico they are not as friendly about it but as there is no alternate road, it is permitted. The Tour group continues to ebb and flow but three will not be showing up here in Silver City. Liz had a dental problem and has pushed on to El Paso. Michael has gone to Taos and will not be seen until . . . ? Michael is carrying a six-by-eight-inch computer and a printer. I have checked out the word processor and believe that I can eliminate the printer if I just use a phone wire to FAX the stuff to my home FAX machine. So I asked Chas buy a Zaurus 1500 for me.

Spot, my trusty bicycle has just visited the bike shop and the total repair sum since San Diego is $234. But everything that can be replaced on a 12-year-old bike has been replaced except the bottom bracket which they assure me is as smooth as silk. When they say such things the part praised for its trustworthiness is sure to be the next to go bad. At least the sealed bearings that die and the wheels that go bad do it slowly so I can get to a shop for repairs.

Spot, the Wonderbike, points out the grinding noise from the bottom bracket of Jim's new, expensive, titanium bicycle with a "see there" attitude. The titanium has some sort of thing where you squeeze in fresh grease from one side and the dirty, ugly, old grease comes out the other side. The bike shop guys praise Spot's joints and assure me, one more time, that Spot is the way to tour.

They are astonished that the people on mountain bikes are using knobby tires instead of the faster road slicks. The mountain bikes all have knobbies because Ole said there would be a few dirt roads. Frankly, I can't picture any more dirt roads now that the plan from the brochure is finished and the group has taken over the making of the route.

Actually, I had left Spot to rust the last five years and done my touring on Green, the Magic Mountain Bike. I had adapted the mountain bike by putting on bull horns and aero bars and road slicks. The bull horns give more grip and encourage the biker to tuck out of the wind rather tan sitting up like a billboard. The road slicks gave me the ability to go "off road" when the 18-wheelers were chasing me down. I could go into a ditch and come back out without having ruined the bicycle. Spot can't take that kind of abuse. I am using Spot because she is comparable to Helen's Schwinn Voyager and we should be able to share parts. Green, the mountain bike waits patiently for the call should Spot fall completely apart.

Spot has a theory about mountain bikes. Most mountain bikes are driven to a remote spot where the owner forces them up nasty roads and down sylvan paths. When the derailleur is crushed by a rock or a stick rearranges the spokes, or the chain is tangled around the handle bars, back goes the mountain bike on the car and is driven to the bike shop, no problem. The heavily weighted World Wander mountain bikes are going through sand which is a cancer in the innards. The bottom brackets grind. Ole's $600 wheels continue to break down under the weight he is carrying, which includes some 40 lbs. of books.

"Mountain bikes are not touring bikes", says Spot with a disdainful sniff.

The ad hoc map committee met and laid out the route to Tupelo, Mississippi. There the group will be split with some going on up the Natchez Trace and on through the Appalachian Mountains to New York. The rest of us will stay flat around Atlanta to the coast and up to D.C. where we will enplane for the British Isles. We will all meet in London on July one.

Talked to Chas. He has bought me a Sharp Zaurus ZR 5000 for my writing. We will meet in Austin and head into Louisiana and perhaps take a bus or car to New Orleans. If we are fortunate enough to arrive on a weekend, there is an ad that says we might be able to catch the jazz festival featuring Branford Marsalis, BB King, James Taylor, etc. in addition to the local jazz people and excellent gourmet food at the festival for a mere $7 per day.

On one of our many days off in Silver City, Helen and I rode out in a car with a teacher from Albuquerque to the Gila National Monument in the Aldo Leopold Primitive Area. The road is so narrow, mountainous, and twisted that the Park Service doesn't even charge a fee. Cave dwellings there were used about 40 years by about three dozen people. They were in a lovely spot with fresh running water not too far away. We were allowed to climb around the ruins, perched high on a cliff. I tried to imagine living there. My theory is that they were abandoned because it was such a long way to the toilet. On a dark night climbing along the face of the cliff, that first step could be really bad. The area is dedicated to Aldo Leopold. He founded the Wilderness Society to raise money to preserve wilderness areas. A number of areas were chosen but by the time he had raised the money only the Gila was still wild enough.

I bought "Pilgrim at Tinkers Creek" by Pittsburgher Annie Dillard at the Visitor Center and am enjoying her description of an area we may bike through in southwest Virginia. Helen bought Leopold's great classic, "A Sand Country Almanac".

March 28, 1995—Deming, New Mexico. It was a windy 52 miles from Silver City to Deming. The wind was out of the east and while my group went east I was going alone, southeast. So I parted from Helen, Jim, Liz, John and Cynthia and the main group because I just didn't feel like going over Unnecessary Mountain, especially when it involved going up to 8000 feet when we are in the grip of a cold spell. The other John and Ole had biked out to the Gila and John said their water bottles had frozen over night.

The Continental Divide was beside my road for a while. It was a pile of earth that was so even it looked as if it had been bulldozed.

There were high peaks all around but this unassuming hump divides the waters of the Pacific from the Gulf of Mexico. It is surprising to see how much of the area is flat with jagged peaks and ridges thrown up all higglidy-pigglidy. One doesn't really have to do mountains and mountain passes to go east.

The day seemed hard and I am tired. Probably the biggest advantage of the group is hearing the rest of them moan about how tired they are. Actually, I like being alone. The group plows the same themes until they are pulverized into dust.

Michael appeared in Silver City only to break a tooth and leave for El Paso and Liz's dentist. I, too, am headed for El Paso after which all of Texas is ahead. A pretty scary thought.

The push to leave earlier for Europe succeeded by moving the departure to Dulles Airport rather than—how nuts can you get—Kennedy. Ole wants to take a loaded bike through New York City? Now the push is to get a date for collecting in London or perhaps at a town where a ferry departs for Europe. A date of July 1st which would give those of us who would like to cut the US to three months and tour England or Scotland before July 1st, I'm one of those. I need to put in some time doing route planning for myself. I have no enthusiasm for Ole's planned route through Poland.

Mustang Sally's Guide to Journal Writing: Read. Reading Annie Dillard gave me a real boost. My high school English teacher had said I had a talent for the humorous, personal essay. So here I am, trying to be funny. Anne isn't particularly humorous but she is frantically first person. Her enthusiasm for being able to see new things is pleasant for a traveler. I try to see road runners and coyotes but they elude me so I shall stick to the slower mesquite, creosote, yucca and the flowering California poppies. Most of the days I travel between fences with not even a cow or horse in sight. When I finally encountered a herd of skinny cattle, they looked at me curiously but ran away when the camera's telescope buzzed and I didn't bother to take a picture of their rumps.

I think of all sorts of interesting things when I ride along so I try to remember what they were when I get someplace where I can write. It is pathetic. I say the same boring things over and over. I have a tiny tape recorder and tried that but it is terrible. I say the same things over and over. Did I notice that I say the same things over and over?

I am happy writing in restaurants and cafes and park restrooms if it is raining. But I say the same thing over and over. If all you have time for is to write is letters or cards to the home folks, ask them to save the communications and give them back when you return. That is much better than nothing.

March 29, 1995 Deming, New Mexico. Early in the morning, I cruised the town of Deming. Most store fronts are functioning and the few buildings are two stories high. Small groups of Mexican men collected at certain places as they did in California, waiting for rides to work on the ranches. I didn't see much farmed land but perhaps it is east toward the Rio Grande.

A buoyant group of mixed young and old, male and female, Mexican and Anglo came in the breakfast restaurant and my guess was that they were teachers on in-service day. I have been there, done that. They are working today and I'm not. Yo! When I pass a school with the yellow buses lined up I'm enormously cheered. They are inside, peering out the windows and I'm outside, finally. I spent so much of my life in school buildings while my heart was roaming the hills! Now, I'm glad I did because I really did love teaching and the kids, and now I'm healthy and financially free enough to, . . . just think of it(!) . . . take a bicycle trip around the world if I like.

Money. Finances may be the deciding factor for some of the group. One can live cheaper in one's own country because the knack of living at a low level of lentils and rice and camping wild is fairly easy to achieve. Europe is expensive which is probably why Ole's plan is through the cheaper countries like Poland and Czechia. Ole and his tough-it-out group bragged that they didn't have a shower from Phoenix to Silver City. Ole won't even camp in a KOA because it is so expensive. He allots $2 per night and a KOA camp can run me, camping alone, up to $18 or $20. That is more than a hostel. He could stay free in most hostels because of being an AYH employee but spurns that sort of comfort. The other bikers are scattered along a continuum to Regina, Jim, and I at the highest-on-the-hog level of cheap motels when I'm alone. Regina scorns my Bombay palaces and heads for the Hilton in the larger cities. Those who sold stuff to finance the trip have to be the most careful because the tendency is to blow the whole thing early on.

The ATM is my best pal. Push the card in a hole in the wall and money comes out, money that the government direct deposited. Magic. Works everywhere but India. Long story later. If you keep falling asleep and don't make the make the long story, Citibank has ATMs in India.

March 30, 1995. The route turned east along I-10 or on frontage roads to Las Cruces.

Never thought I'd be so very pleased to see Texas. In the first cafe, it is like being in Mexico. This cafe has a big Viva Mexico! on the walls, everybody speaks Spanish. I have the theory that the Mexicans will take back everything they lost back in 1845 by moving massive numbers over the border. Case in point? Had steak at this cafe.

When a student in Mexico, I and my fellow students would speculate on what kind of meat they were calling steak and would decide it was horse, mule, or donkey. It was about one-fourth inch thick and tough as shoe soles. That exactly describes my breakfast steak. While sawing on it the coffee spilled and the rice and refried beans sprayed over the flowered oil-clothed table. Should I eat the fresh tomatoes and lettuce that garnish the plate? In old Mexico that is a sure case of "la tourista".

The Tex-Mex mermaid in a painting on the wall has dark, almond eyes and light brown skin, like a nice tan. She also has brown nipples. She is surrounded by cattails!!! Perhaps a fresh water mermaid from the pitiful, not grand, Rio Grande. If you grew up beside the Ohio River, The Rio Bravo, is not brave, and is a creek. I assumed that the unfortunate river has had the water sucked out of it for irrigation.

I followed an irrigation canal from Las Cruces toward El Paso, marveling at the fertility it can produce. I breeze through miles of dormant pecan trees then a lush, brilliant green field of spinach. The terrain is fairly flat and winds are calm although reported to be fierce, blowing from El Paso to Las Cruces. Los Cruces means the crosses. They were put up in honor of whites massacred by the Indians.

The waitress in one restaurant was a lovely, slender, shy chica who had to wait on a bunch of macho idiots who were humming little love songs to her. They stared and four heads followed her as she moved around.

An old but mouthy lady at the counter turned around and dressed them down. They laughed and blushed. It was all very friendly and the men went back to talking to each other.

At one of my many stops I met a fellow tri-athlete; a teacher (18 years) who has done the Hawaii Ironman (1993: 15 hours/10 minutes). When I told him that I had 1996 Ironman ambitions he said to get into the lottery. He was full of intelligent questions about bike touring and then dragged himself away to his school. My advice to him was to keep the nose to the grindstone. In twelve years he can be retired and free to travel. He will be in his fifties and still able to trek.

Chapter IV

DEEP IN THE HEART OF TEXAS

March 31, 1995 El Paso. Slow start today, I debated about holding up a day to rest and go across the border to visit Ciudad Juarez. I'm tired and shaky in a sort of long lasting bonk. Ended up spending an entire day getting my essay off to Health and Fitness. This is the third day. I feel better when I'm riding than when I'm sitting but the queasiness persists. Should have had that gall bladder out? It is sorely stressed by spicy Texas cooking.

The group collected here at the hostel yesterday after finishing a 90 mile day. My little group was not awfully friendly. Perhaps they are just tired after long miles and little rest. They want to be at the Carlsbad Caverns when Ole's group gets there and so left with a few hours of rest after a 90 mile day and headed off for the mountains again. This wasn't the original deal. It was supposed to be 50-60 mile days and a rest day every fifth. They are coming down with a bad case of "white lining."

Mustang Sally's Guide To Vicious Traffic: Jim was actually hit by a car on the way in. The driver was trying to buzz him and the mirror bruised his shoulder. He wobbled some but did not go down. So what do you do? Try to learn to memorize license numbers. If you can get one of these despicable wretches, prosecute.

Most drivers have been very generous and pull over into the other lane if they can. I try to give the good guys a wave to let them know that their thoughtfulness is appreciated. The least considerate are usually women. Women don't seem to grasp the idea that they can move out and around a slow object. They are "color within the lines" people and aren't quick with something that might force them over a real, yellow line.

Liz and Michael have both had their teeth fixed. Tim and Kevin left with Michael for points east. Ric is back with Ole, Regina, Louise, and John. They are doing the Unnecessary Mountains with snow and rain predicted.

The hostel in El Paso is the oldest, continually operating hotel in El Paso. It had a lot of charm with leather furniture and pictures depicting scenes from Bizet's "Carmen". A sizeable group had collected and we went out to a Mexican restaurant. I had a social life again. Nights alone, I am off the streets by 5:00. The specialty was fish and I sang "Cielito Lindo" with the Mariachis. When we got back to the hotel there was a very noisy restaurant outside the window with a loud Mexican celebration of someone's birthday. It was fun to hang out the window and watch the city. Population 600,000.

My small group stopped at an El Paso bike shop. My problem was a back tire that went down a bit. I was able to bike seven miles to a gas station the day before where some nice Mexican guys put air in it. It held up but was low so I had the tube replaced with a thorn-proof one. I liked the Green Slime that got me into town yesterday but will try the thorn-proof. Third flat. The bike shop did have great display of Campy stuff but when they didn't have a long reach derailleur Spot, regretfully, moved on. We split again as my group headed toward Carlsbad Caverns. On the edge of El Paso I was stopped by a train and noticed a Texas DOT building so I went in. Department Of Transportations will always give you free maps. When I asked for a routing to Austin, they sent me upstairs to the Texas Department Of Transportation engineer, of course he is a bicyclist. He put me on I-10. I-10 is bicycle friendly with fairly decent berms and for long stretches, frontage road. Frontage road is the next best thing to a bicycle path.

The Rio Grande is about 20 yards wide here and the Mexican side is two centuries difference in time. The Ciudad Juarez side was mud huts on the outskirts. I like adobe and conside it a pretty decent building material but where it is good, it's painted. The ones I saw were mud huts with tin roofs, no paint.

On the US side, the border patrol has parking areas with little roofs that will protect the patrol wagons from the summer sun. The old green vans here not like the fresh white fleet of vans in Deming, New Mexico. One would think that the farms here would need a lot of pickers for spinach and pecans. If the border patrol actually shuts down the inflow of illegal aliens, that must present a problem for the farmers. I'll be cycling southeast along the Rio Grande perhaps the deplorable impression of Mexico will be corrected.

The sun is going down in a blaze of yellow with the gold edging purple clouds on a light blue sky, I will be off by daybreak tomorrow to beat the morning rush hour. Senior dinner at Pizza Hut—$2.69. Spaghetti and a drink.

April 1, 1995 April Fool's Day. The best joke I have seen is a street called Fort Aleza. Ja Ja!(Ha, ha) Don't get it? Fort is Fortaleza in Spanish and there is nobody called "aleza" so Fort Aleza is two language joke! Oh never mind.

I can't see all the way to the Rio Grande but the canals I have been following on Route 20 are part of its life's blood. Rich farms stretch, on either side of the road and on the US side climb the hills with roads, railroads and the interstate. On the Mexican side it is the barren, cactus covered hills. Why, when Mexico is capitalistic also? Is the business climate so poor that Mexicans or gringos with money can't make a farm there? Why is it so nice here and so poor there????

Fabens looks very Mexican in that most of the stores are barred and grilled like fortresses. Is the crime level really so high that the reasonably well to do have to put themselves in jail?

A touring couple on a tandem, Peter and Anne from Anchorage, pulled into my motel. They know John and Cynthia because they, too, are cross country skiers. Peter was at the Canmore World Championship Cross-Country Ski races when Chas and I were there the end of February. We took off the panniers and, leaving them in the motel, and rode a couple of miles across the border into Porvenir, Mexico. We picked up Mexican Route 2 north of the town and followed it in. The route number ended in a dirt road at the south edge of the town. Porvenir was in the grip of the siesta and nothing was open. In spite of 4000 people it was wretchedly poor with few shops and a scary looking cafe and no restaurant. A pack of eight loose dogs was near the road as we came flying back but they didn't bother us. The Rio Grande here is supposedly very polluted and not much water at all, but it would have been fun to have had a bird book to identify a wide variety of ducks and plovers that in spite of the pollution, were enjoying its meager pools. Ironically, the English meaning of Porvenir is "future".

Still bothered by the difference between the US and Mexico, I asked a lady at the laundromat and she said that the water in the canals comes from Elephant Butte in New Mexico, not the Rio Grande! An historical marker in Tomillo confirmed that. It said that a US government land reclamation plan back in the early 1900's that brought water from Elephant Butte to the Rio Grande valley and caused a big boom in the 1920's. The depression brought hard times from which the area did not completely recover. They still grow a lot of cotton on the US side. It seemed fertile and prosperous to me. Elephant Butte now has a large lake. It is close to the town of Truth or Consequences.

April 2. Busy barn swallows have just returned to Sierra Blanca. They have two hatching periods in the summer then leave for the winter. They always came back to the same nest. The cafe owner is happy to see them back.

I biked out early to get up a mountain before the heat got bad. The couple on the tandem never appeared. It seems impossible that they could have had a worse time on that mountain than I did but tandems suffer on the ascents. Perhaps they decided to take in a church service. None of the world tour group has made the slightest effort in that direction. Fatigue begins to get a grip on me. I'd like to take a nice Sunday nap. (Met Peter again at the 1998 Cross-Country Ski World Championships in Lake Placid.

They had a back wheel go bad and had returned to El Paso for repairs.)

4700 feet here which is higher than Van Horn but there is a pass between here and Van Horn with the wind blowing fiercely. The owner of the cafe has been having an inner ear problem for six months. She walks as though she were a sailor on a wildly tossing deck. Her helper also is walking strangely.

The cafe owner responded,

"Mountains, I guess", to my questions about why it is so much better on this side of the Rio Grande.

"This is the USA and that isn't.," was as clear an answer as I ever got.

Mountains would make it a bit cooler in summer. The border patrol guy lunching in the cafe was young, Anglo, sandy mustache.

"Politics. Mexicans have lousy politics", he said.

I said that if I were over in Porvenir I would be spending most of my time trying to get into the US. He laughed and said he would also. He'd just keep coming over until he figured out how to make it stick.

It is hard to understand how anyone could be make a living out of any place as God-forsaken as Sierra Blanca but there are a couple of hundred homes (trailers) here. I have now spent an entire hour and $2.75 in this cafe and the tandem has not appeared. The swallows, las golandrinas, dart about the main street.

The coffee is excellent but probably has caffeine and in a few minutes I'll be bouncing around and want to tackle that 32 miles! No. Giving up on the tandem. They were going south from here, following the Adventure Cycling Southern Tier maps. There is a park of note, the Big Bend National Park that is on the Adventure Cycling tour.

April 2, 1995. The month anniversary of leaving San Diego and I have only done 37 miles and am about to call it a day. I was up and onto the road before 6:00 AM so I can at least claim to have put in a very tough six hour day. It is 32 miles uphill and into head winds to Van Horn so I'm getting what is advertised as a $20 motel to lay over. The Wheelmen have the saying that if you are going uphill and into the wind, you must be going the right direction

People who notice bike tourists tell me that evin used Room 21 in the El Cheapo motel last night. He was ill and late arising and I am early and I only missed him by a couple of hours. Michael and Tim had been here looking for him yesterday. So, Michael and Tim are together, Kevin is solo, and headed by the shortest route to Austin. I had heard they were going by way of Carlsbad, New Mexico, the tough guys way. But here they are, wimping out like I am. Taking the easy, fewer mountains, route.

I made a big move to Lina's Restaurant. People here are not self conscious about wearing cowboy boots and hats.

Lose some weight? Eating enough to keep from being shaky at the end of the day or, worse, first thing in the morning, is not conducive to weight loss. Don't know how to solve this one. I have lost about five pounds. For poor performance on the hills son Mac would say "lose ten pounds". The fastest bikers who are also the skinniest, are losing weight and worried about it.

See the World! The Annie Dillard book is as big a help as one could hope for, for really seeing what is out there. The presentations at the national parks are very helpful. Chatting with locals about local conditions is the best.

The local news has been about a beautiful, young Tex-mex singer who was murdered by a woman fan—shades of "Bodyguard" or "Murder, She Wrote".

There is to be a gang summit in El Paso which the local media thinks is proper because "gangs" started there. Really? How could anything spread from El Paso which is in dead center of nowhere? Are these the same "gang summit" people who were in Pittsburgh? Is summitting a career for those dirt bags? Do they wander around the country staying in nice hotels and giving speeches about being a jerk? Probably they are funded by the federal government. On the other hand, it may be cheaper to fund gang summits than to keep them in jail.

Finally it is hot. Actually we had enough hot days in Arizona to get a sunburn which has since faded in the chilly days that followed. California was mostly cold and rainy.

One of Van Horn's early settlers said that with its supply of sweet, pure water, air, the healthy citizens of Van Horn would have to be shot to die. Soon after that he was shot, died, and was the first to be buried in the town cemetery.

There is an old hotel museum featuring pictures of Poncho Villa—the very same Poncho Villa that I had my Spanish students sing about in "*La Cucaracha*". When Villa made raids on US territory to get money for his rebellion, he killed a bunch of people. We sent Black Jack Pershing, hero of WW I, to catch him. Pershing never laid a hand on him in a case of what was, let us hope, intentional incompetence. Villa was assassinated by Mexicans after it was all over.

The Mexican Revolution 1911 to 1921 was the subject of my Masters Thesis. I still like the thesis: that according to Mexican novelists, the peons gained very little in a civil war that cost more than a million lives. The same people were in charge before and after the revolution. Also the theme of *DR. ZIVAGO*. Shall I offer my theory on what is different between Mexico and the US? In Mexico it is like the old American South with an oligarchy running the place. The oligarchy is catered to by a corrupt government and has no interest in change, their life is a pleasant, mixture of country club, ranch, trips to Europe. They don't lend out money for upstarts or new ideas. And the oligarchy runs it all. The peon who becomes our illegal has very little opportunity to get ahead. The oligarchy is provider of all the professional people and fills all the positions of lawyers, doctors, priests, etc.

Back in 1975 when I was a student in Mexico, the government claimed 95% literacy; which was a lie. None of the servants in our casa had ever set foot in a school. Did they mean 95% of the men? Some liberalizing influences try to copy the US but the church is strong and has little interest in democracy or capitalism or educating for anything but the church.

The professors who were judging my thesis were so excellent. But they were so poor. They couldn't even afford a car.

At Kent, a town of 19, the man in the store answered my usual question with,

"Life style. They work all week, drink down all the money they make on Saturday; lay around Sunday and start all over Monday."

"Hand to mouth existence", I said

"Yeah, and the ones close to the border on this side are just the same. The further from the border you get the more decent they live."

That was the last comment I'll get I guess. I'm farther from the border now on the interstate and won't see any more Border Patrol.

April 5, 1995. I'm falling behind my schedule. I am to meet Chas in Austin on April 12. The problem is the spacing of the towns. I don't want to exceed 60 miles but that isn't awfully convenient, so I go short miles rather than long miles. I-10 remains very hospitable. There are the unused frontage roads along most of it. Perhaps they are for the interstate traffic when the main road is being repaired. Actually there are very few road repairs and I miss the orange barrels that bloom along Pennsylvania roads as spring arrives. I am mindful of a statistic that Pittsburgh's Allegheny County has more bridges than all of Texas.

It rained as hard as it can ever rain in a desert between Kent and Balmorhea and was such a downpour that I didn't get to see much of pleasant Balmorhea. It is a real town and attractive with cottonwood trees and a creek and an old ranch house turned cafe with other refugees from the storm and a roaring fireplace. Van Horn to Balmorhea with 71 miles was my longest day. Got in at 4:00.

I am determined to find all these miles of desert interesting. Some of it is gray-blue grasses and barren shrubs that show no sign of life. Further on the shrubs (Chaparral?) are leafing out and the few, skinny cattle look less bored with the scraggly grass.

Fort Stockton used to be called Commanche Springs has a good bit of the fort remaining. It was used to ward off raids by the Comanches who are now pretty much gone as are the springs.

April 6, 1995 Fort Stockton was the site of the "Buffalo Soldiers". In 1866 the Congress passed a law forming four black regiments for the freed slaves who were looking for a career. Before they ever got to Fort Stockton, there was a mutiny and an officer and several men were killed. The officers were white. Eventually the blacks got used to a different kind of slavery and became good soldiers. The Indians called them Buffalo Soldiers because the black curly hair was like the Buffalo's mane. They mainly fought the Comanches and in 1886 went west to Arizona to fight the Apaches (Cochise and the Chiricahuas?).

There are several of the original buildings at the historic site where a devoted local group is restoring the grounds. The gentleman dressed as a cavalry man was named Martin and came from the exact small town that husband Charles' family came from in Pennsylvania, Darlington.

The interstate is very bikeable here. There are long stretches of frontage road. These frontage roads are perfectly good two-lane roads with a wide shoulder. They have a fence between the highway and the desert that would keep out all but the smallest dogs. Most trucks and cars move out into the fast lane when they can when I have to be on the shoulder of the interstate itself. That is good because there seems to be no speed limit. I feel safer on I-10 now than on back roads with their dog hazards. Inertia has set in.

I've done most of my bicycle touring alone and I like being by myself. The endless debates and speculation wear you down. Just do it. Out west here, partner, we gets choices.

Even while in the Rockies, and since Van Horn I am finished with the Rockies, I was biking relatively flat country. The land rolls and it has occasional ups and downs. What is discouraging is that there is so darned much of it. I am trying to do no more than 50-60 miles because that seems to be about my limit and since I opt to go flatter and am at this point in time alone, I need motels, I'm on Interstate 10.

Actually I've become enamored of I-10. We encountered it east of Tucson and it has been my choice of bicycle route ever since. I-10 follows the route of the Butterfield Overland Stage which started here in Fort Stockton and went to California. I-10 still connects the few places out this way that have water. Starting at Fort Stockton and to the East is the other thing that flows from the ground, oil.

And how is Spot my bicycle, doing? Holding air. After three flats and $250 of repairs because she, like I, is old and breaks down. She and I are fine now.

You ask, where are the rest of the group? About six are ahead of me on I-10. The rest are in two groups going up and down in what remains of the Rockies to the north of here. We are to meet at the hostel in Austin sometime between April 10-14. If they don't change the place. I hear you say that if they do change the place or date I might never see them again. Yup! And, they don't feel obligated to let anyone know? Nope.

As I maintain, people who do weird stuff like bicycle touring have devils they hope to conquer by putting out a lot of effort for a lot of time, day after day.

One lady suffers from a lack of melanin. You'd think she'd stay out of the sun, but she looks a whole lot better than the rest of us at this point.

On April 12th husband Chuck will fly into Austin to be biking for ten days. I get so tired. Chuck is my last hope for keeping up with the group. He is a great biker, can repair anything. I can go at a great speed while drafting him. Yo! I wonder if I could just pay him to come along, carry all the stuff, make jokes . . . .

Mustang Sally's Guide to Handling Bad Guys:

April 8, 1995 Sonora, Texas. Yesterday I was up bright and early and by 2:00 had done about 60 of the 71 hot miles to Sheffield when a little old Mexican offered me a ride in his red pick-up. The good advice? . . . . don't accept candy or rides from strangers. Who knows why I took it? Well, anyhow, I took it. It was hot and hilly. I didn't realize until we were flying down the road that he had been drinking. He wanted to know if I was carrying a pistol and said he would buy it. I countered with the true fact that I had no interest in pistols but carried defensive gas and that my terrible tempered husband loved pistols and was a deadly marksman. True except for the terrible temper.

"Do you know that 25% of policemen who are killed in the line of duty are killed by their own gun? I imagine that as inept as I am, I'd shoot myself," I said. "See, this the gas." I had it in my hand.

I continued my lecture on the evils of guns and turned down offers to stop here and there with the thought that the longer we were in the car, the more sober he would be. So we passed up Sheffield and Ozona and landed in Sonora at a Dairy Queen. A bunch of huge Texans in boots and cowboy hats strutted into the Dairy Queen and glared at me. I think it was because I was with the little Mexican. This seemed like a good opportunity to get away from the Mexican, who was still weaving a bit. I stood up and loudly paid him $80—one dollar per mile—and shook his hand vigorously and left. I slid around the corner and down the street to a motel and didn't come out again. I was hopeful that I had made up the lost day and caught up with Kevin.

April 9, 1995. The parched topography changed and went from flat and down through canyon lands to some fairly intimidating hills with thickets of trees and the famous, wonderful, Texas Blue Bonnets as far as the eye can see. The weather reports threaten severe storms. Folks around here raise little bitty mohair goats and vineyards. Today was a good one.

I cruised into a gas station, had a snack and was leaving when I noticed that Spot's front tire was very soft. I commandeered a picnic table, removed the front wheel, detached the tool kit from under the seat and prepared myself to do the first flat repair in many years! I had spotted a thorn earlier and located it again. Suddenly two women were there, firmly taking the wheel, the plastic tire levers and after a three way wrestling match we removed the inner tube. It was the new, in El Paso, tube and tire. Green slime oozed where the thorn had punctured the puncture-proof tube. I located the thorn and we took turns with the pliers until we got it out of the casing. There was also a ten inch piece of shiny wire inside between the casing and the tube! I kept the tube because it was a long way to Austin and a bike shop. I found my new tube and we installed it.

I have a terrible time changing tires since the advent of high pressure tires. I whined "my poor old arthritic hands . . ." The ladies wrestled the tire back on the rim with all four levers in use. Now for the real challenge! They said an "Oh no!" to the available air at the gas station and started the pumping iron exercises with the zefal pump. When one got tired the other spelled her.

"Do you bike a lot?" I asked.

"Not really but I took a course on bicycle maintenance."

With the tire pumped up we all shook hands, the ladies popped back into their car and zoomed up the ramp to I-10, heading home to Boston.

MUSTANG SALLY'S ADVICE ON TIRE CHANGES:

Take a bicycle maintenance course.

I had tried to change a tire south of DC just off US 1 a few years ago. A bright green glass shard had punctured a big fat mountain bike tire. I'm sitting by the side of the road when a lovely black man stopped and offered a ride to a bike shop. I accepted, of course, and the huge fellow picked up the loaded bike with one hand, stuffed it in the back of his van, and drove me to his grandchildren's favorite bike shop.

1:30. Junction, Texas. 59 Miles. It was up and down for a while then flat with a tail wind since the Llano River. I'm ahead of Kevin. He was seen about ten miles behind me!!!

The scenery has made a great improvement. The ground is carpeted with green and acres of wild flowers. There are large trees which have leafed out and the Llano River had a bit of water in it. Not enough to float a canoe.

The pain that had developed in my shoulder was mostly solved by wearing two pairs of bicycle gloves. Two pairs of bicycle gloves are exactly twice as hard to get off as one pair. Each finger has to be carefully extracted from first the plastic or Lycra glove, and then the really snug one of leather and webbing.

The cafe was different because of a variety of vegetables: canned, but at least offered. It was over 90 degrees outside and I was sweaty. Inside at 60 degrees I was getting cold and miserable.

April 10, 1995 I walked into a truck stop in Segovia, there is Kevin having breakfast! He has been alone since Fort Stockton but feeling better. It is his 46th Birthday! I treated him to breakfast and sang "Happy Birthday". We charged on and lunched in Harper, having left I-10 for 290. Little by little, to allay the culture shock from the trailer/TexMex, we were introduced to the determinedly German Town of Fredricksburg. It was charming with Bierhuttes and Biergartens and the appeal only intensifies in the downtown section which is a Texas/Martha Stewart version of Bar Harbor, but without the ocean and lobster. Hordes of tourists jammed the streets. Michael and Tim were there. Brad and Chris had left their bikes and hitched-hiked to a rock formation. Later, Spy, Ric and Gene showed up.

Fredricksburg was jammed with jovial tourists but we found an RV camp south of town. There was a warm front hitting a cold front and winds that shook the trees grabbed at my tent which I had clumsily aimed into the wind. I retreated to the laundry room. It had a noisy metal roof and I spent the rest of the night there listening for the sound of the railroad train that meant that the tornado was upon me and I'd end up like the "Wicked Witch of the West", flying about on my bicycle: cackling.

I breakfasted with the group and set off for the LBJ Ranch. The ranch tour was fun and very beautiful with Lady Bird's roadside plantings of the Texas bluebonnets. The bus driver said that the caddy in the driveway belonged to Ladybird and that she was in there. LBJ was born here and kept buying pieces of it through the years. I liked Johnson and voted for the "Great Society" that turned out to be such a great disaster.

"Owa hawts" were in the right place. In a country as rich as ouhs no one should be hungry. Oh well, back to the old drawing board.

The official word here is that Johnson was not killed by the Vietman War, that he had a congenital, familial heart defect. I still think he was a victim of the Vietnam War. I bought a tape of Johnson telling jokes for Chuck who could use some new (or even old) ones.

Here is a sample LBJ joke: A preacher was annoyed with a parishioner who slept through every sermon so one day he said "Everybody who wants to go to Heaven stand up". Everyone but the sleeper stood up, but the sleeper was waking up. Softly,

"Sit down, now."

"Everybody who wants go to Hell, STAND UP!!" The sleeper jumped up and looked around groggily.

"What do you have to say for yourself?", shouted the preacher.

"I don't know what we voted on", said the parishioner, "but you and I, Preacher, are the only ones in favor."

Medicare was an LBJ thing. My 65th birthday, coming up in May, will make me a medicare person. Ric will be even more annoyed with me.

I held up in Johnson City for the LBJ tour and waited out another tornado warning. The rest of them—those young people—breezed through the LBJ stuff and went on to Austin. I kidded the clerk at the motel about not watching the O.J. Simpson trial on his nearby TV set.

"Ah figger ahl start watchin about Septemba," he said.

I trotted off to my room and did the O.J. trial and the tornado watch for a while and then strolled the lilac fringed streets.

April in Austin

How To Survive Rush Hour

Austin was bicycle trauma. I stopped at a mall on the outskirts at a dentist's who charged me $45 for an x-ray and he said I needed a bunch of teeth capped. I tried to talk him into just a filling but with no luck. Spend big money or go was his attitude. Going on into Austin, I stopped three or four times to try to figure how to get to the hostel alive. Nothing helped: not maps, not asking directions to avoid major, screaming mad, traffic. Finally, after I got a pinch flat from a gas station driveway, I called a taxi and said grandly, "Take me to the hostel."

Now, that is the wimpout that I save for life threatening situations. I didn't feel that I had degraded myself too much because I had already biked through San Diego, Phoenix, Tucson and El Paso without whining and sniveling . . . too much. I do try to do as the natives do. In Phoenix the local bike riders were riding on the sidewalks so I did also. While I awaited the taxi, a hippie biker with dreadlocks entertained me with tales about biking in Mexico and his plans to start for South America within the week.

4.14.95 Austin. Chas rented a car at the airport and found the hostel easily. I was so happy to be with him again. We had a private room at the nifty hostel which is in a park on a pleasant river. We toured the state capitol building and the Governor's mansion. The mansion was over 100 years old and a beautiful example of a southern style with lovely columns, charming, antique decor and careful landscape planting. George Bush's kid is governor there.

The capitol building's dome is ten feet higher than the one at the nation's capitol. How terribly Texan to do that and even more Texan to point it out. We got Spot's most recent flat repaired and bought and had installed: da da da dit da da: a Campagnolo long-reach deraillieur. Spot was delighted and permitted us to drive down to San Antonio to take in the Alamo, the Riverwalk, and an Omnimax presentation of the battle of the Alamo. In the afternoon the bicycle group began to straggle in. We had dinner with them. (Never saw Spy again.) I told Chas to not talk during dinner. We were already the point of some annoyance because we had the one couple's room in the hostel.

Almost immediately most of the bikers decided not to stay for the scheduled Sunday afternoon map meeting. We returned the rental car and put Chas' bike together.

I asked Helen if she wanted to go to lunch with us. Helen said she was going to stay with "her friends" and I had the feeling that I wasn't really included in that favored group.

We met Michael and Kevin in a fast foods place at breakfast the next morning. Michael was using his Zaurus and a small printer to print out letters to what must have been a host of friends. Such a nifty thing. Never saw Michael again. Heard that he and Spy were in Scotland when their bikes and gear were stolen. They gave up the trip at that point. Heard Michael got a divorce.

4.15.95 La Grange, TX. The vicissitudes of bicycling include just the sort of surprise we experienced today. We bid farewell to most of the group at the hostel, including Helen, because Chas' plane ticket back to Pittsburgh was out of Lake Charles, Louisiana and south of the planned route. We had the breakfast and were on our way on Rt. 71 though miles of blooming wildflowers. Leaving Bastrop, Chuck changed his back derailleur and the lever broke in his hands. His Allegro, Big Red, is a Swiss frame and full Campagnolo components. That broken piece of pot metal had Campagnolo stamped right on it! Shocking! After a trip to an auto parts store Chas used a vice grip to hold the lever in a middle position and we rolled on to La Grange.

Chas had ordered the Adventure Cycling Southern Tier maps for me and brought them with him to Austin. Adventure Cycling was organized as Bikecentennial in 1976 and set the first Bicycle Trail across the US, which I did most of that first year. I guess after twenty years the pun wore out and they changed their name. They also have established a Northern tier crossing, a Pacific North-South and an Atlantic North-South. We followed the southern tier trail for the rest of Texas until we had to cut south to get to Lake Charles.

4.17.95 Brenhem, TX. At a Brenhem ice cream shop, we met up with Chris. I had thought that she was gone from the trip but she is back. Chas agreed that she is a very pretty girl. It takes some looking. Her low profile look is a khaki hat and huge khaki tee shirt, and brown shorts. She is so tanned that her face seems to blend right into the drab clothing. She does not get harassed for being a lone female on a bike.(Never saw Chris again. She had not planned to do the entire trip.)

4.18.95 Conroe, TX. Chas and I sat out a rainstorm in a restaurant. Had we known it would turn bad, we could have hung out in the motel but the rain started when we were about two blocks from the motel. The town did not look like much on the map but was one huge traffic jam.

Later, the almost daily tornado warnings having moved on, we arrived in Navasota. We met and were interviewed by Randall Patterson, a young reporter from the Houston Post. This was his first day bicycling out of Houston and we were envious that he had the wind behind him. He was doing a series of articles about biking across Texas. He was pleased we were so happy with east Texas' rolling hills and glorious wild flowers. This easterly part is also lush farm land with forests of towering pines. As the hills flattened. We were, however, tortured by headwinds and threatening skies. When it is threatening here, it is scaring us bikers with thunderstorm watches and the possibility of tornadoes.

Being interviewed by Randall Patterson of the Houston Post.

4.19.95 Cleveland TX Well, poor Randall Patterson. His paper, the Houston Post, was bought by Hearst and closed down yesterday. The TV showed 1500 employees getting their final paychecks. Luckless Randall will have to pedal about 100 miles back to

Houston to get his. Randall will then find an additional problem, the headwinds that we were moaning about.

Today we did another 60 miles of headwinds, arriving in Beaumont by 3:00. We have left the Adventure Cycling route to get Chas to the airport in Lake Charles. The TV news was dreadful. Terrorists have blown up the Federal Building in Oklahoma City. What a sad, wrenching thing. I sat at the TV weeping.

4.20.95 Beaumont, TX. The bombing in Oklahoma City glues us to the TV while tornado warnings are keeping us anchored in the motel. That and Chas' sore back. The weather in Pittsburgh had been so bad that he never got out on his bike to get in shape and now he is having lower back pain.

When people say that they admire my courage, I smile in my most patronizing way and hope that they aren't around when I'm in a total flameout. Today traffic was so scary that I am shaken up. It started with sitting around in a Greek restaurant until 11:00 to wait out the latest tornado warning. When we finally got going the traffic on the Interstate feeder road was so ruthless that we were very frightened. We found a back road out of Beaumont and had a pleasant time into Orange on the now deserted feeder roads. Even the bridge over the Neches River wasn't too bad.

In Orange, Chas got to try a bucket of crayfish. I love them so much I will chance Cajun spices to pig out on them but Chas wasn't all that thrilled. How can one get a big bucket of the little guys to eat, per person? They are grown in the rice fields. There are two crops of crayfish: in the Spring and again in the Fall. There are triangular structures in the fields that look like grey pyramids, about a foot and one-half high. These are the traps for the crayfish.

Chapter V

Louisiana

. . . Born on the Bayou

4.21.95 Lake Charles LA. Now my Charles is having a real problem with his hip. Are we too old for this? Naw. It's nothing that can't be cured by Ibuprophen.

Then there is fear!! Today was the worst. We were as close to the Gulf Coast as possible. The land is totally flat, swampy, intersected by wide rivers over which are long, high, narrow bridges. We started from Orange before sunup in hopes of getting over a bridge on I-10 that has no shoulder. Although we made it to the bridge just after sunrise, traffic was already vicious. We decided to thumb. After 3/4 of an hour with no pick-up, Chas started to wave a $20 bill. An enormous flatbed stopped and we hoisted the loaded bikes aboard. The driver was bound for Sulphur, Louisiana. The helpful guy was a biker who is doing the Houston to Austin MS bicycle ride the next week. His wife has had MS for about 15 years and is still walking well. He wouldn't take the twenty until we talked him into taking it for the MS group.

After that hitch we cruised down the road until we found that the next bridge between us and Lake Charles was not only narrow but goes way, way up in the air to permit the passage of sea going ships!!! Horror on horror. My acrophobia makes any bridge unpleasant but one 30/40 feet in the air and with a huge hill in it . . . too much.

There was a convenient phone so we called a taxi to get us across it. Not a glorious end to Chas' time with me. At the big bike shop in Lake Charles, they boxed Chas' bike and then transported us to the UPS place to mail it to our house. That way he doesn't have to try to wrestle it into his sporty little car when he arrives at the Pittsburgh airport.

The rest of the day we indulged in a really nice motel with palms and a pool and CNN to watch the roundup of the bombing criminals. In the morning they will give us breakfast and shuttle Chas to the airport. I will head north to the Adventure Cycling trail to try to find Helen and the group. With any luck, they are headed for New Orleans.

Mustang Sally's Guide to Cajun Country

4.22.95 Eunice LA. I took off early from Lake Charles. Charles, Himself, and I had a great pig out breakfast at the motel and I had my cry and then started out early to avoid traffic. Rt. 90 was OK but the road to Kinder, Louisiana was kinder. Rt. 190 was OK for most of the way. Eunice turned out to be one of the best stops of the entire trip. I met Priscilla LeDoux, an elderly lady (my age) at the Jean LaFitte Museum. She offered to put me up for the night and my acceptance got me their travel trailer. In 1976, while I was biking across the US, this couple had traveled by mule train to Valley Forge, Pa. Her husband, Boo, had been a rodeo cowboy and they still have a small ranch with Louisiana long horn bulls. They are both Cajun and wonderfully kind. Neither of them had spoken English until they started school. Boo drove me out to the farm to see the long horn cows. I was impressed but also by Boo's striking, hand-tooled leather saddles. He makes them to order. On their suggestion, I stopped at the Jean LaFitte National Park Service Center.

I went through a period in my life when I read everything I could find about pirates. This guy LaFitte was almost as far from the ocean as the Pittsburgh Pirates. The Pittsburgh Pirates were . . . . Ah, the romance of sailing ships. At the park, I met a group of bicyclers on a tour of Louisiana. They invited me to a Cajun dinner and, of course, I accepted. So then I went to a production at the Park Service that was Cajun music. It was being broadcast, was mostly in French, was a blast. People got up from the audience and danced Cajun style. The male person steers the lady backwards in a large, counter-clockwise circle while doing the two step. They were all sizes, ages, and colors. Perhaps you don't absolutely have to be a white, French speaking, Catholic to be Cajun. The music was fairly lively and centered around a Cajun accordion. After an hour, I saw the bike group leaving so I trailed them back to their B&B. They left there to go to the 'Bigger Jigger' which advertised itself as a Cajun bar. The bike group people were dancing with great abandon. I joined in after a discussion with the tour leader about why Louisiana is the poorest state when its oil and rice riches are so obvious.

"Lousy government," was the answer. "You know about Huey Long. He was just one. The Cajuns are happy as they are. They still speak a lot of French to each other."

He refused to listen to anything that would jostle his prejudice against the French-speaking Cajuns. But the music and drinks were great fun. Could we substitute "Mexican" in Texas and get the same answers?

After whiling away an hour in the bar singing "I was born on the bayou," we went back to the B&B and had a great Cajun dinner which now sits heavily. Back at Priilla and Boo's, I called Chas and got the news that Helen and her group have abandoned any thought of New Orleans and are headed for Natchez, so I am off at the crack of dawn tomorrow.

That night there was another terrible, hard rain but I was happily sheltered in the Ledoux' camper trailer. (Oh, dear, the group had a horrible night about 80 miles north of me with tents being blown down, etc., etc. I must try to remember not to gloat about these events.)

4.24.Alexandria, LA The day to Alexandria has been made more interesting by the big storm last night. There are long debates when I ask directions. The problem is that it is very flat here and there is a lot of flooding. Only those who listen to their CB radios know which bridges are still functioning. Thanks to a lot of conferences with the very helpful Cajuns, I arrived safely in Alexandria.

(I biked in Alexandria, Egypt in 1983. I went out a flat road from the port to see a new palace. On the way back I went past a school yard. The sweet little boys who had been playing there came streaming out to the road to throw rocks at me. How come they don't seem to throw rocks at Bettina Selby? You can move really fast under those conditions, they didn't hit me.)

Alexandria, LA was pretty depressed on the side of it that I came inso I ended up at an elegant Holiday Inn because I saw no other choice. It was a crisp 42 degrees that day.

I wasted half of the next day just lying around staying warm and watching the grim reports from Oklahoma City. I wanted to get my moneys worth and didn't leave until checkout time. And anyhow Chas found out from Helen's kids that I am ahead of my group.

Sixty tough miles later I was being ejected from a $32 Bombay Palace motel. The guy took my money but after I got to my room, he sent his pretty little wife to fuss about poor Spot. I tried to explain that Spot had been in a lot of motels: that the one last night in downtown Alexandria cost twic as much as the Bombay Palace and went up the elevator. She was adamant and insisted on putting down a sheetto protect the carpet that Spot was already on. I did that but then made the mistake of grumbling about there being no TV remote. She went back to the office. Next, the guy called from the office and told me to get my bicycle and go! I stomped back to the office and things got a little loud.

"I'm older than your grandmother! Would you throw your granny out to bike ten more miles at 5 in the afternoon?" That didn't work. Come to think of it perhaps he would . . . .

"No bicycles. And you insult my wife."

"If I offended your wife I apologize, but please come and see for yourself that the bike is already in the room and has harmed nothing. It will do no harm. This bicycke has been not only in the Holiday Inn in Alexandria but the Drake in Chicago."

Not quite true: Spot had never made the Drake. It was Frisky, my aluminum racing bike, that had been lodged in my elegant room at the Drake on the occasion of the Chicago Triathlon.

He would not back down from his annoyance with me and bicycles. I told him that he was a really mean man to throw an old woman out on the street (really highway) at rush hour, retrivedmy money and poor spot and went on. Spot was really lively. Being thoroughly angry can really power a bicycle. And we had a tailwind. I stopped in the tourist center in Vidalia to locate another motel and complain about the idiot in Ferriday. The lady there lent a sympathetic tsk, tsk and oh, my, and did listen while I trashed the motel guy. Spot felt a bit avenged.

Catfish Time

I had a pleasant dinner of banana split in the cafe next to the motel in Vidalia, chatting with the tiny, tiny black lady cook and cute, young, white girl who ran the place. The cook was eating catfish. Catfish is everywhere here. The well-groomed, grassy, farm ponds where they are grown are a pleasure in the landscape. However, I grew up by the Ohio River when it was so polluted that catfish was the only life in the river and I have the Pittsburgh prejudice against the bottom feeder. I promised the dynamic duo that tomorrow I would be back at 9:00 A.M. to have catfish for breakfast.

So after dinner I went back to my room and was visited by a cockroach. I had the nerve to complain and got a new room. The very nice Indian lady manager said they have the exterminator in every month. Chas and I have an exterminator every 3 months in our home which is a remodeled barn. A lot of bugs had made their home in the barn and their descendents remember for these many generations. Tomorrow I am scheduled to meet with Helen and the group at a bike shop in lovely Natchez, Mississippi.

I regret leaving the coastal area without ever having seen the Gulf. Anytime I mentioned beaches, the natives curled the lip in are distressed here over forty degree mornings but happy to have the rain cleared away. There is much flooding upstream in Jackson, Mississippi and more expected, but today is just beautiful. After three days into the wind, two sixty mile days and yesterday's seventy miles, I am tired and shaky. I would have thought the fatigue would be over by now and I would be able to handle this better. Oh well. Next week. The catfish was a tad spicy and so delicious.

Chapter VI

MISSISSIPPI . . . the old South

4.25.95 Y'all got to try Natchez, Mississippi. The bridge across the Mississippi is plenty wide enough for bicycles. The river was also wide, brown, and bloated from the recent rains. Natchez is on a bit of a bluff, well out of flood range, but the cliffs are not as dramatic as the ones around Pittsburgh. It is mostly flat here.

I reported in to the bike shop first and found that the group, Helen, Jim, Liz, and Cynthia and John will be here tomorrow. Can they be as tired as I?? After checking prices, I decided to treat myself at the hotel across the street from the bike shop. The hotel is old, comfortable and so elegant. Spot is very grateful that the clerks were happy to cheerfully provide a charming private balcony for Spot to rest on. It is not cheap to sooth Spot's distress after the awful rejection from the Bombay Palace. Spot is pretty spoiled, but is aware that the budget really can't survive much more of this kind of self-indulgence. Actually, the hotel was cheaper than any bed and breakfast in this town of fascinating, ante-bellum B&Bs. I took a horse and buggy tour before my nap and a walking tour afterward. Almost every other shop is an antique store with really elegant and expensive antiques. The tour guide said that the well-to-do people here were cotton merchants who would take a shipload of cotton to England or Europe and come back with superb furniture and rugs. The best time to be a tourist here would be in October when the homes are open to tourists and a series of six half-day tours would satisfy a lifetime of longing for Tara.

About 4:00 a band from Alcorn U. arrived and put on a show. It was for a convention and then they marched off with the conventioneers following. I guess the school is all black because the kids were. They were very attractive and having a fun time although it seemed a bit chilly for the majorettes in their skimpy, gold sequined bathing suits. The music was cheerfully mellow, sort of like cajun.

I took the double-decker bus tour and got a load of statistics. Until the Civil War, more than half of the richest people in the US lived here! Their plantations were as far away as Texas. They owned many farms and many thousands of slaves. Only four percent of Southerners owned slaves! 8000 blacks fought for the Confederacy! Freed blacks owned slaves!!!!!! Natchez surrendered after one canon shot. The shot hit the mayor's house and killed his 13 year old daughter. Magnificent Natchez has over one hundred antebellum houses.

4.26.95 The group arrived and I toured the town again with them. Cynthia and John took off to see Vicksburg. I should have gone with them. Ole and group arrived and we camped with them in wild (no toilet) foulness within the city limits. I was much too spoiled for such gritty living. I never saw Regina again until the finish in San Diego.

4.28.95 Our group of six collected again and had pleasant days biking the Natchez Trace. The Natchez Trace is a National Park that celebrates the return of rafts men to Pittsburgh. I thought this was my Pittsburgh but after I became a Civil War buff and read Grant's memoirs, I realized that the Trace was headed for the Pittsburgh Landing that was Grant's first victory. The raft men would ride the rafts down the Ohio and Mississippi that were loaded with the goods manufactured in Pittsburgh, Pa. Then they would walk back from New Orleans to Pittsburgh Landing where they could catch a boat headed down the Tennessee River which flows north to the Ohio. The Tennessee River flowing north made it possible for a successful invasion of the South by U.S. Grant's Federal troops. The present Natchez Trace ends near Springhill, Tennessee, now known for the manufacture of the Saturn auto. This leaves an eastbound biker on the wrong side of the highest Appalachians. Ole's group of four was planning to go to Springhill and make the assault on the highest part of the eastern mountain chain.

Thoughts on Wearing Down:

The things I have done to try to keep myself even with the bicycle tour group are beginning to bottom out. I am a first up and out at the crack of dawn person. I have a snack of oatmeal and raisins to which I added water the night before. This holds me until the first café where I can get a real breakfast. Sometimes that café never appears. For breakfast, my choice is steak and eggs. Tough on the cholesterol but it gives the energy that kicks in around 2:00 PM. In an hour or two even the late risers would start to pass me. I travel lighter than most, this kept me up with the older, slower for awhile. Now they too are up at the crack of dawn and on the road early and are now strong enough to compensate for heavy loads. Because I was a racer, I have better bike technique: I draft like a sand spur; I can tuck on the hills like Woody Woodpecker on a down dive. But even Helen is learning to draft and tuck on the down-hills. On the up-hills where youth and talent will win, I'm dead stuff. They all leave me behind: stopping and hanging over the handlebars like one of Salvador Dali's limp watches. I hate that when it happens and it happens every hill.

Restrooms are always a problem. You MUST keep hydrated while bicycling or cramps and bonk await. If you over-hydrate you are awash and need to be rung out frequently. There isn't much of a way to judge how things are, you just have to deal with the condition that exists. Groceries and gas stations that sell food and drink to travelers should be forced to also provide restrooms. Mississippi is not a wealthy area. People are not treated with much respect for basic problems. What do the people who sell food think is going to happen to the food and drinks????

It is a pleasing countryside. The roadsides are as pretty with flowers as the Texas bluebonnet country and grassy fields roll away to the horizon in smooth waves. There are forests here and the cut pine logs pass us in huge trucks on their way to the chipper. Whole trains carry the chips away.

We often camp in town parks. Toilets, grass, trees, are all there is but it is free. I keep a better budget now that I am with the group again. The motel I had in Jackson has evened out to $9 per night. I believe I am spending around $20 per day for food and incidentals. With the tent that Chuck brought to replace the bivvy, I am enjoying starry nights.

Mustang Sally's Guide: Socially Incorrect Behavior:

As we were leaving the tiny town of Hickory, Miss., an auto driven by a serious gentleman in fairly official clothes stopped us. He said he had a complaint about **adult people**(!), **bicyclers**(!), who had relieved themselves behind an abandoned building! Jim, our silver-tongued advocate, apologized profusely and swore to never misbehave again while the rest stood in slack-jawed amazement. You know how laughter that you really can't show hurts? Having to stifle and keep a straight face got to be very painful but we did manage to behave (finally) until the guy released us and we went on our evil way. I want you to know that I was not one of the perpetrators. I had used a culvert before the town because I couldn't wait until the town. Old ladies . . . well, never mind.

5.2.95 Eutaw, Alabama. It rained last night and turned very chilly which was good for sleeping and I got the best night's sleep in quite a while. Plans were firmed up and tickets bought to Heathrow Airport from Washington, DC at $323 for the one-way ticket. An outfit I had used called Airlink got this deal. They also got me a ticket from Pittsburgh to Heathrow the same day for $342. So I will go home from D.C. to get my bike worked on at home and a dental problem handled by my own dentist. Also I have to get my drivers license renewed. I planned to drive to DC to get visas.

Chapter VII

Alabama

. . . The place where Bear Bryant
lurked to trip up Joe Paterno

You can see that I know all there is to know about Alabama. Our first day of riding in Alabama was very pleasant. We had been riding routes which parallel I-20. Yesterday we took I-20 right through the middle of Meridian, Louisiana and it was dangerous because of narrow bridges. I may have panicked in front of the whole group. Oops. We camped in a rodeo park in Eutaw last night, clear skies, fog, and dew but good sleeping because it was nice and cool.

My re-entry into the group was somewhat disruptive according to Liz but will settle down in time, I guess. My pushing got the low rate tickets purchased before they were all gone and we have set up a time and place to meet in London. No one has begun to plot the course through Europe so I guess I'll get started on that. I am especially unenthusiastic about Ole's route through Poland, Romania, and Bulgaria when we could follow the Danube from near Switzerland through Germany to Vienna and on down to Budapest and work our way down to Istanbul. Chas has decided he would rather do Istanbul to Athens than Poland.

Mustang Sally's Guide to Deviant Behavior

5.3.95 Greensboro, Alabama. I biked out early this morning while the others were cooking breakfast because my restaurant breakfast was twenty miles down the road. I was followed and circled by what I think was an indecent exposeur. He went by me, went on up the road and turned around and came back and parked his ancient jalopy, motor running, in front of an abandoned house. He got out of his car and went up the walk jiggling his trousers. I decided it would not be a good idea to look at or speak to him. Mamma told me to be careful of bad guys.

"Mam," he called plaintively.

I cranked away while determinedly ignoring him.

"Oh, Mam . . ." plaintive again. I kept going, staring straight ahead.

He got back in his car and went on down the road. Very soon he was back, passing me and pulling in a driveway on the right. I continued on looking straight ahead. The next time he got in his car and passed me again. Calming my anger, I got the last four numbers on his license plate. He pulled out of a side road just as I approached it. I pulled in that side road to talk to a lady in a school bus who had parked there. I told her my problem and gave her the license number. In retrospect, I wonder if the guy hadn't been waiting for her. The big advantage of traveling on something as weird as a bike is that you can be in and out of an area before the uncouth can get themselves organized. Most likely the bus driver would have been his target if I hadn't come along. What good to call the police? Because Momma told me not to look, I didn't actually see anything wrong.

Mustang Sally's guide to inexpensive travel

The small towns that we pass through often have town parks. Bicyclists have a limited range to travel, unlike cars or motorcycles. When it gets dark we need a secure place to camp. Our group's practice is to go to the local police station and ask to talk to the Chief. Then we would ask for shelter. Of the ten or fifteen times we have asked, we have only been turned down once, by a nervous underling. The Chief can always find a spot, sometimes the jail itself. The parks are usually clean and have toilets. Sometimes there are swimming pools and showers.

5.4.95 Birmingham, Alabama. When I got in touch with a friend of son Mac, Joe Beckman, he offered to come pick me up and take me to visit Birmingham.

"Oh, no, I couldn't do that." I said. "I am too dedicated. Besides it looks like rain and I wouldn't want to miss camping in the rain."

We had our little laugh and today I went back to bed in the extra bedroom (there are five or six) over the garage where the rain is coming down and we had to turn off the TV thunderstorm warnings to protect the TV. The dog is looking for comfort and has found me. Tanya and the two children, George and Cary have gone to work and nursery school. Joe's darling wife, Tanya is a physical therapist and Dr. Joe is a Prof. at the University and deep into basic research. He has become an authority on something to do with Lou Gherig's Disease and other diseases because of his unusual approach from the botany field. He travels all over the world lecturing.

Joe's family, seven of them, bicycled through Holland and Germany a few years ago and Joe's input is a lot of help. He has been a serious mountain climber and will be in Zurich for three months this summer. They want me to come and visit there. Small world. The Zurich thing isn't all that out of reason. It is quite flat around Zurich, The Rhine goes that way and then I could pick up the Danube near Switzerland and follow it to its mouth in the Black Sea.

The Romans conquered to the Rhine and set up forts along it by Augustus' decree. He was afraid of getting too strung out. They did the same thing with the Danube and then connected the two with a wall. I have seen a map of that wall but not a picture. I wonder if it still exists.

The bed that I am sharing with the dog is beginning to vibrate. The last few thunder claps are scaring him as well as making me jump.

12:00: Dr. Joe's lab occupies the entire floor of a large building. This is a really high flying place. The research goes in many directions, following nitric oxide, a product of trauma which is supposed to kill bacteria but attacks the human instead. There are a dozen scientists, some of whom must be really important because they can barely manage English, working feverishly to expand the breakthrough in the understanding of Lou Gerhig's disease and possibly Parkinsons. They all shake my hand and are happy to know someone traveling around the world and then take the opportunity to bring something science up with Joe. I am glad these folks are going to make things better for mankind. I got claustrophobic. The thought of being in a tiny room staring at a computer, no matter how exotic, or cutting up a rabbit instead of out on the open road . . . well . . . For one who has spent most of her life in school rooms staring out the window, . . . enough! Give me the open road, the trees, the wild flowers. Joe took me back to Selma where I joined the group again.

I had been all hot to go to Selma and march with Martin Luther King a while back. Then some northern housewife got killed down there, trying to register blacks to vote. Chas said it was too dangerous, he didn't want to be raising three small children alone, etc., etc. I decided that Chas was quite right and didn't go. It is a very quiet town today.

Chapter VIII

Georgia

. . . on my mind

5.7.95 Peach Tree City, GA. Do you have music that keeps you company? "Other arms reach out to me, other lips cry tenderly, da da da da" I get a new song every time we get a new state.

We are camping in the apartment of Helen's son, Denny. He shares the space with two other mechanics who trained at the Pittsburgh Institute of Aeronautics. Denny borrowed a van from a friend and took us to the Delta Airlines hanger where he works and we got to see a stripped down Lockheed 1011. It was pretty intimidating and my acrophobia really got some exercise scrambling around on the scaffolding. The planes have a repair schedule based on takeoffs and landings but is usually about every four years for the overhaul. It takes three shifts working 24 hours over a month to recondition the plane. Denny had just come back from a scuba diving trip to the Grand Caymans. We spread out around the apartment and enjoyed the day off.

5.8.95 I got to lay out a bit at the pool and try to even up my biker's tan. Peach Tree City, an Atlanta suburb, is a harmonious planned community. Its model bike paths, winding through elegant landscaping and apartments, were a great pleasure.

The research on routes in Europe has heated up along with debates. I just may be on my own route. I am still opposed to unnecessary mountains and Ole is headed for mountainous Czech Republic and Slovakia by way of Poland. I want to bike the "world's most used bike path" that is beside the Danube River from Germany through Vienna and Budapest.

5.9.95 Jackson GA. There are six in my group: Helen, Jim, Liz, and John and Cynthia. There hasn't been much camping where my bivvy wouldn't have been sufficient except for last night. The fish hatchery campground we stayed in was pretty but crawling, so to speak, with ants. Ants were on poor Spot.

Chapter IX

SOUTH CAROLINA

. . . Nothin could be finah

5.12.95 Williston, South Carolina. Only two days from Charleston and the sea. It is incredibly hot and some dreadful hills but we are assured that this is the top of the Piedmont and it a gradual downhill to the sea. We tried to get the mayor who also runs the drugstore in this little town to sponsor us. While New Orleans is drowning, South Carolina is in the grip of a drought. We told them how we had brought rain to Pecos, Texas that had not seen rain in four years. We tried to get them to sponsor us so our very beneficial rains would happen here. That didn't work. They have given up thinking about rain. The crops are stunted and dried up. We got free drinks and a chance to sit a while out of the sun in the drugstore that had an old-time 40's soda fountain.

The biking was as dangerous today as it has been anywhere. Trucks are mostly generous with the road but this day we had a couple of those types who use the horn to make you jump right out of your skin. We were waiting for news of Helen's expected grandchild. Her daughter has gone to the hospital and may be induced tomorrow, on my birthday.

We were permitted to camp in the town park. It was so pleasant with a couple of ponds with muscovite ducks and semi aggressive geese. The locals are setting up for a walk-a-thon here tomorrow.

There was a terrible attack of fire ants in Williston They were just everywhere in the morning. The tent was crawling with them and they bit ferociously as we packed the gear. My panniers were infested with the wretched pests and I got rid of every bit of food that I had been carrying and still they appeared in hordes. Finally I found a nest in a small pannier pocket and put a handful of fire ant poison in it and zipped it back up. The other bikers were also attacked but not as badly as poor Spot. I have been remiss in writing because of reading a book called *CHAOS* that I bummed from Joe Beckman. It was like reading a modern Microbe Hunters and I couldn't put it down. I sent the book on to son Tom who will actually read it.

5.15.95 Charleston SC My sixty-fifth birthday has come and gone. Wow. I had lots of company to do the birthday ride of sixty-five miles. For dinner, which was in a state park, my pals provided an angel food cake with strawberries and we all feasted. Finally I am feeling better in the mornings. Not just totally fatigued. Today is a day off to see Charleston and I am really ready for the rest. I have a tee shirt dress that I also use for a bathing suit cover up, and night shirt. The bike shoes I wear with it are not the greatest fashion statement. I will, perhaps be able to buy a good pair of running shoes today. I would like to start running now that I am feeling stronger. I must also buy a pair of strong sandals. I need to get some commitment from the group about whether or no they want to climb Mt Olympus in Greece so that if not, I can quit carrying my boots which I have used just once crossing the US. Oh, yes! We have crossed the US!!!!! My Cateye reads 2370 miles and it has only been working since Phoenix.

I bought Spot a nice bumper sticker that says 'DIXIE! Old Times There Are Not Forgotten.' Indeed. We went cruising Charleston to see how wonderful slavery was for a few people. Fort Sumpter is here and this is where hot heads started the Civil War. It is hard for me to deal with Southerners who claim that the Civil War was about either states rights or tariffs or some other nonsense and not over whether it is right to enslave another human being.

My ancestors were mostly English yeomen. No one's boss and no one was their boss. They fought to free slaves.

5.16.95 Charleston SC There was yet another terrible storm. We were in a KOA and the owner was worried about our being in tents and permitted us to use the cabins. Tornados touched down a couple of towns away. We never got to Ft. Sumpter. Jim rented a car so we could go to the fort but the group settled down in a grocery store to write cards and by the time they finished, Ft. Sumpter was closed. I found that annoying. The downtown had glorious blocks and blocks of fabulous old houses that were somewhat like beautiful Natchez but different. These are more for a city. I took lots of pictures. Charleston was pretty well destroyed by the Civil War, which she started. She recovered from that and hurricanes too and is a real beauty.

5.18.95 Myrtle Beach State Park. What a neat idea. A State park right at Myrtle Beach. When we arrived in town there were lots of signs that said, Welcome Bikers! Nice. Unexpected. Oops! Not our kind of bikes. Harleys and Hondas by the thousands. Staying in the State Park with us. Actually they were curious about us and if they just hadn't been roaring around in the wee small hours, it would have been pleasant. In the morning they were going up the two lane street four and five abreast.

Chapter X

NORTH CAROLINA . . .

I must go down to the sea again
To the lonely sea and the tide
And all I ask is a tall, tall ship,
And a star to guide her by

John Masefield

5.19.95 Supply NC We will catch a ferry at Cape Fear, nineteen miles away. Cape Fear is on the Fear River. Scary movie. It has been in the 90's and sweltering. Got a motel last night just to get out of it and get a decent night's rest. I actually slept in this morning.

We met Dick Vara, a bicycler from Boston. He is seventy and in great shape. He is headed for home up the coast also, from Florida. Through Jersey and New York?

5.22.95 Morehead City NC We should get to Ocracoke today. The coastline has been palmettos and live oaks. Most of the time we followed the Adventure Cycling Route 1. It is sometimes busy and the last couple of days have been exceptionally beautiful. I like the greens and beiges of the big expanses of marsh land as much as the purple heather moors of England. Daughter Kitty has made elaborate arrangements for the group in Ocracoke.

Chas and Bill will be joining us for sure and Alma, who hiked across England with me, may join us there. Somewhere I hit upon the idea of going through France and both Alma and Chas think they will keep me company there. That would be so great as Alma is fluent in French and a seasoned traveler, not by bike but by hostel.

Helen and I found that we prefer different modes of travel: she is for camping and I am for traveling by hostel. For one thing, hostelling frees everyone for the day. The destination is set; you just have to get there. So if some want to wander through castles and others want to do the cafe scene, it can work for everyone. The camping mode, it seems to me, leaves one totally involved in the mechanics of finding the campground, the food, and getting it all together there. As we have been doing it, the mechanics of bicycle travel and camping are the only thing. There isn't much else. Last night Jim and I motelled about a block from where the rest of the group camped in a really grungy spot, with some pretty low life people. We were off the bike route and trying to camp in a state park that didn't allow camping. I was so tired when I got the motel that I was in bed at 8:00 and didn't take my mandatory walk on the beach. So, I was up again, writing, at 2:00 AM. One of the best things about a motel is solitude and the comforts of late night TV or a table and chair for writing and no one bothered. I'm spoiled. Sometimes I just feel that there isn't any dignity at my age while crawling in and out of a tent. Camping is OK in an area where everyone is camping but a trailer court where we were tonight, I wouldn't get "no respect."

I need to get some sleep for the race to catch the noon ferry. I don't think I want to do part of Europe with Helen, she is a determined to follow Ole through povertyville. But I would like to join her in Budapest. I doubt that she will miss me in any case.

5.22.95 Ocracoke Island, NC. Another beautiful day in Ocracoke! I am thinking about trying to sea kayak but so far am so fatigued that thinking is an effort. We arrived yesterday. I had tried to explain the "*Got to catch the ferry*' syndrome that attacks people who have missed the ferry and spent an entire night in mosquitoville instead of the bosom of the family. I ran it by the group once and they didn't catch it so I just took off with a '*See you in Ocracoke*' warning. Of course they missed the ferry. The next ferry was only three hours later and they were honored with wonderful Ocracoke hospitalit.

They got a darling, authentic cottage with three bedrooms and two dining tables and wonderful stuff. Tonight, if it can be arranged, a sunset cruise on a sailboat and Wednesday a potluck supper. They have been meeting some of the town characters: Al Scarborough, Russell Newell, David Senseny, and of course my daughter Kitty, her husband Gary, and little Katy are quite the characters, themselves.

I had Kitty hang on to Dick Vara so that we could talk more. He had traveled through Poland and Bulgaria just the year before. He thought that it was very doable.

Bear stories: These are from an old friend, Russell, who hangs out at the Island Inn on Ocracoke Island. He has brightened our days while visiting on Ocracoke with a sparkling Irish wit and amiable stories. He started writing them down and getting them published in a local paper. Also he would go out looking for new stories and told us over successive visits about the bears in North Carolina. They are black bears, of course and seem to be fairly small and of a more likeable disposition than the average grizzly. Russell was always on his way to interview a lady who lived alone out on the edge of Fahfrum, NC.

"She has this littl ole cabin aweigh out theah. It is so fah out there yew don think of gowin out theah in anny thang but one of then fouh wheeled cahs. The road quits a long time befo you kin get there. Eastern Noth Carolina does hav its shah of beahs." He pauses and reflects on why he hasn't been to visit this lady who is such a good story.

She beats on a pan and the beahs jest come right out of theah for the food. They come when she calls them. Can you beat that? Have yew evah heard of such a thang?" We agree that we haven't and he abandons even the thought of a lady in the wilds with bears for watch dogs.

"Oveah Plymouth way theah is a story they tell about the town drunk. Seems Ol' Willet had a pretty good snootful as usual and he is walking along the railroad track when he hears somthin behind him and feggers it is a dawg. But there aren't too many dawgs that grunt and he looks around and not twenty feet away and coming right for him is a black beah. Well, he jumps about three feet high and lands runnin. His shoes wasn't tied because he just wasn't the most careful about his appearance. One shoe started to fall off and he ran on the heel of it for a while and then kicked it off and is running down the track toward town. The other shoe sort of turned sideways and he kicked that one off, too. A couple of the town folk saw him running and stopped to look. They saw the moving scahscrow frantically running along the tracks, puhsued by a scruffy black beah. The beah stopped to sniff somthin that they later decided was the first shoe. Then the beah starts up after Ol' Willet agin and humps along until it comes to somthin else and stops to sniff. Then the beah picks up the second shoe and turning back trots along the tracks for a bit then dives into the scrub and disappears. Ol' Willet arrived in town as sober as a judge and shoeless. The beah was neveh seen agin nor the shoes and Ol' Willet had to put up with a lot of speculation at the local bah about how bad thet shoe of his would have been foh a beah."

5.29.95 I hadn't made many entries in the narrative since I got to Ocracoke. My excuse is the usual Ocracoke ennui wherein one spends the first day or two reading or staring at Pamlico Sound. Actually, the second day I bestirred myself enough to take a sea kayak out from the rental place. It was terrific arm exercise. I couldn't even lift my arms after ten minutes. I know a wonderful lady who is a breast stroke world champion, by a lot. She does a mere 1500 yards a day in a pool but spends many happy hours out in her rowing scull cruising the Florida canals. The paddle action of her scull is what pleasantly builds the world champion muscles. She was seventy when I saw her last. I think a scull is too expensive and too tippy for me but I can almost drag the sea kayak around. Lowering my stiffened butt into it isn't pretty but it is very stable. I could paddle it and dream dreams of world domination. We had a canoe at Ocracoke and it was not good because with all that freeboard, it was so hard to turn if the wind came up. Tony, the owner of the kayak said he would sell it to me for $200. Not too bad for the number of times I would use it in Ocracoke.

Sweet daughter Kitty and her husband Gary held a pot luck dinner for the bicyclers and locals and wonderful food was had by all. My favorites were teriyaki chicken by bicyclers and shrimp and grits by the islanders. We watched the sunset from the deck until the mosquitoes attacked us. One guest was a lady in her seventies who brought fruit that she candied and another was a ninety year old guy who had always lived on the island and another islander who had circumnavigated the world in a small sailboat. Ocracoke is one of those places that collects interesting people.

I don't keep notes well when M'love is along but must mention that on Hattaras Island we stopped at a campground near the first flight area and Chas went up in a plane that was just like the Red Baron's, wearing a leather cap with ear flaps.

Chapter XI

Yes, VIRGINIA

. . . there is a . . .

5.29.95 Surry VA. Waiting here for our little band of adventurers to come by and decide on another excellent restaurant or just make the run for the Jamestown ferry. Yesterday Chas, Alma, Jim and I were holed up in a McDonalds, waiting for the rain to stop. Bill had lagged behind with the car because he is crazy about Ocracoke and hates to leave. I had serious, sharp, knee pain. Serious pain is the kind you can bike with but it is definitely no fun. Alma, a massage therapist, diagnosed it as anterior cruciate ligament. We started calling motels, (can you tell that Alma is along?) finally taking a very expensive one in Smithfield. We were concerned about the expense until we were coming down a small hill, across a bike friendly bridge toward a really handsome Coast Guard Station turned motel, in an abruptly torrential rain. Suddenly it was much cheaper than it had been. In a downpour, any price is right. The motel turned out to be a great pleasure. The rooms were much too good for Spot, the Wonderbike, so we put the bikes on the balcony and enjoyed more space in the rooms. We were right on the water and dined on sea food in high style. Later Bill joined us and we had a dry night in a most charming place. For breakfast I had crab meat Hollandaise. No eggs, just crabmeat. It was so deluxe. We saw Helen and Co. just before breakfast and they didn't think they could make the campground on the other side of the Williamsburg ferry so we don't know where they are but hope we will catch up with them in Williamsburg.

5.30.95 Williamsburg Virginia. Such confusion. I ended up driving Bill's car so he could put some time in on the bike. For some reason I am spending the afternoon alone in the Williamsburg Campground. There is a dog show here. There are such darling puppies. So elegant and such variety. I am hesitant to select a camping spot because there will be complaints. I must learn to be brave about these things. Helen's group seems to have gone right on by. I don't understand the hurry. We have weeks to get to D.C. and it is just 2 days away.

5.31.95 Williamsburg, Va. We camped at the campground and then met in Colonial Williamsburg for breakfast. It is a lot easier to bike into Williamsburg than to drive Bill's car there, so they were all waiting around for me for quite some time while I searched for the authentic colonial restaurant. No one wanted to explore the area, so after breakfast, Chas, Bill, and Alma took off in the car, headed home for Pittsburgh leaving Jim and me to catch up with Helen, Liz, and the Olneses. Parting from Chas was just as sad as usual.

6.1.95 What is so rare as a day in June, then if ever come perfect days, when Heaven tries Earth if it be in tune and o're it softly her warm ear lays. And whether we look or whether we listen, we hear life murmur or see it glisten. And every clod feels a stir of might, an instinct within it reaches and towers and groping blindly above it for light, climbs to a soul in grass and flowers. And there is never a leaf no blade too mean to be some happy creature's palace. I made that up. Sure. But I do carry it around in my head and can produce the pleasure of its company any time that conditions warrant.

Jim and I have not yet made contact with the group but expect to meet them in a campground which is south of Fredricksburg. The traffic has been pretty heavy and the headwinds persist but we must be getting tougher because we keep moving along fairly well. This part of Virginia has rolling hills and pleasant forests and broad fields of peanuts and wheat. I bike through here a lot and always enjoy the warmth of the land. Jim and I shared a motel room once. I like to watch TV and he doesn't. I can't sleep well and get up in the middle of the night to write or read. This does not make me popular with Jim. So once was enough. When I shared a room with Helen, she drove me to distraction by cooking her morning coffee in the room with the flowing flame from the Whisperlite. Watching the flame on the Formica got me fired up. Especially when there was free coffee in the office. Everyone gets so picky. Even me. I get picky.

It was miles out of their way for Helen's group to meet us at the campground but they did. And the campground was nice but expensive. So, again, I wasn't very popular. While they cooked breakfast, Jim and I set off early to get breakfast in Fredricksburg. This is my route for biking from Pittsburgh to Ocracoke. I used to get Chas to drop me off at my school, north of Pittsburgh, with the bike loaded for camping on the last in-service day of the year. At 2:45 I would turn in my grade book and grades. At 3:00 PM, I would start for Ocracoke, right through Pittsburgh's Golden Triangle. Hilarious. I would be the only thing moving in "Downtown's" gridlock. By the witching hour of 5:00, I would be on Rt. 30 south of the city and find a motel. The next day it was over the Alleghenies past Seven Springs Resort and on to Meyersdale. Meyersdale to Cumberland was a challenge with the reward being a glorious 15 mile coast down Mt. Savage across the state line into Cumberland, MD. This is now, incredibly, the GAP bicycle trail. After Cumberland, the C&O Tow Path is 176 miles of off-road bike path into D.C. Then I head south on the Adventure Cycling Bicycle Route 1. I had a favorite restaurant in Fredricksburg right on the Adventure Cycling route, Actually it is the only breakfast spot in town. Jim didn't like it.

We set off for D. C. and when we got to US. 1 met with the group and they decided to go north up US. 1. It was a much shorter route than Bike 1 which goes around Prince William Forest Park but I had been on US 1 just the year before and knew it to be terrible.

The good thing about things going bad is that it gives you something to write about:

6.2.95 Mustang Sally's Guide to *PANIC!!!*

What, me scared? Well, from time to time I get a bit nervous. People ask touring bicyclists, "Aren't you afraid? I'd be scared to death to ride in traffic."

Well, we are not stupid. We get scared.

Coming north on Bike One, the Adventure Cycling (used to be Bikecentennial) route from Boston to Florida, US 1 seems very tempting. Usually a road that hugs an Interstate route (I-95 here) is pretty good for bicyclers. For example, I 20 in Mississippi and Alabama was great for us, we rode Alabama Route 80. A lady truck driver told us that through trucks were NOT ALLOWED on Rt. 80 except for making deliveries on it. Route 80 was pleasant and peaceful and had service stations, restaurants, and camping. Very nice. But I-20 isn't I-95.

US 1 as you approach Washington DC is Hell's Main Street: 30 miles of shopping centers, horrible hills, and vicious traffic. I had tried to talk our group of six out of doing US 1. I had been on it just the year before. I truly knew how bad it was. But they, led by Helen, who is impervious to traffic, couldn't see going Adventure Cycling's extra 15 miles around, through bucolic Prince William Forest Park.

"We are three weeks early getting into D.C. What was the rush?" I whined.

I can't help but envy someone who doesn't even notice traffic. I'm at the other end of the fear spectrum: jumpy and inclined to hysteria when stalked by an endless line of dump trucks. Perhaps dump truck and garbage truck drivers have failed the 18 wheeler test and are bitter toward the world or perhaps they really do have a horn where there should be a brake.

It was a Thursday. I got up, ate a granola bar, and biked 10 miles to breakfast in historic Fredricksburg, Virginia on Bike One's pleasant and fairly flat back roads. In the old section of town was a great cafe. Corned beef hash and poached eggs substituted for my usual steak and eggs breakfast. After breakfast we suffered the first real hills since Charleston, South Carolina on an otherwise delightful back road. I was tired when we hit the intersection with US 1 and gave in to the "It is 15 miles shorter and how bad can it be?" and started north on US. 1. After about 5 miles I was in a cafe trying to figure out why I had the bonk and how to deal with it. I was shaking all over, hands, knees, and stomach vibrating. I had been biking for three months, almost 3000 miles without getting into this condition. My companions had gone on their way leaving me to deal with the increasing traffic congestion alone. Alone is not good in traffic. At least in a group there is a perceived safety in numbers. Traveling in a group you have to think that the trucks are not going to want to mess up their day by having to fill out all the forms after they run over you. Cleaning the blood and innards off those huge tires has to be a nasty thing, not to mention what Spot, the Wonder Bike, would do to their tires. Then, too, if you aren't the last, you have comfort in the idea that the Death Truck has to get the last guy in line before he comes after you. Sort of like a school of fish mentality: just mere numbers means they can't get us all. I had coffee and a sugar jolt of sweet roll for the bonk and plowed on with greater courage and determination. For a while.

I was having more and more troubled with the unrelenting hills. The shopping centers increased until they occupied all but the steepest hills. Sometimes there would be a shoulder to ride but then it would abruptly disappear leaving only the road which the traffic was not in a mood to share. I went off into the gutter several times and started screeching in fear every time a vehicle came near me. Then I started doing sidewalks and finally I was such a wreck I got off the bike and went and sat in a Friendly's Restaurant to sniffle, convinced that I was so cowardly that I would never be able to get on poor Spot again. Oh, poor me. By this time I had caught up with the rest but was mentally blaming them for my not doing what I knew was right for me. I was really angry as well as afraid so I wouldn't even talk to them. Well, hey. Irrational is as irrational does. So they left and I sat there in a Friendly's trying to get my act together. It didn't help that there was a three car accident right outside and bodies had to be pried out and ambulanced away. Finally, a very neat policeman with a sparkling white shirt and neat black moustache came in and sat in the next booth and looked at me with concern. He didn't look as though he had been involved in the mucky, sticky, gory mess outside. I finally realized that the people in the deserted Friendly's must have called him because I was behaving so strangely. Maybe they thought that I had caused the wreck and was feeling guilt. Who knows? Anyway, I got out of there and started biking through endless shopping centers and ignoring the road as much as possible. When I had to do road, I walked the bike.

I finally got to Bike One and its pleasant back roads. I rode excellent bike paths to Alexandria and a motel without further problem, got a good sleep in a motel and rode to a bike shop the next morning where they charged me D.C. prices to box and ship Spot home by UPS. I caught a bus and then the subway to National Airport and a flight to Pittsburgh. The tour group is two weeks ahead of schedule. We leave June 20 for London.

In Europe two of us plan to part from the main group of ten and do our own little tour through France, Switzerland, and Austria and join the main group, who are doing Poland, Chechia, and Slovakia, in Budapest. Friend Alma and husband Charles will be along for most of France. It will be Alma's first real bike tour but she is very knowledgeable and speaks French and German, has been a tour leader before and is enthusiastically buying gear and laying out a course through Brittany and the castles of the Loire Valley. Chas was pretty ho-hum about the trip until he spotted towns named Brie and Chablis on the French map. I could feel the sudden rush of pleasurable anticipation that he enjoyed. What ever turns you on, eh? With the bad day buried in the past, I busied getting Spot new wheels and drive train and replacing some sun faded clothing and on to Europe. The last plan was to take the bikes, boxed, from the belly of the plane to the belly of a bus to Portsmouth and thence by overnight ferry to St. Malo in Brittany with our first excursion being to the same fabulous Mont St. Michel that was on the cover of the second year French book. I felt that thrill of anticipation. Oh! Wow!

I got my drivers license renewed, entered all the debts and stuff in my Quicken program and drove back down to D.C. I stayed at the International Hostel there and had dinner with Ole, John, and Louise. (That was that last time I saw Ole and John until the finish in San Diego.)

Mustang Sally's Non-Guide to Group Dynamics

I don't remember what went wrong. I remember sitting on the floor of a bare apartment in the hostel while Louise cooked and Ole and John ate. I ate left-overs from my lunch at a Chinese restaurant. I wanted them to understand why I wasn't going to accompany them through the scheduled Poland and Czechia if I could do what will probably be my one and only tour of Europe: through France, Switzerland and Germany. Mainly, I hate poverty and don't consider travel in poor countries that much pleasure. I wanted them to schedule a meeting in Budapest because I really wanted the protection of the group through Romania and Bulgaria. They agreed to a date for Budapest, with the understanding that it was only a target and not necessarily an imperative, hardly a new idea with this bunch.

I cruised the embassy district of D.C. visiting the various embassies and getting a visa from Yugoslavia and literature from Malaysia, neither of which did I use. Then I drove back home. I got there in time for a phone call from Louise. She told me that Ole and company did not want me to travel with them. I would not to be with them after Budapest!

"Wasn't that upsetting: to be rejected like that?"

Well, of course. But being alone seems to be the price you pay for not being either a good leader or a good follower.

PART 2

Mustang Sally's Guide to:
BICYCLING EUROPE

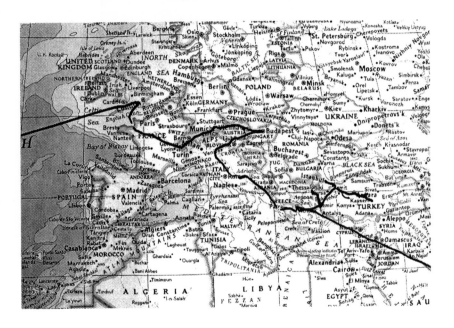

Chapter XII

France in June

"Be an opener of doors for such as come after thee, and do not try to make the Universe a blind alley."

Ralph Waldo Emerson

Instructional aside: MAPPING THE ROUTE

Plotting a route to bicycle is a fine science. First, please try to find someone who has done the proposed route and see what they have to say. You need to screen the commentary a bit because the young, hairy-chested macho types will brag discretely about hauling a bicycle loaded with the treasures of a lifetime over the steepest mountain range. This is not for the aging, gravel-kneed, weaklings like me.

I started in the library. There is a wonderful atlas published by THE TIMES, which costs $100.00. I am only telling you the price so that you will donate to your library and then use its wonderful facilities. This tome is way too heavy to steal. Even if affordable, it would be a challenge to carry, even for Ole or Liz. The Times Atlas has the helpful geophysical maps, which are nicely detailed. It also has roads. The other atlases have one or the other but not both. Geophysical shows mountains, valleys, flat areas, and the most important . . . rivers. Copying sensitive areas from the atlas is usually OK, legal, handy, (the library has copying machines) and may even save on the considerable expense of map buying. For instance, there is a bicyclers map to be bought in

Switzerland ($24) and it must be accompanied by at least a Michelin map to be understood ($9.00). Would you believe that the ever so organized Swiss do not have numbers on the roads? It is a problem about which I will go into in anguished detail later. I copied a map of Bangkok in a library in Pittsburgh that helped me bike in Thailand later.

With the large and heavy Times well supported on a large and strong table, you are prepared to become acquainted with the geography of a place more intimately than most of the natives are. The locals will not usually be able to read a map at all, and if they can manage that, will not be able to understand how tiresome it is for a loaded bike to handle hills.

You need to look at a route as though you were planning to put a railroad through it. Railroads need long slow hills and not too severe turns. Railroads follow rivers. So you look intently at the geophysical map until you begin to see that (oh, WOW!) the railroad engineers have already been there! There is a railroad! It follows a river which becomes a stream which becomes a creek and then it goes through a pass or gap in the mountain range and starts down the other side and the creek becomes a stream which becomes a river to the next ocean. What! You are going to miss the Matterhorn??? Never mind. You will catch Niagara Falls. You absolutely cannot see everything so be content with the zillions of things, great and small, that you will see because you are moseying along on a bicycle.

It is going to be easier to just plain go around the mountains as we did taking the southern tier route through the US. The southern tier (San Diego to Charleston, South Carolina) misses the coastal ranges, the Rockies and the Appalachians. As you approach the East Coast it is fun to be aware of the 'fall Line.' The fall line is where the Piedmont plateau ends and the tidewater flats begin. The Piedmont is rolling and clay soil. The tidewater is sandy soil and not so many rolls. You can usually pick out the line by the towns with 'falls' or 'mills' in their name.

Then it is a matter of finding comfortable back roads and in the US, the Adventure Cycling of Missoula, Montana has done a lot of that for you by planning and mapping a route. The maps, printed on water-resistant paper, are expensive but worth it. They are hard to understand but once you get into the habit of checking and double-checking and then looking carefully just once more, they are pretty good. If you are fully loaded for cooking and camping, they are fine but if you travel with nothing heavier than a credit card, you may have to leave the route from time to time to find food and lodging.

Oh, just one thing about the Southern Tier route: if you are a student or a teacher as I once was and as most long distance tourists are, forget the southern tier. I did it in March, April, and May when a problem was cold and another problem was rain. By June when you are out of school, the flowers that filled the soul with delight are dried up and gone. Some places are so hot and miserable that you can only travel by night and water is a major problem.

So climate is also a factor. The monsoons quit in India in October, just about the same time that the rainy season begins in Greece so Ole had planned a big section of the tour around these immovable facts . . . the plan is for leaving Greece for New Delhi on October 20.

Politics is important. I have traveled in four Muslim countries and found the street people to be disagreeable in two of them, Egypt and Morocco, so from my own experience and from reading the experiences of other women bicyclers I choose to travel in only two Muslim countries, Turkey and India. Politics matters. I had a visa for Yugoslavia but worry about using it when they are ethnic cleansing the Muslims and shooting down our planes and holding UN people prisoner. If things get difficult, I plan to plane or train out of wherever gets uncomfortable to where I want to be. This is no crusade. Can you see the homework assignment of "How I Spent My Summer"? "Chained to a tank in Bosnia."

Then there is the tourist stuff. Info from the various spots to be visited is helpful. A nice brochure about a temple or physical phenomena can help with the choices about how the time would be spent. Could you go through Orlando and not know that Disneyland is there? Perhaps.

You will need to budget for entry fees to various attractions. They will add spice to the trip and may be the only thing you remember years later. The library also carries guidebooks, which are sometimes horridly heavy, and when you finally arrive at a recommended spot, there are dozens of other 'Small Planet' readers there before you.

End of instructional aside.

So with all this in mind I made a plan for France. I have no idea what I meant:

St. Malo June 22 35 miles; Mt St. Michele June 23 40 miles; Rennes 50 miles: Nantes; Angers 375 all routes; Rennes to Bourg-en-Bresse 564 miles. Fortunately, Alma had also made a plan.

June 22. M'love and I landed at Heathrow Airport, south of London, after an uneventful flight. At Heathrow we met Jim who was joining us for the France portion. We greeted Liz and Cynthia and John. Tiny Liz whose bicycle and baggage had come to 160 pounds, had been charged an extra $175 for being over the weight limit. She seemed more amused than chagrinned. The group were headed for London to wait for Helen whose travel plans are always chancy because she travels as a relative of a Delta employee and has to wait for an empty seat. The three of us were going to make for the English Channel at Portsmouth. We didn't know if Alma would make it or not because she still didn't have a ticket or firm plans when we last heard. To our great pleasure, she arrived and we set out for Portsmouth and caught the ferry for St. Malo in Brittany in Northern France.

Jim's bicycle seat had been damaged in transit and we looked for a new seat for him. He didn't find one but I was able to purchase a woman's Brooks leather seat in England. It didn't fit Spot and ended up on Green the Magic Mountain Bike which Chas was riding.

The night on the ferry was spent in sleeping bags and mattresses under a stairwell because the cabins were gone. Teenagers ran up and down the stairs all night, shrieking.

6.22.95 Mt. St. Michele, France. Arrived this morning in glorious St. Malo after the bad night on the over-night ferry. St. Malo is a wonderful city with beautiful beaches and great scenery. The city of St. Malo was not supposed to be bombed in WW II but there was a misunderstanding and instead of just a German gun emplacement being bombed the Allies destroyed the old city. It has been rebuilt to look just like the old city and you could fool me, it looked plenty old with massive walls and turrets to fend off pirates. The beaches are stunningly beautiful with a mixture of craggy rock and shallow sand. Because we are so far north, the tide is very high and the moles are enough to get my acrophobia activated. We are about the same latitude as Nova Scotia and the tide is as powerful. This leaves beached boats at crazy angles during low tide.

Chas and I put up the tent and locked the bikes in a campground and caught the afternoon bus to Mont St. Michel where we hope to catch first a sunset then a sunrise. Alma and Jim had been there before and so stopped in St. Malo to recover from the rigors of the flight and night. Chas and I were still churning along on adrenaline from the excitement of being in France for the first time. It was delightful beyond my expectations. The French went out of their way to be charming. A nice young person even gave up a seat on the bus to poor aging Charles. We also got 40% off the bus tickets for being 'seasoned' citizens.

6.23.95 Mt. St. Michel. Charles et moi sont maintenant en Mt. St. Michel. Cet matin Charles photografie l'Ile tres early, a seis heurs. Il faites froid et windy. Sont beaucoups touristes avec petite cheins. Il est tres belle. L'Ile est magnifique.

The pictures will be wonderful. The monastery was started in 1022 and possibly the Normans who conquered England could have come to the monastery to have their enterprise blessed. The monks are gone now and we tourists have claimed the architectural marvel and spend happy hours clambering around its enchanting nooks and crevices. Chas and I stayed in a motel that had the island as its view and walked in to the monastery and back twice.

Jim, Alma, Sally, and Chuck at St. Malo, Brittany, France.

Back in St. Malo we and Alma and Jim wined and dined French style, spent the night in the tents, and started biking due south.

6.25.95 Dinan. Spot the Wonderbike is upset. Here we are in Dinan with the Tour de France bicycle race to start here on July 2 and Spot is not going to compete. I tried to explain that it is me being slow, old, and female that is the problem but Spot would have none of that. I finally had to crush poor Spot's feelings by pointing out that the brand new wheels are not presta valves. That is a big mistake here in France according to the bike shop where we got the front wheel trued after a rough ocean crossing in a super large Schwinn box. New wheels sometimes have to be trued a couple of times before they settle in and give years of service.

Dinan had a large medieval section which had not been bombed in WWII like so much of France, Germany, and England. We camped in a municipal campground in Dinan, which had a bowling alley and a swimming pool. We spent the next morning cruising the town. From Dinan we caught the bike path south along the Rance River canal. It goes all the way to Rennes but some sections are so bad that one of Spot's front panniers stripped the braise-on and the pack and frame were dragging on the front wheel. A quick repair brought us to the small town of Guilot where our campground hosts were running the sausage and fries concession for a music fest to celebrate St. John, the patron saint of Brittany. We were entertained in the church by an a cappella choir of exquisite balance who sang local pieces like *Amazing Grace*. The townsfolk came out to our campground for a bonfire and *feu*, fireworks. I was still sleep deprived from the flight over and slept through it all. It was a relief to have slept through the event because the bonfire looked like every picture I have seen of the burning of Joan of Arc and I'd be happy to miss that.

The road to Rennes was hilly and I bonked. Will I never get used to the French breakfast of sugar and caffeine that leaves me hanging over the handlebars, shaky, sweaty. I was still trying to recover but weak after a one hour lunch (lamb, red beans and bread) and an hour of rest so I whined and was done for the day. Rennes was full of hippies. They lounged around everywhere, reeking and smoking stuff. We ate lunch at an outdoor cafe that was downwind of two cute but smelly girls whose armpits had great bursts of long black hair coming from them. It was one of those situations where the stomach tightens up and will not accept food.

France is incredibly bicycle friendly. There are bike paths everywhere and half the traffic on the back roads today (Sunday) were guys in racy bike clothes and bicycling groups enjoying the beautiful weather. It is like biking through a Manet or Corot painting. A drafting group passed us and we caught on and drafted them for a while, not an easy thing with a full load and Chas on Green, the Magic Mountain Bike. In spite of everything we had heard about the French being rude, we have yet to meet anyone who wasn't very courteous and friendly with some going a long way out of the way to be helpful. Cars give us a full lane when they can and are thoughtful when they can't. The English and American bicyclers we have met have all said we were really wise to skip biking in England and spend more time in France instead. Southern England is not considered to be bicycle friendly at all.

6.29.95 Saumur. Chas and I spent the night in a nice little hotel at the railroad station after arriving fairly late. The camping was not far away on an island in the middle of the Loire but we have so few days left that we decided to treat ourselves. The meal was excellent, an entree of *Coquille de crabe* and plate of Salmon with boiled potatoes. Chas had a pate (meatloaf) entree and lamb for the plate. We had a nice chat with some Brits who were traveling with a couple from New Zealand. We discussed islands like Borneo and Bali and they said the people were wonderful but you must be careful with the food. Doubly careful in India and Nepal. The lady from New Zealand told me she had read gritty British Bettina Selby's book about biking solo through Afghanistan. I didn't tell her that no amount of money could pay me to go through there, just nodded and smiled wisely. Get a lot more points that way than admitting to having very weak flesh and no spirit at all. When we said that Chas would be going back in 2 days, big fat tears popped out of my eyes and rolled down my cheeks. He swears he won't join us again until New Zealand and that is a long time from now.

Meeting up with the others we toured the castle of Saumur. It is very beautiful with white limestone walls and turrets. Do you remember Henry V? Such a great movie. Sir Laurence at his best. So sweet the scene between Henry and his betrothed, the sister of the Dauphin. She is trying to teach him some French. That charming garden is here, in this aged castle. Henry lived here. Battle of Agincourt? Here. *Lion In Winter* with Katy Hepburn? That was Henry II and Elinor of Aquitaine. Their marriage gave England claim to one third of France and started the One Hundred Years War. They lived here. Richard the Lionhearted returned to this castle after his crusade. The large blocks of limestone make this castle so different from the finer work that came later. St. Joan rousing the French to resist the English? Here. Most of the castle is now a museum and we took the tour (in French) with Aubusson tapestries and lovely furniture and china. There was a horse museum, my second on this tour . . . Silver City, NM has a saddle museum, and then there was the Cajun saddle-maker, Boo LeDoux in Eunice, LA. This one was much more complete with saddles from all ages here in France and examples from all over the world.

We had too much time to sit around afterwards and decided that with train connections to Paris so confusing, that we would start now instead of tomorrow. We catch a train from Saumur to Tour, change for Blois. Leave my bike in the "left luggage" and continue on with Alma's to Paris in search of Charles de Gaulle airport where hopefully we can check in Alma's bike and be free of bikes for a day in Paris.

6.30.95 Blois, Loire Valley. Three chateaus today for Chas and me. That's a lot when one can come down with a bad case of "museum leg" with only one. We had decided to leave early for Paris because of train difficulties and it turned out to be an excellent decision. They only take bikes on trains with baggage cars and they are about a day apart so the original plan would not have put us in Paris in time for the plane. We had to hang up a day in Blois waiting for a proper train so we did the three chateaus.

Chambord is the most wonderful chateau. First of all, Leonardo may have designed the intriguing double helix stairway. He lived here and died near here. Louis the XIV's bedroom and Maria Theresa's suite of rooms were regally lavish. Well, I'd probably cheered if they'd got their heads chopped off. Put the power of the church behind the divine right of kings to rule and you get these four hundred room chateaus. I grumbled at the 'Lion King' and its insidious political message of how cute it is to have kings. Saves lazy people the need to be informed and exercise their constitutional right to vote. Or even decide what to do with their own life. If Greece is not where the rights of man came from then France?? Or was it John Knox of England? These chateaus and the ostentatious display of wealth and power must have affected some of the thinking that finally over threw the mighty nobility. But not completely, like England, French cling to their classes of society.

The region produces that wonderful white limestone that has the chateaus all sparkly even after so many years.

We stayed in another French inn and arranged to leave Spot there in Blois while Chas and I went on our first trip to Paris.

Chas: Madame.
Madam: Oui, Monsieur.
Charles: Je voudrais voyons a Paris avec mon espouse et madame retournee en deux jours pour le velo.
Madam: Oui, Monsieur.
Charles: Je vais au L'etats Unis par avion et madam umh um . . . .

Madame: What you wish, Monsieur, is to leave here the bicycle while you go to Paris with the Madame. You will fly to the US while she returns here for the bicycle. N'est pas?

Charles: Uh. Yeah, that's right.

Madame: Fine. You can leave the bike here. No problem.

7.1.95 Paris. Charles 68'th birthday was a zinger. We spent the first part of the day getting Alma's bicycle to Charles de Gaulle airport, packing it and leaving it at the 'left luggage.' Then we were free to locate a cheaper room, Hotel San Severin on San Severin Rue, and cruise the city. We chose the Musee D'Orsay over the Louvre because of its devotion to the impressionists. The museum was marvelous beyond our imagination. Sisly, Corot, Pizzaro, Millet . . . the Angelus and the Gleaners are here, not in the Louvre. Cezanne, Monet, and Monet, and Monet. Dr. Gachet, The church at Auvers, and Vincent's room in Arle. We rented cassettes and did the whole 2 hour bit in only 5 hours. There is something about the impressionists that captures the cheerful buoyancy of the France we have bicycled.

Everywhere we meet and chat with Americans who seem to be wandering along with mouths agape like we are. Last night we took the water cruise on the Seine which was a terrific way to get an under view of Notre Dame up to the Eiffel Tower. This evening, after a nice nap, we turned right out of our hotel and found a place to eat on the Ille de la Cite. Big mistake! Had we turned left we would have been in an area of ethnic restaurants that reminded us of the Placa in Athens where people stand at the door of the restaurants and try to talk you into their restaurant. Many of them were Greek restaurants, real Greeks, complete with bouzoukis and line dancing.

7.2.95 Paris. Seven in the morning and the street people have stout green machines that make a good bit of noise as they sweep the streets after last night's people madness. There wasn't anything special going on but it was jammed with strollers and feeders looking for the best restaurant deal. It was a great spot for people watching. This morning the cobbled streets are bare of people but lots of litter awaits the green disposal machines.

One last hug and Chas disappeared down the metro and I walked down the quai, weeping. It will be a long time until we see each other again. That was the start of a bad day.

I met a couple of American kids: one was to bicycle the Dordogne Valley. We sat and chatted a while then the train left. My seat was in a little enclosed room with one guy. While he slept and before Orleans which was the first stop, my left knee swelled to twice its normal size and hurt a bunch. I can't think of anything that I did to cause the swelling. Walking was fairly difficult. I got to Blois and retrieved Spot from the hotel, had lunch, and awaited the arrival of my friends. Probably I would be able to bicycle with some pain. It has been three days since I had been on the bike so the sore knee didn't seem bike related. Lots of cross-training believers got to be that way after an injury kept them from doing their usual sport. And, well, darn. To make everything even worse, it is raining for the first time in France. It rained a little last night in Paris but that didn't count. Nobody even moved fast on the crowded streets. Actually, the French aren't paying much attention to the rain here either. Sun came out. I guess they know what they are doing.

It is hard to tell the average French person from the average American. I look at the shoes. The French women wear sandals and the American female tourist is wearing sensible walking shoes. I have achieved a certain level of gauche by wearing socks under my sandals. I must do this because the sandals are new, and make instant blisters. The swelling in the knee seems to be going down. I can bend it.

3.6.95 Billeyeux. Near Chambord. Met the others as planned in Blois and biked about 20 K to this little town where they met up with other bikers they had met before so we had dinner with a couple from Iowa. My knee was still very painful. The couple seemed to me to be very patronizing. They asked me,

"What is your favorite thing in France so far?"

"My husband," I sniffled and a big tear rolled down my cheek. They looked at me as if I had announced that I had the Plague.

I took a bunch of Motrin and limped a lot but was able to bike. The knee could bend but was still swollen out where it should have been dented in.

We toured the chateaux again that Chas and I toured. Francois I's treasurer skimmed off enough from the building of Chambord to have a nice little palace of his own.

Camped last night as usual. It is heavy overcast today. We are going to have to skip Orleans and head east to make up for time we have lost. It is so scenic that we are doing less distance during the day in order to take in all the chateaus. Frankly, I'm about chateauxed out.

7.7.95 Paray-le Monial. However much the split with Alma and Jim was my fault, it was basically this: I never could adapt to the French time sense. I am up at the crack of dawn and out on the road before traffic. When the traffic gets bad I try to find a restaurant and hide out doing breakfast until the rush hour is past. I'm done at five. Eat and be in my snug little bivvy by eight. If you know France you know how they don't think of dinner until I am in bed. Alma and Jim were able to adapt completely. They also laid around in the mornings until the dew had dried from the tents and grass. By 7:30 AM I would be packed and getting grumpy if my companions were not stirring. By eight I would be sour. By nine I had given up on life and joy. In the evening, I hated trying to stay awake at eight o'clock. I usually ordered the Plate du Jour and house red and lived with whatever that might be. If the wines were too dry, I ordered the Coke du Jour. I think of McDonald's as ethnic food. I'm such a slob. I am to the point where I can't take any of French food. It gives me instant heartburn. I order the house cola. I avoid making a decision about dinner by ordering the Plat de Jour, usually the cheapest thing on the menu. Well, guess what? They have had enough of me.

Today, even with a 10:00 start, we made 50 miles. We were in time to enjoy a nice swim in the campground pool. The camping has been spotty but this is a really nice one on the outskirts of an industrial town. I took a picture of an old cathedral and its cloisters from a bridge. Perfect reflections and flowers in the foreground.

This is our last day on the Loire. We will miss it terribly. Tomorrow we start climbing hills to Macon and from Macon it gets really tough all the way to Switzerland.

In one of these castles the claim was made that Lancelot lived there. Perhaps Abigney. Wasn't The Idles of the King, a fictional thing? I could look it up. Saw the Duke de Nevers Castle and the Cathedral. Wonderful stuff and Nevers a charming city.

Split from Alma and Jim in Decize because Alma wanted to go back up a hill we had already come down. She was very upset with me. I was just trying to save my knees as usual. As I went along the canal that day and the next, I left messages for them at every campground and cafe.

7.8.95 Fourchambault. Near Nevers. Still split from Alma and Jim.

I am close to Nevers where they are having a huge St. Bernadette pageant tonight. It would take a taxi and almost $100 US to swing it so I guess I'll pass it up. Everything would be in French anyhow. They do a lot of stuff in French here.

How could I forget my second indecent exposeur!!

I was walking around the town after dinner and came back into the campground which was quite large and nice near the river. I walked around the outer road with the idea of cutting through a gate to go out along a path to enjoy the river. When I got to the gate there was a jogger, waving his masculine gender at me. I giggled. I said excuse me, thinking that I had intruded on him when he had stopped to tinkle, and walked away. It took a while to realize that a discreet piddler wouldn't do it by the gate, especially as the jogging path was higher than the hedges and he could see me coming. Oh, well, I muttered and went back to Spot and my bivvy, strategically placed beside an older couple. This French pair had been to San Francisco and the Grand Canyon.

It was pretty standard for us to be asking people what would be the best way into Switzerland. The lady pointed out my eventual route to Geneva. Actually it was the same route Alma had planned except for one day.

7.9.95 Macon, France. I spent part of the day going to see St. Bernadette. She is laid out under glass in a chapel. I couldn't get very close because a busload of Japanese tourists were crowded around. I tried to meditate a bit but the Japanese tour director was giving a loud lecture in Japanese in the chapel and it was a bit distracting. What I could see of her seemed a bit on the greenish side. I saw Mao in Tiananmen square and he was pretty green also. It was almost as noisy as a Mexican church. I am always astonished by lack of decorum and sometimes outright commercialism in Catholic churches.

Two mountains yesterday and I am really tired today. Spot and I are at about 1500 feet and contemplating the assault on Geneva, Switzerland. The route proposed by the lady in the campground is through Bourg-en-Bresse (20 miles) then a little flatter stuff then up what looks, on my Michelin map, like a river valley to Nantua.

Alma and Jim caught up with me and we shared a camping spot. I had dinner with them one last time.

The Very Last Supper:

Part one is finding seats.

The table linen was faultlessly crisp and white. The glasses, good quality and sparkling, were properly arranged for the meal. We had chosen the oldest and what looked to be the most prestigious of the hotels in this small French city. After the usual debate about seating: should be as far as possible from anyone who even looked as though they might smoke . . . we settled into a comfortable table. One of the wonders of these restaurants was that they rarely had tables big enough for all the glasses and dishes with which they were adorned, and no room at all for my elbows.

Part two is the waiting for the menu.

I suppose that I might have been drumming my fingers on the table. The endless, but intrinsically French fussing around was so annoying at the end of a long day. Why can't I just get my order in so I can get to the toilet and find comfort? Why is there no McDonalds in this town?

Part three is the menu.

A French menu still looks like the opening of a scrabble game to me. Alma, calmly and patiently, explains once more what the offerings are. I usually settle on what will be the least worst. Sometimes it is the least worst financially and some times it is the least worst taste-wise. I had been trying to resign myself to vinegary salads (instant heartburn), watery soups, and tiny main dishes, not to mention the bagettes which are like chewing sticky air. I needed to lose weight, of course but two spoonfuls of noodles smothered by one spoonful of meat always seems ridiculous.

Part four is deciding on the wine. Wine gives me heart burn.

So perhaps I am a tiny bit sullen when Alma and Jim go on and on about the wine. When the waiter finally arrives they go on and on some more about the wine. It invariably came down to which local (cheapest) wine, red or white. That always depended on what color the meat was. I could not see much reason for the fuss because any meat had been creamed and mashed and beaten beyond all recognition of its original self.

Lately I had been ordering steak and fries because they were at least identifiable: the steak so tough, the fries so greasy that it was a creative experiment in bad eating. Worst of all was knowing how much cheaper and better it would have been at home.

Jim decided on a wine and Alma, in a burst of self-righteous economy went for a carafe of tap water. I ordered brown beer and went off in search of the toilette.

When I got back to the table they were finishing their soup, a really delicious looking concoction with mussels floating in it.

"Good soup?" I am trying to be friendly although fatigue has me in its grip.

They smiled and said that it was really exceptional.

Damn. Something that I would have really liked.

They chattered on excitedly about the main course while I studied my beer.

Surprisingly they had chosen the roast beef, not something the French do well, particularly if you are from Kansas like Jim and a self-proclaimed expert in beef. Probably it was to try the

Charolait after biking past those winsome bovines all day. The French have the gall to claim that these Cafe au Lait beeves are better than Black Angus! There had been one barn that I passed that afternoon that afternoon that had several Charolait steers poking their heads over a picturesque stone wall. A great calendar picture. I wondered what the steers would do if I tried to scratch their heads. It was one of those precious moments that make bicycling so special.

Part five The plat

My pitiful handful of Stroganoff just barely soiled the plate. Their piece of roast beef was as fine a thing as you could imagine: thick, juicy, done rare to perfection. Damn. I messed up again. It would definitely be worth the bank loan that they would have to pay for it.

Part six The critique.

They started criticizing the wine first: the body, the aroma. Then they moved on to the beef, the only decent cut of meat that I had seen in France. Perhaps they were trying to make me feel better, me with my spoonful of Stroganoff. The beef was too tough, not warm, fatty . . . they went on and on. It seemed to stretch the meal into somewhere beyond midnight, an agonizing endurance trial. I found myself being torn apart by huge yawns. Fatigue won out, settled in to the very bone marrow and my head drooped to my chest.

"Perhaps we should send it back." This from Alma who had been getting good at sending wines back.

"Yes," Jim almost shouted. "We should sent it back."

He was galvanized by the thought, glowing. I was jolted into wakefulness. I gaped in amazement. They had devoured all but a few scraps and were talking about sending it back?

"How are you going to send it back? In a barf bag," I snorted. I was relentless.

"How about a simple X-ray to show the damage to your alimentary canal?"

Alma gave me a look that meant that she had not found me amusing. I was cowed back into my gloom.

Part seventeen was dessert. Jim settled down with a deep glow of contentment saying,

"I was thinking of having coffee and dessert. I don't want to keep you up."

"Yes," I responded, "that would indeed be a massive pain in the ass. Au voir."

I made a hasty exit, leaving Alma to pay my bill. Having had a nap, I lolled along the ancient street admiring the bursts of color from the geraniums that filled every empty nook of the old town. I was drawn to the bridge, built in the Roman style with sturdy, stone piers. As I clambered down the stairs to the canal that sparkled under the bridge, I decided to take a couple of Ibuprophen for my poor old knees. They had suffered more than they should on the small hills that day. The campground was by the river and very pleasant for one of the city campgrounds.

I had won a small war there, defending my assigned spot, right on the river, from a red-faced tourist who was hauling $20,000 worth of caravan who became enraged that a one night tenter/bicycler should preempt him. I was pleased that I stood up to Monsieur Beer-Belly and won. As I was strolling down the canal a British woman invited me to her boat for a beer. She and her husband told me about the big decision, four years earlier to buy the boat and live on it in France. We were joined by two other couples and it progressed into a very pleasant party. There are 8,000 miles of canals in France that are navigable. Many of these canals have converted the old towpath into a bicycle path so France is also wonderful for bicycling. These Brits head for the Cote de Azure for the winter.

Alma is going by train to Switzerland to spend time with relatives and Jim, if you can believe him, says he is headed north, for Alsace. So, I am the one and only to make the assault on the Swiss mountain fastness. I'll probably hole up in Bourge to rest because I am so shaky. I will also check the Gare (train station) here and at Bourge for the train schedules in case I wimp out. I had better get going now while it is still cool. It is beautiful countryside and beautiful hilly towns and chateaus.

7.9.95. Bourg (en Bresse) A lot of Bourgs in France, I guess, so this one is the one on the river Bresse. What a nice quiet Sunday ride. The roads are a lot like home with corn about thigh high on rolling hills. There are long lanes of huge sycamores which are very close to the road for a red road and give a lot of welcome shade. The farm buildings themselves are endlessly fascinating, old and charming. I'm having the Plat de Jour at a quaint restaurant. It is not easy to get in before the opening hour of noon but the restaurant folk were as agreeable as usual and I am out of the heat. I heard from many people that it is difficult to get something to eat Sundays and Mondays but so far I am not starving. The BAR TABAC which reeks of smoke also has, quite often, a well hidden back room where numbers of people are eating rather well.

Today I am again on the greatly feared red roads on the Michelin maps. It seems that there are red roads and red roads. If there are two near each other, the winding, hilly one will be as free of trucks and cars as the usual yellow road. There is a foot or so of shoulder.

I am planning to stop early today and maybe get a cheap room somewhere before I start up the mountains. I can see a blue line of mountains in the eastern sky now.

I'm doing OK with the language until I try to get them to discuss roads between here and Switzerland. Perhaps they just don't want to be the bearer of bad tidings. I am only about 40 miles from Geneve. Should this be so much of a problem? Just do it!!!!

The Plat du Jour turned out to be: first an appetizer of jellied meat with tomatoes and lettuce and a dressing that may get me to doing dressings again. The main course was roast beef with a couple of unknown veggies in lovely sauces. Bagette of course. Dessert is a white thing with sour cream over it, not sweet but refreshing. They said it was cheese.

Later: I have found a cheapie motel (in the $30 range.) after leaving a campground that looked as though it was filling up with gypsies. This motel was recommended by the understanding owner of the campground. It is brand new and has TV. After a long nap I watched my first rock and roll video. Mercy. There was Michael Jackson on a potty. It always seems that everything imported from the US is this kind of garbage. I look for the Herald Tribune because it has crossword puzzles. In the usual kiosk there is the Wall Street Journal, and the Herald and the rest is Hustler and Penthouse and worse pig slop. No wonder foreigners think we are awful.

On the TV, I found an archeological comparison of stone masonry in France, Peru, and Algeria. I took a shower. It was a real challenge to find out how to turn it on. I am highly mistrustful of showers anyhow. They can turn evil and either flash freeze or boil you without a glimmer of conscience. This one and the toilet and the sink looked as if they arrived as an afterthought. They are a plastic unit that sits about six inches high in the corner of the room. After searching vainly for the faucet to turn the *"douche"* on, I got all dressed again to go down to ask the girl at the desk to find out how to turn the shower on. Do I like looking stupid? Just for laughs I fiddled with the faucet on the sink. Guess what? That's where they hid the controls for the shower!!!!

My outfit for tomorrow has bee carefully laid out for the assault on *Geneve*. My Alma Mater was Geneva College. The Beaver Falls, Pennsylvania, Reformed Presbyterian, Geneva College was named, no doubt, in honor of this Geneva, a theocracy established by the French protestant, John Calvin. Geneva, Switzerland, when I flew in and out of it in 1979 it was surrounded by beautiful, snow-covered Alps. I hope to find the way into the mountain citadel that many French kings would have liked to have found. The route that I have chosen has only one tunnel. It follows very winding streams up and over a mountain range to Nantua. Nantua is on the Rhone River which rises in *Lac Geneve*, also known as *Lac Leman*. I may try to find a train in Nantua. I don't think that this part of Switzerland is all that high. We were there over for Christmas in '79 and the sailboats were sitting out in the lakes. The thrifty Swiss would not risk their craft if the lake iced over.

I am really looking forward to Switzerland. In my memories it is the most beautiful of any place that I have been. I laid out my fake blue jean tights, a white bike jersey, and my running shoes as if I were preparing for a race. The last time I walked a couple of mountains I got heel spurs so I am being extra careful to wear the shoes with the orthotics in them. I have a friend who says that getting old is not for sissies. Orthotics. Glasses. Fake teeth. But, it beats the alternative.

7.10.95 Nantua, France. Tomorrow will probably be my last day in France unless I make a big effort to get back to Evian for Bastille Day on the 14th. Every little town has been promising *feu* and I'd like to make up for the lack of anything at all on the 4th of July. Today's trip started out in Bourg-en-Bresse which is a major manufacturing center (Renault trucks), and therefore a bit grubby and not as quaint. France is just so pleasing and adorable and lovable, especially here in Nantua. As I left I met a peleton of Sunday riders. They tried to chat but when I got out, "*Je suis Americaine*," and therefore hopeless at languages, they gave up easily.

When I ask about the difficultly of the Mountain passes, the French don't seem to think they are bad. You really miss that "Yew aint goona make it up that there mountain. Yuk Yuk", that we get at home. Here they see the skinny little racers, an endless line of them, skipping up the toughest mountains on their tiny hairpin-like *velos*. So it doesn't seem as hard to the average Frenchman. The sight of me pushing Spot up miles of 10%, 12%, 15% grades today must have been an oddity. Most of the other bike tourers that I met today were headed north up the mountain valleys as Jim says he will do. What I was doing, going East up and down huge mountain ridges, seemed pretty dumb. Even to me. My erstwhile partner headed up one of the valleys and will tour Alsace instead of Switzerland. So what got into me?? I'm the world's biggest wimp. Don't know, so I pay the price.

Chapter XIII

Switzerland

The world is not yet exhausted; let me see something tomorrow which I never saw before.

Samuel Johnson

Informational aside:

Switzerland's history is a bit hard to follow. 1215 was the big year when a bunch of Swiss farmers demolished a force of Burgundian (French) knights with a battle formation that was a square with a bunch of pikes sticking out of it. The Burgundians had just been passing through and were a lot the worse for the battle. After the battle, three cantons got together for a mutual defense pact. The Swiss claim that their country started then and that their democracy started then. From that time on, no one went through Switzerland and no one conquered this tight little confederation. Women didn't get the vote until 1971 but that is a minor detail. There was one civil scuffle when Lausanne and several others tried to pull out of the confederation.

There are quite a few Generals who have achieved eminence and their claim to fame is that they kept Switzerland out of war.

Most tax money goes to the Canton. The Swiss around the Neuchatel area that I talked to seemed to feel that too much was going to welfare and that they had a problem like the one in the States. Their other big problem is that they have not joined the EC. CIBA the huge drug industry in Basel may just skip over the line to Germany and save heaps of money.

Over time many other cantons joined the federation, the last being Geneva. To make this more clear, think about Liechtenstein, a land-locked, independent country on the border between Switzerland and Austria. If Liechtenstein felt threatened by Austria, it could take itself and its stamps into the Swiss confederation. It would maintain its language, customs, government and by contributing 2% of its yearly taxes to the federation gain the defense of the most respected army in the world. The Federation would use the tax money for roads and defense and very little else. No federal welfare programs.

The German speaking people dominate Switzerland through sheer size of their lands and the numbers of their people. The country is about evenly divided by Protestant and Catholic. They had religious wars, the theocracy under John Calvin, and now the major religion is banking. There is a bank for every 2400 people and 10% of the working population works in banking.

The banking got its start in the 18th and 19th centuries when the highly trained Swiss soldiers were rented out by the cantons to other governments as mercenaries. The only remnant is the Swiss Guard at the Vatican. The money gained from these efforts was put into banks by the cantons and the major industry was born.

End of informational: My reference on this is *Place de la Concorde Suisse* by John McPhee.

I looked for the Protestant churches but didn't see many. When I asked the Swiss architect what makes Switzerland work so well, he answered, TOLERANCE. Since the horror of the religious wars, they seem to have learned a lesson and pretty much have learned to live together. Of concern for even the most tolerant are the numbers of North African Muslims who have moved into the Geneva area. In a land of nine million people, one million are foreigners who do not share the centuries old traditions of thirty-four years in the army for the able-bodied man. Every Swiss man is in the army and does have a highly effective ouzie type gun at home. The ammo is sealed and he has to account for it if it doesn't come back to the practice sessions just as it went out.

7.11.95 Geneva, Switzerland. Still huge from the meal I ate trying to get rid of my French francs. Everything was absolutely drowned in oil. Oh well. I should have sent it back to the kitchen with a stern remark. Guess I never will get to be a connoisseur.

There was a climb out of Nantua but not bad and a very long downhill into Bellegard. Then was a steep climb out of there and again a big downhill to the dreaded tunnel at the defile into Switzerland. The tunnel wasn't long but it was narrow and I put on my lights, especially the little blinker that I wore on my back, and pushed Spot through the tunnel. Spot is now resting in the basement of the hostel. This hostel is in a much better neighborhood than it would be in the US. The really grand hotels are just around the corner on Lac Leman (Lake Geneva). Everyone speaks English here, and the hostel carries CNN so I got to hear a state department guy mush-mouth about poor Sarajevo. Looks like the Serbs will have it soon. I will try to make a reservation for the hostel at Lausanne for Thursday night. Have to check my schedule, but I think that I am right on.

7.12.95 Geneva Switzerland. I went to visit the UN with my new friend from the hostel, Angela. She is an ophthalmologist from Australia. She isn't great with maps and finding things and we had a lot of laughs about a lot of stuff.

Angela Wang and Spot in Geneva, Switzerland.

Geneva is a big city masquerading as a resort town. The lake is beautiful, the mountains are gorgeous and it is truly worth the trip to just be here. The hostel is OK. It is very pleasant to have someone to talk to. However, when I wanted to collapse and snooze for a couple of hours after lunch at the ethnic cafe, (McDonald's) the hostel is closed. Hostels do that. They close between 9:00 A. M. and 5 PM. So, I am taking a cruise of the small ports on Lac Leman. I watch the scenery go sailing by me instead of the other way around. Meeting Angela again for dinner and perhaps we will travel together to Lausanne tomorrow.

7.13.95 Lausanne, Switzerland. Actually we weren't in the high rent district of Geneva, that was across the Rhone, in the old section. The shops that sell Rolex watches and French Haut Couturier clothing were really a wonder to behold: gorgeous jewels and fabulous furs. This must be one of the watering holes of the very, very rich. On the boat tour that I took they pointed out the mansion of the Rothchilds. The Rothchilds, Jews, were brought in to Switzerland from France to help establish the banks. How ironic that the Swiss banks should later be discovered to have cheated holocaust victims. The UN buildings sprawl across the skyline. Local children play on the sidewalks and streets going at breakneck speed on bikes and roller-skates. There is a beach, marina, and diving platform right in the middle of the city which gives it the feeling of a resort. Back a couple of blocks you find industrial grunge. There is an impressive fountain that, given certain conditions of wind and temperature is spraying its great amount of water into the sky. It is higher than the buildings and can be seen for miles as we boat down the lake to Lausanne.

I couldn't resist taking a second day off the bike to enjoy a second boat ride and the company of my friend Angela. She was one of those people who know the places to go and things to see. We have no place to stay in Lausanne because the hostel is full. Angela doesn't believe that but we will see. The hostel in Geneve was comfortable and lots of interesting people.

Angela Wang was wrong. There was no room in Lausanne so we continued down the lake to Montreaux

7.18.95 Angela Wang was one of those treasures that you can find in a hostel on an excellent day: someone from a completely different culture who is also entirely agreeable We were both going to Lausanne and decided to travel together. She had been born in Shanghai. Her family were doctors who decided to try their fortunes on mainland China because they were dedicated Communists. Being a doctor there was no treat. She had great responsibilities but no more pay, and no technical updating in her field of ophthalmology. When the cultural revolution came along, even doctors could not escape and Angela spent three years in a commune, working in the fields and, she said with her mouth down in a scowl, getting her brain retrained. When they were finally able to leave China, her family went to Australia. She has been in Australia for seven years and is retraining to be a technician in the ophthalmologist field. The head of her hospital in China is also in Australia and sweeps floors there because he is not qualified to be a doctor in Australia. Asked if she would go back to China, she grits her teeth and says harshly,

"I will never go back."

Angela is fifty and looks much younger. She is a tireless traveler. It was her suggestion that we do the UN building and that was a rewarding experience. It is such a wonderful thing for countries of the world to sit down to talk about peace and disarming. May their efforts help the megalomaniacs of the world restrain themselves from their terrible acts toward their fellow man. The UN emphasis was on land mines and the horrible cost in innocent lives in so many lands. The much photographed Princess Diane was their celebrity advocate.

7.15.95 Montreaux, Switzerland. If I ever become incredibly rich, I would like a villa here in Montreaux. It is steep as it rises out of Lac Leman but the beauty of the snow capped mountains and the lake seem like a dream from a Maxfield Parrish painting. There is world class skiing just a short distance away at Chamonix. There are palm trees by the lake. The Montreaux Jazz Festival is about to start. A quartet from Madrid, a Tuna, fully togged out in medieval costumes arrived and I had a good time with them. They let me sing "*Cielito Lindo*" with them. I couldn't quite admit to having been a *maestra* of Spanish, but they did understand my Spanish and I, their Castillian.

Angela and I took a narrow gau ge train up into the mountains to see the little villages up there. I took a lot of pictures. It was Bastille Day but I couldn't talk Angela into boating across the Lake to the French spa, Evian, for the *feu*.

7.15.95 Angela wanted me to go with her to Chamonix where she was meeting friends but I had my schedule and thought that she would be speaking Chinese with them and I would feel left out. Her suitcase was huge so I put it on Spot and together, laughing, we transported it up a Swiss hill to the train station. When I later read the much recommended *Three Swans*, I felt that I really knew one of those poor souls battered down by Chinese communism.

7.16.95 Lausanne. Yesterday was hard on me and I wanted to take a very short day to rest up. I had started from Montreaux with intentions of taking the shortest way to Neuchatel but was seduced by the lovely parks along Lake Geneva. Earlier in the day, in Vevey on Lac Leman, I bicycled into a Saturday market with rows of veggies and fruit and a large area where you could sample wine before buying from possibly thirty wine makers. I didn't get involved in the wine but did enjoy a concert by a seated marching band.

A little further on, I chanced upon a campground where I spotted the very distinctive $1000 gortex tent that belonged to Jim and Jim's $5,000 bike, left all unguarded. I rolled in and found some British bicyclers who said that the old fellow (he's five years younger than I) had gone off to the mountains for the day in a car with a red haired lady, (could this possibly be Alma?) and her aged mother. I left a note begging him not to drop out of the trip and giving my approximate schedule and when the group would assemble in Budapest. To no avail. He did drop out. My selfish disappointment was that he was carrying repair equipment so I had not bothered to bring any. Thanks the gracious god of bicyclers, Spot hung tough for the rest of Europe and I had no need for repairs.

I had so many miles to go and so little time that I passed up the usual collection of brown signs indicating tourist attractions like the Olympic venue. The last hour into the hostel, where I had a reservation, was really a bear I had only the address to show the local people and as I did they gasped, sighed, grabbed their heart, and with hand clapped on forehead, dramatically pointed up an unspeakable mountain, covered with huge factories and chateaus. Finally, I get the "Yew aint gonna make it up that there mountain" from a Swiss. Well, it was getting dark, but I did, pushing Spot every inch of the way. One compassionate young man on a motor bike led me the last mile rather than try to explain where the hostel was. The girl at the hostel desk had saved my reservation even though I was an hour late. None of the usual crowd of oldsters had made it to the top of this mountain and I had no one to talk to. Only one more day of French and I get to struggle with German, which I have never formally studied.

7.17.95 Neufchatel, Switzerland. I breakfasted in an outdoor cafe in Lausanne that had metal chairs. I somehow pinched a finger in a chair so hard it bled. I got a band aid from a helpful girl there, and went bravely on my way. The British bikers at Jim's campground in Cluny had a bicyclers' map of Switzerland. Using it, I pictured a small hill separating the two lakes, Neufchatel and Leman, and that was right. However, I had not figured on Swiss roads not having any road numbering system. Imagine! So what is the system? You find the fifteen or twenty roads going in the direction that you are going and stare at the town signs until one comes clear. Heaven only knows how you would find time to do this in a car.

Then there is the problem that there are two roads going to the same town and the bicyclist wants the least busy. Which one will take you to the autobahn and which one to the pleasant country road? Well, at this point in time the autobahn is relatively new and so its signs are the newer ones. If this seems vague, it is understandable that I could lose a frustrating half-day back-tracking and wandering. I had been trying to buy a bicyclers map of Switzerland since I saw the one used by the Brits at Jim's campground and knew that there was a best route through the tangle of roads northwest of Lausanne. My (wrong) road turned out to be a rustic 15% grade around a mountain with the (right) choice, stream hugging, white road in view as I pushed Spot up Unnecessary Mountain. I was rewarded for stupid perseverance by a little town at the top that was celebrating a wedding.

The sound of brisk drums attracted me to a little plaza with an incredibly old, yellow, sandstone church, very humble and modest with a crowd of patiently waiting people. Part of the crowd was a uniformed soccer team and they lined up in front of the door in a double line but second to a uniformed drum section of a drum and bugle corps. As a bell chimed three o'clock, the traps and big bass drum took up an emphatically enthusiastic beat. The door opened and the bride and groom strode out and joined in what had become a reception line for the rest of the party and all the people in the church. She was lovely, dark-haired in a shining satin gown of shimmering white. He was handsome in a blue tux. Except for the ear-splitting drums it could have been any old small town wedding in the US. Bettina Selby, who writes the charming books about bicycle touring, would have wangled an invite to the wedding dinner that I passed later at a restaurant in the valley. I ate alone.

7.18.95 Solothun. Today was rainy and I had a reservation at a hostel only 10 miles away. It has rained every night since I got to Switzerland but most of the days have been nice. I am loathe to leave the shelter of this restaurant and brave the elements. I could hang out here for sometime then take a ferry down Lac Neufchatel to somewhere.

You know how it is with European cafes, they are never plagued with the flies that make our attempts at ambiance so pitiful. Well, the flies are in this one, accompanied by adorable, brazen sparrows that walk up to your plate on your table. They don't mind the large, scruffy, black dog that comes right in the door to stare at you with sad eyes.

The guidebook said that for the price of a cup of coffee you can sit all day in one of these cafes and I may take that to the limit.

Last night at the hostel cost $27 for the night, a dinner of sandwich and drink and this morning's breakfast. Not bad prices for Switzerland.

7.18.95 Solothun, Switzerland. I enjoyed a second breakfast in Neuchatel after getting a bit wet. I had a long lunch in a charming little hotel restaurant while it poured rain. Later, as I was approaching the Solothun hostel, I asked directions of a young girl who had been mountain biking and was all covered with mud. She invited me to her parents' home for the night and I gladly accepted. The apartment is very modern and has some great artwork done by her father who is an architect. Bettina Selby would have been proud of me.

Do you know Bettina Selby? She is a Brit who can bike in places that I don't even consider and be given housing and food and companionship every where she goes. She has written lots of books about her travels. Could she possibly be stretching the truth a bit?

7.18.95 Solothun, Switzerland. It occurred to me while conversing with the kind people who took me in that German would be a lot easier to learn than French. French has such a unique intonation, a lilt, that I could only master on my most cheerful days. The intonation of German is a lot more like American: slower, flatter, more deliberate. Let's say, grumpier. The Berlitz book on languages that I am carrying says that in 1781 when the US was just getting organized that German lost out to English by only one vote as the official language. Well, I'm glad of that because I might have missed Thomases Paine and Jefferson, not to speak of the *Autobiography* of Benjamin Franklin. Not to mention living in the world's greatest democracy.

However, looking back, the Metzger on my father's side, the France (corruption of Frantz) on my mother's side, probably weigh heavily on my Western Pennsylvania tongue. I like the German and will enjoy learning a couple of dozen words in it. I contacted Joe Beckman who said that he had finished his teaching duties at the University of Zurich and he said they had a large and luxurious apartment in the good part of town so come and visit.

I have been following the delightful bicycle path along the Aare River, going down!!!! Is it possible that I have crested the top of Europe and the rest of the trip is down hill? It is only 430 meters of altitude here. On Lake Geneva there were huge southern-type magnolias, and a couple of palm trees. This is not all that much higher than Pittsburgh. The bike path seemed to be marked better than the road. I'm on Bike 1. It is flat, down, tailwind, and perfect weather. The bread (brot) changed with the language from the mostly air baguette to a sturdy brown bread with a lot of flavor. I met one young US biker who said that his budget was so tight that he could only afford to eat baguettes in France. He now hates French bread and loves the heavy *brot*. Me, too.

Having lunch: potato soup, cold plate of the usual nasty pickled veggies and ham and hard-boiled egg. $14. The pickled veggies are beautiful but give me instant heartburn from the vinegar. It is like eating acid. Poison.

Forgot to pay!!! I was messing with my bike in front of the restaurant when the owner came out and indignantly informed me of the oversight. I apologized and paid immediately but he continued to grouse and went out to the bike and was writing things down. The guy was as sour as his inedible food. On his street were telephone poles with storks nesting.

This day has been just another day of fascinating to adorable old Swiss towns. The bike path was very pleasant but a tad slow. It went on bike paths, bike lanes, forest roads and around most towns. It utilized some farm roads that went between the house and barn. Between house and barn is dog land. Any dog worth his kibbles is going to keep strangers out of such an area. I was very nervous but had no problems with loose dogs.

The most charming thing today was the many large houses attached to large barns. It sounds bad but they are beautiful with the usual array of shutters and flowers.

Spent a night in the hostel in Zolfingen. Son Mac had spent some time in Zolfingen coaching triathletes. It could have been right here at the hostel which is large and near some soccer fields. There are both male and female athletes lodging here. The next

day I biked a while toward Zurich until it got too busy. Finished the trip in by catching a train into the city as Joe had suggested.
7.19.95 Zurich, Switzerland. Just had coffee with two professors from the famous university where Einstein taught. Joe Beckman is here for the summer and I have been enjoying two days with him and Tanya and the children. Dr. Joe has finished teaching and is now working on a couple of chapters he is doing for a textbook. James Joyce and Richard Wagner had both stayed in the house where their spacious apartment is. It was a gasthaus at that time. It is a really nice rest for me. Tanya and I take the children to the park or do a little shopping. Prices here in Switzerland could almost spoil the joy of being here. Many things seem four times what they are at home. Nevertheless, Switzerland is my idea of heaven. You can comfortably bicycle along the rivers and lakes, you can ski in the winter, and you are surrounded by such beauty. After doing some research, I am still somewhat confused about why Switzerland works so well. The nation started as a confederation in the 1880's when Germany and Italy were also forming as nations. French speaking Geneva was the last to join. The position of neutrality has kept them out of the wars which devastated so much of Europe. Banking is the biggest industry with 500 years of security to boast of. Almost 10% of the workers are in the banking industry *La Place de la Concorde Suisse* By John McPhee was Joe's book. I spent two nights reading it on the couch in the living room. I think I love John McPhee. (I got to listen to a lecture by McPhee in Pittsburgh and bought a couple more books that may take me the rest of my life to understand.)

I am so excited today. I believe that I have crested the top of Europe and from here on out, will be headed down. I'm in Switzerland where it is as I remembered, fairly flat if you stay out of the mountains. From Lake Nuechatel I have been going down. If this river that I am following, the Aare, empties into Lake Constance and the Danube River starts near Lake Constance, I have indeed been clever. Time will tell. Actually the Times Atlas would tell but I'd have to get a trailer to carry it.

Joe and son George were so sweet, showed Spot and me
how to ride the trolley to the end of the line.

It still took an hour to get out of Zurich. It turned out that the Aare River empties into the Rhine and the Danube starts a short distance away so I am substantially correct and most of the rest of Europe will be down and should have a tailwind. Was it Augustus who built a wall from the Danube to the Rhine? Is it still there? Life is made interesting by all the stuff I don't know. There is a bike path by the Danube from where it begins clear to Vienna. This is great route picking for lazy river lovers.

I will probably change the route and instead of going from Fussen north on the bike path will probably just forget Fussen and cruise along between Munich and the mountains. There are a lot of little lakes and some swamps and Obergamerau. I love the name but am unlikely to do the uphill meters to see a passion play. Not my passion. The Hostel is a lovely old building but I am back up under the roof where my sweat pours out in rivers. The whole day was pretty warm. The locals are swimming here in the lake but dinner is at six and I probably won't get my act together enough to swim.

Later: As I walked along the lake, a young woman drove up. Stopped. Got out of her car and took off every stitch of clothing. She put on a bathing suit and waded out into the lake for a swim.

Chapter XIV

GERMANY

. . . Unt chu vill enchoy id!

7.22.95 Fussen, Germany. Such a day. A whole entire vacation could have been on this day. It started at six o'clock in the hostel in Constance because I had requested frustuch at that hour. Then I was headed for Kempten. At Isny I picked up a bicycle path that went all 29 Ks to Kempten. Most of this was a rail/trail conversion that climbed an enormous mountain and then descended even further through cool green spruce trees. I arrived at Kempten pretty well whipped and covered with welts from fly bites. I tried to get a room at several places that said 'Zimmer' and was told to come back at five o'clock. The Germans take a siesta. They close stuff for a while and then open again later. I wanted to take a nap too, or just quit for the day but the ladies who ran the Zimmers were in the midst of their naps and didn't want to be bothered until 5:00 and so I decided to go the rest of the way to Fussen by train.

Spot and I had one of those worst trips when the second train we took had only one car for a half-dozen bikes and way too many people for the space. I spent the hour hanging over the engineer to brace Spot. The track was small and the engineer slowed to an almost stop on every corner. There was no place to stay in Fussen. Summer weekend. Everything full-up. Fussen was just another adorable German town but with great cliffs for a background. I could not remember why people had told me to not miss Fussen. Too late I was reminded that Bavarian hostels don't take anyone over 26. Bavaria is where hostelling originated and is determined to maintain its youth oriented function. So while wandering out of town I found myself on Koenig Ludwig Weg. Now I know about Crazy King Ludwig and the Disneyland castle but imagine my surprise when I looked up and there it was. Got there too late to do anything but look around outside the amazing castle. Missed the interior tour. This longest day was far from over.

The second campground I tried gave me a spot and I settled in with an American couple. There were three or four acres of campers stuffed in so compactly that there was no room for trees or even grass. The management entertained a large crowd with a local band who appeared to know how to play polkas but were forced to do Beetles and John Denver over huge loudspeakers. Little puffy clouds grew black and settled heavily down over King Ludwig's Mountain. Then it rained. It got dark and really poured.

My camping spot quickly became a puddle, no, a pond. I grabbed my bivvy and found a huge split log bench under the eave of a boathouse and settled down. The band continued through the rain until after midnight. Teenage hordes used the boathouse where I had settled in for something that didn't sound like a rowing event. They were there jabbering and giggling long after the band quit. I had moved Spot under a porch thing attached to a trailer thinking that no one was home. As I removed her the next morning a head popped up inside. Oops! Spot and I left and are headed for Munich. If it is raining there and no shelter, we will go straight on to Salzburg in hopes of finding shelter. I know there are several huge hostels in Salzburg and it is Sunday so I am expecting it won't be as hard to find lodging as Saturday night. I swear that I will get into the hostel system and start making reservations and keeping them. It has now settled in to rain steadily. I am so glad I got up and to the train during a tiny break in the weather.

7.23.95 Munich, Germany. The nice thing about a big train station like Munich is that it is open on Sunday when most things are closed down. As I stood in line for a ticket to Saltzburg because I couldn't think of anything else to do . . . who should walk by but Liz! My mind had become so much like concrete that my thought was . . . I'll lose my place if I try to catch her. I gave my brain a good shaking and chased her down. We had a great time catching up on everything. She has been traveling alone since Brussels and says that she is having a wonderful time. Says it is the first thing she ever did on her own and she is loving it. She is heading for Warsaw. It doesn't seem that she would be able to make Budapest by the August 7,8,9 meeting period but she isn't concerned. Says she wants to do Bulgaria and Romania alone because it is a challenge. Liz, Helen, and the Olnesses had done southern England and then ferried to Belgium. Liz was armed with a big, heavy collection of Lonely Planet guide books when she and they hit Belgium. She announced that she was going on her own. Olnesses then decided that they wanted to be alone. All this left Helen alone. In other news, Jody had left her white water job in Maine and was now in Europe with Gene and a girl named Michelle who had joined up late. Olnesses managed to see the Tour de France go by and then headed for Poland.

Liz said that she and Helen parted because Helen hates maps and was always asking directions. One of the (seemed sensible to me) dictums from Ole was that you don't tell anyone your proposed route because people with bad intentions could be waiting for you. Liz was upset with Helen because she would always ask directions and go into a long thing about traveling around the world. Liz felt that that made things more dangerous. (Actually, Helen's is the Bettina Selby approach that gets you free housing and free dinners. It worked well that way for Helen.)

Liz and I did the city tour of Munich. We dined at Burger King after lunching at McDonalds. We enjoyed the nice toilettes and the ethnic food. I wanted to try some German beer in Germany so we sat in a bar, I, with a beer and Liz drinking water from her water bottle. The waiter kept bothering us. The Tour d'France was on the TV and we were enjoying watching it. I thought they were hitting on Liz, but what finally happened was they threw Liz out for not drinking their drinks and me too, for having such a friend, I guess.

She showed me how to take the subway, with bicycle, by taking the handicapped elevator (or freight elevator) down to the proper level and just get on the one you want, with the bike. It is OK to do this if it isn't rush hour.

Then there wasn't any use to hang out anymore so I got a room in the YWCA that she recommended and she went on to a campground. It was still raining and I wasn't up for the campground.

I'm back at Burger King today because I am really goofing off today. Liz recommended Dachau but the guide guy is closed Mondays and after serious consideration I decided that it would be worth it to stay over a day. Liz had come up the Rhine and said it was great, there was a bike path the whole way. Then she started down the Romantic Road and got as far as Augsburg before dropping it in favor of Munich. From here she goes to Regensburg then the mountains of the Czech Republic to Prague. I was headed for the Romantic Road but on her recommendation decided to skip it and will be heading straight for Saltzburg, hoping I can catch Ludwig's last castle on the way.

Fantastic news: Michael and Kevin were traveling together in London. Of the original 19, all made it to Europe except Tim, who had left his wife and business behind. Ric will meet us in Athens!!!!! And we picked up three more, the couple from North Carolina on the tandem and Michelle, a lone female. It should be fun to meet up in Budapest because more people are maturing to the idea that group travel is a pain and independent travel is an adventure. However, in some areas like Bulgaria and Roumania there would be safety in numbers.

There will be a bunch of Americans on the bus to Dachau tomorrow. Perhaps I can make a connection to Saltzburg with somebody. I stayed in my first *pension* today. It is a nice simple room that I can get into all day and take a nap, lock the door. I just wallow in the luxury of it. It is only 10 DM more than the YWCA bed with three others in the room, but still twice as much as you would pay at home . . . if you could find a room without bath or air conditioning in the US. I will try to do a half day of biking tomorrow and get down in the area of Ludwig's castle and then one more easy day (with luck) to Saltzburg.

Alan Wissenburg, guide at Dachau.

7.25.95 Dachau, Germany. My head is swimming with the stark horror of Dachau. The only statistic that stuck was that even after the camp was liberated, over 3000 died because they were beyond help. Films from those days showed piles of dead being taken out for burial by the local farmers who were wearing oxygen masks. The Germans themselves suffered terribly for following Hitler. Munich was almost leveled by bombing as were most German cities. What I saw on my city tour was mostly reconstructed. Munich was, is, the capital of independent Bavaria. There are a number of enormous palaces and public buildings including a bunch of museums which were closed Sunday and Monday. I found the city to be intimidating and was lacking the courage to walk much yesterday but did get to the plaza of the city building and sat there like the rest of the large crowd waiting for the mechanical little people on the clock to do their thing. Finally I finished my sketch of the people on the clock and went back to write up an article for Tom on Switzerland and one for Health and Fitness on The Route. I have to have a day in a private room to do my writing because I am so easily distracted.

I am having trouble expressing the pain that Dachau causes. It is an anguish that asks, 'Would I have been a Schindler or would I have been like most Germans, closing the eyes to what was happening? Would I have been like 95% of the French, collaborating or letting it happen? I remember reading *Babi Yar*, the hero saying that:

> When they came for his neighbor he closed his eyes,
> When they came for his family he closed his ears,
> When they came for him,
> There was no one to hear his crying.
>
> Babi Yar was in Russia.

I took a picture of the statue and sign that says, '**Never again**'. It has been 50 years. Can Europe now look at Sarajevo and not see? Not hear? The wonderful, impassioned young American who was our tour guide, Alan Wissenberg, said that the Dachau experience stands alone and should not be compared with any other, but it is hard not to. He was particularly inflamed by revisionists who want to deny that Dachau ever happened. Almost every German school child is brought to Dachau or one of the other camps and the story is told to them. It is against the law to deny that the holocaust happened in Germany. It is considered an offense against the dead, who cannot defend themselves. There is an American who sends hate mail all over the world from the US who is being held for extradition in Denmark (an EC member). If Germany gets him he will be fined heavily and sent out of the country. Oh, gee. That would hurt.

"Schindler's List" is becoming a requirement for those graduating from school in Germany. It should be a requirement in every school around the world.

Tolerance makes things work for Switzerland and intolerance brought the wrath of the free world on Germany. It was Germany's hate that leveled her cities and defeated her army. Fifty years later the scars of the war are gone but the scars of the Holocaust are scarlet across the soul of Germany.

"Throughout the world, the name Dachau is equated with the deepest horror of an inhumane government in Germany. Dachau has become the emblem and symbol of a murdering terror and of a loss of freedom." The quote from the Lord Mayor of Dachau.

Chapter XV

AUSTRIA

. . . The hills echo back the sound of music

7.25.95 Saltzburg. Mozart. I have come to worship at the birthplace of my favorite composer, but I bring with me rank, musty traces of Dachau death camp. At the hostel I met Carl Dalke, a Chicago person, an ex-GI over here on the fiftieth anniversary year of D Day. He had been with the 101st airborne at Bastogne and had suffered terribly there but survived. There was another battle which he felt he was lucky to have survived. Then 24 of the 101st were sent to see if they could catch Hitler at Berchtesgarden or the Eaglesmere. They heard about Dachau and stopped there long enough to get some pictures which Carl was still carrying. He showed me fotos that were sickening originals of heaps of dead at Dachau. He said that he feared that he had caused some of the poor wretches to die because they couldn't handle the army rations that he and his men handed out to the starving skeletons of people.

His soldiers were in a jeep and a truck. The group would ride into a German town. Carl would announce in German with a loudspeaker that they were the US Army, the place was surrounded, throw down weapons, and surrender. Lots of the old men and boys of the Wermacht did They would be told to march up the road to a prisoner camp and their guns were torched. When the Wermacht got to the spot and no one was there, they would just go home. Carl could speak German because he grew up on a Mennonite farm.

At Berchtesgaden, Carl's group arrived quietly and fanned out. Carl cautiously entered a hotel and heard German voices. He crept up a stairway to listen. He had no trouble understanding their plans to fight to the death. He entered the room with his Thompson machine gun and ordered the German officers to get down on the floor and throw in their weapons in his fluent German. He had captured twenty-two SS officers. Many SS officers were tried for war crimes.

Carl Dalke of the 101st Airborne finally
makes it to Eaglesmere

Eaglesmere is on the top of an Alp. You walk in a long cave into the center of the mountain and then take an elevator to the top of the mountain. There is the wonderful view, a great spot that had been enjoyed by the really bad guy who had the bad vegetarian breath. When Carl was here in 1945, they took the jeep up the road up the outside of the mountain for a distance but at that time, the Eaglesmere had been destroyed by allied aircraft.

After we returned to Saltzburg Carl headed out south on a train. I decided to brave the night and go to the *Sound of Music* dinner and show. At $52 it was a bit pricy but I loved it. Six young singers did Richard Rodgers and every now and then one of the

Strausses or Mozart. This was not going to cure me of my "*Sound of Music*" passion. I'm off early tomorrow to tour the places where they shot the movie. "*Sound of Music*" is the most popular movie in the world. I absolutely love Saltzburg. So Precious. Such fun.

7.27.95 Saltzburg. I Love Saltzburg. I had an entire day of Sound of Music again today as I did the bus tour to the places where they shot the movie. Saw a lot of other stuff and the lakes that I will bike by tomorrow if it doesn't continue to rain. Big thunder storm here this evening and I jogged a mile or so in it to get back to the hostel. Met a lovely lady from Cheyenne WY who is with a council on aging and thinks what I am doing is just great. I will try to keep in touch with her. My room at the hostel is full of tiny undies for tiny Japanese girls. They asked if they could cook in the room and I said OK not realizing how their spices would stink up the room. In a hostel, there is always a kitchen where they could have cooked

The Sound of Music story does complete a circle from Dachau. 1938 was when the Von Trapp family left Nazi Austria. Had they not left when they did, their story would have ended in Dachau!!! I had been to their Trapp Family cross-country ski area. Maria was still alive when I was there.

In the rain in the train: 8:30 now and it is very hilly. I would have been a wreck. The train was a good choice and I'll try not to feel the guilt. Maybe this will give me enough time to jog up to Prague.

7.28.95 Linz, Austria. In a complete funk about bicycling. It rained and thundered all night and is still heavily overcast. And, somehow, I have mislaid my rain jacket and the cover for one of the front panniers. Rain is just cooling at this point of the summer. Feels good. Well, not if it is in your face all day while bicycling. People who run Zimmers don't thrill to someone who looks like a drowned rat.

Austrians get almost seven weeks of vacation every year, paid. They get health care. They pay 35-50% of their income to taxes in addition to a value added of 17-20% tax. One of their holidays is a celebration of the day the allied forces left, 10 years after WWII finished! Makes it sound like they liked Hitler better than they liked us. Tourism is the No. 1 industry. You never meet Austrians traveling. I think that with all those taxes they can't afford to go across the street much less travel. However, I like it here. I'd come back any time.

There was a terrorist bombing in Paris at the subway station, St. Michael, where I tearfully parted from my beloved on July 2. On the TV it looked really messed up.

Chas and I had been in Linz, Austria in 1993. We were at a X-Country ski Championships in Germany and took a day to tour Linz. I went back to that same post office that we had used 2 years before to make a call to Chas. They put the phones in the post office so that they can charge a local rate while you are also being billed by MCI. All sorts of paper work. Makes the whole system seem antiquated; tin can and string level. I am so happy. He will meet me in Istanbul on September 3 at the airport at 10:00 AM.

Later. It was another dumb rainy day. I found a few dry hours to bike down the Danube bike path about 15 miles to Melk. This is a town with the outsides of the buildings painted with great imagination. The small hotel that I am in has carved wood beams in the ceiling, wood paneled walls and marble floors. The beautiful white cliffs above Strausburg were marble so it is plentiful around here. It is pouring rain again and a jolly bunch of locals from outside have crowded in with even the women smoking cigars. It is loud to earsplitting but I am tired and will be happy to go to my cheering room upstairs and enjoy my antique carved bed and marble floors. There are six varieties of pork on the menu unless I want pork sausage. Think I will go with the nudelsuppe. I had the worst goulash in Saltzburg. It was water with canned veggies.

Spot is in a tiny garage in back of the hotel that holds, with incredible neatness, the extra food for the restaurant. It wasn't locked so I think Spot is probably safe in this little town. The room has a sink and cost $30. Shower and bath are in the hall. This is the little town you hope to find when you set out on a bike. The bike path itself is just great. Most of the time the bike path is very close to the water on an old railroad bed but occasionally it takes interesting excursions into the towns. The Danube moves briskly and isn't a bad color, however it is more green then blue. It has a lot of traffic going up and down. I raced a barge and got ahead but it might have been slowing down for the locks at the big dam.

7.29.95 Grien on the Donau, Slovakia? (No one was checking my passport.) I guess the most amazing thing about this 'World's Most Used Bicycle Path' is that it goes through four countries: starts in Germany, most of it is in Austria, goes into Slovakia, and then into Hungary. It is like bike paths everywhere, a conglomerate of rail-trail conversions, farm lanes, country roads and made to be bike paths. Actually the worst of these are the made for bike paths. They don't have sufficient base to take the frost well and end up bumpy. I'm not really complaining, relief from traffic is relief from traffic, but a few miles of bumpy will begin to shake loose all the nuts and bolts on the bike. This bike route is endlessly varied: towns, cities, fields of corn and fields of wheat ready for harvest. There are lots of castles and fortifications. I have not been able too get anything in English about them so they end up being a blur of quaint and fascinating stuff. A major part of the bike path is on the dikes that line both sides of the Danube, a very controlled river. There are a number of dams and a lot of commercial activity but not much sport boating in this area.

It threatened rain or drizzled for most of the day. I encountered an American Elder Hostel group headed in the same direction. They were going to stop at Melk so I decided to stop there also on the slight chance that I might bump into them again. It is so good to have someone to speak English to. And they can talk bicycle, too. I registered in a hotel that seemed nice and then the van came up and unloaded their stuff. They seem to be fairly lockstep in their bicycling. They are trucking along at 11 miles an hour and there are no stragglers which is amazing considering their ages. I'm 65 and they looked OLD to me. We met a different Elderhostel group in France and it was pretty much the same there. This group had collected in Munich and started biking in Obersdorf. They have been on the road for some days now but will turn the bikes in at the next stop and bus into Vienna.

Later now. The Elderhostelers have been closeted all evening, learning about the stuff that is such a mystery to me. It is almost 9:00 PM. No wonder they weren't getting under way until 10:00 AM. We oldies need our sleep. Alma and Jim are ready for Elder Hostel. I wandered up the hill and came on to an interesting production of *Faust* that utilized the scaffolding on a monastery to introduce the devil and Faust arrived in a wagon pulled up the hill by a tractor. These actors went through a gate and the crowd followed them in. Everyone was carrying blankets so I guess the production was outside but they wanted a ticket and the German was quite beyond me so I passed that one up.

This is a great spot to bike. Everyone should try this kind of biking, so different from home where it is not bike friendly. I should make Vienna tomorrow.

7.31.95 Vienna, Austria. I am sitting here with my first cup of Viennese coffee in an elegant hotel right across the street from Loren Maazel's Philharmonic hall. Imagine his leaving here for Pittsburgh. He'd have to be nuts. In Vienna he is king. Or is this true? I read something about how hard it is to get along with the Austrians at the opera and at the Philharmonic. The Philharmonic is owned by the members of the orchestra. They hire the conductor. Anyhow it is a great place and, wow the coffee is strong and bitter. I'm used to instant decaf, not the gourmet here that costs $5.00! That will teach me to sit in a fancy hotel cafe. Looking over the bus city tours I can take, I am charmed by them all. I'll take a tour this morning and then opt for something with music for later. I got lucky with the hostel, $16.00 for two nights and breakfast at the grocery where the food is better: yogurt and bananas so far.

My companions at the hostel this time are young, exhausted, bedraggled blonds. They carry huge packs that topple them over from time to time and seem to be in frantic pursuit of something. They come and go without, unfortunately, the beneficial effects of bathing. The Eurail Pass bunch seems to feel that the more countries 'covered' the better. If you question the wisdom of one day per city, they explain, tersely that this is an 'overview' and they will better know which cities they will seriously tour later. Then they slide down the wall and fall asleep at your feet. I am pretty tired myself, having pushed poor Spot eighty miles yesterday. It wouldn't have been nearly so far if we had not ignored some arrows coming into Vienna and ended up on the totally wrong side of the city where after asking directions and receiving some good ones, headed off in the exactly wrong direction again. I never get lost . . . only two hours of extra sight seeing. It is awesome that Beethoven, Shubert, the Strausses, Lehar and Mozart walked these streets, conceivably sat in this very spot, slurping $5.00 per cup coffee. No wonder they died so young and poor. Their memories live on and melodies fight it out for a spot in my head. This is the city to bring a head that has been furnished with the world's great music. I have a passion for Vienna. The building that I am facing, at the back of the Philharmonic hall, has a group of caryatids across the top that are just exquisite. How to describe Vienna . . . overpowering.

Later, having done the city tour, ich ben in Schonbrun Palace, Emperor Franz Joseph, and Belevedere (the guy who won the battle of Levanto and saved Europe from the Muslms) palaces, then another tour of the Vienna State Opera house where they do Die Fledermaus every New Year.

Now I am seated at a free concert in a park and will surely have to take some coffee in order to use the chair. The coffee is probably a bit expensive. Get the coffee and thus the free concert costs $4.00, not bad for a bunch that plays Johann Strauss in the very spot where he gave concerts. Made the acquaintance of another ex-GI who was doing the 50 year tour. He was in the band of the 100th which took Paris. We did the Strauss handclapping song a couple of times. It was so pleasant in the park. I bought a ticket for Lehar's Merry Widow. I don't think I have seen that. The other choice was Don Giovanni but, I have seen that at home with Sherrill Milne. I took a subway into the downtown this morning for $6.00, so I walked back tonight and it was a lovely walk. I located the concert hall for the Lehar tomorrow night on the other side of a park where a jazzy band was playing "Mac the Knife".

I like Vienna but am getting antsy, eager to get on my way and on to Brataslavia which also has opera. And is even cheaper. The food here is all pork and sausage but I found a Lebanese restaurant today and enjoyed a good meal.

8.1.95. Vienna, Austria. Took a really strange bus tour to the Metterling which was the spot where the Crown Prince and his mistress did themselves in at the hunting lodge. No one could understand why. Emperor Franz Joseph, the father, was shattered and the place was torn down and a nunnery built. The brother, Arch Duke Ferdinand, was assassinated at Sarajevo and that started WWI.

Then we went on to a monastery with a lot of great wood and stone carving. Then on to what I thought was a natural grotto but turned out to be a mine that had been a gypsum mine but was used by the Nazis in WWII to build, very secretly, jet fighters. About 100 were built but never used. They were built with slave and POW labor. We toured the mine in a boat, huddling in blankets. They said the latest *Three Musketeers* was shot in the mine.

After going to the US Embassy, I learned that you go to the consulate, not the embassy to find out if it is safe to go through Croatia and Yugoslavia. They let me use the phone at the embassy to call the consulate and after such a long time on hold . . . how can I miss the USA??? . . . the guy who answered the phone practically shouted,

"No. No. Not Croatia! Not Slovenia! Not Yugoslavia!!!!!"

So OK. All right. I never seriously considered it anyway. Yo, settle down.

I am back to trying to figure out Austria. I thought WWI was about Germany but now I think it was about Austria. Austria is now 1/8 the size it was before WWI. The Austro-Hungarian empire fell apart because it was no longer needed to defend Europe from the Muslims (Turks). The Turks collapsed about 1880 about the same time that Germany, Italy formed as countries. I must get something in English and try to make sense of all this. Vienna was more the intellectual and arts capital than Paris until . . . . Must straighten this out.

A book that I read before the trip was written by the first guy to bike around the world. 1885. His bike was a "bone crusher." Great read. When he was biking through Yugoslavia, he found a Muslim mosque that was totally covered by Christian skulls. And we are on the side of the Muslims in Yugoslavia? And the Europeans are sitting on their hands while Muslims are "ethnically cleansed"? What a surprise.

That night in Vienna I saw a delightful *Merry Widow*. We clapped in unison for the cancan. The day before we did the unison clapping for that J Strauss tune that everyone always claps for. I must be really simple because I love that stuff. The widow was beautiful and her gowns were great. The singing was fine and they had a real orchestra on hand because they do this a couple of nights a week. It was a terrific production and I hummed right along with Villa, Maxims, and Girls, Girls, Girls. We should do a tourist attraction like that in Pittsburgh, after all we have Steven Foster and Victor Herbert. One of the Show Boats could do Steven Foster and some nice little hall perform Victor Herbert. How about *Flash Dance* at some scummy Liberty Avenue dive. Atmosphere, and fun. I grabbed the first taxi after the performance and didn't have to walk to the hostel in the dark. I had walked the streets in the daylight and knew them well so I could trust the cabbie, an Afghanistani.

Chapter XVI

SLOVAKIA

. . . Czech it out

8.2.95 Bratislavia, Slovakia. Actually it did not look cheap in this restaurant. Should have guessed. By the time I had used the calculator on the Zaurus to figure out the money system, I had paid $36 for a steak dinner. But, it is really very nice here. I like it but I had better think in terms of a hostel for tonight.

Figured wrong, the steak dinner was less than $10. I got a room for less than $20. The two maps I bought were as much as the dinner. I studied the map to make up for today when I got lost twice. Even with doing 5 miles back and forth in Vienna and another excursion on a dirt path over a hill accompanied by one of the world's great collection of mosquitoes, I made it into Brataslavia by 2:00. There doesn't seem to be a lot of anything between here and Budapest. I thought I would be very soon in Hungary but most of the way is in Slovakia so I hit up the bank again because it is bad when you are starving, dying of thirst, and you don't have the right kind of money to manage with. They are playing a string version of Bach's Toccata and Fugue. Not dramatic but nice. This town has all the bad features of Vienna, namely, they are revamping everything. The streets and the sidewalks are all torn up. Scaffolding hangs from half of the buildings and the other half need it. Let's be nice and say that it just isn't Saltzburg. It has the same grubby look of most of our cities . . . like the windows need to be cleaned and the streets really swept. I see the first window screens that I have noticed in Europe. I am amazed at how little attention they can pay to flies crawling around. I like the music they are playing. US I guess. That I don't know it is doesn't say much. Everyone recognizes me for an American. Is it the sensible shoes or that I always tell my hair dresser that I want to look like Murphy Brown. Hey, I have fewer neck wrinkles than she does. Really tired tonight. I walked all over this town. It is full of young persons who do a lot of kissy-face. There is the biggest K-Mart I ever saw right in the center of town. It is four stories high. I'm drinking a Budweiser that is imported from the Czech Republic. I'm told that this is the original Budweiser. Coke is $.50 in this bar.

Chapter XVII

HUNGARY . . . Not really, thanks, I just ate

8.3.95 The bike path today did not win cheers for Hungary. Some idiot had graveled it with the kind of smooth pebbles that are the worst for bikes. The tires sink down into the pebbles and every pedal is a struggle. Leaving Bratislava, I had a choice of west side of river or east side. I hadn't had breakfast so I took the west side which appeared to have more services. It did but it also had Hungary and the Hungarian style of not marking paths. Had I not made a big effort to buy a *Radweg* map I would have been totally lost. Even doing about ten miles of odious pebbles, I got to Gyor by 2:00 and started looking for a Zimmer. Nothing was available in the city and the clouds that had been threatening all day were really piling up. I finally got a room by just moving on and then taking the first available Pension. It was nice, my own shower and toilet in a pleasant, new house. The lady who runs it is very hospitable, giving me a coke and mineral water. There was a restaurant within walking distance.

Problem. The bike path lead me to Gyor which is a long way from the Danube. It is on a direct route to Budapest because the river does a big loop here, (around a mountain?) The landlady has a great geophysical map of the country. I'll ask her about it.

The most excellent gentleman who was the head of the foreign languages at North Hills Schools, where I taught Spanish was from Hungary. He was a Latin teacher in a girls school in Hungary when one day the Communist thought police came to see why he had complained about changes in the textbook. He isn't too tactful and ended up doing time in the gulag in Siberia. When he got back to Hungary, the 1956 revolution had started and he headed for the border. His name is Molnar and one of the little shops where I bought food today was owned by a Molnar. I tried in vain to find someone who could speak English to tell Ernie's story but could not find anyone. Charles Berlitz says that Hungarian is not like any language around it. It's family is one other language on the far side of Russia. Some of the finest linguists in the world are Hungarian. Ernie says that he had to know the language of his village, Hungarian, German(was recruited into the German army), Latin (they start studying Latin in the 5th grade, and he was a Latin teacher). Then he had to get by in Russian, and after his escape, Italian and English. Seven languages in all!

Ernie went to the University of Pittsburgh to get his Latin certification and got a masters degree also. When he tried to go for a doctorate, he ran into the resident Communist named Colodny who angrily told him not to try for the doctorate because he, Colodny, would prevent him from getting it because he didn't like Ernie's politics. Colodny would probably have been happy to send Ernie back to the Gulag. Ernie would shake his head sadly:

"I have my Cecilia and my little girls and I will not fight that fight anymore." At the U of P.!

The Hungarians consider Attila a big hero. I'm about historied out, maybe some gossip about Zaza or Eva or Arnold would be nice, Dahlink.

Dinner was an exercise in wishful thinking. The beer was an excellent pilsner. The only thing I recognized on the menu besides the beer was Beefsteak or a version thereof accompanied by Tartare. Well. It turned out to be a huge patty of raw or marinated beef surrounded by pretty little piles of spices, salt, paprika, raw onion, horseradish, mustard, something hotter, and pepper. There was a little pocket in the middle in of the beef in which was a simply delectable raw egg yoke. Son Mac would have appreciated this. He has the alarming practice of grabbing raw hamburger out of the refrigerator and eating it. I was not happy. I tried get them to cook the hamburger. Cook the egg. No and no. I managed to get down a bit of the egg, onions, and some salt. I ate about half the meat. Oh for a Burger King. I didn't doggy bag the unfinished portion. In Gyor they name things after Liszt and Bela Bartok.

Chapter XVIII

SLOVAKIA . . . Czech is out!

8.4.95 Komarno, Slovakia, again. Is this ever one of those days when I wonder just what the heck am I doing here? I managed about 30 miles before I died. The heat, I guess. I'm shaking all over. Had lunch, excellent souvlaki, and it hasn't helped. Flaked out in what appears to be the only hotel in town. Either $15 or $28. I can't figure it out. It is too much back and forth from Hungary, just across the Danube, and here. If I can find the bike path, I'll take the boat to catch up. Not behind really just feeling desperate. What if I'm sick . . . .

6:00 PM and still wobbly. I'm trying this wonderful combination . . . Beer with Pomme frites . . . why? Because I know what it is. The raw beef last night has cured me for a while of flying blind in menuland. I'll have a banana split for dessert. Why? I can read it on the menu.

Can't believe how starved I am. The fries are great and just in time . . .

I can't find the boat. There are a lot of boats here, but I can't find the dock for the passenger one. I was sketching out of my window. What great spot. The window opened clear to the floor and no one looked up all the while I was there. There were clouds of smelly pollution stuff blowing by every now and then. This is the most pollution I have seen in a long time. I looked for an advertised hotel on the Hungarian side but did not find anything nor any 'Zimmer Friea' signs. Makes me nervous about this part of Hungary and I'll try to stay on this side of the river. Met a couple of Brit boy scouts. They had been walking the bike path on the Slovakia side but it had so few facilities that now they are walking the roads on the Hungary side. The fries seem to be doing the job and the shakes are going away. Or is it the beer? Finally I am an alcoholic on one small beer a day. Beer is supposed to be good to replace needed electrolytes. I managed to miss the grocery stores this afternoon. That means that I ride with inadequate food again tomorrow. The gas stations here, Shell and Esso, are carrying Gatorade. Gatorade's electrolytes would have helped today if I had just remembered to buy some. Maybe I wouldn't have hit the wall (got the bonk) today. Sometimes I get cheap and pass up necessities to save money.

8.6.95 Budapest, Hungary. It was nice riding the early section on the Slovakia side but spooky. No one else out there. Nice tailwind and on roads for a lot of it. On the trails, the gravel spreaders had invaded from Hungary with those awful pebbles. In the fields are mostly mechanized stuff but in some, men are hand-scything huge fields and raking mountains of straw. In one field were dozens of people scrounging for something after a harvest. I finally figured out that it was a sunflower crop that had been harvested. The people had come on bikes and cars . . . with cars not a big item here that is a surprise. Tried to photo a group of storks that were on the trail but they took off. The roads are so free of traffic here that a bike path is superfluous.

By noon I had reached Sturovo, Slovakia and crossed on the ferry to Estergom, with its overpowering Basilica. After checking around about ferries, because none had been available for a long time, I was suddenly offered a trip to Budapest for $12. One and one half hour later we had hydrofoiled into spectacular Budapest.

HUNGARY again?

I had such a problem getting windblown Spot off the hydrofoil. Everyone had disappeared and all gates were closed and locked, leaving me in the limbo of the customs area by the river. Finally a pleasant, muscular, young fellow showed up and carried Spot with all her bags up the stairs and out. Once on the street after about 25 times saying, "Wow!!!"

Now, even though I had recently been in Paris, Zurich, Munich, and Vienna, Budapest is a "Wow!" Big old buildings, broad pleasant streets, variety, lively street people. Budapest is really impressive, and bigger than Munich or Vienna. The Danube is wide and deep where it runs through the city. Magnificent buildings line the river in a much more imposing way than they do in Paris, especially coming in here as I did, on the river. Let's just say that the Danube makes the River Seine look like pitiful little creek.

I bought a map and started to look for a hostel. It was Saturday and housing always tough on the weekends. A young man, Albert Joseph, approached me and insisted that I rent a room from his mother. While he was peddling the room a girl came up and offered hers. I thought I had the making of yet another operetta with the two getting louder and louder and nose to nose. Albert Joseph was the more insistent and we went around the corner to his mom's apartment. $22 for the night which is a heck of a bargain when you are a block from the Marriott and McD's at 1/2 block.

Prices vary. I'm in section V which is the big tourist center and the Marriott is $175 for a double. Others I talked to could get nothing in this area at any price and are about ten miles out and over $100. I had the local version of a McMuffin and chocolate milk for $1.20. A nice dinner in a restaurant that had live musicians for $7 and a show (Lehar again) in a music hall more gorgeous than the Vienna State Opera for $27. The Hungarians, unlike the Austrians, were happy to be liberated from the Germans.

Albert Joseph's mom's apartment was on the third floor. It was an apartment of dilapidated elegance with massive furniture and paintings and rich carpets but there were mysterious people there. I guess I didn't want to be in a place where they would allow someone like me in their apartment. Also such fussing with the security system was involved that I felt imprisoned and made my escape the next day. The hostel was across the river in what seemed to be a university dorm. I had a room to myself. The others of the bike tour group would stay in a hostel on an island in the middle of the river. I preferred my dorm room. Good choice, they had thieves.

Later: Did the city tour. It is such an impressive city. The war damaged many buildings. Some buildings are still scarred but it is not depressing. 300,000 Jews and gypsies were killed by the Nazis.

The Hungarians were happy when the Russians liberated them from the Germans but the occupation turned into a horror. The entire section where the Hilton is now was destroyed . . . fanatical Hitler youth held off Russians and Allied forces until the entire section of the city was destroyed. I still haven't figured out which side is Buda and so I don't know Peste either. Went through palaces, Cathedrals, Kafka's little house.

It is very pleasant here where I am having lunch. Small group playing . . . Moonriver. Add Henry Mancini to the list of Pittsburgh musicians to be honored . . . Perry Como . . . It would be a great treat for tourists. I'm happily doing the Herald Tribune crossword puzzle.

8.7.95 Budapest. Just talked to M'Love. He says that Helen called and is with the North Carolina tandem couple. They will be in Budapest on the 12th. That gives me a couple of days to scoot up to Prague!!!!!!!!! Yow! I'm packing now.

Later. Had ticket to the folklore dancing group. It was in a non-tourist area but I braved it out. I bought a 3-day transport pass that works on all public transportation. I scouted it out in daylight then had enough courage to tackle it at night. It was fun. The guys were the big item, slapping their legs a lot while jumping around. They never did get totally down in a deep knee and do the Russian kick. The girls wore fetching, bright costumes and spun around a lot. They did one little dance with a bottle on the head. It wasn't as showy as the Mexican bottle dance I used to teach to my Spanish students. Don Swanson was a North Hills student who made it into the Tambouritzens. Not from my instruction. As I recall he didn't get along with them, dropped the scholarship that Duquesne U. had given him and ended up in New York, as the star of the Dr. Pepper ads. He was a better dancer than the guys last night. He could jump like Barishnikov. I tried to get him to jump on the track team but the kids harassed him and he dropped out. Sister Sue still teaches dance in Bellevue. I should stop in and find out what happened to Don.

Chapter XIX

CZECH REPUBLIC

. . . the other part of the now parted Czechoslovia

8.9.95 Prague. Sitting in a box I snuck into at intermission. Probably get thrown out but one has to try.

My cousin used to take me to see shows at the old Nixon Theater in Pittsburgh and that was what we did. If no seats became available, we stood. Fine with me. I still like to stand at the theater. The old "buy the cheapest ticket and move down at halftime" game. This theater was worth the price of admission. It is the same theater, unreconstructed, for which Mozart wrote the opera being performed tonight, the *Clemency of Titus*. The plot was enthusiastically explained to me by a cute French girl. The hall is all baby blue with gold leaf everywhere. They usually do *Cosi Fan Tutti* because it is so well known but this year are going with the piece written for the hall for the coronation of a king. Mozart himself came here to stage and conduct the first performance. The singers are quite good except that most of them are women, two of the major parts being boys played by women. I was in the 5th balcony which has great acoustics but not great view. Now I am in a box on the third. The orchestra is back. Sounds like it depends on old instruments. A little harpsichord sounds before each recitative to give the girls a cue. European singers are generally better than ours and these are no exception, however they aren't putting much emotion into it. The costumes are a little hard to understand, partly Roman, part weird, the chorus is in peasant Bohemian costumes and the lead lady looks like the harvest goddess from Crete but all black. The King has a gold painted face??? Anyhow it is great and the Mozart is meltdown. Nobody threw me out and I luxuriated in the baby blue velvet box. If Prague is where they shot the movie *Amadeus*, this would be that charming theater shown in the movie.

8.9.95. Prague. Can't locate what I wrote this morning. I had to change batteries in the Zaurus, maybe I lost the stuff in the exchange. Two AA's cost $2.00. Well, I have done the city tour, located a new hostel, which is worse than the old one. For $10.00 a bed in an old gymnasium where the men's is separated from the women's by a blanket. I didn't have enough courage to check out the toilet. The one shower was being used. It is on a horrid alley leading to it where street folk have been sleeping. I don't see many men going to work here, only middle aged, overweight, short, determined women.

I spend more and more time in the ethnic restaurant (McD's) because Ronald will feed you at almost any hour of the night or day, and, of course, the flush toilet. I am not the only one looking for something real to eat at 7:00 AM. Most of the customers are local folk. The rest of the day, when the cafes open, they are filled with people drinking beer or wine. If you want something to eat at noon, or 5:00 it's McD's. Lord knows when these people eat dinner. Perhaps I've been in bed an hour when they get around to it. Unlike the French and Swiss who can eat an endless line of fries and sauces and still be slender, the Czechs have a tendency to pork out. I try to eat my big meal around noon when it is cheaper and then just soup or pasta at dinner time, my dinner time. If I try to adopt the later lifestyle I will be biking when it is hot instead of getting the miles in while it is cool.

The River here is called the Vltava. Perhaps Smetena's *Moldau* dried up. All sorts of stuff is dedicated to Smetana and . . . get this . . . *Amadeus* was filmed here. The castle in which the president still lives reminds me of the Alcazar in Toledo. The one in Toledo was rebuilt after the revolution in 1930's destroyed it. War has never destroyed Prague and the cafes where Kafka and Goethe held forth are still here. Hopefully with improved plumbing.

After yesterday's miserable train ride, I updated my ticket back to Budapest and will take the sleeper. Schlauffenwagon. Ya. Gut. 8.10.95 Prague 3. Can you believe a choice of two versions of the Mozart *Requiem*! I chose one that started at 5:00 because I have to catch the train at 10:30 PM. Sat beside a young American who came to try his fortune at piano and directing. Prague is good choice. There is a lot going on in this city. The performance was wonderful. The twenty-four in the orchestra and thirty in the choir seemed perfect in the church where it was performed. The lady conductor was very much in charge of a flawless and emotional rendition of a favorite work. The soloists were superb. Each portion was cut until the entire mass was completed in an hour.

So now I have a couple of hours to kill. The train station is full of human debris, the kind of aimless youth and adults that lay around on the floor after too much booze or whatever. I just can't see how they are so stupid that they can't see a correlation between their ugly scene and the organized crime uglies? There were hordes of them in the main square. Anyhow I am holed up at a Greek restaurant watching a guy who plays Fred Astaire records and dances. There was an unappetizing sword swallower at the other end of the restaurant but he is gone now. To the hospital???

Still Hungary?

8.11.95 Budapest. After the terrible train trip up to Prague, I cleverly upgraded my return ticket and spent the night in the schlauffwagon/couchette. I was on the bottom bunk and two little Italian girls were stacked above me. There was a tiny sink where I abluted but the WC was down the hall. No shower, well, gee, it is a train. The gendarmes of a dozen countries beat on the door and demanded passports at frequent intervals but I slept well anyhow and arrived back in Budapest fresh and relaxed.

I went to the station where you get the three day pass and started riding the subway, first one-way then the other. It isn't easy to travel around when these people persist in writing everything in Hungarian. The escalator to the metro is the steepest and fastest

I have ever seen. I watched little old ladies with canes negotiating moving stairways that would intimidate downhill skiers. Some how they survive, and the poor starving gypsy with her horde of starving children negotiates it also. I hung out at my favorite cafe and chatted with a German who loves paintings. We discussed the plight of the Hungarians with earning about $200 per month and half of that goes for housing. The people here are working hard to spruce things up for next year's celebration of 1100 years as a country.

I met with Helen, and Charles and Lisa, the tandem riders from North Carolina and Michelle, the racer, from Connecticut at the hostel. No Jody. The big decision has already been made to go through Slovakia and down the East Coast of Italy instead of Rumania and Bulgaria. I expressed my delight and approval of this option by jumping up and down accompanied by little screams of joy. I ran right out and got maps of Slovenia, called Hrvatska on the maps. Even Hungarians don't try to pronounce that.

Helen's group had improvised a satisfactory method of camping: they get some English-speaking person to write out a little note in the local language that says that they are on an around the world trip and would like to stay in some farmer's field or other free camping spot. This works very well for them and the hostel here was the first one they had stayed in since Brussels. They do all their own cooking and Helen has yet to have her first flat tire. This is first rate Bettina Selby. (Do they ever bathe? Have they tried Beef Tartare?)

After guestimating the time it will take me to get to Bari or Brindisi in Italy where I thought I could start catching ferries to Istanbul to meet Chas on the 4th of September, I decided to take off today and not wait two days for the other bikers. This bunch are talking about doing some hiking in the mountains anyhow. No way I can do that, the change of route through Italy means it will be nip and tuck getting to Istanbul in less than a month. In the mean time it gives me something else to think about. They planned to go to Trieste and catch a ferry to Istanbul. I thought I could catch a ferry to Istanbul just anywhere. Wrong.

I petted a Bernese Mountain dog puppy yesterday and started to cry because I missed my dog. I try not to think about how much I miss my husband.

Ole's group had told me they didn't want me riding with them. So I wasn't to expect to ride with them after Budapest. I can camp outside and tough it if I have to. I don't have to, and don't really want to. They also told Michele, the racer, they didn't want her. Then the Olneses told Helen they didn't want her, and went off by themselves, swearing never to see Ole again. They hadn't seen him in quite some time anyhow. All this upset and grumpiness is just so typical of bicycle tourers. Getting along with people over an extended period of time is difficult. There are additional stresses for some. Michael and Spy had all their gear stolen in Scotland and have gone home in disgust, or at any rate, disarray. All these people are neat, fun people, the kind you like to be with, but not for so long. To me having to negotiate every bathroom stop, every photograph, is so annoying. I get up and going at dawn so I can take advantage of the cool of the day. I can't travel with people who don't get going until eight or nine, or, can you imagine staying in bed until 10?????.

8.13.95 Leaving Budapest. Let me start by saying that I am not a bigot. I am not prejudiced. I just don't understand Europeans. Now, I do realize that even among Americans I am pretty weird to be up at the crack of dawn and enjoying the fresh of the morning. Not all Americans are like that. But some. There are enough of us to fill up most early restaurants with the early risers. For instance, I am up and out on the road leaving Budapest at 6:15 A.M. I am out of the city and into the country in an hour and begin looking for just anything to buttress the cup of yogurt that was breakfast. Some restaurants are open, I know that because there are people sitting there having their first liter of beer for the day.

If I stop at any of these places they shake their heads at even the thought of frushtuk (breakfast) but I could have coffee or a coke, so I have a coke to pay for the use of the toilette. The little grocery stores are open at 6:00. The quality of these varies from town to town. The one this morning offered a sparkling choice of motor oil or dried up fruit. I did find a Snickers. So now it is 10:00 and I have had yogurt, coke and a snickers. Health food for sure. The real restaurants are beginning to open. The umbrellas are out, the cute waiters in their white shirts, black ties, and black pants are setting up the tables with cloths and flowers and glasses. So I wheel in and find a seat and ask for the menu. But they are not serving food yet. Everyone sitting around is working on their second carboy of beer and could care less about my problems or about eating. At this point they don't even care about their own problems. So I "danke" them in hopes that they will attribute my little tantrum to just another rude, German traveler.

The restaurant of choice for me is McD's because they will feed you at any hour. Believe me there are a lot of people in Hungary in McD's at strange hours snarfing up whatever is offered. Some open early but don't offer breakfast but will serve up a hamburger at 7:00 AM without gagging a whole lot. I predict that Mickey D's will change the lifestyle of Hungary, and for the better.

One o'clock and I am brave enough to try a restaurant again. It is serving and has an English menu. The chicken paprika turns out to be a cut I couldn't recognize: a two rib roast with about 3 grams of meat on it. Perhaps there is one less sparrow in this town today. Shortly after I leave, this restaurant, at some unknown hour, will close for siesta, opening sometime later for drinks (don't ask for food), and still later will double the prices and serve dinner. By then I am in bed. I LOVE McD's. And they are going to end up with every sober Hungarian as their customers.

Nice day today, did 66 miles by 2:00 and started looking for a place to stay. I had a number of interesting conversations with ladies who were hanging out in the main street of this resort town (on Lake Doborny). They wanted to rent a zimmer and I wanted to rent one but it always turned out that (in Hungary, mind you) they would only take Deutsch Marks and I am carrying Hungarian Florints. Also their room is large with many beds and they can get more money if they rent to a group. So after 15 minutes of their pretending not to understand my German we auf Wiederzaned. It took some time to work my way down to a campground that was nice but must have had 5000 people in it. I kept searching and found a charming hotel that also serves dinner (When?) and I went to the beach in my stars and stripes bathing suit. I go down for dinner at 7:30, trying to be fashionable but the Europeans dine sometime later. They will be slowly sipping what appears to be the last vat of beer for the day, but I don't really know because I'm off to bed, hoping not to be wakened by drunken noises as I have been so many nights.

8.14.95 Balonfenyeves, Hungary. Just totally wiped out by the heat. Did 35 miles and the hostel jumped out at me, and dragged me in and I have been lying here for two hours unable to move a muscle. I can see the end of the lake where I will have to choose which way to go to Slovenia. It was so warm in the sun but I was able to move along a lot in the shade. It was so pleasant cruising down through all the resorts. I groceried and the hostel cost $6:00 for what appears to be just me in a four bed room, clean and neat. I'm HUNGRY.

Went looking for food and found a restaurant in the hostel building where I tried the goulash again. It was a little spicy but delicious with chunks of beef and lots of it. After dinner I went wandering and next door is a three piece band, drum, keyboard and fiddle. They are playing stuff that might be upbeat gypsy. What did the guide in Budapest say? That the gypsies would not learn Hungarian and were therefore unemployable . . . unless you can find a use for 500,000 violinists. I had a dessert with a recognizable word, annas, which did turn out to be bananas on chocolate on raspberry crepes. I guess it was OK. It is only 7:00 and there are people here eating dinner! Now they are playing *Jealousy*. Not well. Gypsy tango. The vacationers continue to play in the calm, shallow waters of Lake Balaton. You can see them way out there, thigh deep. At Ocracoke you would think them clamming. The water level in the lake has dropped about a foot recently. If it drops much more you'll be able to walk across it. The weather has been great: lots of sun, if a bit warm. According to the TV it is hotter still in Italy. I can't wait. I am seriously studying Italian and coming well with it. I always think that until I ask for the "Toilette" and they stare at me blankly. I have taken to ordering tonic for a drink. You can't down it too quickly. Sipping a drink gives an excuse to sit through the sunset over the lake.

Chapter XX

Austria again

8.15.95 Graz, Austria. During the night, there was a sound like rain or perhaps the wind in the poplar trees that kept waking me. When I got up, very early, I found that the wind had risen and whipped the moss green surface of Lake Balaton to a froth. Luckily, it was a tailwind so off I went. Somewhere I changed my route three times during the day and found myself on the way to Graz, Austria by train. The trains are still pretty inexpensive and so I decided to solve the whole Slovenia problem, hills, unfriendly borders, etc by going clear around it into Austria. I will be arriving in Graz late and without Austrian money. I'm getting the idea that they don't like Hungarian money even in Hungary.

Lots of very sweet people helped me through this train thing. I should have worked harder on the German. It is still relatively flat and we are into Austria. I was trying to avoid mountains but so far there haven't been any. The Slovenia borders problem was a lack of roads into the country. I could only remember biking in Greece back in 1980's near the Albanian border. The Albanians had shut off all roads to Greece because they didn't want anyone sneaking into the "Workers Paradise." There seemed to be only one road into Slovenia along a long border. What if when I got there it was closed? And then there was the guy at the State Department . . . . Former Communist countries could be strange. Ole and his bunch went through Slovenia, no problem. This took them to Trieste where they caught a ferry to Istanbul.

8.16.95 Somewhere, Austria. Does the title give the notion that something is awry? Never the cleverest traveler, today has been right up there with the bad ones. First of all, they have lost Spot. I don't ever expect to see the Wonderbike again. Then I, myself, was badly mislaid. That's why I'm here in Somewhere, waiting for the 6:10 to Toviso. I was in Somewherelse, Austria for an hour after I missed one of the five train changes so far. I have to take the bicycle through customs into Italy which is why I am going to Taviso. The bike had to go as luggage because that is THEIR deplorable system here in Austria and so THEY were making the shifts of the bike from train to train instead of my making them. The last time I saw Spot, she was on a cart headed, I presumed, for my train to Wherever. THEY didn't take her off and she is probably in Innsbruk where that train was headed. I have never been to Innsbruk but Spot has. Austrian conductors are cute and very neat and well groomed. That about ends the good things I have to say about Austrian trains.

This town, as was the last one, is nestled in the Dolomites, the mountains at the top of my must see list. They have a pink cast (from the magnesium) and are so very steep that great sheets of jagged rock glow, yes, glow, in the sky. Today has been rainy and occasionally the sun comes out on a distant mountain and it lights up with an internal incandescence that delights the heart. It is like heaven, everything but the harp music. There a bicycle goes by and I am lonesome for Spot. All those touchy feely psych courses taught me a few things. One thing I tried to adopt as a life style was "Winners have alternatives." So if Spot is lost beyond all hope, and I am but a day's journey from Milano from which come all the best of the wonderful Italian bikes (and Campangnolo) . . . . Just a thought. The people around here are really good looking, in shape, blonds. Are we thinking Arnold Schwartzennagger? They seem as prosperous as the Swiss.

Chapter XXI

ITALY

. . . Dove il . . . .

8.17.95 Tarvisio, Italy. So you are dying to know what my favorite spot is so far. I now have an answer. Italy. Whom do I like best? Italians. Does the Italian spring to my tongue after four days of intense study??? Well, maybe tomorrow. I have been here for three hours and met more fun people and they have been so nice and incredibly helpful and it is so beautiful. Still in the Dolomites with the screaming white crags towering over this brilliant little town, Tarvisio. It is holiday time in Italy and the resort is booked solid. In one place that I tried, the cook got on the phone and called every pensione and albergue in the town. It took her a half hour but she found a place where the people who had a reservation did not show up by 9:00 so I was given their room. It is just different here. These folks are really having fun. The guy at the counter in the grocery was so cute and laughed with delight at everything I said about being an American on a bicycle. He would repeat everything for the people in the store, about five of them and they would all laugh uproariously, too. Is this fun? Yeah. Do I feel good and loved. Yes. And how about the food? The only thing I have had so far (because by the time I found a place it was after 9:00 and the restaurants were closed) so I went to a cafe and had a totally divine chocolate cake with vanilla gelato . . . . They have stuff like spaghetti . . . . The people here are very stylish and attractive. I am so glad to be here in Italy. Did I mention that I love Italy . . .

Spot arrived at Tovino around 6:00. 6 hours late. I grumbled at the Austrian railroad people that they were just like the airline, losing luggage, but bought a railroad ticket to Trieste. It was dark so I walked Spot over the border into Italy where everything changed. This is the quietest town I have been in. Rolled up the streets at 9:00. It's not Roma. But, I love Italy.

8.17.95 Tarcento, Italy. Not an ordinary day. After sleeping late because it was so quiet I dragged my reluctant body around Tarvisio trying, weakly and ineffectively to locate a train for the coast because I did have a ticket to Trieste. I had been told that Spot couldn't ride the trains and told also that bikes were acceptable but I never did get to a station that was open so this could be straightened out. Instead I was so enthralled by the gigantic mountains that I just kept moving along the road. At the top of the only hill I had to climb was a civilized bicycle shop where a nice fellow stopped the back brake from screaming and got everything trued up in general. From there it was 50 miles downhill through the greatest scenery in the world. Beautiful chalets on a toehold with the sheer mountains behind them. This stopped abruptly about 10 miles back and turned into a fairly industrialized but flat area. When the 50 mile mark hit, I pulled off at a hotel as unbusy as last night's resort had been nuts. $21 here for my own bidet, toilet and one of those showers that soaks the entire bathroom. I am learning to not go into the city because the prices always go up. There is not one thing even worth taking a walk for in this town but I have a TV and already watched a movie that INTRODUCED Danny Thomas. In Italian, I guess. The picture and sound are so bad that it is hard to tell. When I stopped for lunch at Chiuseforte, it was the same wildly Italian babble and cheer and when I explained about the bike trip to one fascinated lady, she grabbed my chin and shaking it back and forth like a dog's, said "Beautiful, beautiful" I really like this place, did I say that?

After a long discussion with the waiter/concierge bartender/ cook, we settled on spaghetti, after mentioning salad and steak. It took a while but he brought out all of them. I guess I need to work some more on the Italian. This is the first time I ever had an entree in Italy since the appetizers always fill me up. Will they never get steak right?? This one was 1/4 inch thick and . . . I can't remember, which cut of beef is it that looks like a map of Greece? I tried to make the big leap and try to call Chas. Phones don't work here.

8.18.95 Writing this on a morning when I am locked in my Italian hotel. This is a serious violation of wisdom that is practiced throughout Europe. How can you tell an American? He's pushing the wrong way on the door. We have panic doors, they open out. The European doors open inward which should make it nice for screen doors but I have only seen one screen door. When you go in a hotel room you have to lock yourself in and unlock it to get out. Stupid. In Joe Beckman's apartment in Zurich, you lock yourself in the building as well as in the apartment. It may be that none of these buildings burn. I now have a fellow trappee here who is beginning to pound on things. Now he is exploring the kitchen. Now he is calling on the phone. No answer, the phone system is out. Perhaps phones don't work when you quit paying the bills. Now he has invaded the sanctity of the office and is going through the keys. Hey, wait, my passport is there! I have found that usually you can keep your passport by paying ahead. Why don't they just get the money ahead like in the States? Especially in this hotel where the phones don't work???? Am I preaching to the choir? We can all be grateful that in the States we do a lot of things better. Did I bring up air-conditioning yet? Or screen doors? A waitress has arrived with keys and is letting out the kittens which have been trapped here all night. One of them is too smart to go out in the rain and eludes the best efforts of the three of us and bounds up the stairs, leaving us laughing. The Tunisian waitress, with a scarf on her head, gives us breakfast and we haven't burned to death and I am soon to be faced with the prospect of riding my first rainy day in a while. If I can get to Udine, I still have a ticket for Trieste. Riding trains is something to do in the rain.

Unlike the Austrians and Hungarians, the Italians don't drink the enormous quantities of beer. However, one of the reasons for the insane driving is that they can get real booze in the gas stations.

Now picture an ESSO station with a dark oak bar, bartender and patrons who drink tiny cups of espresso with a couple of hearty slugs of booze. The Italians have lots of really nice cars and are in them with a heavy foot to the floor even on the back roads.

8.18.95 Aviano, Italy Spent the night in the only open hotel in the area. US Air Force is quartered here. One young officer (female) said that they were on a higher alert this day than the entire year that they have been stationed here. The Air Force is concerned with Sarajevo. Two weeks later, they were bombing.

8.19.95 Venezia, Italy. Spot was able to keep up with a real bicycler (he had shaved legs) today. We drafted for about 5 miles before he had to turn off. He seemed to be happy to tow on old lady.

Coming in to Venice over the bridge by bicycle lacks the glamour of arriving by train. Then there was the problem of poor Spot. The hostel is off on another island so I had planned for Spot to rest up from the rigors of bicycling in a downpour in the 'left luggage' of the Venice railroad station. However, there we were on the car park area on the island end of the causeway and none of the car parks want poor Spot. So at great expense, to avoid dealing with four bridges (all steep with steps), I rented a private motorized scow for Spot (Venetian equivalent of a taxi) and off we went to the railroad station where the Wonderbike was bedded down in "Left Luggage" with thousands of enormous backpacks. Then I caught a ferry to the hostel and got myself settled and rested. The hostel is wonderful. It is just across the bay from St. Marks. I am thinking about doing the city tour tomorrow if it isn't too expensive. The hostel and breakfast total is $14 and lunch and dinner $12 each. . . . in Venice, the most expensive city in Europe!!!! So shall I blow the budget with the city tour or not? Well, of course I will. I sat on the quay in front of the hostel and watched the sun go down. Sunset watching is big with us Martins. This was one of the better ones with some pretty impressive cumulus clouds catching the pinks and greys and golds above a silver-blue bay and the line of exotic building shapes, St. Marks even, between. The hostel is impressively clean and neat in an ancient building retrofitted as a hostel. Walk in the front door there is a division and the first thing you notice on the left is a sign saying, 'Women only. No Men'. Humph. Just the most basic of security. The next sign warns that a non-sober person may be denied entrance.

8.20.95 Venezia, Italy. Venice is so unique. So wonderful. The hostel has a window that looks across the sparkling water to St. Marks. They brought St. Mark's body here in 828 and built a church which later burned and the present edifice was built in the 1100's. The part that was shrouded with the infamous green netting when I was here last has been revealed and the mosaics (Venetian glass) are fresh and glistening. The church is closed to tourists because it is Sunday but there was the once a week flag raising at 9:00 that used medieval costumes and flags. The tour of the Doges' palace was a trip back to the 1400's. The Doges were the mayors of the city, who were usually given the job in their old age, so they died in the palace. It was and is still the place where the government does some of its business. There were collections of horrid looking weapons and torture instruments that have to be seen, and the old prison. Now, wasn't Marco Polo himself in prison here? Wasn't his biographer a Venetian and the biography done here? Polo was to establish business ties with India and China but had a tough time doing that from prison.

The museum has very large paintings by Tintoretto and Titian on a grand scale. Most of the paintings were the Doge worshiping the Virgin but one showed the victory at Levano that beat back the terrible Turks. The Venetians also claim the battle outside Vienna that defeated the Turks and won Prince . . . of Vienna the beautiful Belvedere Palace. Let's blame the Turks occupation for the present problems in Bosnia. Let's wonder why the Muslim countries do so little to help their fellow Muslims in Bosnia. Is it the attacks on Kadaffi and Saddam? We are talking about 1300+ years of religious wars. Is that why Europe refuses to help stop the slaughter of the Muslins?

That Venice became incredibly rich from her conquest of the Mediterranean is undeniable. The wealth displayed here is boggling. The beal'utiful fortresses in Greece and Italy testify to the sense of beauty that has always been a part of Venice. It is still a busy, highly industrial area where time is money.

I'm going to pay for the privilege of sitting in a tiny bar, having a precious pizza with fresh tomatoes and herbs piled on a slab of cheese, washed down by a capuccino. The bar is mahogany and mirrors, red leather, with a brass, sighing espresso machine, American music I don't know . . . Dire Straights?

It is just around the corner from a glass factory where a craftsman blew a glob of glass into a fragile pitcher with a fluted top and graceful handle. The shop was like a threat to sanity. I could only remember friend Dolores' tale of knocking down an étagère of glass in Amalfi and the owner calling the police and the trouble they had staying out of jail, not to speak of the expense. So I was careful with my backpack and got out of there but the glory of all that gold and color and glass is still making me vibrate. The table top here is a sienna and white marble. Actually the people who are my fellow customers seem very colorful. They are tourists, of course, some of the 50,000 who pass through everyday. This is August and the Venetians themselves are in some Torvisio enjoying the holidays. The guide assured us that Venetian women are the best groomed, most beautiful in the world. The posters of Carnival are an invitation to return to see the Venetians at play.

"Notice," says our lovely and beautifully groomed guide, "That we do not call ourselves Italian." Italians seem to do a lot of Italian bashing.

Lots of English is spoken and there are interesting people to talk to. The guide said that Romania and Bulgaria were dangerous. An English teacher, who wants to retire, knew all about the ferries said there were ferries from most of the cities down the coast so I'll try not to worry about getting to Istanbul on the third. An Australian teacher, on leave from teaching and serious doubts about continuing, said that those many kinds of poisonous snakes in Australia are very rarely seen. Not a problem. We had a great chat about teaching and the world. I meet so many teachers traveling and they seem to be universally distressed about the profession, the society, the lifestyles of the poor and confused. I don't think I am feeding this to them, they just seem to be looking for someone to whom they can express their distress. If I had it to do over again, I would not be the grass bending in every wind but a rock. I must confess that I thought of my family as the career. I wanted the money from teaching to help put three kids through college.

8.21.95 Rimini, Italy. I grabbed a train to Rimini through an embarrassingly flat part of Italy. The sun is shining brightly also. No rain. So there is no excuse for being on the train except that it was the only way to leave Venice without going back through the expense that got Spot to Left Luggage. I thought that as long as I would be on the train anyhow why not take the pressure off by getting a little closer to the ferries to Greece/Turkey. It pleases me enormously to do this. And then, the real truth: I love trains. I guess it gives me a feeling of being in control of my destiny. Ferrari. Just looks like another RR station and on we go to Bologna. I have to change trains in Bologna so maybe I can get a local sandwich and make observations about what is not my favorite edible. The Italian train people are all carefully dressed and since good old Mussolini, the trains do run on time.

I was able to totally complete a Herald Tribune crossword today which is a measure of something because they are tough. How do we know that it is Monday? We can do the crossword.

I might meet a Franchesca in Rimini. I don't know anything but the name of the opera, not the composer even.

Later. Well, here in Rimini are all those Italians from those closed up towns and cities. They are stretched out under umbrellas as far as the eye can see. The beach is paved with chubby bodies and lined with tall condos and hotels. Rimini is totally tourist. The traffic is totally dreadful and no room on Rt. 16 for bicycles. Hopefully it will get better after the airport. The hostel is full of strange teenagers and has a sign that says "one=one. Intolerance=0." I am puzzling over that one. Security seems pretty good. However, I don't feel too safe in this atmosphere. The young people hang out here for a month with nothing to do. No, this is not the best atmosphere.

The Adriatic seems clean and comfortably warm. Perhaps I will try biking in the bathing suit again. Up on Lake Balaton where there were plenty of places to just pop into the water, I didn't. When you've been a life guard, you aren't too anxious to go in where there are no life guards. There is just lots and lots of everything here. Old geezers playing bocci. Lots of people in the restaurants and shops.

8.22.95 The Lato is a huge ferry that is bound for Corfu, the Greek island. I'm trying to think of a good reason for having defected from Italy. My right ankle, for no reason at all has swelled up and is causing me pain when I walk but not when I bike. My back is a bit sore. Probably from holding up that big tummy that has been stuffed so with wonderful Italian food so frequently. I'm spoiled. I'm taking the long way because I have never been to Corfu and it is supposed to be one of the good ones.

I will, perhaps, have five days on Corfu because there is no transportation to Greece until Sunday night, arriving in Patras on Monday morning. The other choice has me arriving in Patras at 12 midnight and I think that that is not a good idea.

It was pretty crowded biking down here today. I made good time, sixty-one miles by 2:00. There was a tailwind and I was able to draft a couple of serious lady bikers (shaved legs). It was a long line of beach resorts with lots of traffic though the worst of it was out on the autostrada.

I paid for a four person room in the Lato, but so far I am the only one. What I mean is for one person in a four person room. A bargain. If there are no other single ladies, I may luck out. It is a pleasant room with its own little shower and toilette.

While waiting for the ferry to leave I chatted with a Canadian/Croatian who had gone to Croatia to check out land that his aging and senile grandmother is to leave to him. He had been up to the battle area and seen a bunch of burned out villages with a cousin who was in the army. The Croats are pretty pleased with how things went. "The Serbs have just left the area." It worked for Spain to be totally intolerant with their religious cleansing. In

1492, they ended 700 years of war against the Muslims and then insisted that the Muslims convert or leave Spain.

8.21.95 The Lato Next day. I slept in to eight o'clock, perhaps because the time changed. Finally a time zone change. I missed breakfast while I reviewed the smattering of Greek that I have struggled so to learn. After my eyes fuzzed out, I went up to the lounge where I worked on repairing my fanny pack/purse. The stitching had gone bad in three places but it has taken a lot of abuse very well. Carrying the camera in it is what made it start to go bad but I take a lot more pictures when I carry the camera in the fanny pack.

I spent several hours conversing with Kieth, a carpenter from South Carolina. He is a devout Christian, on his way to the Holy Land. He and his Christian friends had spent some time in a commune some sixty miles from Prague.

"Aren't there a lot of naked people in Europe?" was the way he opened the subject.

"Why, no," I responded. "Only the nudist area near Vienna. Which had to be pointed out to me by the bicyclers who were showing me the bike trail. An overweight, middle-aged couple." Actually there had been the well-endowed gent who was sunning IT by lying on his back fairly close to the bike trail. I try to pretend I don't see these things but . . .

The young man then launched, hesitantly into his reason for being in a commune near Prague. He and his friends had set up a tent and a cross and endeavored to have Bible study sessions in an area where everyone was wandering around naked and chanting stuff and having religious experiences. I threw in that I had seen an extraordinary number of filthy young folks in Prague. I now assumed they were overflow from the "experience." Now that Jerry Garcia is dead, perhaps the Dead Heads can come here for renewal.

Love in a commune seems so phony. When love is a casual thing experienced with the help of drugs like the Dyonisean orgies, what then is an old timy thing like marriage? What is help and encouragement and sharing that goes on with one's chosen mate? What is the caring of the older generation and the raising of children? It seems to me that thrill seekers are apt to miss love entirely.

The born-agains got a few takers. I forgot to ask if they were naked, too. This is beginning to sound like a plot from 'Rain'. Lord. Now I have to search the ship for them to find out if Kieth and his Christian pals were naked.

Later: Finally tracked Keith down and after sitting around for a while was able to elicit that he and his fellow Christians did keep their clothes on. They also do Christian Blues . . . Yet another strand of US music with which I am unfamiliar. I forgot to ask if the sinners that they were trying to save were naked. Let's hope so. Otherwise why go to all that effort??????? Make the sacrifice of sitting around all those naked folk? Why, indeed.

We have a bit of land on both sides now. I would think that it must be Albania. If Albania comes from the Latin it would mean 'White Land' and it would be well named. Big white mountains are reaching to the sky. The famous Mistral is a cold, wet wind from these mountains.

Albania was still under a very repressive regime when we were here last, sailing small sail boats from Parga, Greece. No one ventured very close in a boat because the Albanians would start shooting. (Blow you out of the water.) The commies were keeping foreigners out of the peoples paradise. Little clusters of what look to be five or six story buildings appear in the middle of even the tiniest spot of green on what looks to be a barren land. Coming into Igniomitza, Greece, now. No roads connected Greece and Albania when we were here before on yet a different trip, bicycling in Northern Greece.

Chapter XXII

GREECE

. . . Mens sana in corpore sano

A healthy mind in a healthy body. / A sound mind in a sound body.
My stoic mantra.

8.24.95 Corfu, Greece. Coming into Corfu at 10:00 at night didn't seem like the best idea. I had no place to stay. Alone. Old. Female.

As I was pushing Spot down the dock, a little old man said, "Room? Room? Yes?"

He was being accompanied by two sturdy young women who said that they thought he was OK so we followed him to a very humble home on a back street. It was cheaper for them than for me. I paid $20. They each paid about $16. The old fellow and his little old wife obviously needed the money as the young women pointed out. The women were Swiss from German-speaking Basil but could manage English very well. We dumped our stuff and went out for something to eat. They were both lawyers. One of them asked, a silly question, what had I done on the ship. Forgetting the three movies I had seen, I said,

"I met a group of 'born again Christians' and they were so interesting that I couldn't tear myself away, and went on to tell them about Keith and the gang and the problem of nudity in the world." We were laughing so hard that people were staring at us.

8.24.95 Corfu, Greece. I had decided, more or less, to stay in the city of Corfu because it was so great and it would be so nice to just sit around and do some sketching. I even found some oil crayons to add color to the sketches and the information office which had been well hidden on a back street. The traffic in Corfu was unnerving. Things pop out at you from everywhere. At first I went down a one way street by mistake but then I decided that it was a lot better to have traffic coming at you from one direction than just everywhere. Except for, of course, the others going the wrong way.

I was on my way to the recommended whatever to stay when I was waylaid and kidnapped by a not-to-be-denied lady with a campground in the north.

"You do want to see the North Beaches." Not a question, a statement. Now, after wild ride with ten other kidnapees in a Volkswagen van through some steep mountains, I have settled into a charming taverna, in the North, to contemplate this turn of events. A canary is chirping in its cage. Bougainvillea and trumpet vine form the wall of the taverna. The girl that came to wait on me said at first that they were closed but decided that she could manage mousaka and Greek salad. This done she and her mother went back to their chore of hosing down the throw rugs, an operation that had them yelling at each other and ending up soaked all over. Not too awful for as warm as it is and they giggled a lot and a couple of men showed up to sit around and offer advice. I have already wasted an hour here and am trying to figure out how to stretch that out past the heat of the day. The campground turned out to not be on the water and it looks like a scorcher getting down to the beach. The camp lady, SHE WHO MUST BE OBEYED, said that I should come here because I would want to see the north beaches and lord knows that is so but I don't want to fry the delicate parts that are usually covered by discrete bicycle clothes.

I have the feeling that the beach everyone went off to at noon was the topless one and I am not about too part with my blue and white, starry, high necked top. Nor the red and white stripped bottom. Might be some born agains there trying to convert the libertines to the straight and narrow. This is the toughest time of day for me to be camping. I want to take a nap in a nice, cool, bug free area and there is none. Guess I'll head for the beach and hope it isn't a pebble one. Please let it be sand. And no gorgeous, naked, young things.

8.25.95 Sidri, Corfu, Greece. The Greeks seem like the most exotic people in Europe. Is this because bazookie music comes from every radio? Poor Greece has been invaded by the bare-breasted hordes from Europe and caters to them to squeeze out those drachmas. Corfu, so close to Italy, is so thoroughly Greek in its beaches, wonderful food. The lady who owns the campground where I am for another day just works so hard to make things nice. She is about a mile from a fairly decent beach but she provides a free of charge ride. There were 13 of us in the back of the volkswagon van who went to another beach a 10 K away. Will they give me food at some weird hour? No problem. Do they take an afternoon nap, yes, but not if there is someone who wants something. The desire to please has them hopping and scrambling at all hours. How relieved they must be when winter rains drive tourists away. The waiters in this taverna have on decent running shoes. They need them.

The beach here has been carved by the waves from a soft yellow rock. The taverna is perched on the top of a twenty foot embankment overlooking the sparkling blue water that is in constant motion. The umbrellas are my favorite orange and white. Right next to my favorite red and white umbrellas. The chairs are those universal (EC?) formed, stacking resin ones. Wish I had invented them. Only Coca Cola is more common. The white and orange set off the shimmering blue of the water. Small palm trees adorn the patio, stuffed into pots. After wading through acres of bare breasted Brits and Swedes, I swam some distance with one of the girls from Budapest. They were tastefully clothed. We were trying to go around one cove to investigate another cove but it got so cloudy and threatening that we retreated to the beach. If they don't catch and bring my lunch fish pretty soon, I'll sit some more waiting.

I am writing creative stuff now. I have finished one short story and am into the second one. Problem: when I am so new to plot, etc.: how to also include the exotic settings in which I am writing without being too wordy. A solution comes to me: Go ahead and be wordy, repetitious even, and edit it out later. I feel really good about writing and can't stay away from the Zaurus. Waiters are beginning to notice that it isn't a game and ask me about it. One wanted to know how much it was and after I figured it out in drachmas, wanted to know where I was staying. What if I had told him? Why did he ask that?

8.26.95 Corfu, the city, Greece. The city was so charming that I had wanted just to stay here and sketch or write but was waylaid by the lady with the 'beach up north'. It was a night to forget last night at the campground. Like the campground at Fussen it rained and they had entertainment that lasted until 1:00 but here it rained and the disco lasted until 3:00 AM. I was the only person over thirty there. There was no use to try to invoke common sense or sense of decency or any of that. It was just lay low and try not to miss the 5:30 AM transport to the city. Also I was sleeping in a borrowed tent which was permanently stationed between the toilet and the 100,000 amp speakers in the disco. Now, was this my own fault that I was not at the far end of the camp in my own comfortable bivvy? Well, OK but there really is no way to say comfortable bivvy when you are having a serious thunderstorm. This is a repetition of Fussen. So was it my fault that the lady derailed me from my intent to just enjoy Corfu City . . . Was I being a sightseeing pig????

Anyhow, I got very little sleep last night but am still so enthused at being back in Corfu City that I have done two sketches of the old fort already, going through all the pencils.

8.27.95 Platanos, Greece. Lovely spot on the Pelopenesian Peninsula. I did so enjoy biking here from Patras after a lovely night on the ferry. I had biked it in 1982 when I came here with Classic Bicycle Tours. We did the Pelopenesis and Olympia. I remembered some of the churches and back streets.

In spite of my declarations to the contrary, I am at a campground again, in a cabin. This one has British school teachers from Athens. Two groups have asked me to stay with them in

Athens and I said that I would. What a nice opportunity. Ho ho Bettina Selby. Nicole is a Greek, born in Budapest because her parents were political refugees.

"Communists?" I blurted out.

"No," she snapped. "Anti-American."

Her husband, Rashad, is a Muslim from Aman. Brian is English, a Phys. Ed. teacher and Mike is Irish, and an English teacher. The road that I am on is very pleasant but they tell me that I would be wise to entrain to Athens from Corinth. So tired. 9:30 PM and time to hit the hay. I met an Austrian biker on the way today. He had done Romania and Bulgaria. Said that it was difficult to find food in Romania but Bulgaria was OK. He said no one seemed very happy and the Rumanians were glum. He didn't feel threatened but then this young giant was six-six and very fit. He was really handsome and fun to talk to. He said he had been out 20 days and I was the first bike tourist he had encountered. I wished he were going my way.

8.28.95 Corinth, Greece. I have such great memories of Corinth. I'm held up for a couple of hours. The advice from my new friends, who live in Athens, was to take the train in from Corinth. So Spot and I await a train that will take both people and bike at 3:30 P.M. or the 'Baggage Only' that Spot will take if there is no room on the people train for a superbike. I'm too tired to sketch although this is a lovely place. The striking church across the street is very dramatic . . . sparkling white with black doors that have shinny brass decorations. I told the "born agains" to go to old Corinth. Made a big point of it. It took me all this time for my cluttered brain to come up with the reason. Corinthians II, Chapter 14. In Paul's second letter to the Corinthians. It is a fairly long passage that begins "Though I speak with the tongues of men and angels and have not Charity, it profith me nothing . . . and ends with 'Faith, Hope, Charity, these three. And the greatest of these is Charity."

When we sorted things out in my college freshman dormitory, we had two Sallys, and a Faith and a Hope. So guess who got

Charity? Hope Powell King still comes out with 'Charity' every now and then when we meet at the AYH meetings.

When I was in sixth grade at the Lincoln school in Beaver, Pa., Mrs. Reed, our terrifying teacher, had us memorize the passage. I don't know if I ever tried to get her to clarify "see through a glass, darkly," but I know that her rendition of this fine piece of English is the closest that I have ever come to making sense of Christianity. So, anyhow, it is meaningful (almost) to me. Imagine the delight of finding the passage written out in Greek on one side of a slab of marble in the churchyard in old Corinth. And on the other side, English. King James. I don't know what Madeline Murray O'Hare would have done to Mrs. Reed for having us memorize that passage (and be graded . . .) but I took a picture of that stone and the picture ended the slides that I showed my Latin students about Greece. I considered that historically memorable because when the Romans conquered Corinth, Greece faded from the pages of history until the late 19th Century when the Turks were defeated and withdrew from Greece. And I read Corinthians II, chapter 14 to them. Nobody ever called to complain. Thank goodness they never told Madelyn Murray O'Hare about my reading the Bible in class. They never even called to complain about the first slide of my slide shows which was Polydorus and his sons being killed by snakes that had been sent by Athena. That was from the Illiad. It was full frontal masculine nudity. After the gasps and snickers, I would explain that the statue was done by Michaelangelo. The 7th graders could breathe easier.

"And, the original is in the Vatican Museum." Big sigh. Approved by the Pope himself. After that they accepted the nude statues very well. I never ever had a problem. Culture is culture and lifestyle is lifestyle. And religion is a big part of that and should be taught in a class like foreign language or English or history or literature. But not in science class, please . . . no way!

One time when I was on a bicycle tour in Old Corinth, the one part-way up the mountain, I went out early in the morning to inspect the Roman ruins and had a Fellini moment. There was a conference of Greek Orthodox priests in town. These old testament guys have long beards, black, bowl-like hats, and long, black robes. The ruins do not cover a very large area and were without fence at that time, mounds of white marble and alabaster columns scattered about. The priests had scattered themselves around the ruins and were standing stock still, facing the rising sun. At a signal they started chanting. It was one of the most beautiful moments of my life. I think that I was the only observer.

It may have been that same trip that four of us who were joggers decided to run up to Accra Corinth, the ruins of the city that fell to the Roman, Mummius, in 290 B.C. and ended Greek dominance of the Aegean and Adriatic seas. Now there is a gate and tourist center but in 1980 there were only ghosts in the dusty ruins.

The train to Athens. At least I am sitting. When I was on it before, in 1987, I had to stand from Athens to Patras. I doubt that they have cleaned it since. The workers are unshaven and grubby, with no sense of pride in the operation. No Mussolini success here. The seat is jumping around so much I may have to quit typing on my Zaurus. The newest Corinth, the one down on the Gulf, is nice for a larger town and the area around it is pleasant. We must be approaching the bridge across the canal. Did I tell you that the canal was put off for ever so long because the ancients were afraid that one body of water (Aegean) was higher than the other (Gulf of Corinth) and they thought the cities along the Gulf would be inundated?

I really should look up the hostel and get a taxi there. I'll check out the ferries first. Perhaps I could find one to spend the night on. I got the view side of the train but it is also the sun side. Roasting. I am very happy to be on the train, really. I like trains almost as much as ferries. This one cost $4.75 for Spot and me. The dollar is suddenly power.

8.29.95 Piraeus, Greece. Got new batteries for the Zaurus yesterday in Corinth. Actually the road between Corinth and Athens had 0 traffic. I could see it from the train. Same beautiful road we biked in '80. It would have been fine to bike it in until I couldn't take The traffic anymore or was totally lost, then take a taxi to Piraeus. That is what I did anyhow, took a taxi from the train station to Piraeus. Arrived too late for the ferries so I'll hang out here until 6:00. The cheapie hotel last night was OK but I didn't sleep well. Even called Chas in the middle of the night. He is fine but Tom & Terry's invitro didn't take, and Tom is out of work and looking again. With any luck he will come back to Pittsburgh. Jerry Fields has lung cancer and is taking therapy for it and has lost most of her hair. Why am I here doing this crazy thing? Trying to be super healthy??? There is Martha with her broken bones, Marie with the ear problem. They are worried about me because I am traveling? My only problem is the pollution from the ferries. I have been searching vainly for a USA TODAY. I will probably give up soon and head for McDonalds where the pollution is something I can handle. Actually I am looking for a tape of Greek. When I say something even as innocuous as *"Kali mera"* to them, they pretend to not understand me. The book I have is way out in left field, discussing children etc. when I need to know the word for 'train' Actually it turned out to be "Train,".

I wanted to leave Spot at the Ferry Left Luggage but they were such a horrid looking group I decided not to. Hah! I could try the left luggage at the train station. Then take the city tour,(one more time).

Spot is at the left luggage at the train station, and I am just wiped out across the street, touristed out. Found the USA TODAY and here is a great quote: 'you don't love your enemies for their good, it is for our own good—to keep from becoming the enemy.'.

Later on the ferry Samios on my way to Samos. Tourist batteries are completely restored after a day of reading US papers, and enjoying the cruise down the Attic peninsula. I kept having Optical confusion. Would look at the top of a hill and it would move rapidly to the right while the left moved rapidly to the left. The clouds were low-hanging and seemed to be towed by our ship, swirling in imitation of the land masses. Don't know if the promontory that looked like Sunion really was. No one could tell me.

9.30 95 Samos, Greece. Enjoying yet another rest day. It is tough to come into such a spot and not stay a while. Nice hotel, probably the best in town, with a balcony, electric fan, the works. I have had a refreshing nap and washed my clothes in a machine, for the first time since Budapest. They are retrofitting the lovely building next door. I guess it will be quieter tonight. The floors are marble, the staircase is beautiful marble, and my balcony is even marble. I did minimal anything today. Just tired. Bought a new Greek book because I don't seem to make progress with the one I have. Going through and cleaning out stuff. Ferry tomorrow to the hinterlands of Turkey. I am pretty nervous about that.

The question asked by fellow World Wanders Louise or Regina when I would talk to them on the phone was,

"Are you having a good time?" I never seemed to have a ready answer. I should have said,

"Are you having a good time?"

Probably they wanted to tell about their good time but I didn't have the wit ask so I don't know. What to answer? A good time is a sort of set up thing like a wedding or a party where everyone is bound and determined to 'Have a good time.' I have a good time with spouse, Charles. He is amusing and we laugh a lot. He is pretty much my definition of a good time. But I am here and he is there, showering his puns and silly jokes on what I am sure are unappreciative audiences. So if bicycle touring is not really my idea of a good time, what is it?

(1) I get great pleasure from traveling and seeing new, beautiful things.
(2) I really enjoy meeting new people, hearing their stories, seeing how they live.
(3) I am a map lover. I stare at maps, trying to imagine getting around in exotic places.
(4) I like studying words and foreign languages. It was my profession for quite some time and though I am just feeling too old to keep up with young people to pass it along, I still

like to spend hours studying languages. So, I'm happy and fulfilled. Having a good time? Still not sure. Maybe tomorrow.

8.31.95 Ismir, Turkey. After the simple passages from one EC country to another, it was a shock to go through the ridiculous procedure at leaving Greek Samos. Greeks and Turks don't even try to get along and there aren't many places where you can go from one country to the other.

I had to leave my passport with the ticket agent who said he would help me get it back from the port police the next day. Be there at 7:30 AM. So I am there at 7:30 AM but he is not nor is his across-the-street-office open nor is the 8:00 car ferry that I thought I had a ticket for at the dock. So I go to the Port Police along with a lot of other concerned citizens and wait. One of the officials comes out with a handful of passports, some the beloved navy blue. He calls out Greek names and people answering in Greek grab those navy blue passports. So I am back to the barred window again and show my ticket. It is now 7:48 and I don't see my ship. I wave my ticket in the window again and they seem to make the effort to look for my passport.

"Two minutes," they tell me.

After five minutes I see my much stamped passport come through and a couple of guys look for a place to stamp it, find a place and stamp it. I wave the ticket through the window again, pointing and claiming my visa. Now the rules are changed and I have to go in the door. A man who looks no more suspicious than the rest of us is ushered into the back room, never to be seen again. I get permission to grab my precious passport and run for the boat. Which boat?? The only one there is a fast boat and I like the slow boats.

So now I am on the fast boat for Turkey, skimming over the sapphire water with blue mountains on either side. The fast boats are very small and slender and on a windy day like this one, lurch a lot. No food on a hydrofoil, but I was smart and went to the grocery and got a couple of bananas, a yogurt, and a carton of orange juice which I enjoyed out on the sea wall in the fresh of the morning before tackling the Port Police.

Turkey and Greece are bitter enemies and had a huge ethnic cleansing in the 1920's. The Turks threw out the Greek speaking and the Greeks threw out the Muslims. One of the people I knew as a child was an Armenian whose family had escaped an ethnic cleansing by the Turks in the 1920's. He had a dramatic escape, swimming to an American warship in the harbor of . . . was it Athens? I can't remember any more but when I read "The Mask of Demetrios," I put our Armenian friend in as hero and forgot the real life details. The Armenian married a tiny French woman, Vera, who was so meticulous in every way that she became my ideal for an older adult. My mother thought that Vera was outrageous to diet. Vera was the only person who dieted when I was young, though a book was out about looking younger and living longer. I think the author had the misfortune to die fairly young which didn't help book sales.

Chapter XXIII

TURKEY

"Let me not pray to be sheltered from dangers, but to be fearless in facing them. Let me not be for the stilling of my pain, but the heart to conquer it."

Tagore

Later. Ismir. The boat stopped in Kadisha (or something like that. I have yet to purchase a map of Turkey). I was approached by a charming young man of, perhaps, ten years, who wanted to be very helpful and kept saying, "Thank you. Goodbye." until he finally left. Lots of people could speak English, and the town was charming with a zillion hotels that looked quite nice but I decided to push on to Ismir. Ismir can only be reached by bus. After a bit of a ride and push, Spot, the much admired, and I arrived at the bus station and purchased a ticket. I wandered off to toilette. It was an American style throne, I have only seen one of those dreadful holes in floor of the toilette that the French have so many of. Those things that the French have the nerve to call "Turkish" toilettes.

When I went back to the bus, the first beggar arrived, a ten year old boy. So I ignored him. Wrong. He was an assistant bus person who solemnly helped me strip Spot and load the poor baby, prone, into the belly of the bus. This means that all sorts of stuff will be piled on top of the bike and bikes are not built for that kind of stress. Feeling guilty, I hopped into the wrong seat from which I was later evicted and we were off to Ismir. The little fellow acted as steward for the rest of the trip and did an excellent job. He took it very seriously and the passengers took him seriously.

The landscape was, after the first long hill, fairly flat and farmed. The houses don't look as much like Greece as like Italy because they don't have the shutters that make Greece so charming. Without shutters the houses are plain, sort of boring earthen houses. Ismir appears to be an industrial city: busy and crowded.

I inquired about the train station and no one seemed to understand English at all at the bus station. When you ask directions they wave their arms in vague, don't really know, circles, so I decided to just take the bus instead. The fellows at the kiosk were so nice. They offered to take Spot for the day while I went wandering in the city. So Spot scrunched into the kiosk and there I left her, poor abused bicycle. The roads don't look too bad. Sort of like Greece, narrow with a shoulder that disappears when you really need it, in the cities and at intersections. The landscape is quite pleasant and warm looking. Wheat fields, orchards, vineyards, and the biggest crop, unfinished buildings. They always make me think that the builder had relatives who could do foundations and rebar and concrete but the window and door people have left town. Perhaps in earthquake prone lands they just sort of marinate the building structures to see if they are worth finishing. Turkey is big in this field. There are really sizeable numbers of unfinished buildings. Let me guess: Government project.

There is not a large number of cars here. A lot of taxis. I could have tried the taxi system where everyone piles in one cab but chickened out and took a solo for 70,000 Lire. At 46,000 to the American dollar, that is $1.52 for the expensive cab I think I will like it here. The bus ride to Ismir was 100,000 Lire =$2.17. The ride to Istanbul is twice that. $11,000,000=$239 was what I could get with the Cirrus/Mellon Bank card. I'm not used to dealing with all the zeros and it confuses me. A single room in this nice hotel would be $58 = $2500000 Lire, making the exchange rate here 43104.44 lire to the 1 US dollar. Finally some respect. So each $1,000,000 note is $23. I paid $600,000 to get me to Istanbul ($14) for me and the same for Spot. Perhaps Spot will be in the next seat. It will be an overnight trip, leaving here at 10:00 PM and arriving Istanbul at 7:00 tomorrow morning. Finally I can live on my Social Security.

The zeros are so confusing that I had to get out my calculator and multiply 100,000 by 10 to find out if that is what makes a million. It is.

Since I stashed Spot, I have been to a fair that is held in a large park right in the center of Ismir. Ismir seemed big and it is, 3.5 million. And Istanbul at 8 million is very large.

The fair grounds were so extensive that I was worried about being lost but popped into a building devoted to selling books. The clerks there sent me quite some distance to check out a university bookstore where they shook their heads. No English to Turkish books. No. Back at the fairgrounds a bookseller came up with one with tapes and I went away happy, until I checked it out and found that it has no English. Perhaps I can put enough of it together with the Berlitz book (no tapes) that I have.

So I wandered down to the Hilton to check it out. There they had a display of 'Building Running' and I got some pictures of a guy coming down the side of the building from the top of the sky high Hilton on roller blades. With ropes, of course. He almost landed on me so the pictures should be entertaining. Before that I had a couple of shots of the rollercoaster at the park.

I was given a copy of the London Telegraph's Weekend edition which had a fascinating travel section. The writers rambled on and on and most often in first person. It was a revelation. Since then I have been going on and on about what ever interests me at the time. I will even risk being repetitious. There is a TV News camera eyeing this Chinese restaurant!!!! What! They are coming in to the restaurant. Maybe it is the food editor. A TV is in here. A lady with a butch haircut is talking while the camera checks out a table setting. He is taking pictures of everyone but me. And I am such a media darling . . . I'm glad that Spot isn't here to be embarrassed by this omission. Now he is carefully photographing the artwork. Well. He did take my picture, as I sat here sipping tea and writing. Now he settles down to eat. The waiter comes over to check out the Zaurus. When I showed a Greek waiter how much it would cost in drachmas he got overly curious. Won't do that again. I was just showing how clever it could be, doing the addition and all. He wanted to know if it did games because there are little computers like this one that do games and when I said no he lost interest. I wouldn't think the light in here really sufficient for good television TV but what do I know? It is 7:30 PM and I'll start to look for a cab to the bus station.

9.2.95 Istanbul. It was the first and second days in Istanbul and I was tired from the overnight bus trip. I encountered two sick girls in the hostel, and two more since then which is 4 sickies so far on the entire trip. I am in a holding pattern here because I don't want to go to the attractions without Chas and he arrives in two days.

9.3.95 Istanbul Teeming is the word that comes to mind here. The eight million who live here seem to be out in the streets at all hours. Their clothing is mostly European but tends to be darker than you would expect in a warm country. Actually we're having a cool spell and I am most comfortable in long sleeved shirt and long tights. Strolling the streets, once past the phalanx of English: "Where are you from?" and "Can show you Istanbul?", it is a matter of surviving the crowd and paving. It is like being back on the Appalachian Trail where you don't dare gawk around but must watch your footing every step of the way or risk death or dismemberment. Actually this is most dangerous thing about Turkey so far. Paving is a variety of passable to broken to nonexistent to great holes that appear where your foot was about to land next. The worst is either unprotected stairwells or the open manholes. The manholes are really shocking. They always did have a rather slow looking fellow sitting near them, probably to report on how many people disappeared into the manhole during the day. What is down there anyhow? Never mind. I don't really want to find out.

I love Turkish food but have become nervous about it since the sick girls in the hostel. I am concerned about how long the beautiful dolomites and stuffed peppers and all that have been sitting there. So I eat at the hostel where they grill stuff when you order it or at

McDonalds where, I am finally beginning to understand this, they throw away stuff after a certain amount of time, and it isn't a long time. I ate in a nice, upscale restaurant last night and was served cold fries (picture McD's doing that!!!!) and shiskebab that had mostly nice lamb but toward the end of the skewer was really tough and gristly. It wasn't a popular restaurant.

There is a folk festival going on in the city and groups from Eastern Europe are performing by the Blue Mosque. I didn't buy a ticket for a seat but will try to get there in time to see the show, standing. There was a Russian group with a very handsome young blond man who spun a huge sword around the stage. I must remember to not sit in a front seat. Chas comes tomorrow and I am sort of on hold until he arrives. I talked to a travel agent and he said that with ten days we could see most of the goodies but if we tried to do it by bicycle it would be just out to Capadoccia and back. For $550 10 days of touring and hotels. I have decided that I do want to go to Gallipoli. I am such a movie addict. *Gallipoli* was an Australian movie that was like a remake of "All's Quiet on the Western Front." I saw it on TV and got hysterical and cried for an hour. Australian kids there in Turkey fighting the Turks for . . . . what??

Must research this but what I remember about modern Turkey from Semester at Sea is how desperately hard they are trying to make this a democratic country. After they lost their empire, after the WW I, Kemal Attaturk, at Gallipoli, stopped the Brits and Aussies from taking the rest of Turkey. They set up a democratic system with elections and all. After some 10 years it was so corrupt that the army stepped in and took over and slaughtered bureaucrats, thousands of them, (Timothy McVeigh?) and took over the running of the government again. After a few years they again have elections and civil government takes over until it becomes too corrupt and the army steps in again with a big slaughter of bureaucrats again. We are in a civilian stage now but some people think it is pretty shaky here: The economy is down and anarchists arise. But the Turks are tough. They went nose to nose with the Russians for a long time and the Turks never blinked. Now they are concerned that the US will desert them in order to help Russia. Saddam Hussein is a fun next door neighbor in the other direction. If the Balkans go up in smoke, they will stand clear. It is the mess the Turks made and they don't really want to remind Europeans what a threat to Europe they were for four centuries. They face Europe, not Asia and would like to belong to the EC as they already belong to NATO. They love blue jeans and the most worn garment by women here is stretch jeans. Most of the young people look trim and fit.

9.4.95 Istanbul 3. Himself has arrived! We had discussed the problem of being able to recognize each other after such a long separation and I said that he would know me by the ragged bike clothes. When he spotted me, he got a small photo of me out of his pocket and before even a small smooch checked it out carefully. Now that is thorough.

9.7.95 Nevsehir, Turkey. We had the mother of all bus rides last night. Our choice was a jammed forty-five passenger bus with just one five year old who may not have been smoking or talking loudly. The cheap tour is just that. Nothing first class. Thank goodness we didn't have a lot of luggage because we have walked a lot where we were expecting rides. But fun. This is an interesting desert town. As Benny Hill is our tour director, it will be an experience.

Actually, the room is nice and our guide is really good. This is an exclusive tour, just us and the guide, Mustapha, in a taxi. Mustapha is very knowledgeable about the history, geology, and arts of Turkey. Capadoccia is famous for its strange geological forms that were carved out and lived in by early Christians. The Hittites were the first people here and that takes us back to as early as the early Cretan civilizations. The Hittites, the Persians, the Romans, the Ottomans (is that more correctly Ottomen?) were the successive waves of conquerors. With the Ottomans (to be poltically correct, Ottopersons?), the Turks set out to conquer the world and did a pretty good job, Balkans, Greece, Romania, Bulgaria, Hungary. With the loss of the empire and the overthrow of the Ottomans in 1914, the

Turks had to fight hard to maintain their present borders. In 1924 there was the order from Attaturk that Turkey was going to modernize and anyone who didn't want that could leave. They exchanged Turks for Greeks and others were forced out. Ethnic cleansing?

At the present time there is a lot of tolerance in Turkey and for bicyclers and that is good. However a reactionary group of fundamentalists may get voted in next election. If it does, the army has said it will step in and run the country again as it has before when groups who are anti-capitalist and anti-democratic have come to the fore.

We made the switch from Spot, the Wonder Bike, to Green, the Magic Mountain Bike which Chas retrieved from Alma. Spot has been wonderful. Don't tell this to any dedicated bicycle person but . . . Spot was cleaned 0 times in Europe. She had that one flat very early in France, where the racks rattled loose and had to be tightened a couple of times. Nothing. The perfect bike. I am being very brave, sending her home also the sleeping bag and bivvy. I used them twice since I got to areas with hostels and 'rooms'. This makes my load much lighter and the thought of mountains not so scary. The roads here in Turkey are not too good and the drivers pretty scary, but there are not that many cars and now I have a bike that can ride for a very long way on the unpaved edge of the road when I get chicken and wimp out.

9.8.95 Nevsehir, Cappadocia, Turkey. The lady troglodyte who was the owner of the cave house was so charming that I actually bought a scarf and she showed me how to drape it and tie it on with another scarf. Hers was the ultimate stone house, carved out of tufa. The big attraction of this area is its extraordinary stone cones which have been home to pigeons, Christian hermits and monks, and even the Ottoman tribe which ended up in the opulent palaces in Istanbul.

It is a semiarid region but the local grapes and melons are ripe and sweet.

This morning at 5:00A:M., even Chas and I weren't up when the muezzin cranked up his speakers for the first call to worship.

We had counted eight mosques from the window the night before. The first one we couldn't even see, too close. When he started it sounded like he was right in the hotel room with a megaphone. The rest of the callers jumped in at different times with different chants until it sounded like city traffic when it all got going. Cacaphony is the word that comes to mind. It went on for a good half hour. Himself and I enjoy having a lot of time to get caught up on things.

9.9.95 Ankara, Turkey. We are taking the day bus because we couldn't sleep on the night bus, so we slept 12 hours on the day bus already. We are on the route of the ancient Silk Road that went from Europe to India. It is flat and the wheat has been harvested and the potatoes and peanuts are being harvested. The peanuts have been pulled up and are drying in the sun. Later, they will load the peanuts and the plants on trucks, pile them very high, and with a couple of kerchiefed ladies holding things down, head for market. Closer to Nevsehir, there were wide fields of pumpkins. They only use the seeds from the pumpkins and throw the rest away. It seems that they have not heard of pumpkin pie.

Later, in Ankara, as advertised, a very modern city with a really wonderful bus station that can actually hold the Turkish style bus system. All the gazillion busses are privately owned and the busses are nice. . . . I like a little more shoulder room, especially when sharing the space with Himself. We went to the toilet when we got here, went to information, went to the company indicated and the next bus left 2 minutes later. This is snug but I like being close to the man.

Hours later, and still hours to go to Canakkale. Through some miscalculation we forgot to ask when we would arrive. It will probably be around 10:30. We had a 1/2 hour to grab some food at a gas station and use the adorable Turkish toilettes, the holes in the floor. Tomorrow will be interesting too as we try to cram a lot of stuff into the last day for Chas in Turkey. It is so hard to see all the stuff we want to see here. Since the only thing we really knew of importance was the movie, *Gallipoli*, we are trying to get there.

The movie was an Australian one, asking why Aussies should go to die in such a place.

9.10.95 Canakkale, Turkey was a trip. There were huge posters across the streets extolling Mel Gibson. Who knew that he was the kid in the movie Gallipoli? He must have been the teenager that I sobbed for. We took a ferry across what may be the Dardenelles that Lord Byron swam. Not that far, I could make it. The battlefield of Gallipoli was very moving. The Turks moved a signal that the Brits had put out and the Anzi went up a cliff into terrible destruction instead of an easy beach. The monument put up by Kemel Attaturk makes me cry all over again. It says that the Anzac dead will be honored as much as the dead of the Turks.

When we found that Troy was nearby, of course this old Latin teacher had to see that. Heinrich Schliemann decided that Homer had been telling history and started poking around the area described in the Iliad, and there, by golly, were the ruins of ancient Troy. The ruins are still being explored. There are something like seven different layers of the old city. Scandal: Heinrich Schliemann's wife was seen wearing jewelry from these digs. Everything was supposed to go to the Turkish government.

9.11.95 Istanbul, again. Puttering around today. Tearful good-by to Chas at the airport. How I will miss him. I am always depressed for a week or so after he leaves. He has spoiled me for tent touring. I had him take back the tent, bag, and mattress along with a bunch of horribly spotted clothes. I wore out two pairs of shoes. I could hardly bear to part with them, they were so very comfortable but when your toes begin to stick out they can be trippers of the bad sort.

Won't see himself until New Zealand. That is a long pull, almost 4 months. We have maintained our relationship very well through many phone calls and together tours. It is just lovely and romantic to be meeting all over the world like this. I didn't want to take the time out of being with him to write so I have a lot of catching up to do. So let's go sideways to Capadoccia. Capadoccia isn't a town but a region south west of Ankara. The town we stayed in was Nevsehir. This is part of the area between the Tigress and Euphrates, that is the cradle of our civilization. The area has caves carved out of tufa in which lived some early settlers. Actually the Hittites moved in about the same time as the older civilizations on Crete and there are the always older civilizations in Egypt. The Hittites, to my recollection, were the first to work iron, and we are still in the iron age . . . at least Pittsburgh was until the 50's. The area is sometimes hilly but a lot is fairly flat and there were many invasions and many conquerors. Persians, Alexander the Great, Romans, Somewhere in there the Byzantines. Mohammedan Arabs, Crusaders, Ottomans Ottomen? Ottopersons?.

Change of venue. This restaurant is called the Orient Express. I had heard that the Orient Express Railroad train was being revived after some hiatus. Actually, even now I wonder if it goes to Bagdad. The railroad station is large and if it were carefully cleaned and tended might have its old glory but as it is it is a bit dark and gloomy, even in the daytime. My map doesn't show the railroad going over the Bosphorus and I wondered how it would be done until I saw a barge with railroad tracks pull up to the rail yard here and unload a bunch of cars. Nothing as fancy as the Orient Express, just some ties for roadbed repair, but the barge could be used to take fancy cars across the Bosphorus to go on to Bagdad. Home of bad guy Saddam. I don't want to go there.

There is a waterfall bubbling behind me. I am placed strategically to keep an eye on Green who was just fished out of 'Left Luggage.' The guy who runs 'Left Luggage' was very sweet and gave me the traditional cup of apple tea and I sat and sipped while a trainload of raucous ladies were dragged off to Romania. He didn't even try to sell me a carpet.

Now I am in an elegant restaurant enjoying a perfect Persian melon washed down by ayran. Ayran is a combination of yogurt and water that tastes a lot like buttermilk and although Chas hates buttermilk, he liked ayran. I am the only customer enjoying the lighted restaurant. We, that's Green and I, will have to change in Thessalonika. We are going, by train, to Athens to get some stuff done in preparation for going to India and then to a nearby island to visit some friends from Bradford Woods. This group all went to Carnegie Tech together. I don't want to date them but it was Carnegie Tech back then. I think only one of them is retired, from being CEO of Rockwell. I am always awed by that guy, Don and his wife, who is ever so much quicker with a joke or pun than I am. Tish. She was very pretty, too. Funny how some groups like they are stay together, and as couples, stay together. I think of them all as very funny. Is it a sense of humor that makes for the best relationships? I think so. Flush of homesickness . . . That's what I love so much about my husband. He makes me laugh. As we were going through the underground city in Capadoccia, the caves were very snug and we'd remind each other to "duck" which being so frequent soon disintegrated to "Quack, Quack". Perhaps we are easily amused.

We did all the things expected of people like us in our generation, a 'Father Knows Best' sort of thing, getting married, getting a house, three kids, an unending stream of dogs, cats, cars. When I decided that I wanted to work, he was very supportive and helpful.

There is a really nice Van Gogh print of a cafe at night on the wall in front of me. I don't ever remember seeing it before. Two more hours until we entrain for Athens. The stupid train leaves at 12 midnight and takes 24 hours to get to Athens, arriving at wonderful 12 midnight. I would take a ferry but they don't go to Athens from here, Greeks and Turks don't get along.

Anyhow we did all the right things to have a good American life and it worked well for us. We worked out individual lifestyles while becoming very close. Why does it work??? We spend time with each other. We are very individual but have a wealth of shared interests. Every now and then we make a big effort to understand what the other one is doing, I study art: he is learning the computer. I took up crossword puzzles (in the USA TODAY and the INTERNATIONAL HERALD TRIBUNE.) He has been doing them for years and knows three letter words for almost every thing.

So now we do them together and have a grand time with never a cross word between us.

Article for Health and Fittness

"Now that I am in Turkey and can see Asia, I want to comment about Europeans.

First. Europe is so incredibly beautiful that it is hard to understand why so many left to come to the States. There are many handsome cities right on a lake or ocean or river and the people seem to have a sense of proportion about allowing prime enjoyment land within walking or biking distance for city or town dwellers. As I sit in my latest venue, in Istanbul, in a delightful restaurant, I look through the autostrada at the Sea of Marmara and the Sultan's palace, and then across at the Asian side. Kids are jumping off the wide seawall into the polluted but beautiful water. It is peaceful and gorgeous in this city of 8 million. If I trudge up the hill to the Blue Mosque, I will meet with the teeming tourist hordes. They are here. Since Greece, people in restaurants are willing to make money feeding people at any hour of the day. I love that.

Second, the bicycling: the French, Swiss and Germans are at the top of the list for bicycle friendly. They have bike lanes, bike paths, bike maps, good paving. Italy was tops for the sheer quality of roads and paving, but although they make what are probably the world's best bikes, they don't mark lanes and they have just SO many cars and manic drivers. Greece is Italy with bad paving, but the ambience is wonderful. I just can't seem to get bored with riding gently rolling hills beside a sparkling, cobalt sea. Greeks are my kind of people, up there early and want to make that tourist buck.

Lots of Turks speak English, or enough English to say "Where are you from?" "America, you from America?" Now I know that their secret agenda is to sell me a carpet but it does seem a bit pushy. How do they know I am USA???? It must be the sensible shoes.

And now for the bare breast report. Those you who have requested a frank and forthright report on our European cousins, here it is. Item one: the male chauvinist pig who said don't bother to bring your bikini top to Europe? He lied. Most Europeans are modestly attired. Item 2. Corfu is the tops in topless. There is acre after acre of scantily clad ladies. None of them are Greek. Coming up the Gulf of Corinth, which is also Greece, sorry to disappoint those inclined to stare and leer but these are Greeks and modestly clothed. On the beaches of Turkey they were all topless; but none of them were women.

My personal bathing thing is a stars and stripes number which does stand out on the beach. I don't undrape, not out of modesty especially . . . as a triathlete, I have run through the streets of major cities in very little. I just think that nudity is wasting a natural resource that should be saved for . . . .

Then there is this thing they have for wearing surplus or unsaleable tee shirts from the USA. Like DENVER BRONCOS, SUPER BOWL CHAMPS. I'm sitting across from a fairly grungy guy in the Budapest metro who is wearing a nice Penn State tee shirt.

"Penn State." I said to him. He stared at me for a second and looked away.

"Joe Paterno." No response. No way he ever heard of the place. A normal graduate of Happy Valley would have spent the next hour bragging about our beloved lions.

Later. Grumbling and groaning, the train finally pulled out. I seem to have a room all to myself. The advantage of starting at such a rotten hour, I guess. I can see some of Istanbul at night that I had not seen even in our night on the town with the belly dancers: mosques outlined by tiny bulbs, the shipyards brightly lit. I think I am going to be very comfortable on the train."

Chapter XXIV

GREECE, again

9.12.95 En route to Athens. World's slowest train. It stops and pulls off every five miles. There must be a faster train. Perhaps I can upgrade. I have entertained myself by copying the Greek words from the textbook three times. It is a good system. The pronunciation of Greek is almost as tough as the alphabet and the attention to detail is making things come clear. The little that I had so painfully learned is coming back. How much I enjoy being alone is something of which I must remind myself now that my love has left, going seven time zones away.

I always had a desire to write but the chief block was that writers are such lone souls. Every time I would try I would be driven back to the company of hordes of people by loneliness. I think I have fairly conquered that. I still do my best writing in the midst of people like at a cafe or McDonalds, but I am beginning to seek solitude so that I can concentrate. Also one needs the time to read. In writing you soon run out of words. I remember Cicero complaining about Latin because it had so few words that it confined the thoughts. He also studied Greek, of course. Greek was the Roman's foreign language and I once heard that Caesar's dying words were Greek, not Latin. What a cool guy. I heard that they were really, 'And you, my son.' Brutus was an illegitimate son by an affair. Yet another fun episode in the Greco-Roman soap opera.

I always taught Roman history like a soap opera, and the kids loved it. Is that why I can't remember the dates any more? Everything I write should be researched because I could be wandering off the factual cliff at any time. I should be able to spend many happy months at the library when I finish the tour, trying to weed out the real from the figment of the imagination. I loved Latin. It was just so hard. What a challenge. If I mastered it I would have gone on to Greek, I did take one class of Classical Greek. If I had mastered that I would have gone on to Hebrew. I am to slow at mastering. Can't live that long. And for what, now that I am not teaching . . . . for the same reason as crossword puzzles, studying language, a fascination with words. Himself is such a master of words. He can know three words in a foreign language and make a pun of it. He makes me laugh.

The windows on this train are really grubby and no air-conditioning. The busses are air conditioned. I got my fellow passengers involved in a fly swatting contest.

Later. I'm getting upset. This train was supposed to be in Thessolonika at 5:00 and it is already 7:15. my fellow travelers ETA is 8:30. If I was supposed to catch a train for Athens, it is long gone. Not that I want to arrive in Athens at midnight anyhow. One man here has a deep resonate voice and never shuts up. How can anyone talk for four hours straight? It is getting on my nerves big time. Green is on a different train and probably long ago in Athens. I keep wondering if I shouldn't have gone on Green's train. They said not and all you can do is what they say. Except for one horrendous batch of mountains, lots of tunnels, it has been relatively flat. Well, I am calm again. When I am this tired, things really get to me. The last time I was this upset was in Austria when they lost Spot. Oh, then there was that taxi driver, in Istanbul who pretended not to know where two of the major streets crossed. It was only a couple of blocks from where we were and I knew the way. It bothered me that he went blocks out of the way up hills and places we had never seen. I can usually handle stuff but when I haven't had sleep, I'm easily pushed over the edge. It is really nice and flat here, I have the "Should be on the bike" guilt. I don't know why I decided to visit the friends near Athens. Seems stupid now. I should be on the bicycle. Nobody seems to ride here in Greece. Nobody in Turkey. The last day I did find the bike sale area. What a hoot. It went on for blocks, of course, in the Turkish style. Tiny shops, dozens of them, one after the other. Bikes hanging from walls and filling the streets. Most dealers also sold mopeds and small motorcycles. There were Scott, Specialized. Bianchi, and Trek. It was not too far from the train station but I never did ask prices and the salesmen never approached me. They have never been carpet salesmen.

I spent part of the last day in a favorite restaurant where Chas and I went, between the Santa Sofia and the Blue Mosque. The Blue Mosque is the newest and the most beautiful. The Santa Sofia was finally completed in the 6th century and not too long after that the western side of Christianity disintegrated but Constantinople continued until the 1400's when it was captured by the Ottomans and turned Muslim. The Ottomans went on to build footstools and dominate the Balkans and the near East and even over to Tunisia. They caused what is now the problem in Bosnia by having such a Muslim presence in the area for so long.

And moving backwards, Constantine made Christianity the official religion 410 AD and started what became the Haiga Sofia. After various vicissitudes it was finally finished by Justinian. Before the Roman period, which goes back to 230 B.C. (Look up.) The Romans had a hippodrome in the area and there are still a couple of monuments left in the horse racing area that the Romans brought over from really old Egypt.

9.16.95 Attic Peninsula. Tired today. Started late from Brian and Mike's and the long string of resort towns down the Attic Peninsula were busy enough to keep me on the sidewalks. Three hotels were $40 so I hung on till I found one for $28. I guess that is because the planes are still passing overhead on their landing path to Athens airport and that makes this spot pretty quick to northern Europe. USA Two Days AGO, as Brian calls it is available here so I can believe it is a tourist area and therefore expensive. The beach is your standard beautiful beach with blue, blue water, palm trees, cafes.

Mike and Brian have been together for quite some time. They both teach in English schools and call the kids 'The enemy'. I always tried to think of ignorance and uncouth behavior of youth as the enemy. Mike has been back to school for a week. He said there was an extraordinary event the first day when a new teacher, at lunch time, leapt from a first floor window and fled, never to be seen again. And people think traveling is tough. Mike is planning to work up a new logo for the school of a woman leaping from a window and running for dear life, hair streaming.

These guys were so literary and expressive and had been around so much that I am finding it hard to digest all the info. First: they teach children of incredibly rich Russians and Yugoslavs.

"I lost 93,000,000 US$ last year," one parent told Mike. These people are the so-called Russian Mafia. Probably most of the money they have is US aid money. In Poland, in order to get goods safely to Russia through the highwaymen in Poland they give baksheesh to the Russian army to escort goods across wild and wooly Poland. Joe Beckman had told me about that, too. Said don't bike Poland.

Then, Mike updates a guide book for Thailand and plans to spend Xmas there. They also helped update a Paris guide book. Some people have it tough.

They always spend the last two weeks of August in the campground where I met them and I think I have been invited to join this sanctum sanctorum. I am taking a break now to go walk on the beach. They lent me a travel book on India. It makes me want to get rid of the rest of my stuff before it is stolen. I met a German girl on the road who had spent a lot of time in India. She said that Green the Magic Bike will be stolen. She has no doubt that I will lose Green. The travel book isn't very encouraging either. I didn't worry about that when I was there before, in 1983 with Semester at Sea, but then I was insulated by the bus tour. Actually I jogged the streets alone and was sickened but not afraid.

Sunion, at the end of the Attic Penninsula, my target, isn't too far away.

9.17.95 Sunion, Greece Sitting in a taverna looking at the temple to Poseidon, the god of the sea. It is cream colored, the roof is long gone. It is in a fabulous location on the southern most tip of the Attic Peninsula. It is my favorite Greek temple. I tried to spot it when we were on the ferry to Samos but it was getting so dark by the time we got here from Piraeus that it was hard to tell but I think I saw it. It is definitely one of those things that they should light up at night so that the sea bound could invoke a blessing. When I was here in 1983 with Semester at Sea, I saw where Lord Byron had scratched his name on a pillar but now I can just barely remember which pillar has the famous graffiti. I'd like to hang around here to take sunrise and sunset pictures but there is a big ugly fence and a gate and I'll bet there is no one here to let you in at those hours. Byron found some great spots. This is our fourth encounter. The first was at Lake Geneva, 'The Prisoner of Chalon'. Chalon Prison was just two blocks from the hostel at Montreaux. Second at Dr. Joe's apartment in Zurich where Byron had stayed. Third was Gallipoli where the British didn't do too well but Bryon did Hero and Leander (check this), and swam the Hellesponte. Now here is where he scribbled his initials on a 2000 year old monument. Tsk, Tsk. I'm tired, It is 12:30 and hot. If the little inn down the road isn't too expensive, I'll stay here.

While I am resting in the restaurant, a pair of French women come in. They are dressed, and I use the word loosely, in very French style. Their skimpy shorts droop below the waistline and the very small amount of bra is held over their boobs so loosely that they might as well be naked. They have that very tanned, shoe-leather skin that makes it clear that they tan often and in the nude. They appear to be mother and daughter and are fighting with short, hissy, French snarls. It is not easy to stomp in tiny high heel slings but they are giving it a try. Their small French convertible sits gathering heat in the parking lot. I keep on typing away in my Zaurus, enjoying the airconditioning. Pretty soon a Muslim family enters. They are a man, well dressed in black suit with white shirt and no tie, it is so hot. Two little boys dressed in black trousers and white shirts cling to the mother who is, perhaps pregnant under all those black robes. The husband also defers sweetly to the mother. I am in the ladies room when she comes in. She is very friendly and we manage a few words. Under her veil is a fabulous make-up job with long lashes and eye-shadow. The works. She is truly beautiful, and exudes peace and contentment. Later, in the parking lot, as I get Green, the bicycle, and climb on, the French witches climb into the convertible whose leather seats must have become a fiery hell. They make more French sounds of distress and finally leave with gravel spitting from under their tires. I putzed around, not wanting to be on the road ahead of them. A long black limo slid up to the building, the uniformed driver got out and held the door for the Muslim family.

Reading the guide book that the guys gave me on India made my night fairly sleepless. It is from The Cardamon series which is the one that Brian and Mike work for from time to time. It gave a lot of really lurid descriptions of travel in India. Scary. What is grotesque is that my World Wander companions will be at such a low level of comfort that they will be enthusiastic about sleeping in rat infested places. I just can't do that. If I don't stay with them, I will be a woman alone in India, not an enviable thing. I suppose I can always drop back to the way I went through India before, with a planned tour on a tour bus, not the public one but one of those that would protect from having the bicycle stolen. Bikes are stolen a lot in the States and I didn't worry about it on the trip. The one bike that I lost was stolen from my kitchen, probably by a neighbor kid who was on drugs. That was a lot of years and bikes ago. Now we lock our doors.

There is a mist over the water now and a small breeze. It is very comfortable in the shade and the waiter has finally decided to wait on me. Veal souvlaki and potatoes. And soo-me (bread.)

9.18.95 Rafingen, Sunion, Attic peninsula. I am more and more concerned about India. The guidebook I am reading is just very unnerving. If my companions choose to be in filth, I must do that too. Ole was right to dump me. I don't want to do filth. The alternative would be fancy hotels and bus tours which I did before. I was a lone person then and didn't have much problem with the natives. 'Winners have alternatives.' I will get netting to wrap around me, a rat will have to chew through it. Stay away from monkeys and wild dogs. I used some of my pepper spray in Athens on stray dogs. Perhaps I should get a fresh one of that, dogs all over the world must bark at bicycles and chase them if free. I hate free dogs. There are a lot of stray dogs in Greece, unlike the rest of Europe.

Later: Made it to Rafina by noon. Probably 40 miles. Hills, too.

Well, lets hear it for the old ladies. The ferry for Karistos doesn't leave until 7:30, arriving in Karistos at 9:30! Such a late hour to arrive unannounced at my friends. Better I should grab a hotel room and spring me on them tomorrow morning when they have built up strength over the night. Talked to Chas. Don's mother died after a relatively short bout with C. Chas went to Cliff Ham's memorial service. Chas still has not called the tandem couple Chancellors' sister. No call from Helen yet.

This is a very strange ferry. It is small, rusty, and the nose goes up in the air to allow cars to go in the front. This is probably the kind that sinks in bad weather in the North Sea. Well, we are a long way from the North Sea and it is beautiful weather. Rafina is a nice town. I spent some time talking to an old man who, back in 1923, had to leave Istanbul, where he was born. He was still bitter at the Turks.

My dear Chas has tracked down Helen, Ole, Regina, John, and the Chancellors. They were together in Yugoslavia on the twenty-second of August. What has become of Michelle, the also rejected? Where is Louise? Jody?

They expect to arrive in Athens on the 22nd of October but Liz and the Olnesses will have left on the 20th. Interesting, but strange. I would like to meet up with the Olnesses and Liz and do India with them because they can afford better than the bottom line, won't lie down with rats.

9.19.95 Karistos, Greece. Just read Ole's prospectus again and the guy is doing just exactly what he said he would. He even now has the exact number of companions that he planned, six. I guess Louise and Michelle were told to take a powder. Or they elected to not take the Yugoslavia route. They did not stay at the Istanbul Hostel. They almost had to get there before I did or during the 10 days I was there, or now they are in Turkey, headed for Israel. From reading Bettina Selby, I understand it is hard to get into Israel with a bicycle. I have no enthusiasm for going to Israel. Not wild about India either.

So I am forced to noodle around the Greek Islands by myself. Tough. I am, once more starting a running program in the mornings when it is cool or sometimes I jog in the evenings although that doesn't seem like a good idea when everyone is in the streets. I must swim. I feel so silly in my stars and stripes suit that I think I will buy another suit. I will also get new clothes made in India, culottes that go below the knee but don't get into the gears. I can buy a man's shirt with long sleeves. I always did buy men's shirts because my arms are so long that women's didn't fit properly. Light cotton. Lots of pockets. I will have to send back my other stuff. I would like to send back the back panniers and travel only with a day pack. I just can't do the hills with any kind of load. My day pack has been a marvel. It must be 20 years old. Can it hold warm clothes, rain gear and one change of clothes? I would carry the Zaurus and maps in the across the chest bag. I still don't lock up the bike. I will keep the fanny pack and the money belt then put almost everything on the body. It will be a strain to lock up everything all the time but if you must, you must. It seems that India is full of thieves.

9.20.95 Karistos, Greece. After an entire day of puttering and no one coming on the ferry that Bradfordwoods neighbors Lu and Luke were supposed to be on, I finally accosted the guy at the restaurant next door and insisted on being taken to "the doctor's house on the hill where the "Americans are staying." He said he would call a taxi and did. The taxi was there instantly but it took 15 min. of discussion before he could explain where the house was. The ride to the house was challenging for the nerves of an acrophobic. It went around and around and up and up and then straight up until there was marvelous view of the town's lights. The house was dark and no one responded. so I got back in the taxi and we went down until we saw some lights. 'Americanos?' I said in my perfect Greek. Two people jumped at me out of the dark with a torrent of Greek and the usual windmill of waving arms. I talked one of them into coming to the taxi to tell the driver all about it. The driver waved me in and we turned around and went straight up the hill some more. There was a light at the next house and Spike came crawling out. He was a bit surprised to see me. So was Mary Jane. They are great fun people and soon recovered enough to invite me in to their 200 year old house.

Spike, Mary Jane, and Luke: troglodytes.

I had to remember to stoop everywhere too because the log beams were low. It has a marble sink like the one in the farm house on the bike tour of Zakinthos. The floor was stone slabs and white washed walls. The ceiling was reminiscent of Mexican adobe homes where they used a lot of brush and beams to make a flat roof and over top of that, the Mexicans use more adobe. I don't know what the roofing material is here not adobe, the walls are stone. Chas and I were in a cave house in Capadoccia that was carved out of the tufa stone of the area. It had the same feel to it as the Greek house, but the Greek one was warmed by the wood of the ceiling. The Turkish home was warmed by the carpets. They were both charming and I had a cup of tea in each but Mary Jane didn't try to sell me any handicrafts. She and Spike had toured some of the islands and enjoyed seeing Knossos in Crete. They are trying to figure out what Tish will be able to go see when sight seeing. She has ovarian cancer and is not exactly tiptop.

Found a sentence in the guide book that may save my life. "If you go the convent of the Missionaries of Charity and Circular Road in Calcutta, and knock on the door, Mother Teresa's nuns will put you to work."

9.21.95 Karistos, Evia, Greece. Hiked up the hill with fresh bread for breakfast for the group again. They were in a bit better humor today. We had fun doing a crossword that was a bear. With Don, Spike, Lou and I all struggling with it we finally beat it. Tish is as pretty as ever. She had two near death struggles with the ovarian cancer and still has problems but she is here. Luke's ninety-nine year old dad is failing but they decided to chance coming anyhow. Chas just went to Don VK's mother's funeral. She was 84 and went fairly fast from cancer. And Gerry has lung cancer. I wonder sometimes if anyone will still be around when I get home. Having a bout of homesickness today. Being with couples who get along so well makes me mourn for home and husband. So I called him and he offered to tell me the latest phone bill. I hung up pretty fast and then had a good cry. I just can't sit around with nothing to do. So then I laid out a good biking route around the north Aegean and will not go to those fancy little islands where there is a port on the water and then straight up to a stunning white-washed town, no biking. Going to study Greek for an hour or two.

9.22.95 Karistos. So I spent another day in Karistos learning to say, 'Esthanome arostos. Ekho dhilitiriassi.' (I feel sick. I have food poisoning.') I've had worse cases. this is mild. I broke a rule: no seafood outside the US, and here I am. I had dinner at the restaurant here with the McBeths, Chandlers, and Stitts and I am wondering how they are doing in the cave with their one toilet. Luke was the only one who didn't have fish and he couldn't be a good nurse because he has a bad knee, and moves with great difficulty. I will try to make contact by telling the guy that poisoned me in the restaurant next door to call Christine, the lady next to the cottage and tell them I have not left and am still at the hotel for another day. Perhaps I am the only sick one. I had severe gas pains the last couple of days, it may be just me. I'm drinking my cure all, Coca Cola, and staying very close to my toilette. I went down with the empty roll of toilette paper to get the hotel guy up to speed with my problem. My worst pain is a fungus infected toenail that has decided to do something strange and hurts a lot. I'm going to get the surgical tools from the bike: saw, pick axe. etc. and spend the day doing something I will probably regret, removing more disfigured nail. My only pending health problem when I started this tour was four fungus infected toenails. The podiatrist wanted to remove the toenails permanently because the problem is incurable. Even Dr. Scholl (the only one who understands feet) agreed that the condition was incurable. One of the other bikers said she had cured her similar problem by scrubbing the nails vigorously every day. Scrubbing them vigorously is uncomfortable and I get slack in that department but never the less, the nails do look better. The bottom (plantar area) of my feet gets very tight and shiny and I put lotion and fungicide on them a lot and they occasionally break out in little bubbles??? Not serious enough to slow me down like diarrhea does. Actually I am feeling a lot better and may even get up after another nap.

I spent a lot of time thinking about background and possible plot for my short story. I don't plan out a plot. If I did it would be a remake of Sleepless In Seattle. I think a lot about the characters until they begin to have faces and personality, then when I write they take over and tell me what to put down. It is really a neat thing, I like it.

Later 3:00 PM trying to contact the house on the hill to let them know I am still here. I picture their bodies stacked up in front of the bathroom door and poor Luke, the only survivor (he had chicken not fish) unable to go for help because his knee swelled to three times its size.

A lady who lives in the neighborhood is trying to phone her home so some one there can get one of them to a phone to call me. (None of them got sick.)

Later: 9.29.95 Athens Greece. There are two just wonderful people here in Athens, The fellow who runs the Youth Hostel, and Veronica. The manager of the hostel is very efficient, helpful, kind. I can't say enough for him. He should have the international hostel person of the year award. Veronica is a travel agent in small office around the corner from the hostel, who appears to do everything in the office. She is from the Caribbean and is a female James Earl Jones. She has the same rolling intonation of English and the same stature which is not fat or over weight but presence. She has presence. Her hair is straightened and lightened and carefully coifed. Her clothes are a beautiful expression of her Caribbean love of color, while being very business-like. She is loaded with glowing golden bangles, rings, and necklaces. Presence. She is totally warm kind and patient in Greek, English, French, Japanese and German. She started as a tour leader and traveled the world, east, west, north and south. She says she works twelve hours a day and the only time she takes off is to nurse sick relatives. When she married she thought about settling down in Greece and really did so when the children came. Six months ago, her mother died. She never left her mother's side. For the three months she was in the hospital, spending the nights in a ward in a straight chair. She continually washed and cleansed the dying mother, and held her hand when not tending. She says that when her mother died, she was never so happy because her biggest fear was that she would die first and her mother, having no one to care for her, would have to beg in the streets. That would seem to be a reasonable fear here in Athens where, other than the usual collection of professionally pathetic gypsies, the majority of beggars are very old people. I drop in on Veronica's very busy establishment a couple of times a day and she gives me coffee and I give her stomach medicine. She says she is a very happy person because she loves everyone so much. She works long hours and has the energy left over to give as intensely to her family. She is very proud that she doesn't drink or smoke and eats only healthful food. At fifty, she has no wrinkles and glows with good health in spite of being in an office.

9.24.95 Athens. Lodged in the hostel in Athens.

Health and Fitness article: "It is free day at the museum so I went to review my crush on the sea god, Poseidon. What a guy.

He's in brass so no one was able to emasculate him in a burst of envy. You know, the kind Freud talked about. When Greeks got mad at each other they would knock the penis off of each other's statues. What is the old joke, 'When she married him he was a Greek God. Now he's just a goddam Greek.' The marble statues are nice but, oh my oh, Poseidon.

There is also a lovely brass by Praxilites himself with glass eyes that really give it a live feeling. I wish they would restore Poseidon's eyes. The jockey was as dashing as ever. Such a little kid on such a big horse. Fine detail of veins on the horse. Its nostrils flaring. Then there was a very alive Augustus Caesar . . . well, he had lost his horse somewhere but you can't always have everything. I broke off so I could take a nap before I go to the house of my communist friend, Nicole.

With time to think about that her rude comment about hating Americans, perhaps I should have mentioned that Greeks did have a share in our revolution. Jefferson loved the Greek philosophers. Democracy had its roots in Greece. Was she going to disrespect her heritage by being a communist? Here's something scary: she works for the UN.

Walking down the street for the hostel, it suddenly all went together. Why Greek guys are eternally adjusting the zipper area of their trousers. I thought that maybe they don't wear underwear and get persistent irritation of the crotch. But this is deeper, more serious. This is so basic to the best of Greece. Picture the young Greek boy, taken to the museum to learn about his heritage. The first thing he sees are guy statues with their whatzis missing. Nobody bothers to explain this phenomenon. Panic sets in. What up to now had been a fine thing with which to entertain oneself, is shown to be gone on almost all the male creatures in the museum. The kid checks the zipper area to see if his is still there. It is. Good. He smiles. Oops, another statue with no masculine gender any more. He checks again. OK. He sighs a sigh of satisfaction but anguish has been born and he will check to see that everything is still there at least three times a minute, every waking hour of every day of the rest of his nervous existence. At some point, his granny decides that he will never amount to much if he can't get on to something else, so she gives him worry beads to give his hands something to do. This is comparable to giving up sucking ones thumb for smoking cigarettes. In Greece, flipping, tossing, thumbing and in general getting pretty artistic with an eight inch bracelet of beads is a national sport. If he forgets the worry beads he has a miserable day trying to remind himself that he doesn't have to check IT every thirty seconds.

Now in the land where Oedipus was father to Freud, we have half the population suffering from mass castration paranoia. But it is really a wonderful heritage, don't you think?"

9.29.95Athens Greece. Health and Fittness Article: "The problem of constantly seeing the faces of people I know came to a head today when I stared up Nikis street to see Luke Mcbeth's face looking around in that lost way that tourists have. Nah, I said to myself continuing on my way. Then there was Lou's face too. And the jacket she wears around. Turned out that it was the McBeths and not a figment of my imagination. He has a story to tell of injury and near dismemberment which I will try to record after dinner.

In the meantime, I would like to express my annoyance at Athens traffic which is both rude and unruly. I have backed off a good bit from the posture of tolerance which is the theme of this trip. I have taken to lecturing drivers of various vehicles on the bad behavior that threatens my life and limb. I am a nervous wreck. Istanbul was bad but the holes in the sidewalk were so deep that they kept motorcycles and the like from using them. Not so Athens. The sidewalks are better here and, worse, everyone uses them. Little scooters and big motor cycles escape from the congealed head cheese of trolleys, busses, taxis, and even cars, that sit pouring fumes into the infamous Athens air. Hopefully part of Athens' problem will be solved when they finish working on a new subway. This subway work manages to show up on every major street, squeezing the aforementioned congealed into a smaller sausage casing of lanes, robbing both the motorized and the pedestrian. I, myself, found that if you go down a one way street the wrong way on your bicycle, you only have to worry about traffic from one direction, except here in Athens where lots of people go the wrong way on the one way street. It is right next to worry beads in popularity. Athenians jump for their lives from time to time but they don't scream and shout nasties at jerk drivers like I do. I am alone in this.

If I stayed here long, I would seek a granny disguise: a white wig, black long dress with long sleeves and a black head scarf, and would carry an umbrella with which to get the attention of the rude drivers. I would call myself The Attack Yaya (Greek for granny). Vehicles stopped on the pedestrian zebra would get a lengthy and embarrassing lecture. Miscreants on motor scooters and cycles, all unprotected would get a wake-up bop on head for coming up behind The Attack Yaya, on the sidewalk, and gunning the motor. Those who figure that traffic lights are for everyone else would be video taped by Yaya and after a 10 minute trial, their vehicles would be melted down. No vehicle would ever be permitted to park on a sidewalk. The punishment for this offence, also video taped by The Yaya, would be confiscation, the vehicle painted yellow and put into service so that there would be taxis available even during rush hour.

The Attack Yaya could disappear into the crowd or assume a pitiful position with tin cup on the sidewalk to escape the vengeance of the vehicle deprived.

Probably it is just easier to box up the bike and leave early for Calcutta."

After three trips across the city I was able to get a current visa for India

PART 3

Mustang Sally's Guide To Asia

. . . "Confronted with the pain of Asia, one cannot look and
cannot turn away. In India, human misery seems so pervasive
that one takes in only stray details."
Peter Mathiessen's THE SNOW LEOPARD

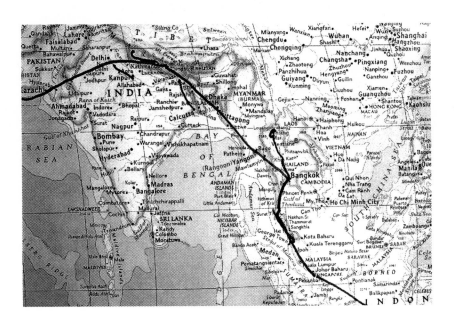

India and Mother Teresa

Instructional apology: I didn't bicycle much in Asia.

Pitiful excuse number 1: The "element" will get lone women. I heard that. Read that. I believe that, in spite of Bettina Selby's books.

Pitiful excuse number 2: I had been disconnected from a group which might or might not offer protection from the "element."

Pitiful excuse number 3: There are diseases and infections there that they don't even have names for.

Pitiful excuse number 4. I, mother of three, teacher, major caregiver, felt guilty about indulging myself in this vacation and felt that working at Mother Teresa's would be a bit of pay back.

Chapter XXV

A Passing Through India

You cannot do a kindness too soon, for you never know how soon it will be too late.

Ralph Waldo Emerson

10.01.95 New Delhi. I arrived at the Delhi Airport, a place mysterious and frightening to even contemplate, in the dead of night. Fortunately, on the plane, I had made friends with a couple of English speakers: a girl with Iranian/Canadian citizenships and a guy from Italy. They were not together but were looking for someplace cheap to stay, as was I. I knew I would be flying on to Calcutta so I wanted to leave Green the Magic Bicycle in the "Left Luggage". The "Left Luggage" was far and dingy across the large parking lot in a murky office possessed by small dark people. Their English rolled softly into the humid air and landed in the ear like a wet washcloth. Reluctantly, I left Green, still in the box, in their friendly care and tagged along with the young people. This should be a different experience.

Back in the main part of the airport lobby, there was a helpful booth that was staffed by two weary women who would be able to go home to bed when we were attended to. They had a list of hotels. We chose a very cheap hotel and the ladies called to make a reservation for us. That done, they arranged with one of the cabs at the taxi stand to take us to the hotel. It was such welcome efficiency for weary travelers. We hurtled through the exotic streets and stopped at a dingy hotel. I told the taxi driver to pick me up at 10 o'clock the next morning.

The hotel we found at 11:30 PM wasn't totally bad but it wasn't good. The two younguns fussed and complained about every little thing but $8.00 for a double with a huge air conditioner and two fans seemed quite reasonable to me. The girl, an "Italian" from Toronto, and I slept on a bed with sagging springs and 40 year old linens. The guy, an "Italian," who was from New York, slept in the even worse bed. The walls were fingerprinted and the plumbing leaked, but were not so annoying as the light of one naked 15 watt bulb that hung from the ceiling by a wire. What really messed up the ambience was the unpaved street outside that was lined with the bodies of sleeping Indians. I didn't see this when I was in Delhi in 1983, only in Bombay.

By the time I was up and about the next morning, my companions had disappeared. Oh dear. Did I snore and keep them awake? Did I scream and holler? When I met the girl later in Kathmandu, I learned that this was the start of a torrid romance for the two of them. They had separated with the aim of meeting again somewhere and had missed that connection and might be parted forever by the ungracious Indian Airline that had bumped one of them from the flight to Kathmandu. Anyhow, in Delhi, the sun was shinning on domes with peeling pink paint.

The streets were the real India. Silhouettes of large or small groups of people are so reminiscent of a book I borrowed once to try to learn how to sketch. The drawings were all of Indian towns, with groups of sari clad ladies like puffs of brightly colored smoke. Every woman in India seems to me to be beautifully dressed and many of the Indian women are beautiful. The Eucalyptus with the mottled olive and white trunks, the biodegradable housing were so charming in the sketchbook. Now, however, I am in the city and the grunge gets to me. I am trying to believe that unpaved, unswept streets are really very artistic. Still, I am getting the urge to sketch and paint. It just died in Greece where everything was so stark. Here where the dust softens the array of pastel colors to a blur, I want to draw. I want to paint.

I bought E. M. Forster's *A Passage To India* and another book *Far Pavillions* by an Indian woman. The taxi driver and I are going shopping to find me some clothing that can be turned over to the Indian wash service, which is down at the river. The river, you must understand, is already indescribably filthy. Women beat the hapless wash on the rocks and stretch the wet wash out on the shore to dry. It would be death by torture for my lycra bicycle clothing.

I met Ishk in the Coffee Shop of the Asok Hotel. He was just bursting with enthusiasm and ideas and wanted someone bounce ideas off of. When I said to Ishk that I did not get the connection between the Aryan Nation type of white supremacists and the Aryan tribe who conquered India around 500 B.C., he launched into a long explanation which I will try to remember. He was born in India but grew up in Vancouver and is a Canadian citizen. He first came to India last year on business and is thrilled at the opportunity for business here. As he says: so 300 million people are hungry, there are another 300 million who can buy some stuff and 300 million who can buy a lot of stuff and, picture this, about 30 M who are very rich. But to get back to The Aryans. They were nomads who conquered a very civilized country and to maintain their top position in the society set up the cast system with each darker color getting lower on the scale. I had never heard of the caste system as racially based but perhaps I am naive. The Aryan Nation apparently had done the proper research. The Dravidians were another tribe here and David Koresh must have been aware of the racial overtones of an entire huge religion based on racial inequality. In spite of the cast system being outlawed, it is, from what I read, still a large part of Indian life. What a pity. It is still unheard of to marry out of cast and young Indians who manage to get a good education abroad often stay there because here in India caste limits how far you can go even in business. So the country deprives itself of many of its best and brightest.

I toured the city with the taxi driver and caught a late plane to Calcutta.

Article for Health and Fitness

"10.2.95 Calcutta I think it is important to get those first impressions down. After they only come once. Firstly . . . YUUUUUK! This place is so incredibly filthy and disgusting. I am trying to keep in mind what one traveler said, 'Things are never as bad as you expect them to be." Oh, yeah?

The airport did have the very nice thing for backpackers that the Delhi Airport had: a list of inexpensive hotels and prepaid taxis. When you arrive in an Indian city in the middle of the night, it is such a comfort to see the desk for hotel reservations. They have the same hotels listed as the guide book that one is clutching (the Cadmon donated by Mike and Brian) and they speak English. You pay for the taxi here and the call to the hotel reserves your space at the advertised price. You can leave the bright lights of the airport for this very foreign land with the knowledge that they are caring for you. The taxi ride from the airport was terrifying.

I had arrived in Calcutta for the festival of Durga Puja. She is the major Hindu goddess of the area and this is the biggest festival of the year. Let's say a harvest festival. The streets were lit up like Christmas, miles of cheerful gods and goddesses in lights. There were the usual collection of poor souls lying on the sidewalk. When I took a stroll around this morning, they were up in a sitting position, begging. In spite of my charitable nickname, I have found that it doesn't pay to give alms because they then never leave you alone. Snobbish rotter in the Raj style, that's me. By this time I can look at a starving mother with a starving child and mutter, 'Not my problem'.

I went strolling and except for the touts who are selling every possible thing, found strolling to be both safe and rewarding. My Astoria Hotel is fairly far from the river, the Hooghly. The hotel that I had hoped would be an old style Raj, Fairlawns. turned out to be another dingy, hole in the crumbling on to the street wall. However, it does have two restaurants, a lounge and a proprietress who looks like Toulouse Loutrec had done her makeup. After shrugging off fifty or sixty touts and escaping from several tailor shops I found the guy who can make the pajama bottom style pants that I hope will be comfortable here. Most of the stores were rejected because they don't have cotton. This fellow is making the pants for 150 rupees or less than $5. I probably should have bargained with him but I just hate that. He has a couple of nice blouses I might be able to get for less if I bargain. I have found that, especially with clothes, you can always get stuff cheaper in the USA. Going to catch up on lost sleep now.

Later. That night I went with Mr. Singh, the taxi guy, and a couple of Austrian lady doctors to see the festival. There are clubs that put up temporary temples around the town. They are large and made of muslin stretched over scaffolding and a great and wonderful art. The outsides look like temples built of sugar cubes and the insides have the goddess with ten arms who is the nice form of Kali. She is pretty active sometimes and vigorously spearing a curly haired guy. There is a lion involved and sometimes a few other gods. Our guide took us about in his taxi through streets that did nothing to cure my panic every time I have to cross the street. The Austrians got into each grabbing a hand and dragging me shrieking and laughing through the worst of the traffic. They are from Vienna and, I suppose, should be able to handle things better than a near hysteric from Bradfordwoods. It helps to be out there with the people. None of these were begging. The Indian women were wearing fabulous new saris that they bought for the festival and were all just beautiful. A sari just doesn't seem as elegant in the States as it does here. Maybe it is the sensible shoes that are worn in the States that spoils the effect.

I bought and started to read *City of Joy* which was about a Calcutta slum. Patrick Swaze movie. How could any plot survive Patrick Swaze?

10.3.95 Calcutta. I reported to Mother Teresa's convent today. It was a short taxi ride from here up really wretched streets to Circular Rd. Circular Road is not so bad. However, horde of grubby, shrieking, begging urchins surrounded the car and actually climbed in. I overpaid the taxi man and fled down the very clean little side street to the door of the convent. Nice little nuns dressed in white saris with baby blue edging let me in and took me upstairs. I waited for a while on a narrow hall that connected an office with a chapel. The clean, whitewashed simplicity of the nunnery was such a change from the dirty chaos outside. Then a very nice and attractive nun with warm brown skin and sparkling brown eyes who could speak excellent English told me to come back and do documents at five o'clock that same afternoon, at which time I could meet Mother Teresa! Then I would report at 8:00 in the morning. I said fine, relieved to put off what I most wanted to do, meet Mother Teresa. Actually I was astonished that I would meet such a famous person.

I left in a taxi that said 30 rupees when I got in and then wanted 50 when I got out. I said 30 is thirty, it can't end up being 50, paid 30 and left. When you don't have exact change it is harder to be tough. But about Mother Teresa? Could she possibly be in the upstairs room where I waited? Could it be that I will meet her this afternoon? I get all strung out at the thought. Ahmed, the Athens Muslim, said he saw her once and although he is a Muslim, he wept. I must take some hankies just in case, I am one of the great weepers of the world. The Convent was the cleanest thing in Calcutta, perhaps in India. The little nuns in their white, with blue stripe, outfits were attending a service and the one I talked to said the convent was closed at this hour. So perhaps at five o'clock I will meet the saint. I am incredibly nervous. What do you say to a saint, anyhow. Good work, Kid. Keep it up?

So, OK. yeah. I met Mother Theresa. Big deal. Like the Taj Mahal is a big deal. And as hard to describe and as much a wonder of the world. She was originally from Albania and is, of course, Roman Catholic. If I expected to be greeted by a yoga, guru type person, tuned out of the world and into herself, forget that. Our Lady of the White Sari seemed to me to be closer to Yosemite Sam in personality. You remember Yosemite Sam? He was a short red-haired cartoon guy with two big guns who would pull them out and start blasting away at the slightest provocation. What got Mother Teresa stirred up when I met her was a young Hindu doctor who had a lot of documents to show her about women who had been imprisoned. She tore into the subject like . . . Yosemite Sam . . . guns blazing.

"Just outrageous," she exclaimed. "They claim these girls are prostitutes and that is ridiculous and even if they were they have been in jail for an outrageously long time."

She took the documents and assured the doctor that she would help. Then she reminded him that the nuns could use the help of a doctor when they went north into the flooded area to inoculate the people there against typhoid. He agreed to help. In leaving he touched her feet as a Hindu gesture of respect.

"Don't do that," she snapped. It's unnatural."

"It is an Hindu sign of respect," he responded. "I meant no offence."

"It's unnatural."

It was my turn to talk.

I babbled a few words of praise for her work and than asked her to pose for a photo which the doctor took. She was very gracious. I guess she has done that a few times.

She turned to the doctor again and said again that she would back his cause. She handed out medals and pictures and lingered as if enjoying our company. I had finally come up with something to say to a saint.

"You are an inspiration to the world," I said.

"I do nothing. Jesus does it all. He works through me. Listen to him." said Mother Teresa.

"What are you doing here?" she asked. I just pretty much stared, open-mouthed. "Do you know that there are 23 Missions of Charity in the United States?"

"Well, I was in India . . . ah . . . and . . ." she patted me on the hand and gave me a couple more medals.

Well gollee, I said to myself. The woman's a religious fanatic. I wept just a tiny bit."

Calcutta doctor and doctor father and mother.

Later, I went with the doctor to his home and met his family. He wanted me to have a good impression of Calcutta and showed me his "posh" home. He also showed me the Ramakrishna place which was 'posh' and thought I should stay there instead of the Victoria Hotel on Suddar Street. He gave me a phone number that never answered. Perhaps he went to the flood area.

10.04.94 Calcutta I'm trying to restore my sense of proportion as well as my equilibrium. I spent my first stretch on the rock pile just down the street from the Convent where there is the children's hospital. There are various Missionaries of Charity hospitals scattered around the city. I don't have it all sorted out yet but there is a hospice for the terminally ill and one for lepers and the one for the children that I went to work at.

Green, the Magic Bike, is in the airplane box. Green's rider is working on a rampaging nervous breakdown, brought on by Indian traffic. Here in Calcutta, very few vehicles are private cars. Most are taxis, rickshaws or three wheeled motor things, trucks and busses. Street cars. First of all, the worst of the British Raj, they drive on the wrong side. Many streets are narrow and the vehicles use whatever is available even if it isn't the proper side of the median. They all tolerate the creative driving that has two taxis racing toward each other to see who gets to an opening in the wall of traffic first. The loser takes it with good spirit and will soon be running another heart stopping race. The tank-like taxis, like everything in India are made in India for India and are as dilapidated, rundown, and run over as everything else in Calcutta. For riding around, nothing smaller than a tank seems reasonable.

Walking is my real problem. Old Smiley Sally, waving and helloing the world, is not in Calcutta. Instead a glum, growling old grouch (in the sack-like clothing I bought here, which I call 'waddling clothes') strides through the pathetic field of waving, fingerless and handless arms, face fixed in a serious scowl. The problem is that if you give beggars anything, they never leave you alone. This is the one place where it is way worse to give than to receive.

Early morning finds the streets relatively clean. The tea brewers start first, heating the water with something which burns with a thick, oily smoke. The Hindus are vegetarians and the rinds and seeds from the mountains of fruit they prepare mounds up in the gutters. It is not long before garbage piles arise, gleaned by the dozens of pariah (ownerless) dogs, crows, people and goats. Do you want to think about the usefulness of dogs in a place where street people have no toilets? I went past one large pile that was dominated by huge black pigs. Even the banks have given up and hide behind ugly barricades and pull down metal shutters that are old, rusted, awful. Very little has ever seen paint, instead a green slime tints the concrete buildings. Sound unappetizing? My stomach is in constant turmoil. Meet a resident and he wants to know if you like Calcutta. He obviously does and will show you one dingy treasure after another if you can't escape. I have yet to get out at dawn to jog. Perhaps tomorrow.

10.5.95 Calcutta and sick.

Dehli Belly caught up with me and I have resolved to never have any salad. At the worst of it I was trying to figure out how to get home or anywhere you could get water to drink that wasn't poisoned. So I have been lying in the dim light reading and reading CITY OF JOY by Larry Collins and Dominique LaPierre. It is the story of a Calcutta slum as told in interviews of some of its inhabitants and fascinating. Horrifying. It is not the thing to be reading while sick. My hotel is not much help to a sickie, and ants have arrived in the third story bathroom, probably my fault because I stored cookies there. It is pretty distressing to see ants constantly in one's tooth brush. I have a train reservation to Darjeeling for tomorrow night but it will take all day to check my pack, check out, get a permit from the Foreign tourists office, get money. I was not able to get a return ticket so Lord knows when I would get back. If I feel OK in the morning I might give it a try. Darjeeling isn't just tea, it was one of the resorts used by the British Raj to escape the heat of summer high in the Himalayas.

Talked to M'Love tonight. Terrible phone connection. No go for Tom and Terry's third attempt at invitro. The main group of world wander bicycle group is now in Athens with Ole. Regina's $5000 bicycle fell apart and they await repair parts. They can't get tickets to New Dehli for the 20th which means that they will miss the eclipse of the sun. Chas going to do the second Governor Ridge (of Pennsylvania) Ride!!!!!! I did the first one last year and it was such fun. I was riding right along with the candidate, Tom Ridge, telling him how the Romans built their roads. Pennsylvania wins terrible road paving contests. My real interest was bicycle paths.

I haven't been writing at all because I have been trying to get through my reference book and, the Dehli Belly. Just killed a mosquito. I don't know where to start. I promised to meet some girls at 5:15 AM at the corner tomorrow and we will walk to Mother's together.

The convent. Being the extreme left wing of Protestant, I haven't spent much time in convents. One would suppose that this one is ordinary but while other orders are having problems getting recruits, this one has a living saint to ignite and fire enthusiasm for the nun's life. I don't have the figures for all the missions in the Mother network but it is in the hundreds, including twenty some in the US. My guess for the mother house is thirty nuns and sixty novitiates. The nuns have a blue stripe on their white saris while the novitiates are plain with two styles of the veil over the head. The novitiates are scrubbing their saris in buckets on the bottom floor when we get there at 5:30 A.M. Some are already assembled in the prayer room. They are in neat rows of kneeling Madonnas facing the very simple altar which has a simple cross and a statue of The Madonna, standing with palms down and forward. The service is read and chanted in what turned out to be English, with a Bengali accent. The novitiates chant and sing and eventually the nuns are assembled. and finally a priest comes in. With head properly bowed I enjoy his delightfully Irish accent. When I lift my eyes I behold . . . a Bengali man! He carries on the Mass, getting out his paraphernalia. Finally he offers the Eucharist and in a very orderly way, the nuns go up row by row and receive the body of the God. I'm grumbling to myself about Dyonisian rites and 'New wine in old bottles' but when my section gets up I get up too and take the first communion in, maybe, 45 years. The walls did not crumble at this piece of hypocrisy. I was telling myself that if I were at a Hindu or Buddhist affair and invited to join, I would. Somewhere along the line I had decided that the reason I was here in the chapel and would come here often for some time to come is to study these wonderful women and try to understand how they can be so selfless. Actually they spend a great deal of time concentrating on selflessness and it is that focus, perhaps, that enables them to do the wonders that they do. They return to their positions, backs straight, I do this, too and my rotten knees cause some pain. Even they can't all manage the knee position for long without pain, some sit side saddle and some sit on the arches of the feet as many Asians do. Mother Teresa enters quietly and quietly prays. In neat lines the nuns leave the prayer room and when we get back down stairs, having retrieved our shoes, the nuns are back to scrubbing saris on the main floor. We volunteers have a breakfast of tea with milk, banana, and bread. A little chatting and much passing of information among the volunteers. I am going to the children because as a retired teacher I feel that is my place. It is a short walk down Circular Road. At the children's hospital, the children are divided into the orphans on the first floor and those who have parents on the second floor. The floor I was on, the children who have parents, was divided again into little babies, little bitty babies, bedridden and getting around and older, say, three or four.

Photo by Linda Schaefer

Nurse Mary Hjeilm of Calcutta, Portland, and Seattle.

The first hour was the worst. I started to change a diaper and a volunteer, Mary, a nurse from Seattle, said,

"Don't change the babies. Let the local girls do that. That one has AIDS or hepatitis."

I did have the presence of mind to put the child down carefully. Then I fled to the sink to scrub. I was advised to use rubber gloves when I touched the children. There were none around. There wasn't even much soap. I hit every drug store in town and found no rubber gloves. The most desperate looking infant had eyes like white marbles. One of the local girls carried that child constantly. I fed a preemie who was as skinny and frail as a baby robin. He sucked desperately on the bottle. The life force was strong in him.

I looked at some pustules on a child's stomach and asked if the child had chicken pox. Mary said,

"No. Look at the scalp. Scabies."

So many have limbs pathetically twisted by rickets. There is a whole roomful of those sad, twisted children. They are in cots in rows and will never be able to leave the cots. They stare vacantly at the ceiling and are, again, cared for by local girls.

The Children's Building is fairly small. The floor I am on is for children who have parents who are unable to care for them. The newest is a tiny preemie whose fontanel has not closed because he was born with rickets. I gave him a bottle which he took greedily; I fed a couple of babies who were up and sitting on the floor.

I ended up moving in with the older children. There were many just lying in beds, their bodies and minds crippled beyond any mobility. I went on into a third room that had a lot of beds and also a small area where kids could play. I sat and watched them play. They got along pretty well. The oldest girl and leader of the pack had a rosary and spend a very long half hour doing the rosary while her adoring followers listened intently. Excuse me, but that is about as exciting as watching two guys fish. Eventually they wandered off, I know not where. I was adopted by Gustav first. I don't know his real name. They don't seem to go by names here. Gustav is actually chubby and the only athlete in the place. He kicks a ball around, throws stuff for the sheer joy of it. I picked him up and hugged him and he tolerated that about as long as a kitten would and, kittenlike, went back to rough and tumble playing. When I could grab him again, we did the "fall through the knees game". He loved it. He is such a stout little fellow with all limbs intact.

A terribly crippled girl of maybe five, comes to have herself lifted to a standing position and walked on long walks. She has what is either a nice grimace or a nice smile and occasionally tries to bite. Her legs are very twisted. I try to get her to hold on to a crib so she can walk herself. Her hands are weak and twisted but can hold mine. It seems to me that she could hold the crib and hold herself upright but as many times as we tried this she didn't get the idea. Perhaps she never will. She reminds me of Andrew Wyeth's painting, 'Cristina's World'.

A girl comes up with a picture puzzle. We work it a few times and I get her to put her frail, twisted hand up in a 'high Five'. She likes that. Then I point out the cactus in the picture and try to get her to say "Cactus". In this jungle place? Then we put the puzzle together again saying, "Cactus, cactus". Then I show her the camel and the same process. Then we try the blue sky. She is beginning to get it. Now she can put two pieces together. She loses interest and wanders away. At this point, Blue Boy appears. He is a very normal looking child and he wants to work on the alphabet. I give him a hug. He is what I have been waiting for. His book has letters on big lines and a child can practice making the lower and upper case letters. He has N and remembers how to do it. He learns the high five. We are both enthralled. Gustav comes back and wants the fall through the knees game again. Smiley wants to be walked, but blue boy is not distracted. He goes over and over the letters. He gets a better copy of the book with more pages intact.

A beautiful Indian lady bountiful in a heavenly blue sari appears like a magic fairy in the small room. She takes a picture of Smiley and me parading around. Another lovely Lady in exquisite sari hands out some kind of goodie carefully packaged. I didn't get one. Gustav works on the ties of his until he has it free and there are goodies all over the floor. The ladies bountiful leave. I guess we a part of a tour. Someone snatches Blue Boy off and I am left to walk Smiley around until she, too crawls off to lunch. At lunchtime we leave. Mother doesn't think that volunteers can take a whole day of work. I go back to the Motherhouse with the others.

The two Irish girls and a lady from New Zealand who have befriended me want to see Mother Teresa before they leave for their homes. They have heard that she will be going traveling herself. I go up to take pictures for them with their cameras. Fantastic, I am firing away from down close to the floor because Mother is exceedingly short. Her poor old body is bent over into a permanent position of caring. I got a good shot of Mother kissing the medals she gives away and hopefully one with her hand on the New Zealander's head in blessing. I was sliding back out the door when Mother nailed me and wanted to know how many there were in my family. (Catholics, did she want to know Catholics???) I reeled off children and grandchildren and she gave up counting and gave me a fistful of medals and a blessing. A big tear rolled down my cheek and, then, sobbing, I fled.

Walking home with the two Irish girls was long and through a very depressing area. My legs were tired, I felt sore all over. I went to lunch at Fairlawns but couldn't eat it. I had lunch with the Viennese Psychiatrist. She was asking me about Mother Teresa's and big tears came out of my eyes rolled off my nose and dripped onto the plate. I sat there feeling like a fool while she patted me on the arm saying,

"Let it out. Go ahead and cry. Don't hold it back." This is too good and invitation. I get clear into the runny nose stage with muffled sobs. "The pain of Asia . . ."

I'm sick. I have Dehli Belly and an hour or so later the wretched symptoms are upon me. So how was the first day on the job? Let me tell you . . . .

10.6.95 After a large debate with myself over using my ticket to Darjeleen or showing up at Mothers at 5:30, I decided to leave it in the hands, or arms, of Morpheus and he let me sleep until 6:00. So I am now at the famous Fairlawns Hotel. The garish green pillars are as soothing as the raucous birds that hang out in the few trees here. Someone feeds the pigeons and some nasty mosquito just bit me on the ankle. Fairlawns is as ugly on the outside as anything on Suddar Street and as strange a hotel as you could learn to truly love. The décor is something a fellow lodgee called: Cotswald. Lots of red. Lots of floral. Lots of everything. Like India, abundance, great abundance. The waiter in turban and gloves, seats me with other traveler stragglers so I have someone to talk to at lunch. Everyone has the same menu and it is very reasonably priced. Most of the time it is English food. When I am not lucky it is spicy Indian food. I have met a lot of lone women and men travelers here, all of whom like it because of the opportunity to meet with others. Shortly after the lights go on in the dining room, one may enter to dine. After a while an enormous bell starts to clang and, lo, it is not a fire but lunch.

Later. Hanging out at the Oberlie Grand Hotel coffee shop. I went cruising with Mr. Singh, the taxi driver. We did the post office where I mailed off two rolls of film. They did not want any postage!!!! Then we cruised to the American Express for whom I can express very little enthusiasm. There was a line that went outside and around the corner where you could meet every American in Calcutta. The American Express card only permitted me to cash a check. Do you know how many checks survived the rains that I have been in? I hate American Express. I had to go to an Indian bank to get cash with a VISA. That was a day out of my life. If I had not trashed my Citibank card I would be better off. Citibank has an ATM here. Too many cards I said and killed the only credit card other than the despised American Express that is honored in India. Then Mr. Singh and I did the Howarth Bridge which is quite wonderful. It charges a fee and is devoid of traffic. I got a copy of the Herald Tribune to read that OJ is out on the streets. Had he been a white man he'd be in the slammer for forever. He'd have had no defense at all. Funny how a Mike Tyson can mess with a girl, who put herself in harm's way by going to the bedroom of a brute, and end up in the slammer and O.J. who stalked and slashed is free, his ex-wife irretrievably dead.

The O.J. thing is so typical. People in the slum can watch one guy mug another and not co-operate with the police in order to stay out of trouble, then they complain that they are not protected by the police when that same brute mugs them. They have freed a murderer. Again. It just does not make sense to me. O.J. is the beneficiary of legal affirmative action. Ah well. Glad I don't live in Beverly Hills. I am indulging in crossword puzzle mania. I totally did yesterdays Herald Tribune and totally bombed USA THREE

DAYS AGO's puzzle. Bye. (With Green in the box, I'm beginning to talk to the Zaurus.)

I wouldn't write about this if I had not read all of Bill Bryson's travel books. Bill tells it like it is. If you don't really want to know how it is, don't read this.

I had to get my ticket for the train to Darjeeling. Mr Singh, my dear taxi driver promised to take me to the ticket place and wait there while I bought the ticket. It was a handsome building, built, no doubt, by the British in better times. There were huge, multiple ticket lines inside the building. Perhaps three light bulbs brightened its dank interior. I had need for the ladies room. That is not unusual.

At a huge train station there should be a ladies room. Right? I could not see one and when I asked there were a lot of shrugs. I stood in one line and then was told that I should go to the line that lead up a stairway that clung to an outside wall. So I went to that line. There are special lines for "Europeans." Pain began to wander around my abdomen. First an ache and then sharp pains then distressing urgency pangs. I went to an official, the Boss, who was seated at an aged wooden desk. He was taking in money and handing tickets around to the usual crowd of people who stamp things that go through their hands and then pass them along to others who stamp them also. One must assume that these are all relatives. All are employed. Then the ticket having gone through ten hands and around the room, is finally delivered to the purchaser who weeps with gratitude. India loves bureaucracy and then came the British who love bureaucracy and now, just try to imagine, the communists now rule.

Anyhow, my Problem is becoming very stressful. I go back to the Boss at the desk. He shurgs his shoulders again when I say I need a toilet. The guys on the stair let me go back to my place which has moved by three people in this half hour. I am now grabbing my suffering abdomen and hunching over. One of the guys yells at the Boss and he scowls deeply. Then, with a sigh, points to a door behind him. I hustle to the door and go through it. On the other side is a large storage area full of cardboard boxes. I scramble around them until I come to that very un-British thing, a Turkish toilet. It has the usual foot pad things aimed in no particular direction. I take a second or so to meditate on whether to head in or head out. It is actually the other end that is the problem. I aim my rear toward the wall in case one of the officials comes in to check me out. The explosion of unwanted matter from my bowels could not have been worse, first a fine spray then clumps of distressed, curried vegetables painted the wall behind me. The four inch hole in the floor that is a Turkish toilet is hard to hit under the best of circumstances and when stuff is coming like as from a fire hose, no chance. By now, in addition to the abdominal agony, I'm beginning to weep from the embarrassment of it all and can't see and my nose is running. Here it comes another paroxysm of pain and this time the convulsion is accompanied by a sound that there is no way to muffle. In spite of the usual cacophony of India, I am sure that the patient ticket lines in the waiting room have heard. More tears dribble. Other stuff dribbles, too. I have never, ever, been so miserable. I mop my eyes and look around. The Turkish toilet is usually accompanied by a bucket of water and sturdy scrub brushes. There is nothing here. The usual napkins that we tourists carry are some personal help but I can't even begin to tend to the mess that is sprayed over wall, boxes, and floor. Totally humiliated, I go out the door and shake my head in despair at the Boss. I give him a fist full of rupees. He rolls his eyes and shrugs. I start for the stairs. I have been in there so long that the line is gone and I go right up and get a ticket for Darjeeling.

10.7.95 Train to Darjeeling. Fantastic scenery and I will have another 5 hours of it even after spending all night on the train.

Thanks to Cardamon, I bought a lock and chain just for this ride so that I could chain my most treasured possessions to my body while sleeping. I picked out a nice Pullman type bed on the corridor because it seemed better than sleeping in a cabinette with three strange men. One guy argued with me about this for a long time but I refused to move and he eventually gave up his spot to me. Seems the numbers on the ticket said it was his but I never moved. Chaining the backpack seemed to work because I was not robbed.

There are lovely green rice paddies in endless miles. India now feeds itself as well as being one of the top five industrial countries. The views of small villages with their mud and straw huts from the vantage of my train are quite charming. The tiny huts are home to the beautiful brown people in their saris and loin cloths or in the case of small children, nothing at all. I borrowed a guide book from a Brit and the flat land continues until the bottom of the mountains where the Himalayas rise with great steepness out of the plain. Darjeeling was the home of Tsinging Norclay and you can see Everest from there on a clear day and this is the time of the year for viewing. The Darjeeling area is a small niche of India in the midst of Bhutan, Tibet, Nepal, and Bangladesh. This area of the train trip is somewhat flooded. Ah, this is the place where Mother Teresa wanted the doctor to go to help with typhoid shots! The poorer huts in the lower areas are the ones hit worst. Ole had planned to arrive here after the monsoons.

As I look out, there is a green carpet with grass huts scattered at great intervals. Some few fields have a crop of bamboo and bamboo stacks are piled up on the little compounds. Now we are passing areas of better housing, adobe, some are brightly painted. One huge tree has a bright collection beneath of yellow, red, and blue saris and a couple of bullock carts with big wooden wheels. Now white cattle and a lone figure with a bundle on the head. Now an adobe hut with banana trees growing all around it. Now flooded paddies. Now a small pond with a fisherman in a skiff with long points on each end, is it made of bamboo? Others fish with big square nets which are now high in the air, ... to dry? More bamboo or perhaps sugar cane is stacked to dry in the fields. Now straw huts with the sides of woven palm leaf. Now huts with sides of bamboo and bamboo roofs. Now bamboo sides and tile roofs. I can't take a picture through the window of the train because the windows are so crazed and scratched, not to mention dirty.

Now there is a stream with a fisherman throwing a circular net, weighted, into the stream. Now a lone concrete building, deserted, in a field. Now a little clump of banana and other trees underneath which is a clump of huts, all flooded. Now white boats and a farmer walking rapidly through his emerald green rice paddy scattering something white . . . fertilizer? insecticide? A group of huts huddling beneath trees in the distance. how appealing they are. Big bamboo trees with brown cattle grazing beneath. All this is very flat. Miles and miles, perhaps I should say, hours and hours of flat land. Very productive. Two, sometimes three crops of rice. Now a lady with an umbrella and a sari silhouetted against a pond. Looking down at an abandoned boat, wood but not both ends pointed. Coming to a town. The Sikh who was sitting across from me had his beard wound into a tight string on both sides of his face and it disappeared up his cheek and under his turban. He has crawled into the upper bunk for a snooze. The town is mostly red brick. The station buildings are the usual dilapidated scene, yellow with wet orange mold. What grass is there is close cut or chewed. There are some bicycles here, not awfully fat tired, about medium fat. A tray of really ugly bananas went by on a head.

Just finished reading Tagore, the poet. Can't say that I understand it as well as I would if I believed in an anthropomorphic god who is attentive to my every move. Because I lack that, Tagore and I are poles apart. However, here is a lovely poem to treasure, learn even:

> *The same stream of life that runs through my veins night and day*
> *runs through the world and dances in rhythmic measures.*
> *It is the same life that shoots in joy through the dust of the earth*
> *in numberless blades of grass and breaks into tumultuous*
> *waves of leaves and flowers.*
> *It is the same life that is rocked in the ocean-cradle of birth and*
> *of death in ebb and in flow.*
> *I feel my limbs are made glorious by the touch of this world of life.*
> *And my pride is from the life-throb of ages dancing in my*
> *blood this moment.'*

James Russell Lowell'

And what is so rare as a day in June, then if ever come perfect days
.... and whether we look or whether we listen we hear life murmur
or see it glisten and every clod feels a stir of might, an instinct within
it that reaches and towers and groping blindly above it for light,
climbs to a soul in grass and flowers.... and there is never a leaf of
grass too mean to be some happy creature's palace.'

Well, sorry, but Tagore loses to Lowell every time in my book. Tagore feels nature pouring through his body. Lowell observes. Good Unitarian approach to things as compared to the Hindu But don't they each paint a lovely picture?

I love the paddies and the day is sparkling but the windows of the train are so filthy that I can barely see the Zaurus.

The air-conditioning insulates us from the reality of India. In a river there are just heads as the children cool off. An aging goatherd has a black umbrella to shield himself, but mostly the landscape is deserted as the inhabitants, as bright as a cluster of butterflies, huddle under the trees. A water buffalo, true to his name settles down happily in a puddle.

The railroad is on an embankment whose substance came from the nearby marsh so there is a constant pond that accompanies the train. These ponds are worked and reworked by successive generations in order to either increase the land or increase the water. Water lilies move in and offer their white purity to the blazing sun. We are casting a shadow on the other side of the train now. We should arrive in a town where we catch a taxi to a bus in about 10 minutes if the train is on time.

10.8.95   Darjeeling, India. Most places I go I try to acquaint myself with the writers and/or poets of the area. I met a live poet/ painter, Peter, last night here in Darjeeling. We ate and discussed life forces and exchanged poetry, his original, 'Pigeons on the grass, alas.' type and my donation of Tagore and James Russell Lowell.

He rode a bike through India until he had an accident which nearly cost him a foot! He is still recovering from the injury. He leaped off the road to avoid being hit by a truck, slashed the ankle and then a horrid infection set in and by the time he got to a doctors they were in a mood to cut his foot off. He wouldn't let them. They did remove a big piece of bone.

He wrote a poem about being invited to enjoy refreshments (he was bike touring) by some sari clad ladies who went back to their work afterwards. They were breaking big rocks into little rocks. They were truly working on a rock pile. I refer to my time as a teacher as being on a rock pile but to those Indian women it was not a joke.

Peter intends to desert his native Vancouver for Calcutta. He will set up a studio there where the life force can move through him to put paint on Belgian Linen. He is having his first book of poetry published in Calcutta.

The ride up here was one long stifled scream for me. Incredibly windy and twisty with bottomless shoulders, dirt and rock slides onto the road, and lots of places where the road itself had washed out.

This is the Himalayas. This is the town where Tenzing Nortay spend his last days and was cremated. Four of us had rented a minivan and made the trip up the mountain from the train. The young people in the van insisted on having the windows open even after we had gone up a mile or so of altitude and it was very chilly. I have a runny nose and so does every one else. Three of us came to Tower View Lodge. It was full so the lady of the house gave me her room, I don't want to seem ungrateful but I can't stay here. It is too musty, I'm allergic to molds and even the quilt smells musty. It is like a cabin, one layer walls and ceiling, the ceiling I can see is boards, probably covered by corrugated metal. This room has its own Turkish toilet and cold, very cold, water. I am at present waiting for a bucket of hot water. The sun is blazing in one window, which is a heavy plastic. The room will cost me 80 rupees for the night, about $2.30 US.

Later. Checking out a fairly decent hotel. My acrophobia has risen to new heights as I realize that the roof of this hotel is being propped up by bamboo poles. Now, the problem is that although I came in on the ground floor, walked about 20 feet to the steep side of the building, I can see that I am on at least the 6th floor here. Bamboo doesn't grow that big and isn't that great a prop. I tell myself, don't go weird. The building is concrete and is probably sturdy enough.

I tried riding a horse a bit. It didn't work out. My guide, a Tibetan, said he came here in 1943 to escape the communists. He left his parents behind: he gave a graphic demonstration of them being shot by the Red Chinese. He has two brothers here who were not one bit of help with the horses. He said he had been a guide and had been up Kanchenjunga (Kinchenjunga), which is the magnificent scenery here. At 8598 meters it is the world's third highest mountain, and lies between us, the good guys, and red China. From Tiger Hill, a small climb from here, Everest can be seen. My horse guy went up Everest also. With New Zealanders . . . . Is Sir Edmond. ? Yes Sir Edmond also. So I had my picture taken with the horse and Ahman. We are below tree line here.

I went to the natural history museum here and like the one in Calcutta, the huge crocodiles are the most horrifying. Dusty old birds and butterflies are OK but I do hate the snake displays and hope never to make the acquaintance of the 'snot beetle'.

Frankly, my dear, I am discouraged with dirt and garbage. I keep trying to look past it to the heavenly mountains in the distance. Sometimes the air is fragrant with some herb or smoke but too often it is just a pile of rotting garbage. I'm off to check up on my expensive plane ticket to Calcutta.

I did get a different room and it put me close to the real activity of the inn, giggling and huffing and puffing that went on far into the night while the help earned some extra money.

A pair of bicycle tourists arrived and were astonishing. Brits. The girl had on a skirt affair that barely covered her cheeks. She was an absolute doll with long blond hair and blue eyes. I couldn't imagine how she could possibly get past the "element" without being mauled. She said that the only problem was that when she would get off the bike to answer the call of nature, she would think that no one was in sight but as soon as she had assumed the position, a crowd would always have gathered to stare. She and the husband had biked from Bombay. Then the husband showed up and the mystery of how she survived India was solved. He was about 6'6" and built like Arnold Schwarzenegger.

10.9.95 Calcutta. Actually I am on the plane for Calcutta. I can see the flooding below. It is in areas that don't seem too populated. It would stand to reason that not many people live in the flood plain area. Finished my article. Not too happy with it but oh well. Massive flooding below. I would judge from my ears that we are coming into Calcutta already. Better make use of the facilities while I can.

10.10.95 Calcutta. I was hoping that the sickish sort of feeling would go away and leave me and it did for a while, I returned to the Astoria Hotel yesterday and settled in. Then this morning, I got up early, in the third day of my cold, and went to Mother Theresa's. I arrived at the beginning of the morning worship and again partook of the mass. Mother Theresa was passing out the paten this time but just as I was two people away, the priest popped up and I had to take it from him. The sermon was given by a white priest who inveighed against the O.J. Simpson trial and the evils of watching TV in general!!!!!! To Mother's nuns??? Is there no rest from it? Even in Calcutta!!!

I met a writer at the breakfast scene. She was Jewish and told me I definitely should not be messing with mass as I am not Catholic. Some how that doesn't bother me and might not bother the rest of the Catholics in that place. Some cranky old priest in the States who has nothing better to do than make people miserable might object but probably not here where their attention is fixed on a different drummer.

I tried to move to the Ramakrishna Center and arrived there, boxed Green and all, and was not permitted in because admittance is only after correspondence. Damn. It was a really beautiful place and very clean. Later, somewhere, I spent hours in the home of the leader of the sect. It was a museum. The Jewish writer and I hit it off and I was looking forward to meeting her on Friday and going to the Lepers' place with her. That didn't happen but we did go to Kalighat where the terminally ill are sheltered. The men's side seemed the usual collection of human wrecks that you see lying on the streets, and I thought I would be able to handle it. We washed dishes from the men's breakfast and helped dish up for the women. It was a dank, stone area that had a dungeon feel to it. It was even tougher on the women's side. It was filled to capacity with the most wretched of creatures, some were too weak to eat. I thought I could help with feeding the poor things and washed up and got an apron (what rubber gloves?). I marched resolutely into the room. The floor started undulating under me. I took a couple of deep breaths, ran back into the hall, found a chair and put my head between my legs. When I thought that I would not faint, I turned in my apron. One hour. That is how long I lasted at Kalighat. If you're not part of the solution, you could become part of the problem.

10.11.95 Calcutta. I didn't go to the services this morning; intimidated by the Jewish gal, I guess. Went to breakfast at Fairlawn. After reading City of Joy I felt differently about rickshaws and caught a rickshaw to the Convent and walked from there to the children. I had bought a little book about colors and it was very successful. The nuns have a school for the Children called St. Mary's and the older ones can read and have a fair English vocabulary. The little ones were very enthusiastic about learning and when the holiday is over, the older ones will be back at St. Mary's and won't hog the stuff and the time. An incredibly aged white lady who must have been a nanny or teacher came in and rehearsed a little presentation for Mother. There is something big coming up, Mother is having an anniversary or going away. The volunteer was a fierce old thing, reminding me of my few moments with Catholic pedagogs: she picked the children up by the neck and pushed and slapped them around. It did work though and they marched around enthusiastically with their blue and white streamers coming together to make a blue and white flower, and then a song for Mother Teresa. An older group then marched around and saluted smartly and sang a song about the army of Jesus. All this in a space about 12 x 12.

Mimiko, a tiny Japanese lady volunteer wanted me go visit an American with whom she rooms. The older woman was feeling badly. They share an incredibly small and poor abode for 40 rupees each. I am paying 400 Rupees, which I thought was a steal at $12. Gretchen, the older woman, is a nurse from Wisconsin and very depressed. Mimiko thinks she is menopausal. Could be. I can remember menopausal days when I did nothing but lie around feeling desperate. I found that a tranquilizer did wonders for my menopausal problems. Gretchen said that she was recovering from drug abuse and couldn't use tranquilizers. I said I would visit again tomorrow but haven't much idea where their little hole was or what to do about insolvable problems.

Tomorrow is our day off. The weather report said rain and it is doing that but it is cooler so I don't mind much. I have to get tickets out of here tomorrow. It will probably take all day to do that. I plan to go to New Delhi and if the bicycle group's plan to get to Nepal doesn't appeal, take off for Kathmandu by train or bus, or plane, or even bike.

10.15.95 Calcutta. Linda Schaefer, CNN stringer and I went down to the river to the burning ghats and the swimming ghats. My husband Charles would have killed to be here, on assignment, shooting the stuff that Linda was shooting. Oh well, he will just have to content himself with shooting Gov. Ridge and Eastern Pennsylvania. I did a lot of camera case carrying while Linda was banging off roll after roll of incredible stuff. I shot a few myself, enough to make Chas jealous when the photos arrive at the house. I don't get to see the pictures because they go directly to Florida for slide and print processing and then home. Linda's go directly to CNN by an affiliate of FEDEX. She has been expecting a package for a few days now and since it hasn't arrived, she is nervous about the stuff she sent out. I took mine to the main post office and they read the package which said postage free if mailed in the U.S. and I couldn't get them to take anything for postage . . . . Oh well. They were pictures of me and Mother Teresa. Finally the heat and the wildness of the burning ghats got to me and I begged for us to leave. We went to the Taj Hotel to get out of the heat and wow what a place. Reminds me of the fancy hotels in Hawaii, fountains and pools and nice stuff. Which reminds me, I took a dozen or so shots from the hip like Chas does of the streets of Calcutta and will be wondering how they will turn out.

Now I'm back at Fairlawn, rested, fed, and with company. Gretchen from Wisconsin, was very ill and despondent. I invited her over to spend the day in Fairlawn to take a bath and air-condition and eat a meal here. It is a big piece of culture shock after the room she shared with three others which is half the size of this one at Fairlawn. She is better, went to Mass this morning at the convent. So did Linda and I. I had run a couple of miles and was really overheated, then the prayer room was stifling and the burning ghat area was like a frying pan. I am really enjoying the AC, the fan.

Then I wrote this piece of drivel: Calcutta. If five o'clock rolls up and you are a jogger and you are not up, you have to make the big decision whether to jog or not. Traffic, heat and pollution are such that infinitely postponing the jog is the salutary decision. However, I have been converted, as have so many spiritual seekers who come to India, to Jggtrtt, one of the newer forms of yoga.

The chief temple to this new spiritualism is yet to be built but the gods themselves, lacking a temple, can be found at the intersection of Chowringihee and Suddar Streets, right by the Indian Museum.

This is a fairly open area with an expanse of grass and trees struggling for life in midtown Calcutta. As one jogs up stifling Suddar street past the thigh high mound of garbage, slowing down so as to not attract the attention of the pariah dogs who are already ear deep in the pile, one enters the presence of the sexually embracing gods, Nz Clgg and Chst Koff. The air is dark and thick with the emanations of their erotic contortions. They sweat profusely, causing the great heat of Calcutta, even at 5:00 A.M. The worshiper stops at the intersection, and looks back down Suddar Street at the pink of the rising sun. The sun must not see the wrestling pair on Chowringi Road! The two dark grey figures roll themselves up into separate huge balls and sadly parting each rolls away from the other down Chowringhee Road where these gods of pollution then sit graying everything out for the rest of the day. At sunset, they come rolling up Chowringhee Road at each other to race to the passionate embrace. The only child of this somewhat lower than the heavens union is Pst Nsl Drppppp who is the god of Suddar Street.

At sunset the people are too busy opening the confusing collection of shops that line the street to notice the gods. Cries of 'Rickshaw', or 'Change money?' or 'Cash' . . . . did he say 'Cash'or 'hash'??? He said 'Hash?' How nice that they can speak English so well. To buy anything like hash might put you in the eye of the local Mafiosi guy and get you into big trouble. The poor live on Suddar Street as they would in a village, washing, eating, sleeping on the street. When awake everyone hustles except the women with babies and the dying and the limbless beggars. People don't just sit around. Women can get employment as street sweepers or construction workers (passing baskets of dirt from head to head down twenty women, in saris, to a truck.) Money passes through many hands: a tout will get a couple of rupees for finding a tourist for a rickshaw or taxi. It all goes on with good humor and the many low to mid-priced hotels on Suddar Street continually furnish fresh tourists for the hungry of the street.

And the Joggtrtt disciple jogs around the park area, entertained by the people who use the park for their toilette. An army truck stops directly in front of the jogger and twenty army guys pile out to use the ditch for their morning waste. Downtown Calcutta. Paradise of the gods.

Linda thought that little effort was impious. And her point was . . . . ?

10.18.95 Calcutta. Tomorrow is to be the last day in Calcutta and I will spend it going to the Lepers' colony. It is fairly far from the city and is quite extensive when you get there. The ill are given a place to stay and work so that they can be self-supporting. Linda wants me to go to the Varinasi with her and I would like to do that but I have my schedule.

The place we visited today was for women from a prison. These women were in terrible condition when Mother Teresa got them out of prison. They had been kept in a room with no clothing, no sanitary facilities and were in wretched condition. Imagine being in jail in India. Now add to that that Bengal and the jails are run by Communists. This must be the place the doctor was asking for Mother Teresa take certain women from a prison to go.

The sister who is in charge of the shelter says that the women will never leave this serene, clean place. They aren't too swift mentally and haven't the skills to survive on the street. I ask where the money comes from and she says many places. One group of donors are Buddhist priests who send everything they collect on Fridays. Most of the women are mentally handicapped, either before the prison ordeal or from the ordeal. It is a beautiful facility and like everything of The Missionaries of Charity, full to capacity. There are a couple of hundred nuns in Calcutta and 6000 world wide, according to the sister we were talking to. The most astonishing thing is that no matter where you go there is another facility you hadn't known about. Today's surprise was college for teaching teachers for Missions of Charity, again, a neat, clean college. Children at the orphanage where I worked go to school at St. Mary's and there is a a Anthony's High School where I saw Missions of Charity sisters. It is all so well run and so organized. Just to be so clean and decently fed in Calcutta is an operation.

Yesterday I followed Linda to the street called City of Joy. Patric Swazey was nowhere to be seen. Just off this street, infamous for the open sewer and abject poverty, was a place for children with TB, painted white with the baby blue trim that announces Mother Teresa. There are not super sick kids here and classes were being held on the first floor. I had a lot of fun playing Simon Says with the kids on the second floor. They are eager to learn English. I felt a lot of empathy because I had TB as a child. Pittsburgh was as polluted as Calcutta during the WWII years. No one in my family can remember my having it but I have three calcified spots that show up on x-rays and always test positive to the patch test.

10.20.95 How wonderful to be in Delhi. It is beautiful and sane here. The roads aren't all that bad. I'm tempted to drag Green out of the box and go cycling. I'm very happy with the hostel. It is in the Embassy area and quite spacious and with grounds and grass. Calcutta is such a pit. I am waiting anxiously for Liz and the Olnesses. They were originally scheduled to arrive today. The taxi to the plane and the plane were uneventful as was the taxi here. I am really getting to be such an old hand at this travel thing.

The last day in Calcutta was as fascinating as the days that preceded it. Linda and I went out to the lepers' colony. The buildings and grounds were incredibly clean, like everything Mother Teresa touches. It was named for Gandhi. He and Mother Teresa were acquainted. Time sequence: Gandhi was murdered in 1949, the year before Mother Teresa was given the right to start her own order. The idea behind the colony, Gandhi's, was that lepers' needed a feeling of dignity as well as a decent place to live out their lives. So they spin, dye and weave material. There is a strange long skinny building by the railroad tracks that is where the spinners sit and the weavers weave the material for diapers, sheets, saris, and the sarong that poor men wear. The 6000 nuns of the order all have their saris made here. The uncounted beds and baby butts are covered by the materials made here. Most of the lepers were in the very neat gardens tending the vegetables that grow lush and green. Hands with no fingers spread fertilizer. Feet with no toes push the treadles of the looms. When a leper is identified as such, his family forces him/her out into the street. As soon as it is known that he is a leper he can't get work and is shunned. As the disease progresses, the leper becomes more and more repugnant and pitiful. The people of the Leper colony seemed very cheerful and positive.

There are still lepers begging on Suddar Street. They like the freedom of the streets and can make more money than at the colony. The street is the street, filthy. People and dogs use it for a toilet.

Garbage is in huge piles. The lepers must contribute a certain amount of filth themselves because they are not very mobile. When they are beyond help and hope, they go to Kalighat to die peacefully in Mother Teresa's care. I haven't even seen a beggar in Delhi. Ladies from the hostel are sitting out front of the hostel in their saris like lavish, bright flowers in the grass of the hostel. It is cloudy here. If I don't go to Rajastan, I will miss the eclipse. It is very comfortable temperature.

Linda and I went to early (5:00 AM) mass yesterday. Linda showed Mother Theresa a book of photos that Linda took while covering Mother Teresa on Atlanta. I was there to get a picture of Linda with the Saint. I was busily snapping away when I suddenly became aware that Mother Teresa was poking her finger right at me, two inches from my nose and she said, "You are good."

My favorite beggar has the joy of living in his eyes.

I really don't know how to take that but I guess I can accept it. I have been trying to learn to accept gifts with good grace. First the young doctor, buying me roses, Mimiko giving me a picture of Mother Teresa, Mother herself giving me a handful of medals, the jeweler at the corner giving me a bracelet. Then Mother Teresa giving me such a gift. Saying that I am good.

I think the one thing I am picking up from my exposure to the world is Linda's feeling that things are signs. A sign that something good will happen or a warning not to do something rash.

Linda is into Baba Something, a guru in Bangalore and she says that masters like Mother, Baba and the Dahli Lama can see into the soul. OK. But it was nice of Mother to say that.

Just as I was leaving Calcutta, I heard that the woman who was so depressed had attempted suicide and was in the hospital.

10.21.95 Linda was way to skinny to look healthy. She wasn't sleeping too well and having several cases of Delhi Belly just isn't great for the constitution. We met at Fairlawn Hotel where she had come after being thrown out of the Astoria Hotel and I had been thrown out of the Lindsay Hotel. I was still big at the Astoria but the conditions there were depressing and my stomach was continually tied in knots. I had packed up my stuff and taken a taxi to the Ramakrishna Mission International House to stay there but was rejected because I had not first corresponded. So I moved to the Lindsay where I complained about the dirt and was ejected two days later. The soil was human feces in the stairwell. Linda had an air conditioner catch fire at night in the Astoria. When she complained of a burnt finger, she was asked to leave. So we were washed up together at loveable Fairlawns. She said that I stood out from the other volunteers because I wasn't into punishing myself. True. Sally is spoiled. I tell Chas that he has spoiled me. It is his fault that I'm in the two star instead of a hovel like the rest of the volunteers.

Actually Linda was the rest of my ruination because she always had an interesting photo project and I didn't want to miss the opportunity to tag along, carrying camera bags as I have so often done for my photographer husband. So we spent long hours in some fascinating spots in Calcutta. I would get back to my room around noon and spend the rest of the day reading books about India: Tagore; poetry, *The Sun In the Morning, City Of Joy*, and two others that Linda lent me that I can't even try to remember. It was a very strange experience. We would go from the burning ghats with the bodies on view and the mourning family there to the Taj Hotel to recover a sense of proportion and to try to put the experience into words. We finally gave up on the words and hope the pictures will capture what there seem to be too few words to tell about. Linda is into finding herself at an ashram near Bangalore with Baba. Baba means father. Baba hadn't spoken to her this visit in spite of her having been there for a couple of months. She is still grieving the loss of her husband. He was the original follower of Baba.

The two of them came to see Baba when Ron, her husband was dying of cancer and stayed a while. So things were very quiet at the Ashram.

Mother Teresa and I. She gives me momentos.

Linda had gifts for the nuns at Calcutta from the nuns in Atlanta, so she was in Calcutta, shooting the Mother Teresa scene. It was powerful stuff. Mother Teresa is so wonderful against the disgusting background of Calcutta. Linda was very moved by

Calcutta and our precious saint. She decided to do a book later. Her story and photos are to be seen in her beautiful and sensitive book : COME AND SEE.

My last day there, we had lunch with a lawyer from Vancouver. He specializes in human rights. He came to India to help get a famous actor and son of a politician named Santay Dutt out of prison. Santay was in for possession of a weapon. (From the article I read, he was also suspected of causing a bomb explosion.) So Howard was brought over to help with that case. He was spending his time in Calcutta sitting in the courts, trying to get a feel of things. He offered to get Linda into the jails to take pictures and she will be unable to resist that opportunity. I gave her the three rolls of 800 film that Chas had given me. I was packing and she flipped when she saw them. I can hear her now,

"It was meant to be that I shoot in the jails. Sally GAVE me the film. Howard GAVE me the opportunity and idea to go in the jails. It was meant to be."

Howard went to dinner with us my last night in Calcutta and got carried away, as some lonely people do and totally monopolized the conversation. Well, Linda was sitting there looking frail and gaunt and needful. Howard has known Mother Teresa for ten years and has raised $1,000,000 for a AIDS center for Mother Teresa and the Bishop in Vancouver is so jealous of MT that he won't accept it or permit Mother Teresa in his domain. How about them apples? Time the priests realize they have become an embarrassment to the church and let the women shine. They can't stop it and should give in with better grace.

Linda's photos of Mother Teresa were on CNN!! And I was featured on CNN also. I am such a media darling.

10.21.95 Delhi. I bought my ticket for Singapore to New Zealand for January six. Singapore Airlines. That and changing money back into travelers checks from rupees took all day. While at the Ashok Hotel, which has a money changing dungeon in the basement, waiting patiently in the long line, I observed a Russian woman with a 4 inch stack of US $20 bills, changing them into Indian Rupees.

I had just been reading in "USA five days ago" that we were going to have to print up different $20s because the Russians were counterfeiting our bills. Having read about the Russian Mafia, I kept my mouth shut, for once.

Hostelling is so good because you continually meet all sorts of people. I have met such a dear old man in Delhi. Franz Rodine from Seattle. He is the oldest traveler I have met, 87. Same age as Mother Teresa but in much better shape. He is one of those people you hear about who never get sick while traveling, even in India. He travels all the time, using hostels, of course. He has some marvelous tales. He was a professional musician. He played on a ship going from Seattle to Japan to Hong Kong in his youth. He has seen and done everything. We'll eat in a Chinese restaurant tonight and do the Taj Mahal trip tomorrow. He got hooked on travel early and is on his fourth trip around the world. One of the stories he likes to tell is about being in Russia in 1939 and having to get the help of the American consulate to get back to the U.S.

Every year he spends part of the year in Mexico visiting a friend. The rest of the year he is traveling or living with his sister in Seattle. He says that he hasn't gained a pound since he was an adult. That is easy to believe, he is tall and spare. And spry. He can manage a day's tour of the Taj Mahal with no more suffering than the average tourist. He is a fan of hostels. He can remember visiting his first hostel, in Paris, for $.18 in 1939. Now-a-days he buys an "around the world" ticket for $1600 and spends about 6 months a year and $4000. going around the world one more time. He went to the University of Washington, majoring in music. He also spend an entire year in Jamaca researching music for his masters degree at Columbia He also taught at Columbia but retired from teaching in 1939 because he was only making $2000 per year. He got a job as a welder during the war years and began buying houses and fixing them up. He married another musician who also liked real estate and they would buy a house, fix it up and move on to another one. This is the real source of his income. They eventually built a four unit then an eight unit, then an eighteen unit building. All of these are now sold and he holds the mortgages and travels. In a minor way, this is what I have done, so we have a lot to talk about. He has a hobby of framing and selling prints that he buys on his travels. This gives him an opportunity to make more contacts with people and talk about his travels because he sells the stuff at yard sales. It is not hard to imagine him going right on into his nineties enjoying traveling and still mentally alert. He is very easy to get along with and interested in new things and people and has a delightful sense of humor. It doesn't hurt that his ancestors were Swedes and lived far beyond the 3 score and ten allotted.

His beloved wife died 13 years ago and he has moved in with other people since then but is happiest with his sister who 'Takes care of me'. Ever friendly, affectionate, he makes friends everywhere he goes. He left yesterday for Calcutta where he has a friend who has a house. From there it will be Hong Kong, Seoul, Korea and back to Seattle for the joys of a Swedish Christmas with the families of his three daughters. After Christmas he will be off to Mexico to avoid the horrors of a Seattle winter.

10.22.95 Dehli, on our way to the Taj Mahal in Agra. This is the bus ride from Hell. We must be on the Grand Trunk Road and are stopped at a border of Dehli in a really bad area. We got up and waited for the bus which came at 7:30 instead of 6:30. And this is a tourist bus, not one of the really wretched things that are run by the government. I got the reservation from the concierge at the best hotel, the Ashok Hotel. The road surface is bad and we lurch around and really suffer in the ruts and pot holes. There is a window on the bus that does not close and the breeze is actually chilly. I have to go but am too intimidated by the conditions here to even look for a spot. I got out of the bus once but got right back on. Reading in the guide book that the bus will go off without you is not encouraging. The part of Delhi that I'm staying in is so nice that grunge India is a shock again.

The Taj was so magnificent. We stopped at the Red Fort also and very late, a small village. The village was having a festival and I got some great pictures, I think. The Hindu drums are so heart pounding. The decorated animals are just charming.

10.25 Dehli' Have you ever been to the Artic Circle in Finland. You ought to go there. It would be a nice place to bicycle. That was Franz. I really miss him. I go back to the Hostel every day to see if any of the bikers have arrive. There is no news of them. 10.28.95 Delhi. I took a swim today, almost 1500 yards. Left shoulder developed a familiar pain, so I quit. It is hard to decide whether to work through a pain or to quit so it doesn't become chronic. The shoulder pain is such a familiar one. Rotator cuff tear in 1982. Face plant on Cross-Country skis. There were adhesions as it healed and that is probably what is wrong and I should work through it. Pittsburgh had such a YMCA swim team in those years, it would win nationals by a wide margin. So many national champs swimming for the South Hills Y team which was the brain child of Mike Schallenburger and Tom Smith. Tom recruited and Mike did the statistics. The South Hills Y had no pool and probably very little notion of their preeminence in swimming since Mike and Tom ran everything on the side. Rick Durstein, Laura Petrini, Tom, Jimmy Goldman, Lee Osterling, Dan Nadler, Ron Walsh, and a couple of older gentlemen could be counted on to clean up in their divisions and if you could just find four people in an age group who could swim 100 yards you could do well in the older divisions. Ages 20-40 were very competitive but after that the competition thinned out and someone my age could medal just by completing an odious event like the 400 I.M or 200 fly. I competed for the Sewickley Y the last great year that Pittsburgh had and got 46 points all by myself. That actually put Sewickley somewhere in the standings but the ones who worked out at Sewickley Y were all swimming for the South Hills megateam and they won handily without me. Most have wandered off and it doesn't seem possible to get such a team together again. Mike got married, had kids and quit as coach and none else had his devotion.

I always had a problem with swimming because I get black line bored. Looking at the line on the bottom of the pool hour after hour is such a drag. Then, too, you need a coach so you don't spend a whole season doing something stupid that would cost you a part of a second. Most coaches don't pay much attention to the older swimmers, we just get run down by the younger ones. I preferred to spend my winters in the ambience of cross-country skiing and those were great years to ski with a full season of races capped by The Chautauqua Marathon or the Berkiebiener. The camaraderie of the hours sitting around the pool waiting for an event was pleasant. There is nothing comparable in skiing. But swimming is so intense and so available. There are pools and coaches and if you have the time, dedication, and money of a Jane Brunner, you could at least imagine being a world record holder like Jane. It is probably the very LACK of snow, trails, and coaches that appeals in X-Country skiing. The chanciness of the conditions on race day, the total inability to get to a meet if it snows at the wrong time and closes the roads. Anyhow here I am at the YMCA in Delhi, India wishing I were home. All of you who are getting annoyed at the coach, tired of the black line on the bottom of the pool, too pooped to lift weights, be glad you have all that stuff to annoy you. Keeps you pepped up.

10.22.95 Dehli The celebration of Divali (the festival of lights, or, more realistically, the festival of lights and firecrackers) goes on. I need a recovery day today to rest up from the expedition to Agra. Still no bikers have arrived. Tomorrow is the eclipse. Clear sky tonight. Had an interesting conversation, in the hostel restaurant, with a lady from Karachi and Australia and a young Muslim man from England. Not a lot of disagreement among us. The young man went to college in Clarion, PA. How can one sleep with this fire cracker racket? It just goes on and on.

10.30.95 Delhi Last day and my brain is completely free of any ideas.

When new comers want to know what to see here in Delhi, I tell them the B'Hai Temple. It is south of center and far enough out of the center that the B'Hai were able to buy in 1970 a sizeable piece of land. It is surrounded by slums of the most temporary sort. Within the grounds everything is carefully tended. Even the first sight is astonishing, a huge, shining white marble lotus flower rising up out of the ground. It seems to float in the air. Poetry was being read inside. I had a B'Hai pal on Semester at Sea. She was a former Jew. It seemed very like Unitarian. Can this exquisite building be compared to the incomparable Taj Mahal? Well, I would. It is lighter, airier, less self conscious. (I love it when you can call a pile of building material self-conscious.). The big, ugly, fortress which surrounds the Taj is a negative for me. Perhaps one day the B'hai will have to build a fortress to protect their jewel but at this point in time it would be pointless. For one thing, they don't charge an entry fee. So the curious, no matter how poor, can wander through and see for themselves that there are no semiprecious stones to be teased out of the walls by vandals.

10.26.95 Delhi Up this morning before dawn. Then I had to decide if I would jog. My right foot has a long lasting problem. Perhaps a broken bone from one of my stumbles, near tumbles on the broken pavement of a large city. It has a toe with fungus tortured nail that is ingrown despite my gristly efforts to prevent that. But toenail problems shouldn't extend to the joint and the ball of the foot which is swollen tight and has been for some time. It isn't great to walk and stupid to think of running. I should get the bike out of the box and cycle but that involves a zillion details. Go to Kathmandu and throw away the box and bike for a month. That's the solution. I'll extend my stay here if possible and get a ticket for Kathmandu first thing and I'm out of here.

Such a day it became. I messed around with my beloved crosswords. I hate for M'Lov to get to them first because there is nothing left to do while I usually leave quite lot for him. Then I got up and went to breakfast. When I tried to pay for another couple of days they said they had no more room. I protested but had no leg to stand on since I was already one day over the 5 day limit. It was most upsetting because I was so unprepared to move with the bike and all. I finally blew up at the girl at the counter who kept insisting that she had told me about it before. A lie and I got really mad. I suspect that there are not 100 people arriving there tonight as she said. I had complained about a cockroach. That was my evil deed.

So, with not being able to talk anyone into helping me, I dragged the bike box and stuff to a taxi and departed in a high dudgeon. The guide book told about a YMCA with a pool so that's where I am now. I'll swim tomorrow morning for 50 rupees a swim. Somewhat more reasonable than the 300 Rupees at the Ashoka Hotel pool.

The room at the Y is small and the bath is way down the hall but it has a desk and good reading light. And a pool and for $8.00 US, breakfast.

I went walking, or should I say callously wading through a collection of beggars outside the very handsome gates. The Y is close to the center of the city. I slid into a restaurant and met a Brit from Hong Kong. She writes for magazines but is here with her boyfriend and very bored in Delhi. She intends to stay in Hong Kong after the Chinese take over. Said,

"See you tomorrow."

Then I ran into the young Muslim man (went to school in Clarion) and his very attractive model girlfriend. We had a nice time chatting for an hour at Wimpys.

Delhi is a nice city. It is flat and has palm trees. The roads are wide and curving or wide and straight. There are large parks and a lot of green stuff along with a lot of interesting things left by the Moguls.

Chapter XXVI

Nepal

... "Whenever I watch TV and see those poor, starving kids all over the world, I can't help but cry. I mean I'd love to be skinny like that, but not with all those flies and death and stuff."

Mariah Carey

10/31/95 I tagged along with a couple of Brit ladies who had a reservation in Kathmandu. It was in a very pleasant home with a couple of extra rooms to rent. All night the screams of a dog in pain kept me awake. In the morning a taxi took me a couple of blocks to the bus station.

Kathmandu to Pokhara. There was a sort of indicated area behind a shanty to relieve oneself at the first bus stop. At the shanty/shop, I indulged in my standard fare, Snickers and Coca-Cola. The second town, according to the guidebook, exists mainly to sell its young girls to truck drivers for sex. So I says to myself, "What'sa nice girl like you, etc. etc."

There was no respectable place to spend the night except one hotel almost into Pokhara. So much for bicycling here. The bus trip here was cheap, $6.00 but terrible. A bicycle would be more comfortable. The road is pretty bad but I would have been able to bicycle it. The hills are very challenging, and the traffic weird.

There was the road repair crew who were using hot tar to patch some potholes. The tar was being heated in 55 gallon drums that had been cut in half, lengthwise. These were held up over an open fire by piled stones. Now, there's I job that I wouldn't want: carrying buckets of boiling hot tar to the road.

The worst of it by bike would have been finding reasonable places to stay. Green was quite comfortable in a box on the top of the bus. There were several Brit guys who had stored kayaks on the top of the bus. They were going to do the rivers. I would not have tried these rivers. Too roiling, boiling for me. You'd have to be really good at kayaking, not an ocean kayak person like I am. They had helped me lift Green to the top of the bus to keep the kayaks and the people riding up there company.

Chas faxed me to chide me for going to unusually great lengths to not be home when the "Moppets come begging for treats" for Halloween. We used to go to major effort to scare the neighborhood kids and on spook night were pretty good at terrorizing. In later years, after our kids grew out of that and left, we had taken to escaping it all by going out for dinner and a movie on Halloween. One would think that every child along the trail must have read that FAX and is waiting for me with persistent, piteous pleas for sweets or candy or money. The guide book says that we are not to give. Even John D. Rockefeller with his bags of dimes would not be able to satisfy them. They upset me because it is chilly. They are in bare feet and bare bottoms. Their cute little noses run constantly.

11.1.95 Pokhara, Nepal. Things seem to be working out. I met the gorgeous Precious from San Francisco who wants to trek together. Also Ted, a Greek computer guy from Boston who lives in Hong Kong. I have applied for two-week trekking permit. We will walk along the Kali Gandaki River to the Tibetan high plain and then back down. That will take until the 17th of November and my plane ticket to Bangkok is the 26th so that leaves me a few days to mess around here and then take off for Kathmandu to mess around there for three days. There are bike trails around the town that should be fun.

11.2.95. Pokhara. Nice motel with my own bath but they are moving me to another room to make room for someone more important, at least that is what they said. The rugged mountains that surround Pokhara are the Anapurnas, part of the Himalayas.

My main concern for this day is to catch a view of the peaks. There are lounge chairs on the roofs that can be utilized for peak peeking. This is an important activity, not just laziness. In this motel, pleasant young people feed you breakfast in the garden and it is chilly but very charming. They know that I am trying to get a picture of the nearby Anapurnas peaks and let me know when the clouds lift from the heights so that I can climb to the top of the roof and enjoy the view. Hotels advertise their rooftop views here. It gets to be very social whenever the peaks show through and everybody sprints up to the rooftops.

11.3.95 Pokhara. Haven't seen too much of Precious. She is studying for a test that she will take in Bankok to try to get into law school. Her family are all lawyers, even her mother. She has been a law clerk for the day job and dancing at night. I do keep meeting Ted in the various eating establishments. He is from Boston, a nephew of actor Telly Savalis and went to Dartmouth College. I said that Chas had graduated from there. Chas' fraternity, Sigma Phi Epsilon, had been ejected from the national organization back in the early 50's for brotherizing a Negro (as they were known back then, I want to be historically if not politically correct.) Ted said that he belonged to the same fraternity. So, much time had passed, and the Richmond, Virginia based fraternity had relented its exclusion policy. It was now allowing blacks to join. So they sent a representative to Hanover and Ted was talking to him in the living room about restoring the errant group's attachment to the national group when a girl walked through the main hall of the house and went up the steps. The rep looked properly shocked and asked what she was doing.

"Well, she lives here," said Ted. "She is a member." The rep smiled a tight thin smile, said he had to be going, and left.

Ted had found a fancy steak house. The steak was really delicious: thick, tender. My body tolerated the meat for about two hours and then totally rejected it and I vomited it with a lot of enthusiasm into the toilet of my new room.

I spend a lot of the time in a leisurely shopping tour of the small town. Such a treat. Bicycle tourists usually buy food. Only food. Many shops were dedicated to supplying people like me for trekking in the cold mountains. I bought warm hat, sweater, jacket, and boots, and backpack to carry the extra clothes. I rented a pair of cranky, collapsing ski poles to steady my aged body. Everyone promised to buy the gear back when I returned. The dickering was intense. I would go from store to store trying to get the best bargain. The most unique purchase was a lemon-colored day-glow gortex jacket for $29. Along the street, sitting on the chilly ground, are the impoverished Tibetan women selling jewelry. I loved the necklaces and bracelets made from yak bone and actually bought some after hours of bargaining. The Tibetans were driven from their homeland by the Red Chinese. It was rumored that Brad Pitt was somewhere in the area doing a movie about Tibet.

The motel would store my bike and gear. I tried to send FAX mail to Chas but that didn't work well.

11.4.95 Road to Jomson. Yesterday we three left Pokhara and took a cab to Phedi, and climbed a huge hill through farms. The farms are constructed on precarious slopes, painfully but beautifully terraced. As we passed the owner's hut, the mother would come out to order her little ragamuffins after us to beg for candy. Precious could always find something for them. On the way up, a young Nepalese named Shiba talked me into being my porter for 500 rupees ($10) a day. This included his room and board. I knew that the inn keepers along the way would charge me the same for his room and board as for mine. This way he could make his own deal with the inn keepers. They usually took him into their living space and treated him like family so it worked out very well. The careful reading of Ted's Lonely Planet guide book had prepared me to be this canny. It doesn't come naturally.

Shiba was a great investment. As soon as he pocketed the first day's wages, he worked at convincing us that we were on the wrong road. How right he was. We marched back down the huge mountain that we had so laboriously climbed and caught another taxi to Naya Pul where we had lunch and hiked to Tirkedhunga. Spent 133 R. for dinner, bed, and breakfast. Finally I am able to manage with Ole's $12 per day budget. Today was a tough climb. Precious is feeling like a cold and suffering so Shiba carried her large pack up the hill and she carried my small one. Then skinny little Shiba with nothing but those cheap plastic bathing sandals to protect his bare feet, went back down for Ted's pack and carried it up. I just climbed slowly and carefully. While resting at a quaint restaurant, we had a wonderful view of 'Good Anapurna,' Himchuli. Twenty-one year old Shiba had a fair facility with English and was an interesting guide.

Ted and guide Shiba with backdrop of
Anapurna Mountains.

Later. The last hour to Gorapani was the pits. We are 2775 meters. around 9,000 feet which is getting high and cold. I have taken to my bed to get warm. The motel room is a dirt-cheap 25 rupees tonight because Precious is sharing the room. It is nice and cozy and downstairs is a roaring fire that will probably heat our part of the building and the toilet is right across the hall. My little finger and ring finger left hand went numb from carrying the cold metal poles. The poles were constant entertainment: they would collapse if not tightly twisted. The tap, tap on the road caused them to become untwisted. So I would stumble along adjusting them. I shouldn't complain so, except for the last hour, it was a fine hiking day. I am sucking up the Ibuprophen now. Ted's guide book reports that we go down the mountain tomorrow. A break for me because I am a little headachy from the altitude. I can keep trekking instead of holding up for a day to acclimatize if we go down. Nepal is about the least scary place I have been. I really like it and want to return some day. However, if I had been doing this hike alone I would definitely wimp more and be less sure reaching the goal at Jomson. If I were in better shape . . . well, you know how it is.

Article for Health and Fitness

"11.5.95 Poon Hill. So now, in the places where trekkers gather, and make serious talk about where they have been and Poon Hill comes up, I'll be able to say, "Poon Hill: been there; done that." It is a ritual that trekkers do for fun. Poon Hill is comparable to the madness of lemmings running into the sea. You start, at the top of Ghorapani Hill which is over 9300 ft., at four in the morning, and try to climb another 1200 feet, in the dark, up a fairly a huge, steep hill on a primitive trail with hundreds of other huffing, puffing, scrabbling, tortured folk who are doing it because: everyone else is. Part of the problem for me was trying to avoid being be trampled by the hordes who are also struggling upward in the darkness. I get feelings of dark foreboding, impending disaster, dread . . . well, you know: I wasn't up for it. Part of the desperation was the lack of a flashlight. Shiba bolted off with Precious and Ted. I decided that if I just went slowly and carefully the rising sun would soon give enough light to keep me from going over a cliff in the dark. A sweet young English girl in a pink plaid skirt offered me a "torch" and went on by me. Flashlight in hand, I stumbled upward trying to avoid the hobnailed boots. About twenty minutes later, I came across Pink Plaid. She had dropped out of the madness. She pointed to a cloud that she said would cover everything. She said that I should stay with her. I returned the flashlight with much gratitude.

"Compulsive is as compulsive does," I muttered and, ungratefully, continued my gasping, struggling, ascent. In the gloom the top of Poon Hill was a dusky mob of gray, sweaty people. An enterprising Nepali had carried a vat of hot chocolate to the top. I bought Shiba one even though he had deserted me on the climb. The bad Precious gave him a cigarette. Ted further corrupted him by giving him his tape player that was playing U-2. Shy Shiba with the headset, cigarette, and chocolate, was a real guy. After a while everything brightened and there was a wonderful sunrise.

The reason for all this madness is the sun coming up on the Anapurnas, of which there are at least five. The intervening hills are no help and at this time of year the actual sunrise is behind a shorter, brown, snowless mountain. If we trekkers only toiled along the trails, which are in the valleys, we would never see the tops of the Annapurnas. I could have gone to Everest Base Camp instead of here but that is the place where you really can't see Everest, because of being at the foot of the highest mountain. Trekking the Annapurna Circuit seemed much the best option with the amount of time I had. I was still trying to keep to Ole's schedule.

The major mountain up there is the sacred mountain, Fishtail in English and Machapuchare in Nepalese. It has never been climbed because the Nepalese regard it as holy. Climbers have been very close to the top but have, so far, respected the Nepalese and stopped short. It is as sharp and dangerous as the Matterhorn.

Now that I am here I can see that it is very good to climb in the dark and the view is terrific. The cloud is below us, and everyone will tell everyone that they shouldn't miss it. This is one of the few times I miss my tent. Could have come up here at a sane hour, spent the night in the 5 billion star motel and really enjoyed sticking the head out to watch the morning mania. Trekking in Nepal is easier than doing the A-T with a backpack. It is quite respectable to get a local person like Shiba to carry your pack and be your guide. So you only have to walk. There are lots of places to eat and spend the night, so you don't have to carry food and tent. There are lots of people doing it. It is very social. If you are in shape and have prepared carefully, you probably won't be a mass of blisters and muscle spasms like my little group. Trekking books are boring but helpful and do have meaning when you are here. If you have a strong stomach and are not overly depressed by the third world, you will be energized by the prices. It is cheap. Even paying my guide $10 per day, I am still only spending $20 per day.

On the way down, I got into a bad humor from being run off the trail by the descending hordes and twisted my ankle and fell down. Shiba was with Ted instead of me and just as I fell, they were passing me, telling about a better trail. So I scolded Shiba for being with Ted not me and that really put me in a grouch. I met the "torch" lender, Pink Plaid, the English girl with the flashlight, one more time. She was bandaging her porter's leg. So I massaged his leg and wrapped it and thought he would follow me everywhere he was so grateful. I was in a much better mood then. After all, I was a Poon Hill survivor."

11.6.95 Tatopani, Nepal. Talk about exotic. I'm sitting by a roaring river, having a cold drink in a straw tea hut, watching a couple of ladies who will retire wealthily after they have washed my clothes for 300 Nepal rupees. The pit they are using is in between two hot spring tubs and they are using hot water from the belly of the earth on my dusty clothes while the river of melted Himalayan snow thunders by. Cold does not begin to tell how that river is, but magnificent and blue with rock powder. The locals come by to bathe. Being Hindu they must bath anyhow but there is one bare lady who has been in there for so long that I think she is advertising. She tosses her long black air and smoothes it over her breasts. Bamboo trees cling to the rocky hillsides all around and towering cliffs hang over the valley. I just hope I didn't get here too late for my well-scrubbed clothes to get dry. There are only a few hours of sun in this gorge and when the sun is gone it gets very cold.

We descended all day yesterday from 9000 ft. to 1600 ft. Article for Health and Fitness:

"So I am going down a monster hill and up coming is a European gentleman, neat and tidy, all in white. He must be doing the Peter Mathieson thing. He has gone native. In this land where hookworm is epidemic, his feet are bare! I was astonished. Shocked. What a silly affectation. My light Nike trainers are OK but boots would be much better.

"Are you doing penance for something??" I demanded, having taken on the Asian attitude of everybody's business is my business. "What did you do wrong?" At this point I am starting to laugh. "What ever it was you were doing, STOP before it gets worse."

He looked at me curiously because by this time I am really laughing and could hardly stand up. Down the mountain I go with tears of hilarity streaming out of my eyes. The people who came after me didn't remember anyone in bare feet. Perhaps the lack of oxygen . . ."

I stopped short, planting both feet after coming a mile down Ghorapani hill to avoid trampling a couple of doll-sized urchins playing on the dusty road. Both knee caps seemed to shoot off the knees. Pain and panic grabbed me but after a liberal dose of beer and Advil, the knees seem to be doing well. Precious went to a doctor who told her she has tonsillitis. She has decided to walk back to Pokhara, and Ted and I will go onward. I don't like such long days and will probably stop by 3:00 pm because it is still warm enough to bathe at that hour. Later, when it gets really cold I don't bathe because I would rather be dirty than chilled.

So being at the hot springs and a day off have been great. I like this place, if I can just get over my upset stomach and vomiting. Hopefully it is food poisoning not altitude sickness.

Last night, Ted had found another steak house. The steak was again delicious. I kept it until early the next morning when I arose with the knowledge that I had to get to a toilet fast. There were two toilets in the hotel, both busy. I shuttled back and forth between them becoming more and more desperate. Finally, in extremis, I seized a plant that was in a clay pot, pulled it out of the pot, and vomited into the pot. I put the plant back in the pot. No one caught me doing this.

Ted thinks we should have gone up some today to acclimatize to the altitude. Probably. I am looking forward to an air flight out of Jomson to Pokhara, so as to avoid the downhills. The downhill yesterday was unrelenting. As we were sitting around moaning last night we tried to figure why we seem to be suffering more than most trekkers. Precious had not been dancing because of a family thing, Ted came on the spur of the moment and I was supposed to be bicycling from Delhi to Kathmandu instead of riding rickshaws around Calcutta. So we are paying a heavy price for our not being prepared. My legs already feel better. I am drinking a ton of water to flush out the microorganism that is attacking me and Precious is stuffing down the antibiotics. Ted is into delusions: a plan of climbing to the top of something huge. I would just like to climb a flight of stairs without problems.

Later. Precious is worse. Temperature of 100.3 and throwing up. Ted and I have both decided that we can't leave her. So we stay here another day tomorrow.

In the meantime' I am reading Peter Mathiessen's *The Snow Leopard* which I more or less stole from Precious because I never returned it. Before I met her again, I had swapped it in a roadside bookstore. It describes our trek right up through Tatopani. He is a wonderful writer and I was tempted to just pirate his descriptions but probably the difference would show. He is into Oriental religions and so that the reader can understand where he is coming from, gives some info on the local religions. In spite of his vibrant enthusiasm, I look at the local folks and say, "Nope, not a great thing". To have the greatest thing in life be a withdrawal from life . . . Nah. I'll stick with my stoics.

There is a family of water buffalos that live right beside the hotel. In the morning the cow is milked and the bull, cow, and calf are led right through the dining area to the street. Free to go where they please, they head for the riverside or up the hillside to graze. As the town ducks into the afternoon shadows they come trotting back and are again led through the dining room. They are tied up and a young fellow, completely covered by the hay and banana leaves that he holds over his head with a pitchfork, comes along, through the dining room, with food for them. The milk is used and the manure is mixed with straw, dried, and used for fuel.

They seem very tame and polite. They have a very nice life for Nepal.

11.7.95 Dana on the Kali Gandaki. So Shiba and I left Precious who was a lot better and Ted, who was being solicitous. We offered to sponsor her to a plane ride if she continues to Jomson, which has to be an easier walk than walking out the way we came. It would also accomplish the goal. So, because I am pretty slow and seem to be the one with the biggest chance of altitude problem, we decided that I would get a half day start and they would catch me if I just went slowly.

11.8.95 Ghansa. 6600 ft. altitude and it is slowing me down. The hills are hillier. It will be 8300 at Kalo Pani where I will hold up for Ted and Precious. I spent the night at Kapchipani where things were a bit primitive. I asked for hot water and then remembered all the lectures about the environment and felt a bunch of guilt. There is very little wood at this altitude, and the only other way to heat water is by burning dried manure. I didn't use a lot of hot water, honest. I washed my hair and sat out in the open air restaurant in the chill. There were two Israelis there and I expressed my sympathy for the murder of Prime Minister Rabin. They were terribly upset, teary. Shiba had heard the news on Nepali radio and was able to give them some details. They were as astonished that the assassin had been Israeli as we were pleased that he wasn't Arab. Went to bed at 6:30 and spent hours trying to review the day in beautiful English like Peter Mathiessen. Mathiessen has let me down a bunch by describing his experiments with LSD. Then on to his experiments with Oriental religion and so on. I was even less enthralled by his going on and on about his dreams and then the interpretations of those same boring dreams. No longer a fan. It was a short romance. Article:

"Heavens to Murgatroid! I was offered marijuana as we were coming up the hill. Shiba, the guide, picks some dried leaves and hands them to me.

"Eat, eat," says Shiba shoving it at me, "Marijuana, eat."

I, who have never before, in my sheltered life, been offered the drug, obediently stuff the dumb, old, crumby, weed in my mouth and start chewing. But then, I thought of our dear leader, Bill Clinton, that great moral exemplar, and *I didn't swallow!*"

Later: I am sitting at a large table that has a skirt of blanket around it. I sit, wearing my jacket, hat, and gloves, on a bench at the table. The lady of the house comes along with a pan full of hot coals that she puts in a metal bucket under the table. I shove my feet toward the bucket and drink down hot mint tea and soon am warm, toasty, and in good company. We are at 8300 feet and only have to climb 700 feet tomorrow. I am waiting for Ted and Precious. Shiba and I will wait at least one day for them. It is pleasant spot and lots of enthusiastic Europeans. Am I having fun? A resounding yes. My toes are aching but I guess I am better off than Wendy, the Australian who had bad feet and an interesting relationship with her much younger guide back in Kapchipani. Wendy went into a long tale of how often she visits Nepal. She always gets the same, handsome guide, she said with meaningful eyebrows and rolling the eyes at the handsome young guide who was rubbing her sore feet and appeared to be incredibly bored. For him the bloom seemed to have fled from the roses. Shiba would hang out with the locals whenever possible. Even he may have scored that night also. Next morning, ever the early riser, I peeked in his room and saw little, fluffy pink sandals next to his sandals under his bed. I hope it wasn't Wendy.

11.9.98 Kalopani. Waiting for Ted and Precious. Day is breaking and it is cold. I sit, on my bed with my Zaurus on the window sill to write. This is the only way I can still be in my sleeping bag and therefore, warm. I can't see the read out on the Zaurus and will have to go back later to correct errors. This is a nice hotel. It is stone with glass in the windows and a curtain over the window. The bed is wood planks with sponge rubber mattress about 2" thick. A sheet is wrapped around the sponge rubber and on that goes my sleeping bag. A herd of shaggy donkeys trots by with nothing on their backs. The Nepali herding them has bare feet in sandals, a skirt, a shirt and a shawl over his head and shoulders. The street is good here, huge flagstones with four steps of heavy stone, four steps. No car or truck could drive it. No gutter. The building across the street is stone with grates and shutters on the windows. The stone is painted white and the windows black. The slates on the roof are large and not too even. There is a shed roof lower down and the top roof has an extra couple of rows of small stones along the rooftree. My fingers are getting cold so I will warm them up. Light clouds are picking up a bit of pink from the sunrise over the hill opposite which is covered with pines. It is a very sharp hill, as are they all. The trees that edge the top have foliage on the last fourth and the rest is bare trunk. Did some hungry animal or chilly human use the lower branches? The knife edge of the hill looks like a fringe that is going up not down. The balcony railing through which I am looking is painted the popular red-clay color. It is a warm earth tone, like our unglazed clay pots. It is altogether a charming scene.

There was a group of three young Israelis, two men and a woman, who spent the night here. Their wild black hair, dark and scowling faces were scary looking. They had just completed their obligated time in the Israeli army. When they leave the army they have some money so they spent it on the trip to Nepal. Since this is the most economical place I have been in, I assume that their severance pay wasn't huge. When I tried to offer condolences for the assassination of their prime minister, they snarled, chillingly, that it was a good thing. One said, stone faced, that they were sorry that they hadn't thought of killing him themselves.

Two French-Canadian trekkers go by the window. They are more French than Canadian but still more or less pleased that the separation from English speaking Canada will not happen. When all the rest of the world is determined to learn English, it is a shame to have such an avoidance.

There are white, resin, stacking chairs on the balcony, just like the ones at home and in Europe. A clothesline holds a line of clean, drying socks and underwear. Between my window and the view is that miracle of miracles, electric wires: new, thick, bringing the blessings of electricity to this mountain fastness. The power comes from Topopani where we were two days ago. It is hydropower and only turned on for a few hours a night. The turbines were in view at the bottom of a waterfall that seemed to start in the sky.

Porters are stirring. The girl from Slovenia passes by, in a rush. She has perfect gear and is carrying her own pack. The sounds of passion in the room next to mine are very clear because the wall is the thinnest wood. Going to warm up again.

Later. Waiting again. Why does none of this read like *The Snow Leopard*? A small patio on the front of the building is receiving a bit of sun and I will move there from my shelter here in the dining room if it continues. The clouds are getting thicker and it looks nasty out there. I bought Shiba another layer of clothing and socks and boots. You can't buy these things for the guide too close to home because he will sell them and give the money to his family. Shiba's choice of clothing was a shiny warm-up suit by Nike.

We plan to wait here until noon and, if Ted and Precious have not arrived, do some hiking up hill, just to keep limber if it keeps on being so cold. There is a fine Rhode Island Red rooster on the roof across the street. He has just hopped out of a window of what seems to be a barn. Two trekkers pass by, headed up. They are bundled up but look very cold. They were both carrying two sticks. I don't feel strange here with my two hiking sticks. Where they serve me best is crossing streams. Down hill they help the balance and up hill I use them just to keep my arms built up. I bought a pair of gloves in Tatopani so they are better to hold.

One of the roofs across the street is woven straw, or is it bamboo splits? We passed a man cutting bamboo yesterday, and another making the big baskets that the donkeys carry. There are cherry trees in bloom. The cherry trees make no sense. It is fall here. A local girl runs by in sandals, bright green slacks, plaid coat, and shawl around her head. Did she receive a package from some church? Even guys wear skirts here. Two trekkers are repacking, getting out warm stuff for their guide. I have only the poncho to give to silly Shiba who bought a warm-up suit instead of something warm. Marigolds are blooming on the little patio and my fingers are too cold to type but now I have packed my sleeping bag and paid my bill in anticipation of the arrival of Precious and Ted. High living Sally had to pay 370 rupees or about $6 for dinner, breakfast, and bed. After all, this is the best place in town. Heated table and all. The walk this morning was absolutely fascinating with shy Shiba at last opening up and talking about his beloved country. I kept pointing out similarities between his country and Switzerland and how well Switzerland has done under similar circumstances. In Nepal, 90% of the people own their own land. An excellent start. This is similar to the yeoman spirit of England where capitalism had its start. I work for no man and no man works for me. We are equal. In Nepal there is a benevolent king. His line has been ruling since they united the country over 100 years ago. One really interesting similarity is that the Swiss used to rent out their soldiers. The money from the rented military was what started the Swiss banking and now 10% of the Swiss work in banking. The Nepalese make money from tourism as does Switzerland, utilizing the mountains. The Swiss process things highly and then charge outrageous prices but people pay them because it is the best. The Nepalese rent out the Ghurkas for protection. They are mainly sent to the Arab Emirates. Anyhow, when I could, I had Chas send Shiba a copy of John McPhee's book about Switzerland that so impressed me. I never got a reply. I suspect that Shiba may be a Communist and such enterprise as the Swiss show would be unintelligible. McPhee isn't the easiest to read.

And then we had settled into a really nice hotel in Tukuche. I had hardly finished my lunch when I was dragged to a Buddhist temple where they were chanting from Tripritic book, or something from the Dali Lama. Buddhist stuff is exciting, with huge drums being enthusiastically beaten and reed flutes and some untuneful horns. It all works very well together and the pulse does pound. The festival is called Sangha. If we would stay here one more night, there would be dancing by ladies in beautiful costumes. When we walked today it was down off the hillsides, beside the beautiful river.

11.10.95 Tucheu, Mustang, Nepal. It is already 7:30 and no breakfast. No Shiba. Rain. The clouds that are soft cotton daubing the tops of the mountains with new snow, are raining here.

Sprinkling, and not seriously. The rain is over for the season, right? No more monsoon. Yesterday there were so few trekkers it was like the end of the season was the day before yesterday. I was the only person in this very nice hotel, and they are trying to get me to stay for a couple of days in order to take in the Buddhist festival. The weather only makes me more determined to get going. I may have to wait a long time for an airplane out of Jomson. There was only one plane that went up yesterday. There could come the day when no planes fly at all because winter is coming. Shiba is up and about now and anxious. He says we should go. Rain will be bad. I don't have anything covered with plastic. It is going to be an interesting walk.

11.11.95 Jomson, Nepal. Still very cold today but the rain of yesterday has stopped. A big grey cloud is hanging over the mountain opposite and is probably snowing. Coming into Jomson was one last stream whose water had risen from the rain. It was really scary. The plank that was usually there had been washed away by the torrent. Shiba went back and forth a couple of times to show me I could make it and then hung on tightly while I waded across. I was so happy to put my wet feet under the covered table and warm them up in the inn in Jomson.

I was too lazy to bathe last night when the electricity was on and now, no electricity, no hot water. My room is the nicest that I have had in Nepal, with bath and the toilet is a throne. The streets in Jomson are flagstones; the buildings are stone painted white. Jomson's misfortune is that it is so bleak a landscape. We seem to be in an area that has few trees, just semiarid growth looking careworn by the cold. I would think we were above tree line but I can see a forest of pines on the hill opposite. It rises up to the snow-covered trees and there are chutes of snow trailing down from the snow area. When the sun shines on the snow-covered peaks, it is the breath-taking view that we have come to see. The roofs of the town are mostly flat, paved with flat stones. The people going by the window are very grubby with a collection of brown rags wrapped around them, Tibetans. Last night the young Canadians were talking about the possibility of a road being built to here. They were against it even though the people here are so out of the mainstream that everything that gets here is carried up on a donkey or a bent human back.

"Well, yes but that is employment. Without the need to transport things by back or donkey, think of how many people will be out of work."

I guess I have a different feeling about these things. Any change from poverty has to be an improvement. Any coming into the modern life is better than living your life in such forsaken circumstances.

Shiba and I have given up any thought of continuing up to the next village. (I saw terrific pictures after the World Wanders got home, that Liz took when she hiked to that next village. I don't know if she was there before or after I was.) Some others that tried it were almost caught in an avalanche

So, Shiba is leaving to go back to Pokhara. It will take him three or four days to walk there. I got the name of his school and will try to send $20 per month to the school so that he can complete his teacher's training. This will be my contribution to Asia: bigger and better than the gift to Mother Teresa, Shiba will help bring the education that is so desperately needed here. I thought a lot about it and decided to send the money to the school because, families being what they are, if I send the money to kind, gentle Shiba, it might be begged from him before he could use it for school.

Looking down the Kali Gandika the valley is filled with clouds and the peak of Nuilui. These are the very clouds that are keeping even the helicopters out of Jomson. The airstrip is too wet and soggy for conventional planes and we heard that the helicopter that tried to fly here only got as far as Ghorapani before it had to turn back. I have a ticket for Tuesday, the 13th and am on a waiting list for Monday the 12th. The Everest Air hopes to make three flights tomorrow to unclog the backlog of people who are waiting here for flights. I have finally found myself a warm comfortable spot to write. The Hotel has a solarium that looks out on the main street and I can watch the passing parade of trekkers. A guy up the street looks so much like Ted without a beard that I feel like checking it out but then it is so nice here in the sun.

Later: It wasn't Ted although it looked like him when I was right next to him. The clouds are lifting down the valley and patches of very blue are getting bigger. Someone who saw TV said that the storm was all over Nepal, India and Indonesia. A dirty little child with no underpants squats and shits diarrhea and pees on the street. Another ragamuffin has a crust of dirt on her smiling face and hair gone to dreadlocks. These are the impoverished Tibetans, Buddhists, who do not have to bathe frequently as do Hindus. No bright saris, just drab baggy pants or skirts and shawls. Last night I was telling one of the Canadians who wants to go to be with Mother Teresa, about Calcutta. After I went to bed I cried for a long time about India, Nepal. I vowed again that Shiba is going to be my contribution. In some of the towns below here there were children not more than eight or ten years old who were carrying large baskets of logs and fuel. Most of the time you get tough and can just walk by all this but sometimes it gets to you.

The big mountain opposite has been approached by big fluffy clouds that are reflecting the sun back on to its dark side. It is so steep that climbing it would be impossible for a trekker. Perhaps one could ski but here you have to be up to an unhealthy altitude to get to the snow, around 15,000 feet. A string of donkeys goes by tended by women. Women doing men's jobs here tend to be gypsies, according to Shiba. He says they came from Egypt many years ago. They always beg from him. Now the mountain is making clouds, or so it seems. The gentle wind blows the cloud off the face but it clings like a lingering lover to the mountain and looks like the source of the cloud. Getting drowsy. Maybe a nap and then I will be inspired to write about trekking, or plagiarize Mathiesson.

Later: Across the street, below my vantage point, a couple of Nepalese dragged two small, white goats to a pole and tied them up and the men went away for a while. The goats looked around for something to eat, and finding not much, settled down to rest. A pleasant, bucolic scene, I thought and began to sketch it. When the men returned, they had a couple of knives and very quickly slit the throat of one of the goats, skinned it, gutted it, and hauled it away. I will always carry the picture of the second goat in my head. It was terrified. It knew it was going to die. It struggled and struggled against the rope. The men came back and killed it quickly and humanely, but I know that goat knew that it was going to die and it was very much afraid.

11.13.95 Jomson, Mustang, Nepal. More rumors and some BBC News has 13 or 14 Japanese trekkers dead in a landslide in the Everest region. It was an organized tour and presumably had not done anything wrong except camp in the way of an avalanche. Four tourists and about six Nepalese killed in the Manang District. The newest rumor for the tragedy in this area is that it is not German trekkers but Canadians who started out to cross the 14.000-foot pass in two inches of snow. The Germans are always unpopular and if anything bad happens . . . . The story today is that the Canadians, having started in the snow, continued in a whiteout. They encountered two Australians and all piled into a small tent. In the morning, a Nepali was dead and the Australians had left and have not been seen again. The Canadians will/will not, be held responsible for the death of the Nepali? The law here is that you must care for your guides. If anything happens to the guide, it is your fault. You are legally responsible. As I came back form the post office, the door of the police station was open and peering in, I could see the legs of a dead Nepali guide laid out stiffly on a table.

This all had seemed very removed from the peaceful, sunny scene at Jomson. Trekkers are not climbers and do not really expect to be exposed to danger. A landslide took out several walls of a hotel in, Kagbeni but no one was injured. Yesterday three climbers, not trekkers, came into the solarium, asking permission of the owner to sort out gear here. Their cheeks and lips were spotted with black spots. Frostbite. They spoke so little that I don't know what their country was but they spent three quarters of an hour shuffling things without a word. Two men and a woman. Those of us in the solarium kept an awed silence.

There is an Irish trekker girl here with a torn ligament in the back of her knee. It caused her ankle to swell also. She politely ignores all advice to stay off the leg and even talks about walking out instead of waiting for the plane. Night before last I played cards with three Canadians and an American, and last night the same American, a Harvard educated New York lawyer and an Ohio nurse with her two daughters who have a bakery in Eugene, Oregon. The lawyer and I are killers in the game of hearts. I stayed up until 10:00.

Nepal is pretty elemental. I was stuck in Jomson for five days, waiting for the plane or helicopter that would save my knees from having to walk back down the mountain. There is no phone or FAX in Jomson so I sent postcards to everyone I could find an address for. I seldom write postcards, and now that I had something newsworthy to talk about, I tried not to mention the disaster that surrounded Jomson. I didn't want anyone to worry.

11.14.95 Today, Tuesday, my ticket to fly in the regular airplane to Pokhara came due and, full of hope, I started packing up at 5:45 AM to be at the airport at 6:30. When the Limo didn't arrive, I hiked the 1/2 block and got a boarding pass and put my backpack in as luggage and retired again to the solarium to await the arrival of planes. The solarium is warm and sunny and has a great view of the airport and the valley that the planes come up. The wind was still strong but the landing field was still soggy and it seemed pretty hopeless. About 9:00 a helicopter arrived and Nepali Air's charter passengers got a chance to pay double the $60 price to fly back to Pokhara. The people that wanted to get on that plane were in such a state of desperation that I stayed clear. Perhaps they were somehow responsible for dead Nepalis. The helicopter left around three o'clock, I know because it flew over my head as I was making my way down the valley.

Never one for patience, I had been in Jomson since Friday. When the airline people said that the planes would not come that day and cheerfully refunded my money, I grabbed it and started walking, I walked right out of town and down the hill. I was still very close to town when I rolled my right ankle and went down hard, tearing my pants at the knee and bloodying my right hand. I'm happy as a duck now, in a nice inn with two Advil down.

Coming back down seems scarier than going up. The trail is dynamited or hacked into the sides of straight up mountains. Geologically, these mountains are supposed to be still moving upward and I don't know about that but they certainly are moving downward. Landslides take out the trail and the ever wonderful donkey trains come along and make a new trail through the rubble. This new trail is not a confidence builder. It is as wide as a foot is wide and the fright-filled glance down isn't much worse than the anxious look up that reveals a lot more stuff ready to come sliding down. I watched a trail crew working on an impossible slope with aluminum wire mesh. No ropes, Nothing. If they go tumbling into the Kali Gandiki, they go. The only worse job would be bridge repair on the suspension bridges.

11.15.95 Ghansa, Nepal. Naturally the helicopters are more frequent, three flights today. However the winds have not calmed, far from it. The new guide and I plowed our way through dust storms as we threaded our way through the gravel of the riverbed to Kalopani. Lunch in Kalopani with two Americans from D.C. who are very nervous about being here. Two other American girls arrived with their English and Danish companions, and tales of daring do. They were the first group over the Pass after the snow. They waited a day to lessen the danger of avalanche and then took off. They started at 7:00 and by 9:00 caught up with a group that had started at 3:00 AM, the first group was already exhausted from beating the trail in the 3 ft. snow. It took five hours to ascend to the pass and seven to descend to the next town, where they collapsed from exhaustion. They said it was a great thing to do and are very proud of themselves. They said the descent was incredibly difficult and the girls just slid down on their rears. They were ignoring their blackened lips and cheeks.

This hotel in Ghansa has very primitive facilities and I am unable to buy a flashlight. Oh well, it will be cheap and I will spend a long time in bed. It is really very charming here. Across a flagstone street is a spreading apple tree that is growing out of a spot designed for people with backpacks to rest the packs and let them sit while they take refreshment at the hotel. There is a racing stream and then another wall with ferns and other plants growing out of it. Beyond this wall is an area newly prepared as a corral with a ragged stockade fence. There is a short field beyond this and a towering wall of Himalaya, covered with scrub growth. One wall of the corral is made of sticks that will be burnt for fuel over the winter. Today we passed again the huts of the mountain people (Tibetans) who are moving down hill for the winter. Their huts awaited on the river gravel, below the snow line. I suppose they are so memorable because they are using huge slabs of bark for the walls. I am drinking a huge beer that calls itself Tabor. It helps wash down the Advil. My legs felt stronger today. Not so much pain. The porters have gathered around to stare at the computer and bother me with their smoking. Beyond the wall of firewood is a barn whose roof is piled high with corn shocks and hay. There is a small store next door that does not sell flashlights. It has the usual clay orange trim on a stone building painted white. The roofs are flat with a couple of courses of stone showing at the edge. I saw porters carrying huge slabs of flagstone up a hill today and wondered about a building sized pile of building stone in Jomson. How did it get there? On the back of a burro or on the back of a human burro?

A white pony is tied in the patio of the store next door. He is cleaning up a pile of hay and paper that ended up there. I have tried to take a picture of the dogs; they are very healthy looking and after the horror of the pariah dogs of India. They look like my Bernese except they don't have her white markings. Someone started to braid the tail of the white pony but gave up. The porter here is looking through a dirty magazine in Hindi. The white pony is having a tough time eating because he is wearing a fairly severe muzzle. I am not doing too well social wise. If the Swiss couple is here I guess I am invited to eat with them but if they can manage German with the older Dutch couple it may be pretty boring. I should make a run to the toilet while it is still light and scout the prospects for dinner.

11.17.95 Tatopani repeat. Staggered into Tatopani yesterday afternoon, incredibly sore and beat up. Paid my porter a generous

750 rupees for two days and collapsed into beer and Motrin. After recovering a bit, I went out and bought a novel and buried myself in it for the rest of yesterday day and most of today. I'm running short of cash and the price, $4.00 for a novel seemed outrageous but I decided on something more elevating today and bought *Freedom at Midnight* by the same pair that wrote *City of Joy*. They tell India like it is. This should cover the same time periods as Salmon Rushdie's manic *Midnight's Children*. Rushdie's silly book could have been the model for Tom Hanks' Forrest Gump. The Hotel here at Tatopani is so hard to leave. It has a fabulous garden and wonderful food. I am hooked on their eggplant lasagna. There is a huge, rangy poinsettia that has draped itself over a charming stone and wood garden gate. A white rose has woven its way through a lemon tree to offer a picture of sparkling white flowers beside the bright yellow oranges. Here the limes are biggest of the citrus fruit; oval and yellow green. The lemons are fairly small and orange, and the oranges are dark green . . . . either Mandarin oranges or almost tangerines to judge by the taste and texture. There are lots of blue tables with white chairs on the flagstone patio. Coming down the mile of altitude from Jomson has changed things from around the tree line, semi-arid to citrus and bananas. Lots of trekkers take a day to rest here. One of the amazing things is that there are lots of the young and strong who are laid up with bad legs, blisters, etc. Probably a belief in invincibility has kept them from proper rest and things have gone chronic. Going chronic is the worst. For most injuries it means six month of inactivity while the injury heals. Even the people who did the Anapurnas Circuit are having muscle problems. The change from climbing up to going down is just too much.

The rumor report: A fellow yesterday said he was almost to Besisahar and turned back because the landslide that killed the 13 Japanese and about as many porters, had taken out a lot of the town of Besisahar where it was all soldiers and aid people. And then Manang where four more people died is on the back side of the Anapurna Circuit on my map. Too close for comfort, really. So he somehow got here and is going to Jomson then back down to go over Ghorapani to Anapurna base camp. Getting cold out here, the sun has gone behind the hill. In spite of the citrus you can see your breath here now and in the mornings.

Two English girls that I met in Tatopani had spent some time in London with World Wanderer Jody Staunton who was in the Indian embassy trying to get an Indian visa. They said that she told them she had never been to an English pub so they took her to one and had a couple of small beers. This was about three weeks ago.

11.18.95 Beni. Still glad that I walked back down. The knee did not begin to throb until noon. The estimated time of travel Tatopani to Beni is seven hours so when I made it in eight and one half hours, I was quite proud. I didn't get lost as I picked my solo way through the broad gravel bed of the river that is braiding itself down this valley. Every now and then, there is a board across a strand of the river and you know you are on the right track. I really miss Shiba's confident guiding. Then, remembering that Shiba would ask the way frequently, I started asking for the next town. The donkey drivers and goat herds were helpful and grinning at my pronunciation, would point in the direction I should go. With each new avalanche, the path changed.

I am totally exhausted but sucking down one more coke and Advil. The bathroom is now clear and I am going to try the advertised hot shower, nicest place in town for 80 R or $1.50 US.

Later: So the shower was lukewarm. We are out of the wind here and have descended into a farming area with banana trees. The trail was wider and very busy today with donkeys and people. It is practically a megalopolis of towns strung out along the trail. People who travel it are occasionally dressed in their Sunday best, as if going to a wedding. It is Saturday which is Nepal's Sunday. I tried very hard to get here before the bank closed but missed the closing by an hour. Tomorrow the bank in Baglung should be open when I get there and I will be able to pay for my guide and transportation back to Pokhara. I got a new guide today, picked him up on the trail after not being able to come to an agreement with one that the hotel found. I stuck with $350 R. and the would-be porter went from $500 to $400 then back to $500 as we negotiated.

Iceland, the guide is such a young kid. He speaks English fairly well. He walks right in my way and I have to shoo him off. He is out of the way for a while then he gets lonesome and is back where I trip over him. Oh dear. He is really very nice and I am grateful to have him. It was a scenic walk today but very perilous at times. The landslides are, as usual, the scary part, with the trail just barely beaten in by the donkeys since the last rain.

11.20.95 Pokhara, Nepal. Spent today being good. Mother Teresa would have been proud of me. After going down to the great white way to sell the clothes off my back, I went to Pokhara Campus. I got the bike out first and that involved about 30 Nepalese who had not seen the likes of the rotten brakes on Green, The Mountain Bike. I can never get the wheels off to transport the bike then when they finally are off; I can't get them on again. This is the biggest reason why I like to use Spot, the touring bike. The brakes are not so complicated. Before breakfast, getting up at 4:00 AM, I prepared four Faxes but every line was busy and the FAX man told me to come back later. So I'll try again as soon as I get down the tea that the nice people at the motel forced on me. After the fun time at the bike shop, I biked to the airline office to get tickets for tomorrow morning. I decided to be brave and take the helicopter. The helicopters are large and Russian made.

I missed lunch being good. I biked to the next town and found my way to the Pokhara Campus of Pribohan University. There was an enormous crowd of young people. Turns out there are over 7000 students and I had come inadequately prepared to help the office staff figure out who the receiver of my largess was. A lovely lady who spoke excellent English helped me find my way around and communicated with the powers that run the college. The top man was in Kathmandu. His office was comically bare. It had grubby windows, chipped paint, a single desk with a bunch of files piled on the floor. I did not see a telephone there. I tried to imagine the Chancellor of the U of Pitt in this office.

Then we went to another building with a series of Profs offices and that felt like home, seedy home. At least all the windows were still in. Then we went to another building on the campus that everyone assured me was beautiful. There the staff found Shiba's picture and records and everyone was very happy. I pledged a $20 check every month and plunked down 1000 rupees to fill in any gap in communication. I explained at least three times that I wanted the money to go through the school rather than through Shiba. He is such a mild gentle soul that the average family could easily con it out of him. This way he gets the extra prestige of being the beneficiary of a scholarship. Anyhow it is done. The lady thanked me warmly and bought me a cup of tea. She showed me the library. Not as many books as students. Our Junior High librarian would have sent most of them to the bookbinders or trashed them. However, it really was a good library because it had a copy of Jerome K. Jerome's *Three Men In a Boat* which is all I could ever ask of a library. Most of the books were in English and I imagined setting up a system to send books from Pittsburgh. I could beg a donation from all those profs and students at the Pittsburgh AYH and ship them over or arrange for trekkers to bring them over. (Never did this.)

11.22.95 Kathmandu. Been so busy writing out FAXes that I haven't even written about the wonderful helicopter flight from Pokhara. It didn't crash. I took lots of pictures and believe I got the Anapurnas and perhaps Everest. It definitely isn't Pittsburgh. The sharp hills are frantically terraced no matter how steep. The sun would glint on the snow-covered peaks and everything was a calendar picture. How to pick out something definitive was the problem. I tried getting tops of nearby hills to contrast with the blue-white mountains. Clouds in the valleys with a streak of green-brown mountain between their soft white and the sharp, sparkling white of the Himalayas. So exotic. I have to keep telling myself that, yes it is I. I am here. (Pictures all bad. Nothing but scratched, dirty windows of the Russian helicopter)

I believe I hear a bit of Mozart coming from the restaurant next door. I may weep. Going to check.

11.23.95 Kathmandu. There, walking down the street near my hotel (Star) was that cool babe, Precious. I had not seen her since I deserted her in Tatopani on the fourth day of the trek. She is all recovered from the tonsillitis, food poisoning, and pinched nerve that followed it. She was headed for a free (last time you'll hear that word) lecture on Buddhism. So naturally I tagged along. The lecture was interesting but Buddhism seemed just another guilt trip thing. However, I signed up for a day and a half retreat up a mountain where there is to be a great sunrise view of Everest. I had to go through the renting cold weather clothes thing again. The group meets at 9:00 AM at the restaurant above which is the meeting room. It is just amazing how many people are up and at 'em at this hour.

Precious and Amogochita checking out Mustang Sally.

I'm in Alice's Restaurant where I organized a dinner for everyone who had met Mustang Sally: the Italian-Canadian from New Delhi with her Israeli friend from the first night in Delhi, the two Brit girls from Tatopani who met Jodi, Precious from the bus to Pokhara. Later when we went to a bar so Precious could get them to play *Mustang Sally* for me. There, as predicted, Ted (of Precious, Ted and Sally, the trekking threesome) showed up. He seemed very serious. Most lyrics in most modern songs are unintelligible to me as was Mustang Sally, however, the Ride, Sally, Ride came through and did seem appropriate.

So I am at the retreat. This is fun and I am not so much alone here in Kathmandu. The group of Buddhist novitiates is only five people and is pretty intense therefore. We had one lecture and lunch and the rest are off on a scramble that was too tough for me. The place is indeed at 7300 ft. and chilly but one of the greatest spots I have been to. It is the Nagotka farmhouse, charming with stained wood beams and red brick. The bedrooms and meditation room are all roofed with thatching. I'll try to get some pictures when the sun is on the other side, in the morning. Our leader is a very nice Englishman guru person, Amogachita. I will meditate some more on increasing sensitivity but I think being married to an artist like Chas had done a lot more for me over the years than meditation can do. Looking at all his pictures opens the eyes to a lot. I hope he is having a happy time at Kassabs-in-law for Turkey Day. I sent off two more Faxes today in response to the yards of stuff he sent me. Looking over the hill here, down the terraces, you can see the people living their village lives, see them walking along the dirt roads. One village had little naked children playing in the streets. It is probably in the 50's when the sun is out.

11.24.95 We are back in Kathmandu again after walking down a steep mountain from Nogota. I passed the RESTAURANT AT THE END OF THE UNIVERSE. Didn't stop. The owner at the farmhouse says the owner at the restaurant there goes nuts and puts marijuana on the fire and everyone gets weird. I can't believe that I got this sore walking down a steep road, carrying a light daypack. We got up for a sunrise, which was not one of the great ones, but the view from the Nogatoh Farm house was terrific. Everest is out there somewhere. It is cold, 42 degrees. We did two meditations and I'm beginning to get with it. It is very pleasant to think good thoughts like liking yourself, liking the people with you, and letting kindness spread down the valley like sunshine. Nice. I liked it. However, I just don't go for the 2000 years of demons and symbols. Silly. When the guru guy zeroed in on me, I expressed the thing that keeps such people from asking me for donations: *You live. You die. You are dead.* I owe son Tom for that one.

We are all going out for dinner at a place where there is Nepali dancing. Precious said she got up and danced too. It does sound like fun. Off now for the garden restaurant and dancing.

11.26.95 Kathmandu. It is a better day than yesterday. I confirmed my flight, which is leaving two hours early. Now perched in Alice's Restaurant across from the Star Hotel awaiting breakfast. Daughter Kitty claims that her friend, Alice Rounthaler, who lives on Ocracoke is the original Alice of the original Alice's Restaurant. OK. Small world.

Will stop by American Express on my way to the airport, and check on Challoners, the tandem couple I met briefly in Budapest from the World Wander. Perhaps leave a message at American Express. Every now and then you see a European woman here with makeup on. Startling. Most travelers look pretty drab in their waddling clothes. Just saw a girl who looked like Jody S. and another that looked like Regina go into my hotel. Green is sitting there and should cause some questions if it were they. Boring Nepali music on the radio. It just seems to repeat over and over. Two girls stroll by. One looks so familiar. One of those days that drive you nuts. I should concentrate on the good feeling that it would be to see these people again and enjoy the feeling even though they are not there. Am I becoming just a tad Buddhist? Beautiful blonde came out and it still looked like Jody. Poached eggs and potatoes have arrived. The last day in Kathmandu and I biked around the city. The first target was the American Express message board where I saw Helen's signature and left a message for her about staying at the Bangkok hostel. I checked at the hotel where the Challoners were supposed to be but no one was there. I biked on to the airport and put Spot on the plane British style, without benefit of box. No one seemed much surprised. The tool bag was missing when she arrived in Bangkok.

Chapter XXVII

Bangladesh

. . . Prospering Muslim State?

11.26.95 Dhaka, Bangladesh. When you take Bangladesh Airline you just might land in Dhaka and get a night on the town. Our little group of economizing passengers who were traveling on to Thailand on the cheapest possible airline was transported for free to a hotel. The road in was lined with tall trees and billboards. It was not unattractive and did not look as if everyone in Bangladesh were starving as has been reported. The hotel wasn't bad, nice bath with almost enough hot water. The meal, however was the worst in a long time, not helped by sampling a chili disguised as a green bean and waiters who made fun of me for being old.

A German girl of this group says that there were around 200 deaths from the storm that kept me in Jomson. She was taken to identify a German but did not know him. Most were lost in landslides. She was on the Anapurna Circuit when the storm hit. I talked with an cross-country skier from San Francisco who was in Manang and went over the pass in the snow three days after it fell. Said it wasn't bad going up but the descent into Jomson was really tough.

This part of Bangladesh is low and flat. Lots of ponds and pools. It doesn't seem all that poor. Good roads, industry, enough billboards to make me feel at home. There are palm trees and lots of flowers in bloom on large trees. The airport is nice and the help helpful if a bit slow with the computers. There were no women working at all. I figured that these Muslims are used to the women doing all the work and are pretty helpless when they have to do it themselves. The women in our group are the only ones in sight although there are lots of people in the waiting room. The German girl told about having visited a Japanese hotel at 3700 meters at Namphehr that had a great view of Everest, an airfield, and pressurized rooms so that the Japanese flying up from Kathmandu can be there in comfort. Of course they still get altitude sickness but at least they can say they saw Everest. $10 US for a cup of coffee on the terrace.

The trip into Dhaka seemed to promote the idea that Bangladesh was thriving, not given up by the prosperous countries as a dead loss. OK. Good idea.

Chapter XXVIII

THAILAND

Yes, Siam in Thailand

Thailand is the same exotic place it was when Anna was nanny for the King of Siam's children. That king was Rama VI and Rama IX is now on the throne. The roads are generally good for biking and the people gentle and tolerant. Their driving is more controlled than the mania of India and Nepal. Going north from Bangkok to the mysterious Golden Triangle area of Chaing Mai is well worth the biking. The Thais are into wringing the tourist dollars out in interesting ways. Restaurants and hotels are frequent and reasonable and a leisurely trip up and back can fill in some of the gaps in our western knowledge of this fabled land. Thailand is one of the world's most populated areas so it is exciting to get away from the crowd and trek in the hills where the few locals are tribal and each tribe very different form the other. I used a commercial group for a trek, signed up for it on Kao San Road in Bangkok where there is frenetic tourist activity. Going south to Phuket is chancier because the towns/facilities are further apart but those who did bike it found it to be OK.

In Kathmandu, I had decided to try putting Green on the airplane as the British do, no box. Just the bike. Arriving in Bangkok, the bike was fine but someone had swiped my toolbag and the second Cateye was in it. So I have no idea how many miles it would have shown. The bright, striped plastic bag into which I had bought in Greece held all the panniers and was intact. I put it all together and rode the bike to the hostel using a map I had copied from one at my Pittsburgh library.

11/28-12/1/95 Bangkok. Thailand I bought a Thai language tape and book. It was no help and the only Thai I learned was farang which means foreigner and "mai pen rai" which means "oh, never mind." There was an exciting message at the hostel from Helen saying she would be there on the 2nd or 3rd of December. I could only hope that she was to separate from Ole and I would have a companion.

To fill in the time, I am taking Thai Massage.

The city tour was lots of walking around the glittering palaces and exotic temples. The city is relatively clean and seems quite prosperous. After the tour, I returned to the palace spend another afternoon. I could not stop taking pictures because each twist and turn presented new compositions of color and light. The Thai have covered whole buildings with ceramic flowers, pieces of mirror, gold. It only needs the sun for shimmering, shining glory.

The kings, Rama I-IX, all liked medals and had whole buildings for them. I dutifully admired all these and the gifts from other potentates.

The incredible wealth of the temples always annoys me. After I finish staring at and ooing and awing over a 60 ft. golden Buddha, I wonder why people feel it is necessary to shower their gods with wealth. It can't be much of a God if it needs our hard won food, drink, or money. People come to ask favors of the godlike thing. They have a mass of superstition and mythology to show devotion to. It is such a drag, not at all the pleasant, skull-bound Buddhism of the retreat in Nepal. Looks just like Hinduism to me.

From the hostel I would walk a short distance to a dock and go to the palace by way of the river fast boat. The river seems to be coming up again. It is not flooding badly enough to hurt by anything but mud and the inconvenience of traveling over the wet spots on shaky boards that are supported by bricks or concrete blocks.

I still have a problem communicating with the Thais. I wandered a long time looking for a FAX closer to the hostel. If they couldn't speak English they just shooed me out the door. They don't want to be bothered. Signs in the windows read, "No deal foreigners". The taxi drivers and Tuk tuk drivers are that way, too. Both they and I lack patience.

Himself has not responded to my last three Faxes. How I miss him. Homesickness really gets to be a problem when I hold up for a while in one spot. I was sort of hoping I would meet some people at the massage lessons but I seem to be the only student. Today I took a bus the wrong direction and saw a lot of Bangkok. Missed lunch completely. I had to take a taxi back.

Bridge On the River Kwai

Last night at the hostel, I was chatting with a SHORT Scotsman. When I mentioned that I was going to take a tour to the Bridge on the River Kwai, he told me the story of his brother. The brother, call him Stewart, was also a very short man. He still made it into the British army because he was unusually fit and able. When the Japanese took over Singapore he was surrendered with the rest of his group. They were lined up and a Japanese officer went down the line with his sword and marked certain men, most of them tall. These men were then shot and killed. Stewart had been standing next to his best pal. The pal was one of the selected. He was shot and killed on the spot. Stewart said that he later had wished he had been one of the chosen. The men were then herded up the peninsula in one of those horrible Japanese death marches and put in a concentration camp. The next long years were spent working in the 'Death Railway', including the "Bridge On the River Kwai" that the Japanese were building to facilitate troop and materiel movement into Siam, Malaysia, and Burma. Meanwhile the US was continuing its bloody march toward Tokyo. Bombers had destroyed Tokyo almost completely by conventional bombing. The group that Stewart was with was put in a ship and sent to a Japan to work on rebuilding Tokyo. They never got there.

The ship that Stewart was on, was unmarked by the red cross that the Geneva Convention says prisoners of war should have. A

US submarine destroyed it with torpedoes and Stewart was in the water. Japanese ships came to the area and raced through it to kill any survivors. They missed Stewart and he floated on into the record books as the person to be the longest to live in shark infested waters. He was picked up by a US sub and ended up in the US. Then they decided he was Australian and shipped him to Australia. Stewart was so mentally destroyed that he was unable to help his care-givers. As time went on he got better and was finally able to indicate that he was Scotch. They shipped him to Scotland. Meanwhile, officials had gone to his mother's tenement home and showed the mother pictures of two men so starved that they looked like skeletons. They asked her to indicate with an x which she thought might be her son. They went away and came back later to say that she should abandon hope, they didn't think it was Stewart. Later they came back and had a picture of recovering humans instead of a couple of skeletons. She identified Stewart and he eventually arrived home. His brother was much younger and remembers Stewart as the person whose screams terrified him at night. The younger brother left home after a couple of years. Stewart continued to steadily improve, helped, no doubt by the 17 lb. sterling given him by a still unrepentant Japanese government. Finally he was able to hold a job. Stewart decided to do his best to put those memories behind him but before he did that he went to see the wife of the best friend who was murdered in Singapore. He married that lady and helped bring up the son of the best friend. His story was the subject of a book that my story teller, his brother, cannot remember the name of. Stewart is dead now but gradually his life got better and in a small way he prospered and was content.

Thai Massage

First session of traditional Thai massage. For three hours I got then gave massage. My instructor, Pain, (really Pian) has been to the US to teach and work at Thai Massage, in Akron, Ohio, where she remembers being cold even in the summer. She was also in Atlanta and Arizona which she thought were too hot. My right foot that had a bottle of water drop on it yesterday, seemed better than the left which is still swollen from the tumble I took leaving Jomson, Mustang, Nepal. We did the feet then the legs then the body some and a bit of the back. My ankle is no longer swollen!!!!! I first heard about Thai massage from the Viennese psychiatrist doctor friend from Calcutta who was an her way to Chaing Mai to take a course in Thai massage. I guess I hoped to meet congenial people in the classes. There was Thai massage at the old Palace but it was my understanding that it was done by Buddhist monks and Buddhist monks are not to ever touch women?? The best school was supposd to be in Chaing Mai but I had no idea where Chaing Mai was and wanted to wait at the hostel for Helen. Pian's massage parlor was right on an alley off Khao San Road with squashed masses of people moving by constantly so it seemed safe. I never met any farangs to hang out with but I did like being at the massage parlor and with my collection of masseuses. It was as good a way of contacting locals as I could come up with.

The general plan of attack is full hand pressure on the muscle at three or four points, then finger pressure, then slide the fingers between the muscles until they touch bone, at three or four points on the lower leg. Then gently make fingers meet around the muscle, three or four points. Then repeat in reverse order, deepest to surface. The first couple of times she put a knee into my foot, it was painful but by the 8th time, it was beginning to feel good. There are the acrobatic things where you lie on your back and grab the victim's foot and push with your feet on the victim's leg kneading it with your feet. The best part is the last where you lay on your back, head in giver's lap, and get the head and neck done. After three hours of this, I was so spaced out I could barely walk. I will try for four hours tomorrow. It takes thirty hours to get a certificate. Off to take Advil and a nap.

There was a strange scene . . . I am cutting off the longest fingernails I have ever had . . . Shouldn't I try real estate or being a travel agent again???? I was always sure that the inability to grow three inch nails with perfect polish was, undoubtedly, why I couldn't succeed at these two glamorous professions. I pictured dressing in stylish clothes, instead of the waddling clothes and using my Estee

Lauder BEAUTIFUL (didn't I give it away?), high heels instead of orthotics in Nikes . . . . A dream. Anyhow I am clipping nails because my Thai massage teacher insisted, and this handsome young man is asking if I biked around the world did I know about the Transamerica Trail . . . HE, this charming young man . . . is the cartographer for Adventure Cycling!!!! I told him how enthusiastic I was. How very familiar with the maps I am and how many I have used and how I give the Missoula, Montana address of Adventure Cycling to every biker I can because it is a safer, better, cheaper way to see the USA. I quizzed him about the route that I had heard they might be preparing for mountain bikes through the Rockies and he said that the Montana part was almost ready for printing. I told him that my experience with the Appalachian Trail led me to believe that there were certainly enough logging and Dept. of Agriculture roads to do the Appalachians also and to get to work. Meanwhile nail clippings are flying everywhere.

I worked on massage three hours today. I have five hours altogether now. Day off tomorrow to visit the River Kwai.

12.2.95 Floating market . . . This is a 2 hour drive from Bangkok, didn't see any hotels???? (Two hours in a car is about what a bike can do in a day.) We stopped at a copra growing place and I had fresh coconut milk, and with my trusty Swiss Army knife, teased out some meat also. Delicious. Bad tempered parrot there. We also passed some flats for extracting salt from the sea water. A whole lot more salt at the Great Salt Lake. Now I am hiding out from the Tiger Balm sellers at the floating market.

"Tigah bahm? Tigah bahm?"

"No, thank you. My tiger is just fine."

"Madam. Madam, excuse me," to which I respond in my best Junior High teacher voice:

"You are excused."

This place is so cute. The boats are darling. the fruit is beautiful, the silk fabulous. I bought a lot of bananas for ten baht and am now trying to get rid of the excess. I'm sitting at a table overlooking one of the canals filled with a grey, sticky-looking fluid. It may be water. Flat bottomed skiffs, long and narrow go by propelled by motor or pole or paddle. The boats are stuffed full of fruit or veggies or tourists. It is incredibly full of life and light. Coconut palms and bananas crowd the waterways. It is so like the floating gardens of Xochimilco outside of Mexico City . . . .

12.3.95 Bangkok. And Helen has not yet arrived. Trouble getting a plane, I suppose. I managed five hours of massage today: muscles pinched, mashed pummeled pulled, and twisted. Think I'll have some Advil. Discovered something important: if I do Yogic breathing while doing the massage it helps me concentrate. The girls all do a little 'Namaste' thing before they start. I think translated it goes:

"If I break something while standing on this fat cow's back, may she not be a lawyer."

There was a fat, hideous, ugly German who hung around Pian's. He wanted her fourteen year old daughter for a weekend. They would argue long and loud. Finally the pig went off for the weekend with one of my teachers.

I watched the parade for the King's birthday. Actually it is each corps presenting its beautiful self and pledging loyalty for another year. The Thai love of color and show made me run out of film early. The king was in a small pavillion a half block away.

Saw The last hour of '*Waterworld*'. What a hoot. They show movies in the restaurants on Khao San Road so being the world's biggest movie fan I have switched my allegiance to Khao San Street. The movies are announced on hand written signs giving the time of the showing. Order a meal and you can watch the entire movie. Tourist to the core. I tried, twice to watch a movie called *The Beach* starring some teeny bopper guy when it came out in the late 1990s. It started out on Khao San Road but the movie got so bad that I got up and left; twice.

12.7.95 Pearl Harbor Day for me. Bombed. Sunk. I spotted a post office from which to mail my masseuse certificate and books on Thai massage to home. There was a young couple inside, sending packages, who turned out to be, I didn't recognize them, Chancellors, the North Carolina tandem couple from World Wander. I was so confused. Not recognizing them from the encounter in Budapest didn't help. Where were they staying? . . . In a guest house nearby, Ole and the whole group are there. I should go visit. I guess they didn't know I had been rejected. And Helen Coyne? Oh yes she had been there, too. For days. And had not tried to contact me who had been patiently waiting for her because she had called and said she would be there. Or did she call? Perhaps she who called was Charles, telling me to expect her on the second or third. It is definitely not like Helen to call. Perhaps the mystery is solved. She never intended to make contact. Does that make me feel any better? Not really. I had deluded myself that I had a friend who was joining me. Wrong. I walked off a psychological cliff of instant depression and fled out the door. Gee, it did hurt.

So. The one thing I learned from hours and hours of touchy-feely psych courses is winners have alternatives. No waiting for anyone any more. Ever. Except my dear soul mate. I'm off to Chaing Mai tomorrow at 5:00 PM.

12/10-12/12/95 Chaing Mai Trekking

Hilarious. The trekking isn't too tough. The young folks go slowly enough that I can keep up. The food is a bit chancy because there is no sanitation hereabouts but huge helping of papaya, topped off by an experimental chew of betel nut does make for an interesting meal. Four of us tried the betel nut then got our pictures taken with red teeth. The tiny village ladies are so entertaining. They want so much to sell us stuff and are so quaint in their costumes of silver decorated head dresses and coin waist bands and bright colored outfits. This is just a blast. There is a varied but compatible group of Josh, two Brits, two Swedes, a Dutchman, three Korean girls and a Japanese. All of these travelers spoke English. The guide told us about spending seven years in a school as a monk so he could get an education. He made a lot of fun of Bhuddist monkhood. The Brits are great fun and we will be sorry to see them go tomorrow after the elephant ride.

12.11.95 Chaing Mai. Trekking in such beautiful surroundings. The mountains are small compared to the Anapurnas but are very jagged and picturesque because of red streaks in them.

The area is not as intensively farmed as Nepal, not tier after tier of rice paddies but farming on flat ground. They used to grow a lot of opium here but now the government encourages them to grow tobacco instead and they grow a sweet burly. Josh's job is buying tobacco. Josh and I have a running debate about the future of the third world. He thinks the life style here is cute. I think it is pathetic. He thinks that a simple (non-polluting, not using much material stuff) life is better. So I say:

"Given the choice of a 9-5 job in the city and a three piece suit, or looking at the butt end of a water buffalo all day while wading through a mucky rice paddy, you'd pick the water buffalo? I just think people should have a choice."

The houses are all bamboo huts with grass roofs. They are drying a crop of soy beans now on flat mats around the town. The ladies a charmingly dressed in bright dresses with ornate trim.

We rode the elephants today and I could not have imagined what fun it was. They were huge and graceful. We were way up in the air, rocking back and forth, in the trees. The elephants walked very carefully and after a while you got a feeling of confidence and just rocked with it. Richard, the Dutchman, was on the elephant with me and he is very tall, about 6'4' and I was afraid everything would slant his direction but it didn't. He was very cold last night and couldn't sleep. Tonight looks better because they have mattresses for under us. There is a pack of dogs barking at some girls from another village who have come to sell stuff to the local girls The locals here are immigrant Camer Rouge. The dickering goes on and on and so does the barking. A policeman arrived on motorcycle and was very enthusiastic about our Korean girls, one of them is very pretty. My thumb is still swollen hugely and my feet hurt so I'm going to take a nap until lunch.

12.12.95 Chaing Mai. Back in the city after the final day of trekking. We got up late so we wouldn't start rafting before it got hot. We had a nice 2 hour trek on foot. I have a sore throat. from the wretched miserable ride in the open truck. Cheap. We're still talking $62 for three days of great fun. Yesterday after the elephant ride was pretty calm. We walked to a village where there was a

Buddhist monastery in a bamboo hut. The monk was very nice and friendly and the locals let us take their pictures. They are refugees from Burma (Mayamar) and what ever has been going on there. They grow other crops than opium now and have money coming in all year round, so they like Thailand. I'm propped up in bed, one of my favorite places to write. The bed is in a bamboo hut with floors and walls of split bamboo and roof of grass which has been tied on to bamboo poles. The rafters are, you guessed it, bamboo. The floor and support beams are 6 x6 rough cut wood. The women work very hard here, going out to the fields early with the small children, to weed and harvest. The current crop seems to be several kinds of beans. Back to my bedroom. The two Swedes, the Hollander, the American, and the Korean girls are still sleeping here in my bedroom. We each have a nice spot in the floor with plastic mat on top of the bamboo floor. This is what we decided was a two star hut because it has mattresses which fold up when not in use. These are not only more comfortable than the first night's hovel, but keep a sleeping person reasonably warm. Most of us came off without sleeping bags and so the blankets offered were piled deep for this chilly night. The village and the two Korean girls are stirring and chattering and coughing. The sun has not yet penetrated the fog and until it does, I'll huddle here in my blankets. Last night the little girls of the village entertained us with in their cute costumes with songs they learned in school. "Camptown Town Races". I tried to explain that Stephen Foster came from my town but they didn't understand that. They do a minimal shuffling dance with the songs and some small hand movements but I still haven't seen real Thai dancing. Did a minimal back, neck and head massage on the Dutch person, Richard. He is the huge fellow and it was like culture shock to try to locate spine and ribs in such a person after all those tiny Thai ladies at Pian's. The sun has finally appeared and I'm going to look for a spot of it to sit in. Lacking that, I'll be back to huddle in the blankets. Yesterday we also visited a cave that had a lovely Buddha. The cave itself was very beautiful. It was interesting to see the monk's platform and few possessions there. He goes to the village everyday to teach the children.

!2.13.95 Bangkok. This is your reporter in Bangkok reporting on the arrival of the ASEAN group for meetings. These are the presidents of the Southeast Asia. (The foregoing was interrupted by a Spanish lady, blonde, blue-eyed, who bought me dinner in the coffee shop of the Bangkok Sheraton.) The Sheraton is on the river and has a wonderful coffee shop with a great view of the river and its collection of buildings, the oldest of the buildings are not much more than shacks that are up on piers and covered with corrugated tin or tar paper or slabs of wood. These are right next to beautiful high rise garden apartments and flashy hotels. The express ferries that go zipping through the water light like a dragon fly touching its tail, just long enough for its agile passengers to leap from heaving deck to heaving dock and new passengers to leap and push their way onto the already crowded ferry then off again at full speed to light at another dock a few blocks up the river. This is Bangkok's answer to the lack of subway and you can get around delightfully without the impacted traffic of the major streets. Bangkok is very much a modern city with super highways and broad boulevards but the press of traffic from its eight million is fierce. There are many shopping areas scattered widely, not one big white way. Hotels are also widely scattered. Down in the canyons between the high rise buildings, is the Orient, with its tiny shops that make walking on the sidewalk an exercise in patience. Food vendors and stuff vendors are up early and late, putting out a huge volume of stuff on the sidewalks. Back alleys are lined with more small entrepreneurs. It is all quite fascinating and enjoyable except for the grime that results from the ungoverned businesses. The traffic police wear masks to fight the pollution as do many of the motorcycle riders. The cold that I caught on the ride to Chaing Mai is much better today, sore throat gone and harsh voice cleared up. Two glasses of lemon water yesterday. I have learned to enjoy cities on this tour and Bangkok is a very enjoyable city.

The Thais are putting up Christmas and New Year decorations. The educated ones go to Protestant or Catholic schools so they know about Christmas. They still come out 99% Buddhist!

The guide on our Chaing Mai tour told about how he got his education. In his village, you don't go too far, then you have to go to a monastery to live to get more education, if you are poor. He was seven years in a monastery. The monks live on what they can beg so his diet wasn't great. He was sent to a village to educate the children there and would get an entire month of bamboo sprouts or an entire month of watermelon because that is what the local farmers were producing. The farmers do eat an elephant when it dies.

The Spanish lady who bought me lunch was involved in buying and selling great quantities of things like cement and jute but her main interest was in promoting Spanish produced machinery along with Italian machinery. She said business was booming. She had given up an excellent job in Spain to come to South East Asia with a man who later disappointed her. She has created her job herself and is doing very well as a self-employed person. She has great admiration for American women and the freedom that we represent to the rest of the world. She thought I was just wonderful to be traveling even though married. She has aunts who are not married and they travel but her mother would not think of leaving her father even for a weekend. Yeah. Well. I guess a break is nice but I certainly miss my guy. I just can't wait forever for him to decide get his nose off the grindstone and start rolling. Trouble is, he likes to travel alone also.

Here in the Hostel there is a sizeable family living. A very old man, teenagers, babies. They are back in the back somewhere. This is apparently standard, if you hire someone, you get the extended family too. Also there are sizeable families of cockroaches and rats in the community room. I don't spend much time there. My room is as clean as a whistle and the restaurant is pleasant.

12.15-95 Phuket, Thailand, actually Karon Beach. The bus trip from Bangkok was a horror that was supposed to last 14 hours and lasted 24 hours. There was a nice Brit photographer who helped me with Green the bike and Green made it through OK, riding under the bus. I had a lot of guilt riding a bus on such bikeable roads. My biggest problem here in Thailand was lack of facilities for spending the night. All hotels seem to be clustered around tourist areas which are hundreds of miles apart with nothing in between for the spoiled bicycler. If I hadn't been waiting around for Helen . . . grumble, grumble. Liz reported that she biked solo through the area and had no problem camping solo. Helen was with her group and they had no problem.

The bus dumped me in Phuket on the east side of the island and having heard that Malaysia was Muslim, I bought a plane ticket to Singapore. The bike ride to the resort area on the west side of the island was pleasant. I easily found an affordable paradise cottage and pleasant au fresco restaurant and enjoyed sipping lemon water and watching the sunset over the Indian Ocean while waiting for my grilled mackerel. How could I have wasted all those days in Bangkok? In the three days at the beach I was unable to connect with sea kayakers and paddle around the islands that are so enticing on the horizon. It is my kind of touristy here with lounge chairs and beach umbrellas, and quite warm.

I consider my cheapo spot ideal since there is a resort hotel that is next door that is as fancy as the Hyatt on Kona, Hawaii. My meter stick is the swimming pools, some up with slides to some down. But . . . I forgot the canal with boats to glide you past the shopping area in the Hawaii resort. Naw. Doesn't compare. On the big island of Hawaii, they had to hack the golf courses and pools and all out of black lava. Here there are merely round towers with a balcony for each room with flowers spilling out of the balconies. Palm trees without coconuts abound. A Japanese company seems to be having a convention here and the place is as loaded with Japanese as my little cheapie, next door, is with Chermans. I have now a chest cold which I am hoping to bake out of the system on the beach. I am having steak and potatoes here for $5.00 so it seems to be a bargain. Could have had a nice breakfast for under $4.00 but decided to splurge calories before throwing myself into a beach chair for the day. Some really ugly, starling type birds are threatening the area with their hideous presence. Adorable little Japanese kids are beginning to arrive with pool toys.

There were little puffy clouds hanging around the hills behind all this but they have gone and the sky is clear.

I do not have time to bicycle here. I spent too much time waiting around for Helen who wasn't ever really coming. I am feeling a lot of guilt over not biking in Thailand. (So why not spend today, or at least part of the day biking?????) And I could run. People, probably the Chermans, running all the time here. The Hot House Harriers meet today in the next town and if I work up the strength, I will join them. I have a bad case of the 'I'm getting fat from just sitting around' guilt. I should try to remember that just missing the attack of the Christmas Cookie Lady at home should be worth a month of Jenny Craig.

There are women here with make up on. Backpackers do not use make-up, wear dreary clothing, and in general look like the pits. So this is a change. Might get my hair done here instead of Singapore. I'll get it striped and cut and perhaps even do a perm . . . Nah. Then I need to get back to the rice diet and lots of water before trying to seduce Charles in New Zealand. Maybe I should bike today just to get rid of the steak and egg. The steak was cold, the egg was cold and the grease potatoes were cold. But, the place has a load of ambiance.

Back at my bungalow again, watching a couple of women street sweepers come down the road. Thank goodness they have a man with them to tell them how to do stuff while he stands there smoking.

12.17.95 Karon Beach, Phuket, Thailand. Jogging report. Lovely at daybreak which is around 6:00 A.M. There are other joggers out here at all hours of the day, tall Orientals (Chinese?), short Farangs, no women. There is a lovely brick sidewalk along the beach that the joggers use. It has attractive light posts every ten yards and dugouts for palm trees every five yards so it is broken field running but so pleasant. Between the beach and the sidewalk they try to stabilize the beach with lavender morning glories. There are scattered collections of royal palms on the other side of the road, interspersed with humungous resort hotels and their hard working grounds keepers. The sea is a medium blue at this hour and minimal surf. They tell me that it is great for surfing during the monsoon season when the wind comes from the other direction.

Yesterday I got a ride to Patong Beach to the Expatriate Hotel and specifically the Expatriate Bar where the Hash House Harriers were reputed to hang out. It was a movie bar and I saw Airplane II, followed by an epic with Patrick Swazie that was 'I was a surfer for the FBI' or something equally stupid. The Patrick Swazie could have been filmed in New Mexico where Jannie Leary's hubby flies for the parachute drop crazies. Anyway, the harriers trickled in, smoking, having a few beers BEFORE going out to run at 3:00 P.M. They were British accent and thoroughly tattooed. Most of them looked tough and fit, not young. They didn't talk to me at all even though I was sitting there in shorts, tee shirt and running shoes. I thought that perhaps it was a strictly male group but after a while some Thai women signed up and one red haired female Farang. They had an interesting collection of Harrier Tee shirts, from all over the world. At three they all filtered out and when I followed them, I saw them pile into a rickety bus which wandered off down the street. I went back into the air-conditioning and watched Patrick Swazie come to a well deserved bad end with the red-head who had managed to miss the bus. I decided to walk back to Karon Beach but was saved by a tuk-tuk driver who would no doubt have starved to death had I not forced 100 baht on him for driving me back to Karon.

Met Katy, the Canadian, at the Ocean View Restaurant. When I described my missing husband as a workaholic, she coined a phrase, claiming to be a 'lifeaholic.' We went shopping for a while and I mailed off cards with pictures of Nepal and the Taj Mahal on them. We tackled the USA YESTERDAY crossword but it pretty much won. She was happy to see she had missed a record snowfall that buried Buffalo. She will be home for Christmas after a year and a half traveling and working as a bartender. She bought little necklace things to hold drugs for gifts for her friends back home. She plans to go to Banff to work in a bar in a 'Big Hotel' there so I'll have to try to look her up . . . if traveling with a group permits . . . I'm imagining biking the Alcan Highway with a group.

My feet are not good. New theory: the bunion is pushing the second toe out of line and actually causing a bunion in the joint of the second toe. The chest cold has settled in and seems resistant to large doses of vitamins, Lemon (really lime) water, and lying on the beach. I wanted to get rid of it before going to Singapore or New Zealand.

12.18.95 Phuket, Thailand It is days like this that make me wonder if I'll ever make it as a tourist. I started biking from Koron Beach at a good hour and puffed some on the hills and made it in good order to Phuket only to find out at a late hour that I should have gone north up the beach to get to the airport because it is not in Phuket but on the north end of the island. By this time it was so brutally hot that I decided to take a ride. After going to a hotel which sent me to Thai Airlines which sent me to the limo place, clear across town, I was totally wilted and dehydrated. Could have been at the airport which was on a lovely beach and now has a major sunset working up over the Adaman??? Sea. Never heard of it. Is it the Bay of Bengal or the Indian Ocean? Whatever. It was nice and now they are showing a film about Thailand that has a zillion places I have never laid eyes on.

Chapter XXIX

SINGAPORE . . .

"You can't cross the sea by merely standing and staring at the water."
Tagore

12.20.95 Fantastic. I flew into Singapore in the dark and got a taxi to the YMCA. The taxi skimmed along a beautiful, modern highway. Was this different from India and Kathmandu? It was so different. The night views were of a wonderful, elegant, sparkling city with high rises and neon lights and parks along the highways. Yep. Very different from Kathmandu. The taxi rolled up into a high rise garage and I had arrived at the Singapore YMCA. As it was not a hostel, they were not ready to store Green the Bicycle. We improvised by chaining Green to a post and I went back to the desk to register. There was a bed available in a room with only four women. It was great to have arriving so smooth and simple in the middle of the night.

Singapore is clean, orderly. Traffic is sane, orderly. The teenager who was caned for spray-painting cars? Fine with me. I remember meeting a couple of girls from Singapore in England who were embarrassed about the caning of an American teenage vandal. When I sympathized, they went on to say that cars are very expensive in Singapore, equivalent of $100,000 in our money. What ever it takes to keep the varmints in line.

Anyone who thinks the Orient, just because it is the Orient, has to be dirty, needs to come here. Should I say, I needed to come here. Am I talking to myself? Gee, I love the cleanliness. It is also so amazing to have cars stop for you.

314

The city is decorated most wonderfully for Xmas. Christmas carols are everywhere and frenzied shopping and only 2% Christian!!! Everybody who is anybody is educated in Christian schools . . . and are 100% Buddhist or Taoist or Muslim or whatever they were when they went in when they come out. But Christmas is more fun and makes more money than Buddhist or Taoist festivals. Singapore's religion, like Switzerland's, is money. And then, too, no other religion has anything that is as much fun as Santa Claus.

Went to the historic Raffles Hotel for a break from the shopping malls. One roommate at the Y was a strapping, pretty, and altogether pleasant German girl, Jennifer, who wanted to practice her English. So we went cruising, even going out at night because the city seemed so safe. The Long Bar of the Raffles Hotel is famous. Raffles was the British founder of the city, working with The British East India Company. The bar and walls of the hotel are polished wood and a lazy ceiling fan dates it all as a period piece. It is really appealing, and looks like Humphrey Bogart or Sidney Greenstreet could come around the corner and order a Singapore Sling. What's in a Singapore Sling? I haven't the foggiest idea. It's pink and quite tasty. The Jennifer and I sipped our slings and exulted in throwing peanut shells on the floor. It has to be the only place in Singapore where littering doesn't get you arrested.

Jennifer wanted to hit the Top of the Westin one evening so after being checked out by a guy at the bottom of the elevator we went up. The stomach arrives a bit later than the rest of the body on the trip up to the 70th floor. There was the excellent view of the lights of this superb city. After indulging in our $15 minimum, we felt safe walking back to the YMCA. The Y is in such a handy location, next to the museum, right on Orchard Street. We have walked to most of the attractions.

The Museum next door has a room where you can experience the A-bomb blowing up at Hiroshima, by being thrown about and bombarded by sound. Singapore is mostly Chinese and the Chinese have no fondness for Japan, especially here in Singapore where the Japanese occupation was particularly cruel. So what is the point at this museum? James Clavell, author of *Shogun* tells about spending the war in Changi Prison near Singapore in his book, "*King Rat.*" The prisoners were very much afraid that the Japanese would kill them all, just from frustration, as the war ended. When the Atom Bomb went off, the ending came so suddenly that the Japanese just left the prison camp. Disappeared and left the prisoners alive. The controversy at the Smithsonian to apologize for the bomb seems pretty silly out here or to the guys who were in the Navy like my dear Charles. If we had not used the bomb and had to invade Japan, many, many more Americans would be dead. Charles was on a destroyer headed for Japan when the bomb went off. The father of my children was spared by dropping the atom bomb on Hiroshima and Nagasaki to live a long and pleasant life. A lot of Japs lived a longer life also.

A terrible typhoon struck around that time and took a toll of lives, probably almost as many as the bomb. Before the people who revise history forget, let's remember that before the first bomb, the people of Hiroshima were warned to get out. The first bomb was exploded and Hirohito was given, by President Truman, chance to save Nagasaki. He didn't surrender and Nagasaki was atomized. Did Hirhito ever apologize to the citizens of Nagasaki? They are on his conscience, not ours.

Jennifer and I went touring on an ornate junk and got a good look at the port as well as the various sections of high-rises that pop up out of the low lying land like an architect's dream. We stopped at a little island. There was a cone shaped hill on the island with a Taoist shrine. I climbed to the top of this and put in a good word, and small donation at the shrine, for Tom, Terry, and Charley and their hopes for more children. We picked up with Brian from San Francisco who was a businessman, not a tourist. He and Jennifer went off somewhere. I begged off because of fatigue. Faxed Chas last night and got no reply. Tried again tonight. Bought a book about New Zealand. Lots of stuff in English here.

2.20.95 Expatriate Xmas. I keep trying to remind myself of all the annoyances of Christmas, most of all the probability of gaining an unwanted 10 lbs. while feasting on as many freebies as possible. I have never been known to turn down an invitation to food, or an urging to stuff myself to a point beyond mere pain and gas. That these extra pounds have in later years involved clandestine visits to Jenny Craig who questions every greedy thought I have ever had . . . . The skinny young things who are the counselors are really interested only in the very expensive food they sell but I'm a sucker for this every time because I haven't the after X-mas strength to do the right kind of penance for over-indulgence. What I would like, really, is a scheme for balancing the calories expended in such things as cross-country skiing and the eating of a deluxe lunch at the restaurant in the barn on Rt. 31. Charles confesses that his "downtown clothes" have shrunk to the point that he can't zip them. My first thought was that I haven't been there, he can't blame me for too much fond indulgence. He blames Christmas. Very properly so.

However, to not be home for the holidays is such bad planning. Being without family is just too painful to think about. The daughter and company from North Carolina are going to make the awful winter trip to Pittsburgh with me not there. They will have a real Christmas without me, but I haven't got much going without them. They are going to eat in the restaurant where we take honored guests to Pittsburgh, on Mt. Washington with the unexcelled view of the city. I love it there. Damn. Kitty's group is bringing a Rumanian exchange student. The honored guest. They will also enjoy one last time in the Seven Springs ski resort condo before it is sold.

12.21.95 Singapore. Now that I have done most of the tours, what? Rest day. Swim here at the Y. The pool is on the roof and very nice. Did I mention that Singapore is on the Equator? The weather is great. Temperature great. I jogged already. My feet still feel terrible but the rest of me is good. When I settle in to write on the Zaurus, it is at a McDonald's located in the YMCA building. Here I am surrounded by all the ugliest US entertainers. Can you believe that that slut Madonna sings Christmas? In a YMCA you would think they could discriminate between her kind of trash and the "Jesus Met Me in the Garden," and "He Was Incredibly

Cool, ya ya ya" popstuff that you get for absolutely free in the Y's own cafe. The USA is loved all over the world: Mickey Mouse to Mick Jagger, blue jeans and Coca Cola. All the really classy stuff.

Reading the background of the Moari tribe of New Zealand brings to the fore what the US has to offer the world. The Moaris, like the Hindus had a caste system. People's lack of faith in themselves and a desire to not have to make decisions so often puts them in places where they have no choice about their own life. So many religions, so many political systems depend on this desire to just occupy a niche in the great stream of things and let life happen to you. The contented hordes of Hindu, Tao, Buddhism, look at our movies and wonder and then put on their blue jeans and go back to the slot into which they were born to suck a coca cola. Why can't we sell the really different USA? Why is it so hard to make people understand that wealth is created by individuals that have a great idea and work on it. Well, gee, Tiger Balm. The guy who came up with Tiger Balm and vigorously markets it is now very wealthy. He had no help from the government, robbed no one, is giving lots of people work. That is so capitalistic, so like the USA. The other thing about the US is the ferocious competition to do things well, to be the one who does something best. The real USA isn't Madonna and Coca Cola while it is also, of course, Madonna and Coca Cola.

12.21.95 Singapore, Singapore. Singapore offered to be part of Malaysia but was turned down because it wasn't Muslim.

I did a lot of serious shopping for a camcorder for Chas. I fired faxes to him and he fired them back and we finally decided things were cheaper in the US and the repair service would be better if he just bought it at home. Ever since spending time with Linda, I thought he should have one. I have the idea that we could make travel videos for the grandchildren that might even be saleable.

The stores were wonderfully decorated for Christmas. They are decorated way beyond the stores at home. Office buildings have building high banners. One has huge Disney characters that move. Perhaps I should stay here for Christmas. Jennifer has moved on.

12.22.95 Singapore, last day. My choice for roommate of the year was up at 5:30 to start packing. The moving van will be here soon, no doubt. Could it be that she is moving because of me? I asked the guys at the desk yesterday if it was OK to cook in the rooms. That is all I said. Not one word more. They said no, not permitted and the eyebrows shot up. Oh, now, wouldn't it be terrible if I had caused her problems?

She had completely taken over the room. I put all but the most essential of my stuff in storage so I wouldn't have to worry about it. I slept on the rest of it. My experience with her type of Japanese Princess is that they will also steal you blind. I haven't met anyone as obnoxious in a hostel since Saltzburg. That time, as here, there was cooking in the room, a forbidden activity. There, as here, the tiny, pretty Japanese had filled every space in the room like an obnoxious gas. There, they went through my stuff and took souvenirs, Swiss Army knife, Gortex rain jacket, just some nice things that I wouldn't miss until I needed them. It was a long time before I was able to assess the damage. So, older and wiser, I put almost everything in storage this time. It may be that this royal pain was ill and that is why she didn't get up until noon yesterday. Then she wanted to mess around late but I very firmly insisted on lights out at ten. So she was up at 5:30 this A.M., cooking her smelly food.

I am deep into reading about New Zealand and preparing an itinerary for Chas and myself from Christ Church. Now, if she leaves, I can use the desk for writing. It had been a stove and refrigerator. I was told that bicycling was not allowed on the island of Singapore so I left poor Green to lean against her pillar. Someone came along to paint the pillar white and painted a lot of Green white, too. Should that person be caned?

PART 4

NEW ZEALAND AND
THE ISLANDS

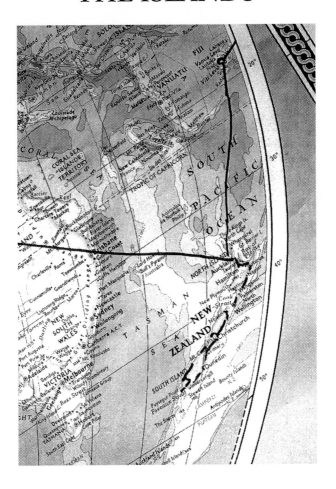

Chapter XXX

New Zealand

"I know God promises not to give me more than I can handle. I just wish he didn't trust me so much."

Mother Teresa

12.23.95 Aukland. Great travel day. I double checked to be sure that my plane was leaving Singapore at 10:45 PM or 20:45 and no problem. It was and did. Thank goodness I made a big effort to get to the airport very early so that I could be only astonished when the check-in girl told me I had only seven minutes to catch the plane. Oh well. Not too tough with Green ready to roll. One of these days I'll be able to manage a twenty-four hour clock. I hate never having been past the 'Mickey's big hand is on the Minutes' stage. Saw a nice, silly movie on the plane about Santa Claus which reaffirms m y opinion that the reason the people of Singapore are so nuts about Christmas is that it is fun. Santa is just more amusing stuff like Disney or Ronald McDonald.

There was a pleasant van ride to a wonderful room at the Aukland YMCA. At $30 per night it is relatively expensive but I love having it to myself, the tremendous view and a beautiful quilt and a great desk with a light over it, looking out on the view. It is on a hill and I am on the 5th floor. I can see across the downtown area to a major bridge that shoots cars over a bay to Northcote, a major suburb. The bad thing is that is like the hostels in England, the windows are wide open and the heat is on. And the heat is needed. After being right on the Equator at Singapore, I feel chilled all the time here. I am constantly closing windows.

The traffic is very light but then a lot of shops are not open because of Christmas. The bike shop was open and Green will get a new computer, her third. I always take the computer off the bike when I leave it. So, one computer went through a washing machine and dryer and the next one disappeared with my tool kit on the plane trip between Kathmandu and Bangkok. $79.00 NZ or $49 US. Since it will give me cadence, hopefully it will be worth it. I walked all the way down town to a bookstore to get a USA TODAY but they just had Thursdays, which I already have. Time Magazine, with Newt Gingrich as Man of the Year was a $1 cheaper than USA TODAY at $3.95 NZ!!!! I may have to live without crosswords puzzles for a while.

Later: Dozed for a while. It has been raining some and the weather report threatens two more days of the same. Rain had not occurred to me as a problem, even after Singapore's daily deluge. It is supposed to be dry season here but the natives say it has been a strange summer so far with cold spells and lots of rain. I ended up buying a rain suit at a store called Kathmandu. It is dark green, not the best color for a biker on a wet road, but I love it and wear it everywhere. I got a hat that says Kathmandu on it. I love the hat, too.

A problem here where everyone speaks English is that the English speakers don't hang together in little knots. I have picked an expensive bar with loads of character that is connected to the Sheraton for lunch. Many of the restaurants and most of the businesses are closed with the notice that they won't open until after New Years! This is not the same money grubbing attitude as Singapore. I should have stayed in Singapore.

On the way here was a guy with a foreign accent who wanted to know where I was going. My snappy conversation stopper to this question is, 'Out.' It was what my youngest kid would respond when I would ask him where he was going. 'Out.'

If I persisted and asked the next question,

"What are you going to do?"

His conversation stopper was:

"Rape, steal, mug, pillage, etc., etc."
To which I could only respond,
"Well, be home by 10:00."
12.24.95 Auckland. I met Lord Auckland today. He is in bronze in a small park. Handsome dude. Back in those days when they did a statue it was to show a guy in his prime, not when he got old and shriveled.

There is a lovely bookstore downtown that has an excellent collection of magazines. In a Kiwi triathlon monthly was son Mac's name for wining the Duathlon World Championships in Cancun, Mexico. Makes a momma proud.

Reading through the magazine, I find that they are just coming into the Triathlon season in New Zealand. What do I do? Triathlons. What have I never accomplished? An Ironman.

What is coming along very soon? The Kiwi Ironman. So, I am thinking of signing up for the New Zealand Ironman which is March 3. If it isn't too late. I am so energized by this. So happy. It just does seem right to me. The Tri will be held in Auckland. Don't know what I will do for a bike. Green is a Mountain bike with fat tires. How about Chas brings Frisky my Vitus racing bike and takes Green back? Too complicated? I am going to try to enter it! There was another newsprint publication that listed lots and lots of triathlons. So, after much pouring over the list, I chose two races to do in preparation: a short one about 100 miles from Auckland and a half-Ironman a week after that in Tauranga. Then I can go on to the South Island to bike with Chas then back to Auckland to work out for the big one. I will have to change my plane ticket again, and there will not be time for Australia.

Christmas Eve, I had dinner in a deserted bar, in Auckland, New Zealand, that was serving turkey. I stared at an old gent with a red nose, his only resemblance to Santa. He downed four glasses of wine and staggered out the door. Then I went down a block to the movie theater and paid good money to get so scared that my teeth chattered as I left the theater. Only an apple pie with rum raisin ice cream and coffee at the Carlton stopped the chattering.

Seven was the name. I only went because I like Brad Pitt and Morgan Freeman. It wasn't nice of them to do a really good job and scare me to the teeth chattering state.

Christmas Day, 1995. Got up early and dressed warmly in running clothes and after making a reservation at the International Hostel for the 26th, had breakfast standing by a trailer on a side street by the docks because nothing else was open. Then I caught a ferry to Waiheke Island. Such a place. A neighbor, Jim Bashford, talks about how nice it would be to live in New Zealand. Yes, especially Waiheke Island. Wonderful. Rolling hills with sheep and steep rugged cliffs and sandy beaches with slow rolling surf and many islands on the seascape. I took a nice long slow jog around the small island. When I got back to Auckland the only place open was a Chinese restaurant and they were closing early for Christmas.

"What do you do on Christmas," I asked, "are you Christian?"

"Oh, no," was the reply. "We just have a family time and exchange gifts."

I forgot to call home where they were awaiting my call! The Zaurus is good for showing what time it is in Pittsburgh but I didn't use it. Depressed is depressed.

From my wonderful window at the Y, I can see not only the harbor, the gracefully curving bridge, a huge billboard that has only a flower on it and 'Flora's Famous Massage' with a phone number. Another place I saw a sign that advertised 'Massage and Escort Service.' My masseuse in Pittsburgh is at the YMCA and very respectable. It is a different world here.

Christmas away from home is such poor planning. How could I have done this to myself? Is it just to complete something I started, even when it has come to seem incredibly stupid? I am still hopelessly in love with my husband and I have left him for such a, long time with another long stretch coming up after a short togetherness. And the worst is that there is no one else to blame it on. I like to get together with my kids more than anything. What am I doing here? Well, forgetting to call home.

12.26.95 Moved to the Hostel to save $12 per day. There is lots of company here. I did a tour of the city with a couple of middle aged ladies and then took a ferry to the nearest island. I was told that I would have to take a ferry to Devonport because bicycles are not allowed on the beautiful bridge that I could see from my window. A Maori ticket taker for the ferry said that he had a relative playing for the Steelers. Said that a lot of New Zealanders were cheering for the Steelers!

On the other side, I biked a few miles to the headquarters of the triathlon and gave them the huge check and got the info. I was just under the deadline. That was my last happy moment.

Since then I have been anguished about finishing the Tri. I will bike to Oputere where there is a short tri on New Year's weekend. I bought a book of bike routes. I will be leaving tomorrow. I will take the train out of the city a while, as recommended by the bike book, then an 80 mile bike.

12.27.95 Thames. North Island. Pronounced Teems. I got a bit lost after the train ride but a nice young man on a racing bike helped me out. I made it to Thames in spite of only one restaurant open all day. Thames is in an area of very high tides and flat beaches because we are so far from the Equator. When the tide is out it is pretty drab with vast stretches of gravel. The town is alright but not fancy. The Backpackers hostel is a notch down from the international hostels. I find it disagreeable because men and women have to share the same bathroom. Stupid for women to permit this. I always complain when ever it happens.

12.28.95 Oputere, New Zealand.

Article for Health and Fitness

I have reached the famed Coromandel Peninsula. I am biking across the base of the peninsula to a place called Oputere. It is quite hilly and there have not been many homes lately. I am on a downhill in a very wild and pretty area of fragrant pine trees. There is a pull-off area on the left side of the road. That is my side of the road because this New Zealand and used to be part of THE EMPIRE. There are three white pickup trucks parked, nose in, in the pull-off. Three men are working on a fence or a gate at what appears to be a driveway entrance. The driveway goes down and is steep.

He was dark, passionate, breathing heavily. He just bumped me to catch my attention at first. That worked. A huge electrifying bolt of energy went through me. I had no time to think, to defend myself, to discuss it with him. I screamed, knowing help was not very far away but I had passed the trucks, was on a down hill, and getting further from the help by the second. I picked the leg closest to him off the pedal and tried to think of how to kick him. That is when his teeth sunk in and I saw blood spurt out of the gash in my leg. He seemed so big: dark brown with black brindle markings. The bull mastiff stopped and I continued on down the hill screaming. I pulled off the road at a wide space and stopped when I was sure he was gone and continued screaming. I saw a truck pull out of the place where the dog had been and start down the hill. I reached down to my leg and touched it and when I looked at my hand it was covered with blood and some lumpy stuff that I figured had come out of my body. I screamed a whole lot more. Two trucks pulled up and their owners got out to confront the hysterical creature that I was.

"I want that dog quarantined. I have to get to a doctor."

"Yes, Mam. We'll take you to Thames to the hospital."

They shuffled around loading Green on the truck and taking a lot of abuse, the full opinion of owners who think they need to be protected from aging grannies by huge, rotten dogs: dogs bred and trained to kill things.

As they tied the bike down, I bitterly pointed out that that self same rope could have been used to tie the dog. That some people have more concerned for their dog to be free than that innocent people be free of dog bites, etc., etc., etc.

It didn't hurt much, just burned. When we got to the hospital I walked into the emergency room, showing them a hand full of blood, saying,

"Dogbite. He got my leg. This is from my leg."

They were very careful with the blood that had soaked my sock and shoe.

"I want the police informed. The dog quarantined. I suppose I have to get rabies shots," weeping some tears of self pity.

The nurse was calm, "Oh, I dint think rebbies."

The guy who had taken all the abuse driving me turned out to be the owner. He had had the dog for two weeks. He got the dog at the pound. It seemed OK, played with the children.

"The only good thing about this is that he got me instead of a child," I said. "A rotten dog like that can really tear up a child."

The previous owner had left the creature tied to the fence at the pound. Golly, who could leave a fine animal like that that way????

The doctor finally arrived. My leg was mauled and swollen but appeared to be mostly there. No stitches. No need for rabies shots. They don't have rabies in New Zealand. Two days off the bike and two days out of the salt water.

"Doctor, I just spend $395 (NZ) to enter the Kiwi Ironman. Am I going to be able to swim 2.5 miles and bike 114 and run a full marathon by March 3rd ?"

"Oh, I think so," answered the doctor. "Just a couple of days off your feet."

And I'll be able to finish an Ironman. Terrific! I never could before!"

12/31/95 New Years Eve. I guess I don't really like parties all that much. I used to like parties but my hearing is such that the noise clutter of parties is just frustrating. Then there is the over-eating, loud obnoxious music. Yeah, well, I will admit to being the over-eater. I was at a charming hostel called Oputere where the tradition is a barbecue for New Year's Eve. It was very pleasant and I lasted until little things started biting the ankles, even in spite of bug spray and socks. So I left interesting conversations to hide on my room, scratching, and finish reading Conrad's great sea epic, *Lord Jim*. I was in bed by 10:00 only to be awakened by the crowd counting down to midnight.

I got up again and joined the group for a ragged *Auld Lang Sang* and a taste of champagne and was driven to bed this time by so called music, very loud, from a speaker with a broken tweeter. It would have been the same at home where New Year's is a much anticipated, full dress bash at a friend's house. Eventually, as the younger folk get drunker the music gets louder and there comes that point at which my roommate and I look at each other and sigh and head for the door. There is always snow and ice in the yard. There is the tripping out to the car in heels, (the only time I wear them all year) and the fur jacket is cold and there is the worry that someone will have slid into the beloved sports car which is usually sitting out on the road. I'm the designated driver but the roommate is still under the legal limit so he drives home.

New Year's Day we have pork and sauerkraut for as many people as we can find, family or friends.

1/1/96 What should come to the hostel but two American women, mother and daughter, on bicycles. Mom changes the dressings on my wound. The daughter says they haven't biked much, they are too unnerved by the New Zealand drivers. They have found the dogs to be friendly.

Mother has a husband at home that she misses, but she hates Christmas, Santa, carols, tinsel, presents and all. A woman after my own heart. New Zealand is a great choice if you are trying to avoid Christmas. Last year she spent the holiday on Maui. Now it is ten minutes to midnight in Pittsburgh. Himself will be duded up in his tux, if he can get into it. He looks so cute in it.

I decided to stay here another day and bus it to Tauranga. I really feel lethargic. Could be the antibiotics. I felt good only on the day I forgot to take them and I sleep like a rock every night with no complaints about screaming from my roommates. I did enjoy taking the hostel's kayak by way of a tidal inlet, to the ocean. If you don't plan the return well, you can get stuck a long way out when the tide goes out and be dragging the kayak back through a mile of mud. Lots of joggers in Wangamata. Scott Tinley???? I'm sure it was Scott. Haven't seen him since San Diego where he, or his look alike, was running in the quay. He is threatening to come out of retirement to challenge my son Mac in age-group triathlons. With the Ironman coming up here in Aukland, it could be the great one. I asked him to put air in my tires at a tri once and he was so sweet and did that.

Later: The ride to Waihi was very hilly with the crazy volcano tops crowded in together and the twisted little road going up and down. The tree ferns seemed to be practicing clever ways to uncurl their new fronds, some up, some down. These ferns are large as trees and are the symbol of New Zealand, not the Kiwi bird which is nocturnal and very shy. The bus took an hour and didn't mind carrying the bicycle. It involved another $10 and wrapping the pedals to get Green on the bus which costs me $11. Biking would have taken me all day. The one good thing was that there wasn't all that much traffic. The road surface smooth but narrow. Waihi's stores have false fronts is like a town in our old West but surrounded by the upside down ice cream cone hills.

1.3.96 Taranga. Not yet there, just leaving Wangamata by bus. I stayed an extra day in Oputere because I felt so tired and besides, it was right up there as one of the best hostels. The managers, a married couple with kids, were the most thoughtful and caring.

1.04.96 Taranga, North Island The reporter from the Pittsburgh Post Gazette called and I spent a long time on the phone with him. Then the local paper came by to interview me. Media darling.

1.05.96 Taranga. A young couple of bicyclers from Seattle arrived at the hostel yesterday and were fun to talk to. Info: Ferries ($300) leave from Bellingham, Washington for Juneau, Alaska on Fridays. You need a reservation to get a cabin or you have to sleep on the deck. Other ferries leave from Vancouver for Ft.????? but then there are more ferries to Alaska. Ferries are no cheaper than the air flight and take three wonderful days. Perhaps Ole's schedule is best after all and one should arrive in Anchorage, Alaska around the first of June. If I could streak up the West Coast and Chas join me for the trip to Juneau then bike to Fairbanks and come back down . . . That was the suggestion of the fellow from Seattle. Some how it seems better to come down from Alaska than to go up to Alaska. Most important is scheduling around the mosquitoes.

I need to get to a library and collect some info on Canada and Alaska. Tauranga is another enjoyable town. It is bigger than any of the other towns I have been in. Lots of restaurants, a movie theater and a couple of bike shops. I came to Taranga to prepare for the Ironman but I am losing heart about signing up for a 1/2 Ironman at the end of the week. I should try to remember that I was the US Champ in 1993 for this distance and my age group. The championship was in the Texas Hill country. I usually take energy bars and cut them into bite-sized pieces. They glue themselves to the bike frame and are there for the tri. In Texas, they fell off and I had no snack. In the run, I saw some pieces of energy bar lying on the street. I was so hungry I picked them up to eat. Mistake. The candy was covered with fire ants.

The local paper came around to interview me because of being so old or foreign or something. Media darling.

I rented a bike that was far from a racing bike but at least didn't have fat tires. It didn't have the gears that I needed for the hills.

1.6.06 Tauranga, New Zealand. Here's how to get an intimate look at Tauranga: a half-Ironman. First 2100 meters of the bay at the foot of Mt Maungaunui: For this I had bought a wet suit at a second hand store. I had a terrible time just trying the wretched things on and they were being especially obnoxious to the dog bite on the left leg. The one I bought was too large for me, had short sleeves and legs. Too late, I realized during the swim that it was trying to saw off my left arm and right side of my neck. Little things bother you in a race. I needed goggles that would permit me to look ahead and see what is there instead of having to look a through a corner of the glasses. Finally a cute girl on a paddle boat took pity on my Mr. Magoo attempts to see and paddled beside me to show me the way. Unfortunately she didn't know the bay too well and we ended up fighting the current while the rest of the competitors swam out of it closer to shore. The swim was, nevertheless, pleasant if a tad long but everyone left me behind. This doesn't usually happen. I am a pretty good swimmer and can keep up. Perhaps it was a measure of how few older people were in the event.

It took me an hour to finish the swim and get myself together for the bike. I wore bike shoes because they seem to be better for my feet but even they caused pain and I had to stop the bike and just stand a while to get the pain in the right foot to stop toward the end of the bike segment. I messed up the drinks thinking that the opportunity offered to give the officials your own drink bottle also meant that they would also furnish drinks like in the US. Not so. No drinks. By the end of the first bike loop I had stomach cramps, headache, severe back ache and shooting pains in the left leg and other symptoms of dehydration. Did I fail to mention cruel neck pain? I wanted to quit at the end of the first loop. I had not bought aerobars. I really missed them. It was a hot, sunny, windy ride but nice and well, I could just hear the leader of our jogging club, Hot Harry, complaining about Pittsburgh's North Park Marathon. It went around the five mile perimeter of North Park Lake five times and Harry said the worst thing about it was having to pass up his car (and the chance to quit and go home) that many times. Loops can be tough psychologically.

I tried to quit at the end of the first 25 mile bike loop but they shooed me on through the turnaround and back out I went for another 25 miles of pain. After finishing the bike, I wandered around a lot at the bike/run exchange, messing with shoes, shirt, hat, and trying to find something other than water for sustenance. I must have been last at that point, because they sent a mountain biker out with me. He had no water bottle or anything to drink. I set off around the dirt track at the foot of the mountain. The mountain is a conical volcano with a 3-mile track around the bottom. It is incredibly beautiful with rocks, pounding surf and twisted trees. It compared well with pictures I have seen of the Monterrey Peninsula. I just puttered along enjoying the view until my left leg felt too weak to run and I got dizzy.

This is your body talking: "quit."

So I did, with 10 miles of running not done. As I was crawling back to the start/finish line in ignominious defeat, I was stopped by some people from Seattle who gave me a beer and I sat and chatted on their porch with them for a while. New Zealanders are mad for triathlons and were in great cheering groups all along the course. I really like being here in such a spirit of enthusiasm for my sport. Sorry I didn't finish the course but it was a good workout. The minute I stopped I felt fine. Tired but fine. As the young Britts would say, sarcastically, "Brilliant."

1.08.96 Tauranga. Housekeeping day. Returned the rented bike and sold back the wet suit. The suit left a rough spot on my neck that several doctors have looked at and have no cure for. It gets rough and itchy in hot weather. I jogged the estuary on the wooden walkways that take you out among the water birds. Every time I am on such a lovely trail I get angry all over again at the demagoguery of the hiking/biking trail opposition in my hometown. The leader of the opposition achieved political prominence fussing about "the element." Leader of the haters. Boss of the bigots. King of the Park Killers.

1.9.96 Tauranga. At the airport where I am a bit early, having coffee. How happy I am. Chas plane is on schedule. Pittsburgh is having terrible weather and the airport had been shut down. He had a FAX waiting when I got up. That does make it a good day. This airport is small but so nice, with one paved (sealed) strip, fabulous mimosa in the foreground and the estuary then Tauranga in the background. Life after the around the world trip has to include New Zealand. How about an around the world X-Country ski trip? Norway, Sweden, Germany, Finland, Siberia, Alaska, Canada. What happened to New Zealand? Too warm.

The plane is a two engine prop. I'm hoping for some fabulous views. Window seat. I am just so happy.

Later: Christ Church, South Island, New Zealand is precious. Love it. It is just like England: cloudy, chilly, fantastic flowers, clean. I biked in from the airport, no traffic, 10k. After a nap, I jogged in the Botanical garden, which is right across the street from the hostel, as is the museum. The garden is just wonderful, from roses to rock gardens to enormous eucalyptus trees. It is quite large and a lot of people jog here. Perfect temperature for jogging.

Later I went for a stroll from the hostel, which is also across the street from the very quaint cafe where I am sitting. This is in a group of teddibly English buildings, gray Tudor. What a great menu. I'm having a baked potato and a glass of milk. Chas will love this. The room in the hostel is so nice. It is an old mansion with high ceilings and we have three windows and a fireplace in our little wing where we are the only ones. It looks out on the cafe which is such a pleasant, green, outdoor cafe scene. It is just the kind of too fussy stuff I like to sketch. I absently ordered milk, making this a half gallon of milk I have drunk today.

There is a personable little stream called the Avon which meanders through the city, lovingly protected by grassy banks and sheltering willows. On this stream you may rent time in a punt with its young man in white slacks, shirt and the hat that is called a boater. *Three Men in a Boat* country. There is a theater connected with the cafe and the play, *Wind in the Willows* is sold out for tonight. Ah Mr. Toad, my hero: Adventure, excitement, change!

1.10.96 Christ Church. We managed to miss each other at the airport, of course, but he found the Hostel easily and we enjoyed all the things that I knew he would like. I had a bunch of reservations and there was not time to bike to Kaikoura so we took the little tourist train. We were able to get on a whale watching boat and were delighted to see several humpback whales. The next day we had wanted to swim with the dolphins but those boats were booked so we went off to swim with the seals instead. Being so close to the seal colony was fascinating. The males grumped at males and females fed babies and occasionally one of them would come in to swim with those of us waiting in the water. They would go by like a torpedo. It can hardly be said that I swam with them but I could see them flashing by under water and that was a thrill. One seal caught an octopus and thrashed around with it, tearing it to pieces and chomping down the pieces.

Chas wanted to go whale watching the next day but the weather turned bad and the boats didn't go out. We went back to Christ Church where Chas worked on the bikes and we dined in the cafe and heard the haunting music of Audiemus that will go so well with New Zealand: *Songs of Sanctuary*. The full voice singing crowd on the tape sounds just like the Maoris but is, unbelievably, only one Irish woman.

1.14.96 Greymouth, Westside, New Zealand. The train took us up and over Arthur's Pass. They permitted us to get off and look around at the pass. It was a ghost town. The gorges were enjoyable and some snow was visible on the mountains. Later, I jogged around Greymouth while Chas caught up on lost sleep. The harbor area was interesting. There are a lot of sea walls to protect the town but it gets flooded anyhow. Seems to me that they could have built further up the hill.

1.15.96 Franz Joseph Glacier. First day of bicycling. Great day, the sunniest in New Zealand so far. It was warm and flat. There were headwinds from about 10:00 AM. We never did get much breakfast until noon. Left Greymouth around 7:30 and arrived in Ross around 2:00 where we waited to be picked up by the bus for Franz Joseph Glacier. We had biked 42 miles and it would have been that much again to get to Franz Joseph, so we were well pleased with the arrangement and also for the hostel reservation system that gave us a pleasant room while others were being turned away. The area we went through was as charming as Greece with the ocean on one side and snow capped mountains on the other.

The Franz Joseph Village had tourist charm and pricey food with scrambled eggs and toast at $7.50. We went to a great omnimax theater presentation that showed flying over the Glacier.

1.16.95 Franz Joseph Glacier. Article for Health and Fitness:

"The Maori legend of the glacier is that a Maori maiden named Hine-Hukatere was a most unusual Maori because she liked to climb mountains while Maoris were fisher and plains people and did not like to mess around in mountains. Her boyfriend, Tawe, was a courageous fisherman and hunter but had a fear of heights. She got lonesome while climbing and issued an ultimatum to him that he had to climb to the top of the mountain or they were through. They went to the top of the mountain. It was a nice walk up and they sat to have lunch and enjoyed the view of the ocean . . .

on the way down . . . he slipped and fell. She grabbed him but could not hold him and he rolled and tumbled all the way to the bottom. She wept many bitter, tears. The gods froze her tears for a monument to their love, and the glacier is called by the Maori Karoimata-o-Hinehukatere or "tears of the Avalanche Girl."

So anyhow, Chas and I signed up for the guided excursion to the glacier, having no idea that this walk was in the same category as hang gliding, sky diving, and bungee jumping (all popular here in New Zealand). We got fitted for REAL hobnailed boots, with nails sticking out of the bottom and metal tips on the toes, and wooly socks and heavy, warm, and rainproof jackets. There was a bus ride to the glacier. The glacier got bigger and bigger as we approached it and the ice was in very large, untidy cracks and crevices. It was not smooth like glaciers we have seen in the US and Canada. As we got closer the cracks became larger and a big, black cave that is made by the river that rushes out from under the glacier grew and grew. A group of people were climbing straight up the blue ice of the glacier.

"Not me. This is not my thing," I said. "Big mistake for me to be here."

"Well, just give it a try," says my soul mate.

The group sat on ice blocks to change clothes. I put on the wooly socks and hobnailed boots. Just as we got to a fragile aluminum ladder that was a warning of horrors to come, a Volkswagen-sized piece of ice came crashing down and landed not twenty feet from us.

"Gets noisy sometimes," said our attractive girl guide with a confident smile.

When do you really detest children? When they are making you feel especially old. Three youngsters scrambled up the aluminum ladder and disappeared up the ice steps. I lumbered up the ladder feeling as graceful as Frankenstein's monster. Then came a short series of steps, climbed with the help of a hand-over-hand rope. This was NOT in the brochure. The steps, hacked out of the ice, led to a crevasse with 3-ft. gap to the ice path on the other side. I couldn't see the bottom of this crevasse because it curved under. One of the guides had been helping every one across the gap but he wasn't there when I got to the crevasse. There was a rope dangling into the crevasse of baby blue ice. If I slipped I would be hanging in it with my weak little hands clinging to this rope.

"Done," I said. "I'm done."

I started back down.

So, now the guide scrambled down to help. I descended carefully, only remembering at the last second that I was deserting my job as camera carrier. Himself had the video and I had the Nikon.

"No problem," his voice slid down the ice from the out-of-sight climbers.

"Go back of the safety rope," advised the guide. Remembering the chunk of glacier that had crashed down, I found my shoes and a nice spot, far from falling ice, to watch the climbers and thought about Mt Kathadin in Maine to which I had dragged my roommate and he had climbed it and I didn't. How is it that I sign up for stuff like this never remembering my acrophobia until I have become totally involved? Then, my spouse ends up climbing to the top of things he never imagined. He says there is a new scientific discovery that people like I am have a weird chromosome. Yah? well, he married me. So what's in his smart alec DNA?"

1.17.96 Hast, Westland, NZ. Day of just enjoying being. Did nothing at all. Sort of embarrassing. We wimped out totally on biking, lolled around in a real motel, and who should come along but a Backroads bicycle group. We had met a Backroads group in Hatteras, NC. This particular bunch was tough. They had done one 100 mile day and tomorrow expected to do a 90 miler over Hast Pass. Today has been just a 20 miler into a very tough headwind and they are tired. We decided to do half that distance by bus and then bike the last half of the day tomorrow into Wanaka

1.18.96 Wanaka, New Zealand. Bussed and biked a huge park today. The bus hauled us over Hast pass and we biked 48 miles to

Wanaka. It seemed hard, probably because we didn't start biking until 1:00. I walked a lot of hills, fulfilling the New Zealand appellation for bicycles: they call them "push bikes." It is so beautiful here, a biker's paradise with blue lakes and skies and scenery like Glacier Park. There are almost as many bikes as cars. The roads are good and the weather great.

1.19.96 Queensland, New Zealand. We biked in and found a really nice hostel. The views of this lake were so fine. We took an antique ferry across to a restaurant and after an excellent dinner were treated to a show by the local border collies who herd sheep.

01/20/96 Te Anau, New Zealand. I bussed from Queensland because of distance and digestive attack. I really must stay away from mussels. We had dinner last night in such a lovely spot that I hate to complain but the mussels were gamey. Te Anu is quite beautiful and we rested. Chas is also suffering from travelers complaint so we are at a rather low level.

The next day we were in great shape to do Milford Sound. This involved a long bus ride and then a mid-sized boat that worked its way out the sound to the ocean. We saw lots of seals and the delightful dusky dolphins who stood on their tails for us. There were outstanding waterfalls with at least a four hundred foot drop into the Sound.

The next day, I loafed on the bus while Chas biked to Invercargill.

1.21.96 The bus rolled right up to the hostel door, just as the driver had said it would and we unloaded our bikes. For the last time. At least I thought it was for the last time.

When I got the dates for Chas' arrival from the US and departure from Christchurch, I set up an ambitious itinerary. As it turned out, there were very few days when we could actually make the distances that I had scheduled. I had confirmed reservations with a series of hostels and after we watched people being turned away from fully booked hostels, we decided that it was really important to be at the hostels at the correct time. Then we discovered the convenience of the intercity bus system. What a break!

I had the very earnest desire to see everything in the brochures and guide books. This began to conflict with the necessarily slow pace of bicycling and I found myself substituting the public transportation for the biking. The first substitution was to take the train from Christchurch to Kaikoura and then back again and to the end of the train line in Greymouth. From Greymouth our first day of bicycling took us as far as Ross where we waited for a bus to take us to Franz Joseph. The bus was great because we would not have had time to reserve a glacier walk for the next day. Leaving Franz Joseph we bussed all the way to Haast and took a day off. The next day we caught the late bus which obligingly dropped us off at Makarora and we biked on in to Wanaka. We biked 52 K from Wanaka to Cromwell and bussed up to Queenstown arriving in time to take the dinner cruise on a boat.

That was the dinner that made us sick and we had to bus to Te Anau hostel or miss our chance to do Milford Sound. John Sinclair was much in my mind as I biked today. He was a neighbor and President of the North Hills JC's when they sponsored and marshaled and helped raise money for a bicycle race that I was in charge of in Bellevue, Pa. So he was a friend and shortly after the race he had a terrible catastrophe. He was a roofer and fell from a three story building. When I visited him in the hospital, he was really a mess, all broken up. He's OK now but was really shaken up then. He said,

"I didn't think of my life. It didn't pass before my eyes. I just thought: "This is really going to hurt."

How often I have thought of that. Especially in India. Riding a bus in from Dehli to the Taj, we had such a bad driver. He must have aimed at every one of the myriad of potholes. We would bounce out of our seats if we didn't brace ourselves to keep from being painfully thrown around. Eighty-seven year old Franz and I were suffering real bruises. Our driver, driver A, would start to pass the bus ahead of us and that would awaken the driver of the bus ahead of us, driver B and driver B would decide to pass the bus in front of him. As driver B started to pull out around bus C, our bus, A, was forced, because our driver was too stubborn to give up on a stupid idea, off the road and onto the hard packed dust of the shoulder, on the wrong side of the road. Now you must understand that this shoulder is the place where the bicycles, rickshaws, people walking and carts dragged by oxen or water buffalo find a fairly safe place to move about. So to warn them that they have been invaded our driver sounds his horn constantly. The racket heightens the drama which comes to a climax when we are suddenly faced with the same madness coming at us from the other direction, dust flying, horns blaring. In these moments of helpless terror I close my eyes and say to my self, "This is going to hurt."

Somehow when I had the courage to open the eyes again, the mess would have straightened itself out and we were all still alive.

Back the US where bus drivers have been scabs for the many years because the regular drivers have been on the world's longest strike, against the only bus company in the US. The substitute drivers are not very professional. On one memorable trip through Indiana the driver of my bus was kept awake by a passenger who screamed at him every time he dozed off. She went to the police at a rest stop and had him arrested.

When in India, I talked with a fellow tourist who had rented a car. He described overturned busses and trucks that they came across. When there is an accident involving injured, they claimed, the driver takes off and is never seen again.

One day at Fairlawns, Hotel in Calcutta, I met the guy who arranged busses for Semester at Sea. He was arranging for the kids to come to Calcutta to meet Mother Teresa. I heard later that the bus crashed and kids and professors were killed!

Nepal was another bus trip. My two hiking pals actually slept on the trip from Kathmandu to Pokhara. My coccyx was so bruised that I could barely walk for a couple of days. One earnest, religious young USA guy who was working in Nepal said that a bus that a friend had been on the week before had swerved to avoid a water buffalo and the bus went into the river and everyone is still in it at the bottom of the river.

Then there is New Zealand where the drivers are a delight and give great descriptions of what we are looking at. The only thing that I have seen that compares are the English and Turkish busses where you are served tea. You also got the refreshing wipes on the Turkish bus. I consider New Zealand to be the tops for busses.

1.23.96 Christchurch. Travel day. We spent all day on the train from Invercargill to Christchurch. Lovely trip. We had a table to ourselves most of the way and could read a well written book about Arab countries by Richard Greiner, *Marrakech One Two*. We decided that Chas' brother, Jim, who had lived in Saudi Arabia would really enjoy it and sort of took it from the hostel. I have also left many books at hostels. Gee. Don't get excited.

The views of New Zealand were great but we had no time to stop in Dunedin to look for penguins. Arriving at 5:00 gave us time to eat at the cafe across the street from the hostel and then take in Wind in The Willows.

1.24.04 Went to the airport with Chas and cried a lot when he left.

01.25.04 Christ Church. Chas had not brought Frisky, the Vitus racing bike because I had lent Frisky to daughter Kitty who wanted to try bicycle racing. She broke a shoulder quite a few years back when some jerk ran her into a curb on her first try at racing. So there was a bit of a hiatus. Anyhow, Chas had not made the trip to North Carolina to pick up the bike so he lent me his, Big Red, an ancient Allegro touring bike. He took Green home with him. I spent a large part of the day in Christchurch trying to buy a wet suit. Wet suits are quite expensive but necessary here in the cold Pacific. Met Sue Bastian today. She is from Bend, Oregon, the Shangri-La of Cross-country skiing. She knows our leader, Dick Hunt. She has been on the bike constantly since she retired. She is meeting another biker here to bike with. She usually bikes on her own and is very nervous about traveling with someone. Yep. She is one of those people who thinks that the US is a big bully in the world and we went around and around. These people can always find some obscure thing that you never heard of to muck rake. I took off, biking north along the beautiful coast.

1.26.96 Wellington. Jumped on a train at Kaikoura to Picton and caught the ferry for Wellington. I have left the South Island

and am on the southern most part of the North Island. My sinuses are aflame and my nose runs constantly. I am a mess. The ferry captain warned us that the recent bad weather had caused cyclones on the North Island and would be causing 3 meter waves. The ferry was huge. There were railroad cars on the level where I was with Allegro Red. That was nothing compared to trying to get to the Trekkers Hotel where I had a reservation. The wind was howling and driving sheets of rain. I had to get off the bike and walk it from time to time because I was afraid the wind would knock me down. Not quite like the storm in Texas. There the wind was an honest screamer that always came at you from the same direction. Here, in the canyons of the city, you never knew where it would come from next. I stopped in a Japanese restaurant and had a fairly expensive dinner. At the Trekker, I reserved a second night in hopes that that would give the storm time to settle down before I hit the road. There are bars in the hotel but they seem noisy and rough. There is an expensive looking restaurant. My bed is very cozy and I am going to snuggle down into it. If it should be nice in the morning, I will take off early.

01.27.96 Wellington, New Zealand. Terrible weather. I did accomplish two things: bought a wetsuit and got medicine. The wet suit was $198 NZ or $132 US. I have two other wet suits at home. This is a full body job and looks pretty snazzy on. It will be huge and difficult to carry. Then, because by dnoz is a bess, I bought a bottle of Vicks nose spray. Ever used that stuff? It is like pouring boiling acid up you nose. I dumped the Vicks and used the sprayer for the concoction that son Mac invented. It is Listerine and Neosporin spray. He says to treat a cold like a brush burn. It usually works pretty well. My cold has moved into the chest and rumbles around there while my nose is still drippy and I woke up with a raw throat. There is a nice desk in this room but I can't get that far and am typing in the Zaurus while lying in bed. I am in a Trekkers and as always the people here seem rough. I haven't met even one person that I would want to speak to. Wellington is noted for strong winds that can knock you down or pin strong men to the walls. I can't wait to leave. Every time I muster the strength to look out the window it is raining. Thank goodness for my rain suit. I need to be training for the Ironman. This is not going well and I am getting down on myself.

!.30. Napier. What a day! The sky is blue, the sun is bright! The Pacific is a gentle rippled green. I never got out of bed until noon after sleeping soundly all night. When I awoke at my usual hour this morning my hands were white and cold and I felt deathly tired. So I read a book, telling myself to be patient. I am listening to my body. Today it said,

"Nothing."

It was unnerving. So I got up at noon, detested the idea of a shower, still cold, am now sitting in a bar, finally warm, and warmly dressed and the sweat is pouring down. As I could not get warm at all under quilts this morning, this seems good to me but the people in shorts are looking at me strangely.

I entered the 1/2 Ironman that will be here in a couple of days. I found a great pool, actually three pools not too far away. I swam 2000 yards in 18 C degree water. After that I was cold with my fingers and toes numbed. I went to bed and slept a couple of hours. After that I biked about 20 miles to enter the triathlon. I planned to run the course today, a mere 13 miles, but here I am, hung up.

I sent a fax to Chas today and got one back. It was a copy of an article about me from the interview in Taranga in the Greensburg, PA Tribune-Review, a paper that is trying to move into the spot left by the departed Pittsburg Press. It was really well done. I am not at all sure that I can handle being a Media Darling. But then, no one that I know reads the Tribune-Review.

So I decided that I am probably depressed because someone was nice to me and I just can't handle that. So, now, I am at the movies to watch the gorgeous Whitney Houston. Only women have come to watch. The endless ads are on, the local ones. The movie was not the one to cure my depression.

Napier is cute. The streets are named Emerson, Tennyson, Dalton . . . who was Hastings . . . Battle of ? . . . Carlisle, Shakespeare. The town was destroyed by an earthquake in 1931 and rebuilt in

Art Deco style which is carefully treasured and maintained. The hostel is Art Deco and winds around and up and down almost as much as the vast Trekkers Hotel in Wellington.

Son Tom, who, poor child, has lost his mind and is running for Congress as a Libertarian wanted me to do some research on the schools in New Zealand, so here it is:

School funding: Since 1992, 70 schools have been taking part in a three year trial of bulk funding of teachers salaries. (Bulk funding . . . do fat teachers make more money?) All other costs are funded by grants to individual schools, with the expenditure being controlled by each school's board of trustees. From 1993, salaries grant for designated management positions has been paid directly to the board of trustees. Financial management of the schools is subject to review by the Audit Office. Education management and attainment is to be reviewed by the Education Review Office. (Excited about this?) Evidence from research on school choice in New Zealand: Choice is more strongly related to social status than to educational resources of the school. This situation is strongly self-reinforcing. Schools with mainly middle class and Pakeha or Asian population tend to achieve better on national examinations because of the high level of educational readiness and motivation of the students, and relatively low levels of social problems that impinge on the educational process. (How well put is that?)

There is increasing social polarization of school enrollments . . . very limited on the high because everyone wants them and lots of choice on the low because so many have left them . . . Choice is an urban phenomenon . . . we do not want to return to the past but the future is unclear. Even political parties which advocate a straight privatization of the education system, with a voucher "safety net," do so with the hope of improving, not narrowing educational opportunities for all groups in this country. What is needed is a policy approach that combines the older social democratic of educational comparability across class and ethnic boundaries, with real choices for families . . . resource disparities have increased. (School based management not always very admirable in my district, the school board chairman ran a beer distributors.) Government on the behalf of the disadvantaged . . . increased social polarization . . . .

Recommendations: Every child should have the right to go to their local school.

Over subscribed schools use a system of balloting.

The policy of exit is inappropriate for the "working class" schools and funding should be provided to compensate for this.

Solving the above conflicts with "cost cutting" in the 21st Century. (So. Vouchers have been tried in New Zealand, and are far from perfect. Good luck with it, Tom. I spent my 27 years watching foreign language standards sink with each new text book. I blame the Universities. Do they have requirements? How long has it been since any college shrank? How long has it been since anyone flunked out of college? There is a basket weaving course out there for everyone. Women's studies . . . what a joke. Black studies . . . Is this what used to be called a liberal education? Education for Libs. Get you a job? Where? In some other university.)

2.4.96 Napier, New Zealand. Bummer. After hiding in my room with a serious depression, I emerged to fall flat on my face in the 1/2 Iron triathlon. But I feel better and will undoubtedly enter the Olympic distance Nationals in Taupo. I'm leaving for Taupo on the bus in the morning and will arrive there by noon. It is on the other side of the mountains that I became so well acquainted with today. I know them well because I pushed my bike up five huge, steep mountains.

It took long habit to get my fearful body to the start line this morning. The little habits of selecting socks, shoes, swim suit, goggles, nose plugs, swim cap, all that went together nicely until outside with the bike, I stupidly put my keys in the hole by the office and then realized that the "bought for the occasion, wet suit" was still hanging in my room. So I woke up the poor hostel manager to let me in at 6:30 AM. Got it and biked the 3K to the start line. Things went well there and the swim was good but in spite of being trouble free, took 10 min. longer than Tauranga. The bike started well although my legs were very tired. Same at Tauranga. I can't remember them being tire on the bike in other years. (Is this because I usually swim a couple of thousand yards every day?) It was nice for a while and I allowed for the first mountain. The walking slowed me some and brought me to the horrid realization that Chas' bike really doesn't fit me. We use the same size frame because we have the same leg inseam but that is, I found, about the end of it. I could not get up the steep hills with his gears, I am a granny and need my granny gears. I had to get off and walk. And walk, and walk. After finally making the top there would be a series of threatening signs about the curves on the down hill. My small hands could not make his brakes work properly and every downhill was an anguish filled session of bad words and desperate battle with the handbrakes. Each of the five long up hills took forever. I finished the 56 bike miles and did one loop of the run and gave up on it. Now that it is over, all I can remember is that it was a gorgeous course. Should have walked that last 6 miles and finished. This not finishing thing is bad for the soul.

2.7.96 Taupo, New Zealand. Haven't been writing because there are suddenly, people to talk to. First a couple of ladies in their sixties who were vacationing together. Both had lost husbands to divorce and each complained about the other. What a hoot. Last time I saw them they were grumbling at each other most miserably. Then there was an American couple. He a retired computer, systems manager and the lady an ex-French teacher. As they both worked very hard to prove to everyone that they knew everything and everyone else nothing. Snore. They did have an admirable grip on one thing, he was a Rotary guy and would contact the local Rotary people and the locals would entertain the touring folk. The guy got to go fishing (his passion) with the locals. That really is good travel.

The atmosphere here is most pleasant except for the dogs that are loose and check out my leg to see if the dog that bit me was a dog that they know. I hope I won't regret the move.

I'm leaving the hostel for a room in a hotel that is all my own and has a desk. The Lake Hotel. It is in a lively area but I have a room that should be fairly quiet.

It rained hard for most of the day and still looks threatening. I used the time go to the library to plot out the trip to Missoula, Montana. By way of Seattle, 2 months. That leaves almost a month to????

02.08.96 Taupo, North Island. The poem about the rain is coming into its own here in Taupo. This is the warm dry season and it has been rainy two of the three days I have been here. I went swimming in the rain and had the first real workout in over a year since I dropped my Y membership in November of 1994. I have swum from time to time but not done a workout where I did a batch of hundreds at top pace. My recent sessions have just been doing the 2000 yard distance. I miss swim team. It really shows when you have been loafing. I did the first sprints running here too. Have not done any real workouts on Red, the bicycle. Then I came back and slept like a log for three hours. I haven't been sleeping very well so I guess that is good. When I woke at 6 O'clock, I smelled steak from the kitchen below so here in the restaurant I am to get some protein. And red wine. The library is open a little tonight so I might go there to read. A computer store may let me use their computer so I really need to rewrite the article for Tom just in case I can run it off.

2.11.96 Taupo, North Island. I started the day by deciding, wrongly, that it would rain and I might as well take the tour some of the wonders. The tour was about volcanoes and enthralling. Lake Taupo is a caldera of a huge volcano that blew up 200 B.C. The lake is warm and clean and I am such a wimp that I haven't worked up courage to swim in it yet. I really must. The area here is in a volcano series that has some really huge volcanoes south of here to some very active volcanoes north east of here. The one that blew up last fall messed up the ski season there but otherwise, not much harm. They have a lot of steamy places and have captured this heat to produce 15% of the electricity through geothermals. The rest is produced by a series of hydro-electric dams on the same river that comes out of Lake Taupo. We saw the rush of the river at several spots and it was very impressive. A world class resort is just outside of Taupo on the river.

When I got back to town, I stopped to watch a group of Maoris, performing for free, followed by British acrobats who were just wonderful. Then I spent the rest of the afternoon at the bar beside the hotel listening to Dixieland jazz group, (white, New Zealand.) Beverly Watson, black, from San Francisco also sang with them and she was scheduled to perform tonight so since I met her in the ladies room and she invited me to come, I spent the evening at her concert and she is terrific. Tanya Turner screamy but a great performer. I was locked out of my hotel! As I am never out late, that was a surprise. A little panic helped and the night man finally appeared. Actually the bar that had the music was part of the hotel that I was locked out of.

Yesterday I spent writing to the sons and did a good bike workout and swim workout. The swim is much longer than the 900 yards we do in the states. Unless the distance has changed there too. It is 1500 meters here, which is a lot more than 1/4 of 3800 of the Ironman. That was fine, I did 500: 100x15 for 2000 and it all felt good. Before that I cranked out to the hills on the bike. So I am giving myself a break today. Doing a track beside a river that I am told is part of the race.

To Tom I wrote that he should above all, be himself, what ever that is. He should be clear about a core of beliefs and able to express them. Told him to read Rush Limbaugh's book to find out about how you succeed in the media. Rush's core is the Republican platform. For better or for worse. Having a talk show would help him to be known and to make his points.

02.14.96 Taupo. My rule is never, never eat sea food outside of the US. When I got sick in Greece, sea food. When I got sick in Tauranga, mussels. When I got sick in Queenstown, mussels. Now here I am again after a seafood pasta last night. I got up with a bit of diarreah but that isn't unusual when I am tied in knots, as I am about going out on the bike to work out. I had a banana, usually no problem but when the body is in crisis, I am almost allergic to bananas. McD's was open so I got large orange juice because my stomach felt bad, I thought food would help. Wrong. On the first hill I got really sick and started sweating in a most unhealthy way. I gave up on the workout and made my way back to my bed. Now here I am, huddled under blankets, sneezing and sweating.

Last evening was most enjoyable. I went to a poetry reading and met two really charming people, Mayke, a nice looking young man who is the co person of the poetry group, and Sharon Roberts, a composer, chellist, who is finishing up on a requiem. A Requiem! Her father will conduct it on March 23.

She read a Katherine Mansfield poem about living alone in a one room situation. I will take myself to the library and try to borrow some Katherine Mansfield for while I am sick. She is New Zealand's person of letters. I've heard of her, of course, but never read her works. I read my opus, which I wrote for the occasion. Possums are in process of eating to the ground one of New Zealand's favorite trees. There are so many dead possums on New Zealand roads that you have to believe that the locals aim for them. But they are cute, even when pretty much mutilated.

Possumtumously
When possums go love mad,
Then comes the liebestod, sad:
A death, not too sweet,
In the middle of the street.
Poor possum, so happy in the trees,
Felt urgings of love from his tail to his knees,
And in order an, unknown lady to please,
Left his safe perch,
Left life.
Splurch
"'She is talking about my life,' said Sharon. 'I live alone with my cello just like she did.'"

When Sharon read Mansfield's poetry, everyone in the small bar listened with rapt attention. She read dramatically, she had practiced with her usual care.

"I can't call him a boyfriend, he is twice my age. We have been friends for ever so long. I call him my partner. He is so sweet and kind. He has been there for me this year. It has been so very difficult. My father is marrying. My aunt died and my sister's baby and everyone counts on me to do everything Then my partner had an operation for prostate cancer. and I helped him get through that. We have been there for each other. My work has taken off. I'm famous. It is wonderful but now everyone wants me to do something for them. and I have two step sisters now. One is very cold. She is like me but I have through all this, learned to communicate with my father. And he has learned to communicate with my step sister because she is so much like me. I don't like her much but she is a lot like me. Somehow they have to quit leaning on me. I have to have time to compose. They think that because I don't work regular hours that I can jus drop everything and do stuff for them. I'm exhausted all the time. I'm up until one or two o'clock every night because that is the only time they leave me alone."

I only have the silly Triathlon to do.

02.14.96 Taupo. Body and psyche came to a screeching halt today. My need for a large dose of courage took me out at the knees. So I bought two self-help books. They involve my telling myself things like,

"I **could** go on a 60 mile bike ride today."

Instead of,

"I should go on a sixty mile bike ride today."

If I don't go, at least I won't be beating myself up so badly.

People, especially women are always saying to me,

"I don't know how you have the courage to . . . ."

Whatever it is I am doing is beyond the risk venturing of most people. Right now it is beyond me. I kept thinking if I just sat around that the courage cup would fill up again but it did no such thing. The courage cup is dry.

2.15.96 Taupo. The last time I had pasta, it made me sick. I have ordered one of the all day breakfast selections here, spaghetti on toast. For some reason, today I started to worry about my cholesterol level, which is never good. Taupo has the usual selection of deep fried junk that you get in the USA.

Breakfast has arrived and is canned spaghetti, warmed and dumped on four buttered pieces of toast. This, with bottle of sprite, no glass, is almost $10 NZ or $7.50 US. It is almost enough to drive me to cook. My companions here in the lunch room are a group of ladies, casually dressed, most overweight and most mostly Maori. They are having a great time. Some of them smoke. The waitress hangs over the group, chatting. The cafe fronts on the lake which is a deep sparkling blue today with baby blue, puffy clouds hanging over it, like a friendly waitress. I did a bike workout this morning but was shooed out of the room by the chambermaid so I retreated to the library where I read Mark Sombody's travel book called *Room Service*. He has a great sense of humor and I make indecent noise in the library laughing at him. I took picture of blooming Acanthus outside the library. I spent yesterday closeted with yet another self help book, Susan Jeffers, *"Feel the Fear, and Do it Anyhow."* I made my own little tape of affirmations, from stuff in the book. It seems helpful. At any rate, I did get out on the bike today with a minimum of dread. The bike course is marked now. I went to the swim venue and was attacked by little gnats. I bought another book of self help and will wander back to the Lake Hotel to read it. While doing a visualization, I pictured having myself with a new career as a Latin or Spanish tutor. The business would be run from the house by FAX and or Email. Rich kids going to Shady Side or Sewickley Academy, Ellis School. Kid in trouble in Latin. I interview the kid and we set up a schedule, on the computer, of when he will have his homework to me. I correct the translation and FAX it back to him, he has to have a FAX at home. He corrects his translation. Writes out vocabulary on flash cards, memorizes.

Studies grammar and writes out the grammar exercises, Faxes them to me. I correct them and FAX them back. He goes to school the next day with a correct translation and a correct set of grammar exercises. If he has studied his vocabulary, he can survive a quiz. He might need extra time when studying for a test but hopefully, by doing the daily work with great care and thoroughness, he does Oli Kala on the tests. For this I charge no less than $25 per hour. As I go on I could figure out some sort of standard. There would be an honor code with this, that nothing would be shared with other students. I can picture the rage of the teacher if he found a crib sheet of my making floating around the classroom. Any such dereliction and the student would be out of my program. Madness. I'm too lazy to do any of that.

What a thrill, a FAX from Precious waiting for me at my hotel when I got back.

2.15.96 Taupo. So the self-help book that I am working with says it is better to forgive. So I write a long letter to Alma. At the end of this I reach the conclusion that she is a dumper and I am a dumped. Just like the Eric Berne's OK Corral. Since this is probably our standard position on things, probably not all that uncomfortable. We are used to it. In the OK Corral she is in the I'M OK, you're not ok, getting rid of position: I'm in the I'm not ok, You're OK, running away, position. Most of my friends are I'm OK, you're not. That is what I am used to. I am comfortable with understanding their weaknesses and ignoring the weakness, just as they probably recognize my wimpiness and ignore it most of the time. How do I avoid being 'dumped'? I leave before they can tell me to. Ole Oleson is a big time dumper and the people with him maybe other dumpers. I can't imagine dumping anyone. Cannot picture telling anyone that I can't stand the sight of them and they must go. I would leave an uncomfortable situation, but not dump.

So what do I do to compensate for this feeling of being a wimp? Triathlons. A-trail. Bike around the world. The self-help I am working with says ignore all the self-derogatory stuff coming from my mind chatter. Drowned it out with 'affirmations'. I have tried this before and it seemed pretty silly but now it makes more sense and I wonder what it will do to me if I change. If I just decide I'm ok. I'M OK.

I struggle with the other self-help book. It makes me feel guilty but I feel guilty if think of dumping it. It might offer some great insight that I am discounting. Actually it basically says that we are our own worst enemy. I have finally left the security of my room and am indulging in a banana smoothie

2.17.96 Taupo, NZ. There had been a little old drunk in the room next to me who had smelly food in his room and who stopped dead and stared at me with bleary eyes whenever I was forced to pass him in the hall. I hoped there was someone in there with him because he talked on and on into the night. What was really annoying was that he smoked and I could see myself being cremated without benefit of funeral. The ladies who clean the room, one pleasant, aging pukhera and one Maori were upset because he swore at them. I guess they wanted me to complain officially because they kept talking about him. I said,

"What ME complain about a falling down drunk who smokes?"

I guess they took that as negative. I spent some more hours at the library, reading Mark . . . 's book, ... *Room Service*. He traveled to New Zealand, US and Alaska and was so British and sarcastic and funny that I kept making more disturbances with my laughter. Going to see Liam Neeson in "*Ethan Fromm*" now. Great Movie festival in town now.

Now at the theater waiting. Went to hear a singer of Gershwin and Cole Porter. He was Mel Torme type and very popular here. From Christ Church. There were two jazz pianists backing him up, one was blind. They were OK for white guys. You know what I mean. No sweat. Too cool. Missing the 'soul' that puts US entertainers on top. Live elevator music.

There was a group of Andean pan flutes, etc playing on the street today that played with such innocent gusto and enthusiasm. Love their stuff. Thought about traveling in the Latin Americas for five or ten seconds. At the library, I picked up a copy of *Travels with Roscinante*. Roscinante isn't a beatup old nag, it is his bicycle, of course. The introduction tells about the bicycler being robbed twice in one day in Guerrero province. So much for Latino America. Spain, Si. Mexico, NO. Ads finished

Geeze, what a well crafted story *Ethan Fromm* is. The cripple man. Knowing that something awful, too awful to talk about with nice people, has happened. Little clues to the future, strychnine, the tree, the increasing passion of the lovers, their choices, how the choices came out. Really a perfect story. Perfect. Hideous ending. Hell is. Wonderful acting of all concerned. The credits said that perfect town was Peacham, Vermont. Vermont is probably kept green by New York money.

I am sitting along Terrace Drive but the gnats are coming after me. Light wind out of the north. Every time you look at the flags, they re headed a different direction. Cool, some light, some heavy clouds . . . Who knows what the weather will be. Only 6:38 PM and everything but the few bars that stay open has closed up already.

2.18.96 Taupo. So, now, I am sitting here with my gold medal from the NZ Nationals for the standard (Olympic) distance. If I had finished Napier I could have had one for the 1/2 iron nationals. I joined TRI-NZ so I could receive this medal. They said I was a former US citizen. Once and future. California here I come. A Fax arrived just as I was starting out for the race and I read it at McD's as I stuffed down my pancakes. It was just so great, from the lady with the Wyoming Council for the aging. She didn't print my article but she did quote from it a bunch. It was interesting and fun to read. It really set me up for the Tri. The tri started under heavy hanging clouds. The 1500 meter swim seemed long but not as bad by a lot as Taranga and Napier. This one was in fresh, warm water. I made the switch to the bike and was actually with some people. There was a three or four mile coast on the bike along the edge of the lake and a climb up a hill and then a dip back into the town. I took out the water bottle from my new water bottle cage and as I was trying to put it back, missed the cage and it went down on the street. My thought,

"I ought to pick that up . . ." was interrupted by the bike front wheel twisting sideways and my body taking a tight somersault over the bars. I landed on my feet on the sidewalk! The bike was crumpled up in the gutter. I was astounded to be so unscathed. I picked up the bottle and the bike. Both were OK so I got on and went on my way. On the ride there were still people passing me. It was really nice in the run part with very little paving, just a soft path beside the lake. There were still people behind me! An older woman came and sat with me during the awards ceremony. She was the next oldest, in the 55+ age group. I was almost an hour slower than she was: I did her times when I was her age. Yuk. She diagnosed my foot pain as a Morton's Neuroma. Said she had hers operated on and it was a snap and very successful.

2/19/96 So I'm chatting with a very nice young Kiwi fellow. He is wearing one of the very popular Chicago Bulls tee shirts. He takes a pouch of tobacco out of his breast pocket, papers put of a jacket pocket and making a neat little trough with the paper puts some tobacco in, licks it, and rolls it, not too neatly, with tobacco spilling around.

"I've seen quite a few New Zealanders rolling their own," I remarked. "I used to roll cigarettes for my mother and father during the big war. I had a little machine into which you put paper and tobacco and rolled up each cigarette. They paid me by the pack to do that. Since he died of heart trouble and she died of cancer I probably helped them to an early grave."

The cigarette rolled in his fingers and his eyes rolled up at me.

"They put somethin' nawsty in the commercial cigarettes. Salt peter, I think."

"You are going to put that cancer stick in your mouth and call it healthful.?"

"Well, it is cheapah."

"Then what happens to the statis thing of smoking because you can afford it?"

"Tell you, Mate. I smoke because I like to."

He inhaled deeply and started to cough then choke as he started to laugh at the same time. Smoke was coming out of his nose, mouth and maybe even ears. When he could straighten up and breathe again, I said,

"First cigarette, huh?"

That sent him off again, choking and laughing.

"The bus is leaving, we'd better go."

He gasped, sighed, looked at the rumpled cigarette and butted it out in the ashtray and we climbed in the bus.

2.19.96 Rotorura. The big decision to really ride the bike to Rotorura was washed out by a downpour. I had packed much too much to be able to ride with it anyhow. Getting a free duffle bag, towel, water bottle and the old Campy derailleur and crank and the very useless handlebar bag was a big messy problem. There are no hooks on the bottom of the handlebar bag, it just flops around so I took it off. Plus a couple of books that I couldn't seem to part with. Anyhow this plus spare tires, and the wet suit, it is all too much. Also I was tired from the triathlon. My back was the sorest. Legs seem ok but they were very tired during the race. I must not forget to report from the swim part of the race the panic or whatever gets at me when I am wearing a wet suit. I think that I am going to die. I didn't warm up anymore than just paddling around. The training I had done was good but the stopping to gasp and choke because of the wet suit meant that any hope of drafting left me. I did catch up with one girl and drafted her for a while when she stopped in confusion I offered to lead and she said good but I never saw her again. My practice at keeping my chin up as I swam helped a lot spotting and I didn't get too terribly lost as I had in the other swims. The tiny suggestion is that it would have been some help to practice in the accursed wet suit.

Arriving in Rotorura, I booked the hostel for two more nights and the Moari dinner and entertainment for tomorrow night and then set out for the Polonisian Spa which is where I am now, enjoying the best meal I have had in NZ. Fruit salad, orange roughy, and for dessert, passion fruit cheese cake.

The spa is very nice and handy to a sizeable Quality Court and there is a Sheraton down the street so we know this place is big time. Just about every motel room has its own natural hot water spa.

2.23.06 Rotorura. Very disappointing day. Got up bright and early and started biking around beautiful Lake Rotorura today. The humongous volcano that blew up a millennia back left a caldera which filled up and is now Lake Rotorura. Then sometime later another small volcano pushed up a conical island on the middle of the lake. Steam from all sorts of geothermal activity is constantly puffing out great clouds. The locals do marathons around the lake because the road is fascinating and not too tough a 25 miles. So I set out, in my wimpy way, on the bike, the sidewalks as long as they lasted. When sidewalks gave out, I hugged the side of the road. There were a couple of sizeable hills on the course but it was generally flat. The first detour was to Hell's Gate where I went through yet another thermal park. It was enjoyable and I thought about writing a poem about Mother Earth having hot gas belly ache. I pottered along to the next roadside attraction which was on the outskirts of Rotorura, Fairy Springs. It was as beautiful as Hells Gate was scary. I took lots of pictures of trout, Rainbow and Brown . . . . huge for trout. Little piggies, wild boar, deer, it was fun. But the Ironman is 4 1/2 times the Rotorura Lake circuit.

So then I got the terrible realization that I was never going to even finish the bike in the Ironman. I looked at the written description of the course in Auckland and it looked pretty terrible. Hills. More hills. I decided I could just forget the whole thing. Why even show up? Then I read where if you want be qualified to go to the Hawaii Ironman you have to let them know by the 23rd so I ran the form to the FAX machine and wasted another dollar telling them I wanted the Hawaii Ironman spot which I haven't a snowball's chance of getting. No way. Too much. Don't know why I keep torturing myself with this Ironman thing. Masochistic. Well, I have been seriously depressed in the last couple of weeks and perhaps this is the mania side of it. I haven't worked out like I should because I got stuck on dead center and could not move a finger in any direction. So I bought the most recent collection of self-help books and have been bucking up my courage with all sorts of positive thinking. On the other hand isn't it positive thinking that gets me painted into a corner like this? Thinking,

"I can do an Ironman. No problem." I'm going to have to find the book that will help me distinguish between pipedreams and reality.

On the other hand, if I had good sense I wouldn't be a New Zealand Champion, would I? It really is too much.

I stopped at the tiny RR Station on the way back and bought myself a ticket to Auckland. Sunday 1:00. Arrive Auckland 5:00 that evening. It is sunny and the wind is very strong. Met a girl sleeping in the bathroom who had been driven there by last night's storm. Been there. Done that. I'll take a nap and then perhaps go to the Orchid Garden for dinner.

2.24.96 Rotorura. Blew a lot of positive thinking and love of fellow man when they wouldn't let me take my daypack into the theater

2.25.96 Rotorura. Have lost all desire for the Ironman. Flat out don't want to continue torturing myself with even the thought of it. Reading Michner's 'The Novel'. Michner writes about good people doing good things. And it is still interesting. His people get up and do their work. They study hard and go to school. They live decent lives. He is the most 'middle America' writer. As I have bicycle traveled through places he has written about, (*Chesapeake*) I could see that the road signs and historical markers are the back bone of his stories.

2.26.96 Auckland. Biked the run course. A beast. The first part runs along the waterfront, flat and then back to the start(14k) then there is a batch of horrendous hills with rough grabby pavement(11K), then back to the start and a repeat of the first loop. I got the bike checked by going clear across the city. They just shook their heads and shrugged their shoulders. I will try to be at the swim start tomorrow for 'dig me' psych out time tomorrow. It is always fun to watch the big timers playing their psychological games. Problem here is I don't know the players except Kenny Glau who had been one of John DuPont's FocCatcher Tri team. He may be in mourning for DuPont, or celebrating that he wasn't there when DuPont lost it totally. Kenny winters here because his wife, Jan, is a Kiwi triathlete. He usually makes expense money in the Kiwi Ironman. (4th this year.) When I talked to him he said that son Mac had introduced him to his wife.

Anyhow, if everybody is in the water at the same time your chances of being shark bait are a lot less in a mob scene. The things one will do to keep from being bored. I'm not afraid. The little worm of fear has died. I'll do what I can and then drop out.

2.27.96 Shins very sore today. What did I do? Nothing. So what am I doing? Nothing.

When I looked for the $300 NZ that I got from the money machine yesterday, it was nowhere to be found. Oh, woe. A line had formed at the machine as I was getting my donation so I just stuffed the bills in my wallet, I guess. Never saw them again. I didn't miss them until this morning. Called the police but they had nothing to report. By then my plan to take the local train to Papakura and do the end of the bicycle course was pretty much blown so I went down to city center and picked up a Cannondale bike box. Pleased to see the box travel from Pennsylvania to NZ and back to the USA again. Bedford to Pittsburgh by way of NZ. Met a DC bicycler named Bob who is aging and very upset with NZ roads. He has been here a month and is thoroughly discouraged with bicycling in general and hates NZ. He didn't even get bitten by a dog. He retired 10 years ago and biked a lot of the US without getting so thoroughly psyched out. He also got sick from food and has spend almost as much time moping around as I have.

3.1.96 Auckland. The anniversary of the World Wander. I'm planning to celebrate with a steak at a loovely puub down the hill from the hostel. This will be the last time to have red meat before the Ironman. Think I'll have a pint of bitters, too. I took the train to Papakura and biked from there to the bike course, 10 miles and then the 30 miles of the course back to the start. Nasty hills. Got lost a lot. Traffic. But all in all, a pleasant day of biking and pretty countryside.

Article for Health and Fitness

"In the suburban train that I ride, the bike goes in the last car and I just sit with it. Unfortunately all the sleaze likes to sit in the last seat of the last car: I had read my positive thinking bit from Og Mandino. I prefer Og to Susan Jeffers and the psychiatrist because he is much more positive. Actually Og proposes to make me into the world's greatest sales person and I have blackened out a few lines that have me mentally grabbing a customer by the lapels on hanging on until one or both of us is unconscious. This leaves Og's positive thinking which sounds quite a bit like the Sermon on the Mount. One wonders if Og knows that he is plagiarizing some pretty well-known stuff. On the other hand what are his chances of being sued by someone dead for two millenia? So, anyhow, I am practicing looking into peoples eyes and mentally saying,

"I love you."

While I am doing this an incredible sleaze gets on the train. On this nearly empty train, it looks like he will sit beside me and Red, the bicycle.

"Get off my train," I am mentally projecting at this dirt bag.

Suddenly I felt guilt. This is a long way from the Sermon on the Mount. Og is right there to nag me about that.

"You are supposed to look in his eyes and think, 'I love you. Power of positive thinking. Sermon on the Mount'."

"Yeah, Og, but you didn't say anything about dirt balls." Maybe Og doesn't meet up with dirt balls.

My mental Og comes up with,

"So, Mother Teresa. She loves the scumballs. Remember Mother Teresa!"

So, still sulking, I tried projecting, "You are a scumball, But I love you."

The conductor, an older gentleman in knee pants, came along and demanded a ticket or money from the young man. None was forth coming. The conductor pushed a button. The train stopped, in the middle of nowhere, and the dirt ball climbed down and disappeared. By this time there were four or five other people watching the scene and they burst into applause. The conductor took a bow and chuckling, went on his way."

Yesterday I did the last part of the Ironman course and caught the train back from Papakura. A lot of students ride the train. At the Papakura station, as I was approaching the waiting shed, a young man rushed by me with blood streaming from his nose and smeared all over his face. I timidly peaked into the waiting shed and there sat five boys, looking quiet and glum. I decided not to sit there and climbed into back of the last car with Red, the bicycle. The boys in the waiting shed were all younger and smaller than the one with the bloody nose. A couple of girls, thrilled and excited by the blood-letting sat across from me in spite of my projecting, "Go away."

Eventually they got off the train and a young mother with three children with bikes sat beside me and told me what a great place New Zealand was to raise children. I wondered if she just couldn't see the ugly graffiti, miles of it, that turned this placid seeming country into a scene of violence.

3.2.96Auckland NZ. While typing this I realized that my ticket home is for Sunday, same day as the Ironman. I had always believed that the Ironman was the 3rd. And I think my case of nerves has given me a rash. I am rough, red, itchy around the neck. Other than that, it has been a lovely day.

I have been reading Shirley MacClaine and . . . . Gee, Wow, it is beginning to make sense. Even before I used Tom as an excuse, I wanted to buy her books. I have always admired her search for self. I can remember saying, years ago, when a stupid movie came out about her search that

"If I had her money, that's what I would do." Reincarnation is beginning to sound not so silly but Shirley has the whole ridiculous thing of aliens etc. All the silly stuff comes in one package.

I had two March 2s. My watch did not recognize leap year and messed me up big time. I had to take it to a jeweler to get it reset but then I was right downtown anyhow when the lady at Air New Zealand helped me to understand that it was my watch that was wrong and I didn't have to change my tickets. Booked window seats while there. Do not have to reconfirm.

3.2.96 Auckland NZ. Experiencing severe chest pain. This pain starts in the heart area and goes up the neck to the jaw where it gets very serious. The jaw feels like it is in a clamp which is being tightened. I have had this pain before and even though I spent 5 days in Sewickley Valley Hospital, there has been no real diagnosis of it. I took Tagamet. I also have that rash on my neck. This nervousness is just not worth it. I took Red, the bike, to the staging area and left him. Reading Shirley MacClaine again.

"When the student is ready, the teacher will appear."
Who said that??? Is wierdo Shirley my teacher? I'm afraid so. I have had a grudging admiration for her luniness, her travels, her search for meaning.

3.4.96 Auckland. I try to reconcile not finishing the Ironman yet once more with knowing that I had shot myself down by not training properly. I did have a fairly decent swim. There again it would have been improved if I had just gone out and done the course once to correctly sight the skyline so I didn't have to stop in confusion so many times on race day. Did the 3800 meter swim in 1 hour 45 min.

So how is it that the Kiwis are so tough in Triathlon? For one, they are determined to make a name for themselves.

Triing Times: Article for Health and Fitness

Feb. 10 The thing is that the US invented Triathlons. The first official one was in Hawaii when some athletes were, heavens, drinking in a bar and got to arguing over who was the most fit, swimmers, bikers, or runners. They got together a horrendous event of swim 2.4 miles, in the ocean: bike 114, and then run a full marathon, all in the same day. The biker won.

The main event, the Hawaii Ironman captured television and the imagination of anyone who had ever biked a century or run a marathon. Lots of competitive high school swimmers were doing 5000 yards daily and could fanaticize swimming the channel or across the Hellespont or Lake Erie.

The Hawaii Ironman moved from Oahu to The Big Island, Kona, Hawaii but maintained its integrity, and broadened. Patience, patience, triathlon is a creature of TV, one tells oneself when being run off the road by the 'Media' trucks. Mark Allen, all-time Ironman champ saw on TV, Julie Moss, in a state if disrepair, crawl across the finish line in Kona, said,

"I can do that," he has won the Hawaii Ironman so many times and married Julie Moss for one of the stranger triathlon stories.

So, anyhow, my great bicycle tour of the world took yet another strange turn when I arrived in Auckland in late December. While searching for a USA TODAY, found a schedule of triathlon events, with the Kiwi Ironman being within my schedule. So I signed up for it. No problem, you don't have to qualify by doing another event well. Or at all. Then I signed up for a bunch of shorter Triathlons to motivate and train my aging body.

New Zealanders are mad for triathlon. It suits them to a T and there are almost as many top Kiwi triathletes in world competition as there are from the US. How can this be? It is our baby. California nurtured and perfected. US is nearing 300 million and New Zealand 3.5 million. Most of the world's top triathletes move to Boulder Colorado. They spend the winter hiibernating or cross-country skiing. They should migrate to New Zealand or Australia and enjoy the facilities of these more 'backward' countries.

Being in the southern hemisphere, the NZ tri season was well under way when I arrived at Christmas time. I suffered the dog bite on the way to Opotere and skipped the first one. Then I moved on to pleasant Taranga, where, in spite of a week of training, I tried but couldn't finish a 1/2 iron on the 7th of January. Then it was off to tour the South Island with my best pal. Back on the North Island alone, depression set in and I had a terrible time trying another 1/2 Iron on Feb. 4. There were lots of short tris but I thought I could handle these. Hah.

So far, the experience has been enlightening. The race officials here are not big on handing out water or food so you have to truck it all yourself. The swims in salt water have ferocious currents to deal with. So far two bike routes were cake, if you don't count the prevailing gale force winds and nasty traffic. The third bike course was twenty miles of straight up and 'DANGER' downhills then out into traffic and gale force winds. So far the runs have been cake except for the slack attitude toward hydration. The 'camelback' water system is very popular here. So, in conclusion: the races are degree of difficulty . . . seven on a scale of ten. The Kona Ironman is 12-15 on a scale of 1-10.

The February 18 nationals at Taupo looked like cake and well planned. I had no trouble getting into it, just sent in the money. You have to qualify for nationals in the US in this distance because the 'standard distance is only a 1/4 ironman. is popular. I have come in second a couple of times in our nationals and second in the World Champs in England in 1992. Anyhow, US competitors are still there at the Ironman distance but are really out of it in the distance that will be in the 2000 Olympics. In Sidney. We will be blown away in our own sport Like losing in basketball or baseball.

So how come? We might blame it on the Kiwis lack of concern for life and limb as demonstrated by their enthusiasm for bungy jumping and skydiving, but triathlon is not your instant thrill. It is a lifetime of hard effort. My thought is the number of clubs. Even the smallest town has a triathlon club and coaches and enthusiastically enters many (money-making) teams as well as individuals. These clubs have the numbers and power to designate swimming pools to lap swimming. The US has numberless pools but the great majority of them are built to discourage lap swimming. Think of the great wet wasteland of all those motel pools with their curvy walls. No, don't. Too disgusting. Little kids floating around with those dangerous float things. Most of them never do learn to swim. High school pools have the motel pool graduates competing with lappers for space. Here, every little town has masters swimming and coaches. I know of only 3 places to swim with a masters' coach in Pittsburgh.

So, OK. The pools at little Taupo, 20,000 pop., are year round but they are heated by thermal water from quiesent volcanos. The lake is also warmed by spa water. Still no excuse. This town has four lap pools. Napier had three lap pools.

So on February .23 I moved on to Rotorura, tourist destination of the North Island. Fantastic swim complex in a town of 60,000. The outdoor lap pool is a 50 meter which has held two all day high school girls meets in the four days that I was there. The other pool has lanes but can also be set up for water polo or water ballet because it is really deep. (Turns out that indoor pool is one of two in New Zealand where water hockey is played.) All of these pools are open 6:30 AM to 9:00 or 11:00 PM.

There are always a number of people using the pool. All pools have been tile in excellent condition. A fair percentage of people swimming are handicapped. Perhaps they lose limbs bungie jumping. I've got my face in the water all the time and don't talk much.

On February 19, Darned if I didn't finish a race. Cake course. The course for the New Zealand Ironman has changed from Aukland to here at Taupo, a much safer and more benign race. The swim was in fresh water with wet suits. 1500 meters. Bike was 40 K, not hard. I dropped my water bottle and while I was thinking about stopping to pick it up, suddenly found myself flying over the handlebars. To my surprise I landed on my feet (no toe clips) with poor Red (the bicycle) crumpled in the gutter. Picked up bottle, bike and proceeded. The run was pleasant, soft ground beside Lake Taupo. Just 10 K. And since this was their national championships, that makes me champ in the distance in which they are really competitive. I was outstanding because I was the only female above sixty who competed. The one lady in the 55-59 group came by to chat. I moaned a lot about my time. I was almost an hour behind her. Used to do her times when I was her age. Getting old is as one wag says, not for sissies. But it beats the alternative.

The above was an article for Health and Fitness Magazine.

3.4.96 On my way to Fiji. Did a pretty good swim in the Ironman, The day before, I took a taxi to the start and the official bus ride around the course. Taxied home and had a nap and then went with the hundreds of other competitors to the carbo load banquet where I was introduced and stood up and took a bow to a big round of applause. Finally some respect. It had been a lovely day and I looked everyone in the eye and mentally said 'I love you.' A Frenchman let me crash the line at the pig out and that was the nicest part.Anyhow, there were lots of Japanese guys behind me in the swim. 47 miles of the bike proved beyond a doubt that

I couldn't make the bike cut-off, and nobody was behind me. I didn't want to go over Snake Hill with its 22 sharp turns straight up and 14 on the other side. Then you turned around and came back. Narrow, horrendous traffic. The bikers who cut corners coming down the hill would never be disqualified for such dangerous behavior and would be likely to collide with me head on. Then there were the cars that were permitted to follow their racers. Very bad, very dangerous. So after all the fretting, I dropped out at the bottom of the hill. I did a 1/2 Iron, almost.

Chapter XXXI

FIJI

*Every new day begins with possibilities. It is up to us to fill it
with the things that move us toward progress and peace.*

Ronald Regan

3.6.96 Nadi, Fiji. Walked the beach yesterday. A little fellow
with a big knife came along and wanted to chat and wanted to
climb the very, very tall coconut palm to cut a coconut for me. I
said no at the thought of his risking his life, and fled. I'm not used
to so much friendliness from a guy carrying a huge knife. Spent
the rest of the day resting from the tri and acclimatizing to the
heat. My motel was pleasant with a single at $17.00 and good,
cheap food. Read James Clavell's 'King Rat'. Takes place in Changi
prison in Singapore where Clavell himself spent WWII.
Autobiographical? Wasn't it a movie with . . . . Frank Sinatra???

I gave the book away today to one of the US Army Corps of
Engineers guys who are staying here. A squad of them are putting
in a drain and building a wall around a school. Humanitarian stuff
which I was assured that they do about once a year in third world
countries. They are stationed in Alaska and were very happy to be
getting a break in Fiji. They buy or contract equipment on location
which is the toughest thing to manage. I chatted with the leader
for a while. He had driven up the Alcan highway last fall. Loved it.
Said it was beautiful the whole way. Expensive. I said I was thinking
of paying the Adventure Cycling Bike outfitters $2600 for 2 1/2
months food and camping, and he thought that was very reasonable.

Fiji is very nice. Warm but not oppressively so. The hills are rugged and have clouds hanging around them that wander down to the plains from time to time to drop a misty rain. There are some fairly high hills but I can't see them from here. The famous Fijian hospitality is OK but I get the feeling that trying to speak English is a strain and they get bored with me.

There are only three of us tourists on the boat I am on for a 1/2 day tour of some island. My neck muscles and back muscles are still sore from the tri but the most irritating is the chaffed raw spots on my arms and neck from the new, expensive wet suit. I have such a rash on my neck. It is so much the same size and shape as the neck of the wet suit that I have to believe it is an allergic reaction to the wet suit. The nervous wreck I have been lately, who knows? I hate it, what ever it is. It itches and I find myself clawing at my throat.

I love boat rides and this one is so relaxed. Some of the crew are playing guitars and Ukuleles. I swam all the way around the tiny island with one of the guides. It is so salty that you float high in the water. Lovely. Paradise.

Chapter XXXII

TAHITI

Enthusiasm is everything. It must be taut and vibrating like a guitar string.

Pele

3.7.96 Tahiti and all I can think of is getting to California. I arrived here at two AM got a bed and breakfast that cost $42 for a miserable thing in the suburbs of Papeete. So I switched to a miserable resort for $30. Everything is horridly expensive and you get very little for your money. The guy who runs the resort has been in a depression since his wife left a couple of years ago. He lived in California a few years, met the lady there and they came back to Tahiti. Why do I have the feeling that she did most of the work? It is the only 'backpackers accommodation' and when he folds there will be nothing left but the Hyatt. I like it though. It is in 4 acres of Australian Pine, orchids, wandering dogs, on a polluted beach. This is the Wednesday after the Ironman and I still seem to be deeply tired. Everyone says don't leave stuff on the beach and I have no one to watch it so even though I am lunching at Mahina Point, famous for being the landing spot of the various Europeans, and everyone is surfing with much enthusiasm . . . . I am cautiously guarding my stuff. It is warm here but since I don't try to do much, not too warm

3.9.96 Papeete, Tahiti. Except for the Hyatt, here, it is so grungy. When I try analyze what upsets me, I come up with the concrete block walls around each little palace. That and the piles of garbage and wandering dogs that are so reminiscent of India.

And there are Indians here. Indians didn't have to bring this crap with them. I am thinking of the huge mansions that I tried to sell, unsuccessfully, to Indian doctors in my unsuccessful venture into Pittsburgh real estate.

Will our Pittsburgh doctor Indians eventually give in to the call of 'nature' and throw up a hideous fortifications of aluminum or concrete block around their castles in Pittsburgh? Preserve us, oh not that. Will they bring their hideous caste system to destroy the freedoms that we offer? Please, no. I don't think it is asking too much if we try to preserve what makes America unique. If we insist on a puritanical work ethic, is that so bad? If they don't want it they need not come. I want Americans to just be Americans. Not Indian Americans. So we come in a lot of flavors. Nice. Good. The spice of life. I have never filled in the ethnic section of anything and no one ever complained. I do admit to being female on government forms because I believe that the best protection for women is being secluded from men in restrooms and dormitories. Ladies, speaking of India, have you ever been exposed to the great morning song of India, the hawking, spitting and general grossness? Imagine having to share a bathroom with one of these guys and your aren't even married? Not even introduced. Am I in a bad mood or what? I just think that the average Tahitian isn't going to shut out his neighbors with the ultimate unfriendliness of ugly 6 ft. walls. Tahitians are curious and wander everywhere and may help themselves to whatever is just lying around. So build the big ugly wall. Anyway, it is ugly here in spite of exotic, ambitious flora that burst hugely out of everywhere. The soil and beaches are black sand which is not easy to get used to. Kids get used to it but I don't. Tonight I leave for LA. Yeah!!!!!!

PART 5

Mustang Sally is pretty burned out but will try to guide you to bicycling:

THE WEST COAST,
THE DEMPSTER HIGHWAY,
AND ALASKA

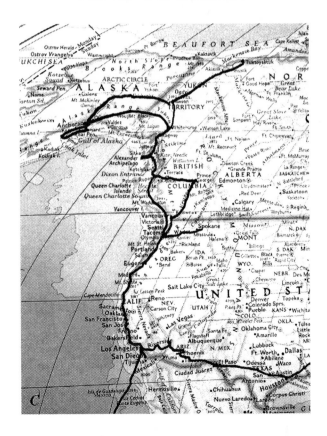

Chapter XXXIII

CALIFORNIA (again)

Hate . . . it's Cold and it's Damp

(Oh, come on. Don't be so sensitive. Cole Porter: "*Hate California, it's cold and its damp, that's why the lady is a tramp. I like the cool, fresh, wind in my hair, life without care, I'm broke, that's OK (oak)* . . ."

You will have to allow that that fits me as well as *Mustang Sally, ride.*) (*I never bother with people I hate.*) Actually, I don't hate anyone, Og, Mother Teresa, I love everyone.

Instructional aside. First of all, if you arrive at LAX by plane, you can assemble your bike in the airport, unpack your rain gear, and head for the ocean. Soon, because the airport is fairly close to the water, you will see a paved bike trail. This is the Pacific Coast Bicycle Trail and it goes, as close to the ocean and wonderful views as possible, to the California border either north or south. If you have your AYH hostel book you will soon come to one of the string of hostels. You will also need camping equipment. Adventure Cycling maps can take you to the Canadian border. (Just kidding about the rain.)

LA 3.10.96 LAX On the plane, I am actually listening to Madame Butterfly and weeping as usual. Thinking about arriving in the US makes me weep also. Filling out the immigration card makes me weep. Been away much to long.

There was a bit of confusion and I was up all last night. I was supposed to be on a New Zealand Air flight leaving Tahit at 2:30 AM. The flight was cancelled and I spent the night in the airport because they said I would ("Un Belle Die", sob.) take another plane at 6:00 AM. 6:00 A.M. turned out to be 10:00 AM so here I am on an Air France with very little sleep, but headed for California. (Lord, how sad.) Saved the article in my treasured one week old TIME magazine about the surviving lady of the ice dancing pair. It was too sad to read in the airport.

Then, on the plane, I had to get my seat moved because I was sitting next an aging dog. I didn't even think about it until my nose started closing up and my head was throbbing When I told the steward that I would have to move, I was moved. In spite of it all, I am sublimely happy. I can call Chas tonight. I'll buy one of those Delta packet of four tickets, and plan a trip home. Easter. Have Chas pick me up at the Norfolk airport and go down to the North Carolina beach as usual. I am tired of spending holidays alone. For this I put all the time, effort, energy and love into my family? So I can be alone? No way. Never again. The US is coming up on the TV map and I may sob. I'm so glad to get back. Crossing the Equator. Did I mention that this is a 747-400 Air France that took in the stranded Air New Zealand people? Star Spangled Banner, Puccini style. We don't come out looking too good in the opera. Only 2700 miles to go. The poor lady dies because of Japanese style "honor". I have a quote on the wall at home from Thomas Jefferson that says, "Pride costs more than hunger, thirst or cold."

The airplane's TV program is in English, Japanese, and French. When in French, meters, when in English, miles. Are we never going to make the change to meters? The change is long overdue. *Iles Hawaii* on our left. We miss them by a good bit.

500Ks from touchdown. Japanese characters all over my beloved USA map. Good. Come. Spend money. The movie they showed had Denzel Washington as a detective named Easy. I read a later book in the series and really liked it. Later in Easy's life. While he's running around doing stuff his wife gets disgusted and leaves him with two kids. I love the character. More, more of these pictures. Jennifer Beals, our Jennifer from *Flashdance* (Canadian movie made in Pittsburgh) was in the movie.

3.11.96 The Santa Monica Hostel is just great. Clean, spacious. I'm in a dorm with 6 other girls. Fun.

'I saw Brad Pitt!'

'So did I,' This followed by squeals.

'He had long hair.'

'No. He had short hair . . . .'

They stare at each other in consternation, realizing that here, so close to Hollywood, there may be just a few Brad Pitt look-alikes.

At the airport was a loud couple who kept yelling, "Any one goun ta San Diego?" How we guna git ta San Diego?"

I offered to take them on my bicycle and this was, unfortunately, greeted with even louder grunts, snuffles, and hor-de-hor, hors. I wanted to tell the rest of the queued-ups that if they had come to see the Beverly Hillbillies, here it is. But I didn't. The other que-ups were sort of hunching up their shoulders and turning the other way.

So, this morning, with a guy from Chicago and his daughter, I caught a taxi ride to Beverly Hills and then a bus or two to Hollywood Boulevard where we walked over the names of the stars to Mann's Chinese Theater. There we were nailed by a tout and given tickets to a free TV show, Mike and Mattie. What with all this excitement, I haven't called Chas yet. Busses require exact amounts. They don't give change.

So anyhow we're sitting here in a TV theater waiting for the show to start, should be in about 6 min. It is a homey little stage with a kitchen, probably a lot like the Today Show. No stars yet. The director might be a very handsome blond guy. No, the director was an unsmiling lady. Everyone else had a great time. The warm-up guy was great. Juggled a bit. Mike and Matty were adorable. I loved every minute of it.

We saw the hotel where they shot pretty woman. Very nice. Also the apartment where she was when he came by for her.

Not so nice. There were the same swanky shops as in Geneva.

One of these is a sex goddess, the other is Mae West.

03.13.96 Los Angeles. Wasted day so far. Waiting for UPS to come and pick up Allegro Red, the husband's bike. I can't leave the hostel because the idiots on the desk won't take responsibility for giving UPS the money. Guess I should have taken the bike in a cab to the UPS office but the place is on the other side of the city. So I sit. Naturally they have all the doors and windows open and it is 50 degrees. I am so tired of being cold. And sitting here. Extended the stay one day in order to take in the city tour. 1:30 P.M. and still here. Saw an UPS truck go by but it didn't stop. I get into such a rage when things don't go well. I must look into myself to find the patience to put up with the facelessness of city life and organization. The people at the hostel are faceless, too. cold. Efficient. Totally rigid. I can't get warm. Catching a cold. Totally miserable with being stuck here in this cold place waiting for the UPS guy. Could have wandered down to Venice to see the weirdoes. Hope to take in the J. Paul Getty Museum on Saturday. It is a replica of a Roman Villa that was buried at Herculaneum. Oh well, if I miss it here, I saw it at Herculaneum, near Naples, Italy, when I was there with the Virgilian Society(Latin teachers. Scary thought? Super group to travel with. Knew everything about ancient Rome.)

It must be that all travelers sit around an awful lot. As I am sitting around here I see others who do nothing but sit. They wait for tickets to ripen for other places or in Santa Monica perhaps they wait for stardom to strike. I must go next door and find that back packer's handbook (can they be as bad in the US as in New Zealand?) and make certain that I get cheapo spots to stay between here San Francisco. Think I'll go now. I think, well, I could meditate but not when every other second my head is flying around to see if UPS is here. Oh, this is dumb.

Free at last. Free at last. Saw Big Red off with Brown (UPS) and went to the bike shop because putting Green, the magic bicycle, together is always a problem for me. I found a huge warm polar fleece jacket for $30 and bike gloves for almost that much. I went to the post office to mail an article to Marion, who wanted me to write something for the Harmony Trail Council. I hope it isn't as nose clogged as I feel. I decided to promenade this upscale area and to cruise the nearby shopping area. I found a lovely Italian restaurant for dinner. Saw Michelle Pfiffer and Robert Redford in a lovely weeper. Did I cry. Can I cry. Bought a book called *Life 101*, recommended by a lady psychologist from Philly that I met while whiling away in the cafeteria. Got her address. I'd like to keep in touch with her. She had come to LA to meet the author, John-Roger, who knows everything about LIFE but John-Roger had a big fight with his co-writer and it went to court and the newest editions don't have his name on it. So maybe John-Roger should read Og Mandino.

3.14.96 Los Angeles. Bright and sunny is the big news today. Jogged on the beach for an hour then later walked down the beach to Venice Beach. Lots of tattoo and body piercing there. The whole beach is just wonderful. A bit of trash but still, just a magnificent sweep of beach. The waves keep rolling in. There is a bicycle path, which is fine concrete and has wonderful signs on it saying 'Bicycles only'. I asked a group of people who were strolling on this bike path if it was all right to walk there in spite of the 'Bikes only' sign and they assured me it was no problem to walk there. Dogs are forbidden on the entire beach. There are some volleyball nets set up and a group of serious players doing drills at 6:00 AM. Volley ball as an Olympic sport? It is like getting serious with badminton. Or table tennis.

I had my palm read on Venice Beach. It seemed like the least threatening thing to do here in marijuana land. It was also the cheapest. I have such strong lines. Aren't they just deeper wrinkles? She said I should be writing fiction. That I am not using my creativity enough. That I have a strong psychic ability but am not using that either. I think she's been talking to Shirley MacClaine. Since I don't have to go anywhere, I think I will take a nap and maybe go to another movie tonight. I am reading 'LIFE 101" by John-Roger.

"Honest criticism is hard to take, particularly from a relative, a friend, an acquaintance, or a stranger." Franklin P. Jones.

Later: Guess what it was doing when I awoke from my nap??? That's right, raining. So I put on all of my clothes and went a half block to a delightful English pub. Shepherds pie. Warms the cockles of the heart for sure. I just love the English atmosphere. Found yet another movie theater and will go to see *El Postiero*. *The Postman*.

Reading Life 101 and thinking of Helen. From what I hear, She is alone now. Her choice. I would like to talk to all the World Wanderers and hear their adventures. Then, thinking about my choice to come to the US instead of doing Australia? Yes. Good. I am happy here after being so depressed in New Zealand and after all that is a very important factor. I need to be good to me. I had very little interest in Australia. Was there for a swim meet in 1988. I was lucky to be on a relay that broke two world records. Flo Carr, Anne Adams, Gail Roper and I broke the old world record by 8 seconds in the 240 age group 200 Medley Relay with 2:51.82. Then we went on to another record in the 200 Freestyle Relay with 2:28.24. It was nice to have a gold medal from a World

Championships in something as competitive as swimming. Flo had been in Billy Rose's Aquacade, Anne Adams and Gail Roper were Olympians. Gail Roper holds all the world records. It was such an honor to be in their relay.

Met a lot of really fun Australians on this trip and will miss looking them up in Australia. So now, John-Roger says, I must let these things go. Throw myself totally into this lovely dinner, the movie and tomorrow the tour of the movie stars homes. The tour was only $30 and takes all day. Seems like quite a bargain. I will be leaving Saturday morning for Santa Barbara. The first stop will be the Getty Museum. Damn. Forgot to mail off the rolls of film I have been saving. They are locked up with my panniers in the storage at the hostel.

This statistic: 1/4 of all the world's Rolls Royces live in LA. I was mulling this over with Green, the Magic Bicycle. Green cost a bargain $300 at our friendly bike shop in Ambridge. Green now has world travel stickers instead of paint. So then I promised Green to not discuss expensive cars any more.

The natives here, with the exception of South Central L. A., the natives here are really rich. OK, South Central does seem to go on and on. The tour from the Santa Monica AYH hostel was guided by a young South African (white) who wouldn't take his nice tourist van even close to Watts. South Central still, even though looking very bombed out, doesn't in any way compare to Tahiti for depressed looking. 20,000 gang members is still only one of every 150 people in LA's teeming 3 million. We toured to the intersection where the riot started. All the buildings there were destroyed and only the gas station has been rebuilt. I don't understand why the families of the 40 some people who died in the riots don't get together and sue the Crips and Bloods out of existence. Class action. Think about it, lawyers. You could do something decent once and a while.

The manic tour guide's South African accent became even, more annoying when he spent hours and hours imitating Beavus and Butt Head. We did see movie star homes. Nice. Well, OK, very nice. Madonna lives in a house built by Bugsy Siegle. Not the house Bugsy was murdered in. We saw that one, too, and I recognized the living room window through which Warren Beatty got shot . . . Bugsy was right there with the rich and famous. Out on Malibu is a house for which Bing Crosby paid $8,600. It is Robert Redford's now and he paid 1.4 M. Location. Location. Location.

Days later, as I sat in my $3.00 tent space in Leo Carillo State Park, $3.00 for hiker/biker, I tried not to feel to sorry for the very, very rich and the problems that money can bring. I didn't even feel sorry for South Central and the problems that viciousness can bring.

A young British guy in our little LA tour group complained incessantly about the US. Too much chance of sudden death with everyone armed. He had been to New York and LA. He worked here and there but didn't make much money. We were waiting for service in the really fun Hard Rock Cafe.

"If you want to be rich," I said, "Go to the library. Read books by people who got rich. They all write books about how they did it. Start with "The Autobiography of Benjamin Franklin."

He puffed on his cigarette and looked off into space. He said that McDonalds was causing all the rainforests to be cut down. I asked him if he had been able to see all the cows waiting to be turned into burgers from his plane window as he flew across the US. I protested that we had enough burgers for the entire world without messing with rainforests. Did he know what comes out of the nether end of male cattle? He ate his very large burger. I had ordered a veggie burger, which I ate with a sauce rich with sanctimoniousness.

3.17.96 Ventura, CA. How to describe this part of California? In a word, wealthy. I figure anyone with a palm tree is rich. Anyone with a sailboat is rich. Where I'm sitting, next to the Channel Islands National Park, I can see a forest of palms and another aluminum jungle of sailboat masts. This is also my idea of pretty. And pretty much money. It is also bicycle friendly. So far almost all of the Pacific Coast Highway has been a bicycle delight. I won't make it to Santa Barbara tonight because I am going whale watching. Grey whales here. Humpback whales in New Zealand.

Like wow, man, like wow! No wonder the inhabitants are reduced to one syllable.

Later: Best whale watching yet. Grey whales, two of them that rolled and spouted for as long as we watched them. They were headed for the Baja. There are some 5000 common dolphins (a small whale, marked like the killer whale but gray where the killer is white) that reside in the Santa Barbara channel. They enthusiastically surf the bow and the wake of the boat so it is easy to watch them. The little dusky dolphins that danced on their tails and did flips on Milford Sound did not let us get as close as these guys. Besides the boat owners on Milford thought of them as an extra rather than the tour de force they turned out to be.

The jaunt through the Channel Islands National Park ends at 5:00 which gives me an hour to eat and get tucked in for the night because the sun sets at 6:15. There is a State park down the road that will, hopefully, give shelter. In spite of the 12 hours sleep last night, I could do with a nap right now.

3.18.96 Ventura CA. Wrote out an article for Marion this morning, getting the money's worth out of my motel. It is tough to get started today. Chilly and overcast again like yesterday. Ventura is as pretty as money can make it. Breakfast at McDonalds. All I need to make life wonderful is a USA TODAY and a crossword to do. Am I talking day off after just two days of bicycling.?

Article:

"BACK IN THE USA

Whenever people ask me what my favorite country is, I answer, "You mean other than the USA?" Home, sweet home is so very superior to just about anywhere. I am so happy to be here. Throw together the bicycle friendliness of France, the dedication to flowers of Switzerland, the ride by the pounding surf of Greece or New Zealand, and you'll have the Pacific Coast Highway. Is it beautiful? Beyond description.

Green and I just can't pass up a National Park. This one was just a tourist center and the park which is five of the 8 channel islands. So I took a boat tour at 1/2 the price of a whale watch in New Zealand and saw twice as many whales. We were entertained by pair of gray whales who were lazing along on their way to the Baja. We also went up to Gail, an oil platform. Gee, I like it when others give names to things. It helps Green the Bicycle to feel accepted. Gail looks like she had been designed for a James Bond movie. A big barrel near it had been adopted by a bunch of sea lions. Best of all were a portion of the 500 common dolphins that reside in the Santa Barbara Channel who came to play with our boat. They enthusiastically rode the bow wave and surfed the wake by the dozens.

How many whale watches between here and Alaska?"

3.19.96Santa Barbara. This is a low profile city. Except for exceptionally tall and majestic palms, the city is short and hunkered down. I think that this is a sign that they are on the fault line and the residents have learned to be careful in the crash zone. There was a hostel advertised, not an AYH hostel although it advertised itself as the International Hostel. It had moved and the new quarters were filthy. I checked out the nearby hotels and they were also not only expensive but very slovenly. I eventually settled on a nice one, a block from the beach and $38 with tax and breakfast. The area was full of quaint and interesting shops and I bought a flashlight that you put on your head. I passed one up in Nepal for $12 and then thought, big mistake. In the outfitters shop it was $36 with tax, but not Chinese. The Amtrack station was right next door so I picked up timetables. You never know.

Later: In Las Gaviotas State Park. Camping. There is a cloud hanging over. I will take a short day tomorrow and stop in a motel. The many other choices of State Park were much nicer than this but this one is at the bottom of a long hill, which has a tunnel coming up tomorrow. The hosts here are nice. I got to ride to the grocery store in Buhlton where I broke down and bought a loaf of bread and a jar of peanut butter. Now, I will never starve. The fog that makes it dark before dark is due, around 6:20. I walked the beach. It is short here, pounding up against uplifted tablets of pink limestone. Red Gum trees (eucalyptus). It is getting really cold now so I'm going to dive into my tent. I am very happy with the day. Rode a lot of miles on Rt. 101, four lane, divided, lots of traffic and Green and I were very brave.

03.20.96 Lompoc, CA. Started out at 6:30 because I wanted to beat the traffic to a tunnel on a humongous hill. Tunnels are really scary. These people are up early. We are nowhere near anything at all but there they were, tandem dump trucks and everything, at the crack of dawn. Actually it was a damp foggy dawn and when I get to my motel, I will have to spread out the tent and dry it. The tunnel was short, had a sidewalk on which I walked the bike. Ear crushing noise. It started a six mile hill of which so much was straight up that I had to push poor Green. Green was embarrassed. It wasn't a bad walk; the views of California ranches were green also. Cattle ambled up and down the steep hills and more than once the road's paving had slid away downhill. Once at the top, there was a downhill most of the way to Lampoc through more lovely ranches and valleys. Lompoc seems as rich as the rest of California (South Central LA excepted). The traffic is tolerant and no one so far has given me the "Git the H (or F) offn the road" that is so endemic to Western PA. I might stay two days here because it is break time and I think I have the time. Lompoc turns out to be the home of the Stealth bomber. Chas has his beloved Dodge Stealth so I send him a post card of the real thing. The plane was so stealthy that I never saw one.

3.23.96 Pismo Beach. Longest day yesterday and the toughest. First there was Unnecessary Mountain which was off of Rt. 1 and climbed a steep hill with many switchbacks and down the other side the same way. I finally made Guadalupe, the lunch stop and looked in vain for an American restaurant. I chose the best looking Mexican and had one of the worst meals of my life. Pismo Beach makes me think I went the wrong way and ended up in Mexico. But it can't be. It is nice and clean. Streets paved. The Restaurant was fairly clean and there was no notice to put waste toilet paper in the wastebasket. Can't be Mexico. I don't understand why the plumbing across the border can't handle toilet paper. Guadalupe will celebrate MEXICAN Independence Day, Sep. 16.

There was a dreadful stretch after Guadalupe with strong side winds blowing sand straight through my body. As trucks passed, they shut off the wind for a few seconds and the wind I was leaning into was no longer there. So I'd lurch left, just as the truck passed and the gale resumed and threw me right. Right off the road on to a sand burm. This happened over and over. I never figured out how to prevent the violence. Eventually I came to another steep hill and a forest of red gum (eucalyptus) which smelled great and protected me from the wind. At the end of 50 miles was the Pismo Beach Hiker/biker, which allowed me to camp out of the wind in a lovely spot for $3.00. This is the first time I have seen the Pacific in days. Also, the sun is shining. It is very cold. The lady who owns the hot dog shop where I had dinner (everything else is closed) was telling me that her son flew, solo, from Oceana to Paris, France when he was 11years old that made him famous for a while. He is now 19 and doesn't want to be a pilot. Thinking about being a para medic. Refused to go to a fancy university for future air oriented because he couldn't have a car and his girlfriend couldn't go with him. The owner's brother had died six months ago of AIDS. She nursed him for about four months.

Met two bicycle touring guys doing motels from San Jose to LA. They said they had met one couple and me. Same story I heard from the Swiss biker who is going from Alaska to Tierra del Fuego.

This is a jolly cafe and I am loathe to leave. I am only doing thirty miles today and don't feel like rushing to it. I will try to take in the mission at San Luis Obispo.

Finished reading John Grisham's *The Rainmaker*. Most excellent. Glad we sued the insurance company that denied our claim when the condo that we had at a ski resort got inundated by a condo two flights up. Should have taken it to court and shamed them. I would think it would just be easier for them to pay small claims but according to John Grisham it seems to be more lucrative to the insurance company to deny all claims.

Later. Lost in San Luis Obisbo. Pretty upscale here. I missed the Adventure Cycling route and the Pacific Coast route that I followed was very nice but has deserted me here in lovely San Luis. I'm ensconced in a mall in a good-for-you restaurant. I shouldn't complain since it isn't costing me any more than the foul meal I had yesterday in Guadalupe. This town is not Mexican. Very blanco with designer blue jeans and expensive sweaters. It is a tad warmer but only just. Tree lined streets and two and three story buildings, Spanish style. Haven't a clue as to where the Mission might be. Chinese family eating here. There's a switch. Very tired today. Maybe I had better mosey on down to Morro Bay and worry about wasting time there.

Later. Morro Bay is so adorable. The Mission at San Luis was right down the street. All kinds of fun stuff going on there. Street entertainers and people selling all sorts of fair type stuff. Mailed the Grisham book to Chas. Must remember to tell him to read it. Very informative about insurance companies. Nationwide has always been on our side. We had to sue the CNA jerks.

The ride here was pleasant, Green and I followed Adventure Cycling's back roads rather than Caltrans' Rt.1. Went over a beautiful hill that reminded me of the close cropped, steep hills of England. No sheep, just cows. Morro Bay is a marsh area which has been designated as a bird sanctuary. There are two State Parks and I am at the one with the marina and cafe. The delightful cafe overlooks the small marina and a cozy bay with dunes on the far side. A tiny US flag clings to the wobbly staff, fluttering wildly. The table I have rented here is a circle of varnished wood, propped up by sturdy 2 x 4,s. The rest of the chairs and tables are the white, stacking resin that I wish I had invented. Wide, clean windows allow the sparkling waves to paint a serene picture. I want to eat my black bean soup a bean at a time but it is too good and I bolt it down, lubricated by a "taste of Pittsburgh," Rolling Rock beer. I seem to be dropping one bean per spoonful on my black tights, then have to surreptitiously recover it and clean off my tights. Green is leaning patiently against a post by the front door. I have already invested the $3.00 for a hiker biker spot for tonight. They have a fish sandwich that is Salmon today. grilled. If I go back and put up the tent, I could crawl in it and nap until dinnertime. So tired.

3.24.96 San Simeon. I'll visit the castle tomorrow. I might run into Patty Hearst, though I probably won't know her without the gun. I think she is out of jail now. The sun is just sliding into the sea. I was so tired when I got here that I watched Kevin Costner as Wyatt Earp again. It was better than I remembered.

This is such a charming restaurant, part of a Motel 6 that bought out a Holiday Inn. A lot more Holiday Inn than Motel 6. Tomorrow's ride starts the 90-mile Big Sur drive that goes up 10,000 feet in 90 miles. I'll try to get an early start. Wish I could dump some of my excess clothing. The waiter here is so sweet. He has been to South and Central America. He liked some ruins in northern Honduras the best.

Talked to Chas. He is working on the videotape from New Zealand. He is able to edit using the old camera and the new together. Great. He didn't confirm anything about Alaska. Seemed rather evasive. I thought it seemed too good when Peter said he would be taking the trip with me. Now I am wondering if there will be enough money. I can't seem to deny myself all the goodies. I probably should be camping more. Will get out all the maps and data and plan as much camping and hostelling as possible. On the Big Sur I plan to motel so that I can get a good rest at night.

3.25.96 I'm not too much into "Lifestyles of the Rich and Famous." They have their problems and I have mine. However, San Simion, the Hearst Castle is something else again. William Randolph Hearst, a modest fellow always called it the Ranch. It started out that way when his very rich father bought up what was to become 50 miles of the central coast of California. The architect for the castle was a woman, Julia Morgan. The original idea was to just build something fairly solid because the family and friends had been coming the two day trip to the ranch and staying in tents. It grew and grew into quite a bunch of rooms and became one of the costliest homes in the world. I would like to live there. It isn't exactly cozy but W.R. had great taste and ripped off from Europe a lot of the kinds of things I really like, tapestries, statues, paintings. He transported or had copied beautiful ceilings, floors, and put them in a place where there is not acid in the air to destroy them. It is all very charming and for sure the movie stars, politicians and just famous who came to relax here must have had a great time. Actually it was a bit before my time but I will try to imagine being here with Clark Gable, Charlie Chaplin and all the gang. The swimming pool reminded me of a picture of the one John Dupont had indoors that the Foxcatcher triathlon team used to work out in. W.R. had bigger things in mind, like being president. He never made that but as a newspaper tycoon, was a great opinion influencer.

The fee charged by the state park was a mere $14 which included a bus ride that wound and twisted its way up the hill to the castle. Could never have made it on the bicycle. My back has been bothering me. Lower back, left side and the knee on that side has twinges. A week's rest would do both a good thing. I only biked about six horrid miles, starting at noon after the visit to the castle. The wind was fierce, 15 knots the TV said. The best thing was the batch of sea lions that were stretched out on the beach, snoozing. You could walk right up and pat them. They could care less. Then came the picturesque light house. It would have been really nice day if I had been going the other way and I did think about it. Especially after I met two bicycle tourers going south who gave me a lot of well deserved pity. I'll be off at the crack of dawn tomorrow and see if I can't make my 32 miles by 10:00 when the wind comes up. Mustn't forget to look for the comet tonight. North East.

Later: Went out one last time to try to spot the comet and there it was. I can never spot those things but it was truly too big to miss. Fantastic. The wind is still screaming in the eves of the building. Oh well, only thirty miles tomorrow. Good rest today.

3.26.96 Lucia, CA. Tough but beautiful day with minimal wind. The coastline is rugged and the most beautiful. There is no rush hour here but traffic does pick up around 9 o'clock. Lots of climbing up hills and down again today. My back and left knee held up but I certainly am glad to get off the bike by 1:00. I had lunch with some bicycle racers. It was fun to talk to them.

They thought I could make it to Big Sur and I probably could but I'd rather take it easy and build up slowly. I am sore today in spite of a relatively (to yesterday) easy day. I planned very short days on the Big Sur section and I am sticking to that.

There are lots of bikers on the highway the last three days. Spring Break at the colleges.

Later: The motel was a ridiculous $60 for nothing. No TV, No tub. The restaurant is a delight, part au fresco and part by a fireplace. It closes at five so here I am trying to eat the right thing because there are no facilities between here and Big Sur. There are whales out there. Pretty far out. There were four of them. The owner here says he had a mountain lion in his garden yesterday and what you don't want to do is run because that is when they will attack. Just look them in the eye and scream and holler and back slowly away. I figure if I ever meet one it will be trying to look ME in the eye while backing slowly away. Screaming. 4:30 PM. Guess I'll go to bed.

3.27.96 Big Sur. Stopped at the first cafe. It is attached to an art gallery and really nice. No breakfast served so I'm working my way through a huge poppy seed muffin. The ride was short and easier than yesterday. I still have five or so miles to go before I really reach the town but I will be buttressed by the muffin and will have wasted enough time that I am not arriving at a motel before noon. The cliffs were beautiful, but it was cloudy so I didn't take many pictures. Took one of a blue flower against the blue sky and blue Pacific. Actually the water is subtle streaks of lavender and gray as well as blue. There is a Cal DOT road crew studying a pot hole where the parking lot hits the road. In Pittsburgh, the owner would have to repair it but it looks like these guys are going to earn themselves a lifetime supply of coffee.

There was only one really big land slide last winter on the highway, south of here. It was cleared in only three days. I have the same feeling about the road here that I did about the trail in Nepal. When it rains, you don't want to be here because the mountainside starts moving. I have spent a lot of the morning on the left side or ocean side of the road because you can see a lot more but also because the mountainsides are so intimidating on the right side.

One workman, ONE, is opening bags of patching stuff and hand dropping and stomping it into one of the puddles. I could watch this craftsman working all day. I feel really good. Depending on the spot I get for the night, I'd like to go on an expedition to see sea otters. Daughter Kitty had an otter that visited the cottage at Ocracoke Island and played by the sea wall. One day she was checking conditions, trying to decide whether to evacuate the cottage because it was blowing hard and the water was coming up. She saw the mother otter, a cub in her mouth swim over the sea wall and right under the cottage. Kitty left the cottage to the storm and the otter.

The road guy is making the second pot hole even bigger by chipping off the edges and shoveling these pieces into the truck. He is getting all wet and dirty. The pines across the road are candling. Yesterday, on a particularly high spot I saw leaves coming out on a deciduous tree. There were a couple of patches of brilliant orange California poppies. Getting the urge to move on. Funny how compulsive you get. Inertia sets in and when not biking you feel a lot of guilt. No reason. Just the inertia of continuing to do what you have been doing.

The workman opens one end of the bag and lets the patching stuff gradually slide out of its package. He has run out of patching stuff and will have to go for more. He gets in the truck and goes back and forth over the patches a bit then takes off in the direction of Carmel.

The art gallery was dedicated to the art of Henry Miller, author of *Tropic of Cancer*. He lived in Big Sur. As Big Sur has a population of 620 people, Henry was most important. Have never read anything of his that I can recall. I'll get to Carmel tomorrow and look for mayor, Clint Eastwood. We were born the same year and month. The downtown area of the Big Sur was a disappointing two rustic buildings, clinging to the side of the road. It said Big Sur Center and this is how I knew I had arrived. One building was a post office, the other a grocery/deli. I had a snack and rolled on down the hill to a lovely campground where I have raised my tent in a grove of redwood trees. If Rush Limbaugh were here I'd commit the chainsaw murder. All someone has to do is mention a tree and he has a sound bite of a big tree being sawed down. Sometimes I just can't take a joke. It is 3:00 P.M. and chilly. Mosquitoes drift around in front of my glasses.

03.28.96 Monterrey CA. Such a day. It started to rain after midnight and at 3:00 am I finally gave up trying to sleep in my leaking tent. The ladies room to which I fled was a long way from the lounge at Heinz Hall. I squatted in the corner under the sink, studying Og Mandino until it began to get light at 5:30. By 6:15 I had packed my soggy everything on poor Green. I hit the road before the sun was up but I could see some encouraging blue in the sky so I rolled right by the nearby motels and cafes and on down to the shore where it looked as if the storm was over until I got beyond the lighthouse. From then into Carmel, it really rained and raged at me. Poor little me with the huge, wind-catcher bicycle. Each corner was a scary challenge because I didn't know where the winds would blow me. My glasses were so wet they washed themselves and were not a problem. I finally gave up riding and pushed the bike up the tight turns and around the tight corners. Then I really gave up, totally in despair, and put out a thumb. It took a while but a couple of guys in an old truck picked me up, loading the loaded Green up over the high side and into the crowded truck. Then we flew. The driver, smoking and sipping coffee, roared through the corners and down hills. I was more scared than I had been on the bike. They were only going about three miles but it was a real blessing to be out of the area of twisting canyon roads. I was headed for the same restaurant where they were going but it didn't open until 11:30 and it was only 8:30 then so I biked on. They refused the money I offered. The road into Carmel was better after that. I tried to think of the white light that John-Roger talked about in *Life 101* and did manage to get a feeling of comfort and safety going. Or was it that things were really better? I eventually got to a service station in Carmel Highlands. I had been wearing my Reebok sandals and the wool socks from New Zealand. I had some silly idea that saving a warm dry pair of shoes would save me from hypothermia. By the time I got to Carmel, the skies were clear and the sun bright on the sparkling white of the waves breaking over the ragged rocks in the bay. I never laid eyes on Clint Eastwood. He's my age. If he has any sense at all, he's resting.

The motel I found in Monterrey, something about Cypress, cost the same as the Motel 6 and was as beautiful any I have ever been in. It also had a tub. When I spread out the tent, sleeping bag, *Life 101* and all to dry, there was redwood bark and needles and twigs every where. The guy at the desk said I was the Forrest Gump of bicycling. I bought a new tape recorder and am playing the *Adiemus, Songs of Sanctuary*. It is based on Maori songs and is way beyond beautiful. Chas is going to use it for background music for a New Zealand show or tape and is having a hard time picking because he thinks they are all very wonderful. He never got to see the Moari dancers that I saw in Rotorura. The music makes me start dancing, not that I would ever manage the hip switching that Maori girls do but the music has the beat and is really wonderful for New Zealand even though done by an Irish pair. I got to see Seinfeld for the first time in a year. Great. Talked to Chas and he ordered a new tent for me from Campomor.

3.29.96 Watsonville. Starting in Monterey,CA I had a breakfast at the motel and am now chowing down at a charming restaurant. There are five very effective paintings on canvas that look as though they were heavily influenced by Monet's garden scenes. They are at least 4'x6' and hanging on an attractive brick wall. What makes them different is that the canvas has been nailed to the frame on the back side of the frame and the side edges continue the scene a bit so that there is no need for a frame. This makes the brick wall become the very effective frame. Planning to visit the aquarium.

Later: the aquarium visit was a disappointment. They were uninterested in my security problems, would not find a safe place to leave Green so I didn't go in. Still it was a nice outing. The waterfront has Fisherman's wharf and John Steinbeck's *Cannery Row*, both huge tourist attractions. Unfortunately I ran out of the supply of film that Charles gives me and got no pictures of this very picturesque area. Since then I have been on bicycle paths through Seaside to Marina. I patronized the Taco Bell at Marina. Just came through Fort Ord. It seems to be one of the army bases that are closing down. There is a large debate in today's local paper about how to handle the problem. Needs just a huge batch of money to move it to local hands. The locals have decided that the only way they can handle it is if the Army gives them the land. It will take $71,000,000 just to tear down existing buildings. It is, however such prime land on the beach that they can't afford to ignore the opportunity. Part of it will be a university. Marina isn't the playground of the rich and famous that Carmel and Monterrey are. It is very lower middle class, as if it had been part of nourishing the Army base and now, what for Marina? It's chunk of federal money and jobs disappearing and this wonderful opportunity opening up.

Lots of bikers on the bike path. One of them said that I had chosen the right time to come up the Big Sur because once the tourist season starts it is really dreadful traffic and not a place to be on a bike. 1:30 and 40 more miles to Santa Cruz!!!! Don't think I will make it. Look for a cheap hotel here.

Later: Tried every Motel between Watsonville and Marina. Very unsatisfactory. They wanted more than the beautiful motel in Monterey for not much. Two of them were Bombay palaces. Why is it so hard to deal with the Indians? Is it because my experience in India (and Mississippi) was that if I had the smallest complaint they pitch me out on the street? The last one had stickers for all sorts of credit cards in the window but when I tried to use one, wanted cash. Problems. Said I couldn't use the phone. Problems. Said that the TV which seemed to be working well had problems and sometimes didn't work well. I just slid on out the door and kept looking.

Missed a great picture today of a guy in total cowboy stuff, hat, boots, and most astonishing, leather chaps. He was on a bicycle and by the time I realized how great he was, I had missed the photo op.

This is another Mexican town in the US. Mexican guys sweetly moved off the sidewalk to let me go by as I was wimping my way through town. There was a no-tell-hotel that was so seedy that I was too chicken to even inquire about prices.

3.30.96 Santa Cruz. Not there yet, just breakfasting. Will call for a reservation before I leave the motel this morning. It is very cold. Low 40's I guess. Hope it is warmer in Ocracoke. Played son-in-law Gary Mitchell's delightful tape when I couldn't sleep last night. What a treat it is. How refreshing and fun. A guy coming in who was here for dinner last night. Guess he doesn't have anywhere to go either. Actually I am going a big 20 miles today to Santa Cruz. 50,000 people so it should have a Motel 6 but doesn't. If I can't get in the hostel I will be in trouble. I went through the artichoke capitol of the world yesterday and then fields of ripening strawberries. The strawberries were in humped-up rows that stretched to the horizon. Strawberries as big as plums burst from the green leaves and flowed down the mounded rows. Lots of pickers and big equipment were in the fields. Watsonville and Pajaro had large facilities for chilling fruit. Don't need it right now, there is a natural refrigerator. I don't even get down to tee shirt these days. The sun is warm but there is a really chill breeze. The ocean off shore uplifts really cold water from its depths and the warm water is pushed out to sea and this causes fogs usually but right now it is causing chill. I have been studying maps, trying to figure out where the hostels are. The one in Santa Cruz won't say, just says call for directions.

Later: Bicycler girl stopped me in Santa Cruz and we did lunch. She wants to tour but is worried about how to start. I suggested

Adventure Cycling in Missoula Montana or Dale Hart's Classic Cycling. Also suggested a tour from D.C. to Pittsburgh using the C&O Tow Path and after Cumberland Maryland, the Great Allegheny Passage bike paths and the Youghigheny River bike paths. She is a teacher and may take some time off to go touring.

I am sitting on the beach at Santa Cruz, waiting for the hostel to open. Can see a roller coaster and stuff down the beach. The other way is the wharf with lots of shops and entertainment for tourists. Al fresco eating which is very pleasant. The busses here have racks on the front for bicycles.

03.31.96 Pescadero. CA Actually headed for the lighthouse at Pigeon Point which is a good bit this side of Pescadero. There is a hostel at the lighthouse. What a superb day. Bright, sunny, brilliant white foam against cobalt blue sea. Rocks and cliffs. And, AND a tailwind. I flew along the twenty some miles to the georgous lighthouse. Produced this for Health and Fitness:

White Light

"Want adventure? The last frontier is the interior."

John-Roger, *Life 101*

As I battle my way up the Pacific Coast Bicycle Trail from LA, I frequently regret that I took the word of an encyclopedia in New Zealand that the winds on the California Coast come out of the West. A little north-west. Then when I arrive on these rugged shores, the information says that SUMMER winds go north to south. So I figure I will find out, by doing, what the winds are like in the Spring. Answer? They are strong and when in your face . . . .

That reminds me, the subject of one of the few short conversations that I ever had with Ole, (the one who had the original World Wander idea), was headwinds and my theory that it makes people crazy to have the wind blowing on the forehead, day after day, unrelenting. Ole responded, as argumentive as usual, that he never worries about headwinds, goes into them all the time. I couldn't ignore this opportunity and said,

"See. Exactly what I mean. It has made you crazy."
He didn't seem to think that was funny. Gave me a crazed look.

"Just kidding," I said.

Some people just can't take a joke.

Me, I'm trying to save my sanity from the headwinds. Southern California is a perfect place to work on sanity. Here in America's paradise there are a lot of other people working on their sanity and you feel very 'in' if you are worried about going nuts, from the headwind or what ever.

I got bogged down on the present self-help book I am working with right after the author praised the other book I got bogged down with.

Here is an exercise from LIFE 101. You picture a safe secure place to be. I decide back in Mom's womb was pretty good after a day on Rt. 101 with tandem dump trucks.

Now, picture a white light that surrounds you and makes you feel really good.

Problem. I can't get a grip on the white light. Is it too dark in the womb? Is it that no one has been in my brain replacing burned out bulbs? I can't get a white light and probably the entire method of retaining sanity is dependant on white light. I dare not give up Og Mandino and swearing to love everybody three times a day because I can handle reading that three times a day. So I try to imagine the white light in the morning because sight seeing on this magnificent, wonderful, fabulous place makes me tired and I am ready for bed at dusk (6:30), As I close the eyes, I can see the day's horde of snoozing elephant sea lions that let everyone just walk around patting them. I can see the light house far out on a rugged point with waves edged in white splashing high into the air. I can feel the wind on my poor chilled brain. The wind on the brain. But no white light.

One of the better things about white light, according to 'LIFE 101' is that you can send it out to make other people feel good. Fantastic. This could put Hallmark out of business. You should be able to put a bright green neon sign with it saying, 'This white light sent to you by . . .' I really must master the white light, or at least get a glimmer.

***There are those who ask, 'Are you having fun with that bicycling around the world?'

Is that a stupid question or what? To bike into 30-mile-an-hour headwinds . . . . To have climbed and pushed a loaded-for-camping bike up the threatened 10,000 feet of climbing in 90 miles area of the Big Sur . . . in hypothermic weather. Fun! It is just a barrel of fun. Actually my idea of fun is family gatherings with guitars and singing, or Seinfeld, or *Naked Gun 2 1/2* So I bike short days and lie around trying to imagine white light.

Adventure is as much hard work as fun. Travel, as perhaps has been mentioned before, comes from the same root word as travail which means to suffer. So if family and TV and movies are my idea of fun, why not just do that? Well. Been there. Done that.

***Went by Esalen Institute and could actually see a building, clinging to the cliff below me with waves dancing up toward it. If I remember correctly this was the hangout (and the building does seem to hang out over the Pacific) of Carl Rogers and Gestalt therapy. I always pictured buck-naked people seated in the lotus position staring out at the Pacific, but looking down, I couldn't see a soul out on the deck. Too chilly to commune with nature, perhaps. Actually, I am jealous. The journey within offered by Gestalt sounds exciting. If I had Shirley MacClaine's money I'd love to give it a try. I haven't been there. Haven't done that.

***Now, arrived in San Francisco, I sit wondering about magical days yesterday and today. Yesterday's brilliant, sunny day offered the first tailwind of California and wafted me to the Pigeon Point Lighthouse with its frothy waves, ice plant covered cliffs, lovely hostel and fun group. At dawn, rains and bitter winds beat on the old buildings and as I grappled with Green the Magic Bicycle, in the parking lot, a truck with a really attractive couple drove up and the driver announced that he had been driving up Route 1 when he suddenly felt drawn to the lighthouse. He slammed on the brakes and turned into the lighthouse. When he saw me with Green, he knew that we were his mission. They hoisted Green into the back of the rusting truck and toasty dry, we rode through the chilling downpour to The hostel at San Francisco's Fort Mason. Is this California, or what, huh?

*　*　*

End of piece for Health and Fitness

04.01.95 San Francisco. So here I am in THE city and it is pouring.

The couple that transported Green and me to SanFrancisco refused the $20 that I offered but I put it under the seat and hope that they find it. There was one stretch of narrow, twisting, no shoulder that made me even more glad to be in a truck. The scenery continued to be beautiful and suddenly we were in the area. (Dale City) about which the song, 'and they're all made of ticky tacky and they all look just the same' was written. It was a shockingly planned area when you are expecting to see one of the world's most beautiful cities. Then past Twin Peaks and into Golden Gate Park with its Eucalyptus trees.

The hostel is at Fort Mason in a great spot on the bay, not far from Fisherman's Wharf. If it ever stops raining so I can leave this restaurant, I will go exploring. I have my rain suit on which seems as appropriate here as it did in Auckland but this is real, serious rain and my feet got wet in the sandals. I'm thinking of swapping them for my hiking boots, or swap the running shoes for hiking boots. Hiking boots keep the feet dry even when riding the bicycle.

So now, I can't put it off any longer, I have to call the local relatives or Precious. Rather call Precious and see if she is still off cigarettes.

Later: In a beautiful restaurant with 20' high windows looking out on the bay. The sun is setting. Because of the rain, I spent the day preparing the article, "White Light" for the fitness magazine. When I Faxed it Chas said there was a streak through it that he couldn't read. So I came looking for a FAX machine but got waylaid by hunger and a beautiful restaurant. Managed to get down half of an eggplant and mushroom calzone. The tables are on three tiers so everyone has a view. It used to be the Galliardia Chocolate Company and is right next door to the National Marine Museum.

4.3.96 SanFrancisco. Arrived at the cable car street and waiting for my steak and eggs. Was San Francisco over sold?. Yesterday, two meals no meat. The day before two meals, no meat. Should be holding my own, weight wise. Yesterday woke up with a new character for my Greek short story that hopefully will save the heroine from a fate worse than death. It rolled along very nicely until the point where the girl must part from her bike pal. And stalled again. But it was a day well spent.

People ask where is the best food in my travels and I answer USA. The steak I just had was huge, a t-bone about an inch thick, perfectly cooked with jacket hash browns and such excellent whole wheat and scrambled. $6.15 in Union Square, in San Francisco. Can't beat that anywhere. How about Europe: contenential breakfast, the day's permissible calories that will bring on a sugar high within two hours and then the sugar crash within an hour of that? How about the Orient and a bowl of rice with something green in it? Now there is a breakfast to dream about. I can do the vegetarian thing and feel very pure but I believe much more in the healing power of steak. Hey. The steer is dead. He doesn't mind. When I have to diet, the first thing to go is meat. When I need strength and energy, I head for the steak house. This one is called Tad's. Across the street is Lori's Diner and around the corner, Louis' something or other. It is very friendly here Everyone is on a first name basis.

A young Australian who seemed very unAissie, sober, in love with life, super intelligent and well educated said he follows the rule of: breakfast like a king, lunch like a prince and dinner like a pauper. I try to get in the three veggies and three fruits a day, preferably raw. This is an attempt to leave no room for junk food.

I also switch to water from Gatorade when not bicycling. Lots and lots of water. Water will cure the tourista, colds . . . lots of stuff.

Granny Report

On TV I saw an 80 year old granny leap out of an airplane in tandem with an experienced parachute jumper. She sort of doggy paddled for a bit then stretched her arms out and flew. She said that it was a great thrill. She was in Picton, South Island, New Zealand. I was very impressed. The grannies I saw in New Zealand play tennis and golf and are sharp dressers. They don't do triathlons. ***Here's a quote from Sophie Tucker:

'From birth to age 18, a girl needs good parents, from 18 to 35 she needs good looks, from 35 to 55 she needs a good personality and from 55 on she needs cash.'

***California Grannies have camper vans. I see them pointing out the window at me and Green the Magic Bike and I can almost hear them saying, 'Look at that would you, Dad! Who does she think she is?' Most of them view me with great suspicion as I clump into Dennys with my noisy shoes and tight tights. When I take off my helmet, my fine, sweaty hair is tangled and squashed into dreadlocks. This is when bad really is bad.

What is inertia all about? Getting stuck in the direction we are going so that a change of direction, taste, clothing or whatever, is just too much to contemplate. Inertia is doing it because it is what we do.

The welcome signs are up for Elder Hostel at the State Park where I am camping, $3.00 in the hiker biker. I inquired about the lodge where I presume the elders are staying and it would have been somewhere around $70 up to around $120 for my one person. I occupied a table in the pleasant restaurant and am having fried chicken, rice and lukewarm warm coffee for $11.00. Hopefully the elders will come tromping in to regale me with tales of everything that I am missing in the area. They enter and do not just fill in the empty tables. They have groups of four or six. One wonders what the pecking system is since they all signed up for the same thing at the same price. They do have wonderful tales about things they are learning: whales and Redwoods.

Bus 30 in San Francisco is the Chinese granny bus. They don't seem over-weight but are still burdened with canes. They don't speak English but have a lot of other grannies to talk to. As we go by a park it is morning and groups of senior Chinese are doing Tai Chi. Looks like they are swatting no-seeums in slow motion. Mao said that Tai Chi was for old people. Perhaps I am ready.

So how is this granny doing? The arthritis pain in my hands has all but disappeared. I can even ride without gloves. I have not lost weight, but what I am carrying is pretty well distributed. In 1994, on a walking tour in England, I fell flat on my face. No reason. Lack of attention. Scratched my glasses, my chin, my nose. The chin and nose healed and I replaced the lens. Much later my dentist suggested that the problem with my two front teeth being loose came from a blow and it took another couple of months before I remembered the fall in England. Now, two years later, the loose teeth are beginning to firm up again and I can almost bite into things with them. My feet are still pretty pathetic. An aging triathlete in New Zealand diagnosed the awful pain that I get sometimes in the toe area as Morton's neuroma and says that it is easily taken care of. The four toenails that have been distorted by fungus seem better and if I live another hundred years, they might get back to normal. In the meantime, I limp a bit.

4.05.96 Ocracoke, NC. Vacation from the vacation. Spending Easter with my beloved husband and daughter Kitty, granddaughter Katy, son-in-law Gary, Bill, Dave the Fiddler, Blue the husky, Momma Cat, and various assorted types that hang out in this East Coast paradise. Today we inspected the unusual building project which has Gary and Kitty's little ole cottage propped up, 20 feet in the air while another cottage is built under it. Then the original was lowered to the top of the new first floor and tacked in and the whole thing sheathed in cedar shingles. It will be a gorgeous house with a recording studio for Gary and an art studio for Kitty, a bath of her own for Katy, a nice big kitchen dining room, and a new screened in porch. We had a fun lunch and then I napped and went out for dinner again. Went through my pictures of Thailand, Turkey, New Zealand, Fantastic. I'm good!

04.12.96 San Francisco. Writing on the plane. Left rather abruptly when I noticed that the departure from Pgh was 10:55 and not 12:40. The 12:40 departure was from Cincinnati. We were settled at Kings with all bags packed and waiting for pal Don to join us when we discovered the error. Chas called the dentist and cancelled the appointment and ran back home for the film he had forgotten to give me. So it was rush, rush, but fun. We did the same thing when we left for Canmore. Are we trying subconsciously not to leave Pittsburgh? We love Pittsburgh.

The ground below looks very dry and forlorn. Will I bike over this? Stupid. There was a thunder storm as we had breakfast in Pittsburgh but it had warmed up enormously. Don bought breakfast. It seems bright and sunny here. I am reading about the Inside Passage area and getting very excited about it. It really sounds like fun. I have come up with an idea for a route to add to the great idea Chas had about going from Jasper to Prince Rupert by train. We love our train rides and this one would be great. Easy on the bikes also. Large dam below. Relatively small river into it. I will try to get to Edmonton for his birthday, July 1. We catch a train to Prince Rupert and are back in USA for July 4. Take ferry to different small towns and spend two days in each, camping if possible. When we get to Skagway, bike to Whitehorse and he flies home. I continue to Fairbanks where he joins again to do Denali. Anchorage and the fiords in that area. I go back to Whitehorse, to Dawson Creek to Edmonton, to Winnipeg to Sault St. Marie to Detroit, Cleveland, Pittsburgh.

None of this happened.

Worked on budget.

Went to library and worked on maps for an hour.

It is beginning to shape up. As usual Chas is not spending nearly enough time with me.

4.13.96 San Francisco. The natives here are a trip. First my nieces and nephews. One normal Mitchell of the three with two kids, wife and workaholic symptoms. One delightful gay guy, beloved of all, who bears my father's name. One unmarried mother who lives in a beautiful house in Berkeley with the father. They are all quite charming, fun people. They think *I* am odd. Old, weird Aunt Sally. They want to know about the family since my brother, a very 'now' person whose now is an agony because his wife, their mother, has Alzheimer's, and has no recall of anything.

Precious is my friend in San Francisco. She and I and Ted trekked together in Nepal. She is somewhere around perfect in appearance, a dancer, with tattoos and nose rings. She is also a para legal, attending law school. She lives with Bob, a school teacher, in Berkeley. Most contact was my leaving messages on the answering system but she is anxious to prove to me that she has quit smoking. Those who work here are hard workers. The one nephew's health food store is in the Castro district and has an average of 500 customers a day.

In the evenings the streets fill up with in-line-skate folk, since they aren't allowed to skate on the sidewalk in the Marina district. The car driver sits in the car in the street pushing buttons and a wall opens and he drives his car into the garage. This is not very picturesque as you would expect such an expensive area to be. In fact it is rather plain and uninteresting. A warehouse for people. Galileo High School which graduated Joe Dimaggio and OJ is just cater-cornered from Fort Mason where my hostel is. It is light pink. Fisherman's Wharf is next door and quite exotic with fish store after fish store and quaint trawlers coming in and out. Cable cars start there and travel adorably toward the sky.

I tried to strike up a conversation with a lone female while waiting in line at the movie and she gave me such an icy, disdainful look that I actually stopped talking. Did she think I was trying to pick her up? I forgot to do my 'I love you' mantra yesterday.

Traveling from the East Coast to the West Coast seems like such a miracle. A fellow on the plane was complaining about the trip (no movie). I was surprised since I think in terms of moving about by bicycle or car. How about covered wagon?

The movie was Robin Williams in *'The Birdcage.'* It was one joke that lasted a couple of hours but I never quit laughing.

Birthday party for my grand niece today. Rob picks me up at 2:30. Dinner with Precious tomorrow. If one of the relatives has copying facilities, I'll try to talk them into parting with a tape or CD so I can give Kitty and Gary's Molasses Creek tape to Precious. Partial payment for *The Snow Leopard*

San Francisco

Sunday morning and there are voices outside the window of my room at the Fort Mason hostel. I try rolling over and ignoring the disturbance but it persists. Familiar sounding female voices of ladies who are ordering grunting, sweating men around with the same patience they reserve for small children. Finally I peeked out of the blind. The grassy area that is sheltered by huge eucalyptus is being invaded by loudspeakers. Might as well get up so I can run when the noise pollution starts.

Meanwhile there is a protest going on right beside the hostel. After breakfast I joined the group outside for a Sunday morning service. The cognoscenti are right here beside me, a lot of women with tee shirts that say they were in Beijing with Hillary or that women should arise in one way or another. Well, I did. I arose. There was a: white Unitarian preacher lady who wanted to preserve affirmative action, gay rights, etc., She was followed by a Jewish rabbi, token male, who said he is the only professed gay rabbi in the world, and who advised good behavior and good manners. The last was impassioned A.M.E. preacher lady who cried for the blood of Bob Dole and Newt Gingrich and then belted out some great music that encouraged LOVE. It was most interesting in the clear sunshine, green grass, fluttering birds, with a backdrop of the bay and the Golden Gate Bridge.

I have a conflict. Being basically conservative, I can't understand why conservatives, whose main cause is less government, have taken up such causes as the so called 'prolife'. Prolife meaning doctor killers and clinic bombers. I think 'Choice' is a conservative position. I always vote by that criteria because women have to take a stand somewhere. I can't get pregnant. My only still fertile daughter-in-law is trying to get pregnant with invitro, which is detested by the 'pro-lifers'. It is all too confusing.

Back in the hostel for lunch, I tried, in vain, to talk a young Chinese guy from Singapore into going to the rally. He wasn't the tiniest bit interested in watching US citizens exercise their First Amendment rights. Two Brit girls who shared my room said they had been watching from the window and rolling on the floor during the morning service because it was so funny. I felt a bit miffed. Sometimes you don't get no respect.

After buying a *'Down with the Radical Right'* poster I wandered down to the newly set up speakers' platform and settled down on the poster to listen to the speakers. A goodly number of people here now.

They were grape pickers, garment workers, AIDS sufferers, marijuana touters, Mexicans, blacks, and Chinese, bussed in from the edges of civilization. The first male is now speaking, has a Arab accent and is opposed to anti-terrorist legislation. Says it is against free speech. Next speaker is HIV positive and wants to prevent legislature that would require pregnant women to be tested for HIV and AIDS. Next is for opposing 'civil rights amendment', what is that? One lass is down to her bra. And what is her point, or should I say points? The drum group has been the best entertainment so far.

The rally was organized by NOW to preserve affirmative action and offered Patricia Ireland, who was as hard to understand as the others. 'Our fight, our lives, our right to decide.' Some just get up there and get carried away with passion, they scream and spit.

Being young in the 1940's with pictures of big time demagogs like Hitler and Mussolini branded on the brain, I have always avoided this kind rally. The appeal is not to the brain but to emotion. Very suspicious. My usual aproach to these subjects is the editorial page.

Here is a rude sign opposing Bob Dole. YWCA VP. Black and excellent speaker . . . Pro choice . . . Radical who? Hey, police beat up whites, too. Lady next to me looks like the Vanessa Redgraves cripple from the anti-Nazi movie, cane and eye-patch. NOW a Lady from Philly for poor. Doesn't like Newt. Stopped the government of PA from cutting health care. We don't have health care in Pa? Shouting, spitting. America. Get to work

Gloria Steinem made the only truly coherent speech of the day. Said that the radical right was trying to take over the Republican Party. This is causing problems within the party and offers great opportunity to the Democrats, particularly Clinton, who now stands revealed as a moderate. She said, 'VOTE'. Hitler was voted in. (This whole thing reminds me of Hitler.) One other thing was that the notion that 'all candidates are the same' excuses voter laziness. But really, how would voters get this notion? Is a response to the horror of October's vicious ads on TV?

She is beautiful. Doesn't shout. She has a well-planned speech. She pushes affirmative action. Affirmative action is about inclusion. .06% of population runs everything?????? (Is she part of that .06????) What you do matters. What we do reflects our values. Flap of a butterfly's wing. (Chaos Theory. She must have read Joe Beckman's Chaos Theory book. How many of us can there be?)

Baptist guy for civil rights. Fiery. 'I'm white and I'm all right.' For sure being white and male needs an apology in this group.

Legal rights for illegal immigrants. Lady Garment workers. Sugar and cream(?) Crema y azucar. Danny Glover. Unite minorities. Defeat CCRI.(?) Large, smelly ladies right next to me. Stopping in a place with no shower are they? Lady who was with Caesar Chavez: Dole, you have brought us together because we all HATE you.

At a second speakers platform the NOW ladies could not restrain from attacking the white males, exemplified by the detested

Dole and Gingrich, even though there were a number of white males (maybe half) present. A lot of speakers got group participation with 'WE WILL—' chants. For me, this was a stretch but I 'WE WILL . . . . ED' and tried to feel love with the rest of the crowd, who pretty much ignored me in spite of urgings from the rostrum to be loving. (Except when HATING.)

I had my sign to sit on and it was pleasant in the sun. We were waiting for Jessie. When he spoke, the presence mysteriously shifted from the NOW ladies to maleness. Jessie had us all stand and hold hands. Jessie is no Martin Luther King and when he went from extolling the virtues of Ron Brown and the other leaders who had died in the plane crash to attacking Dole and Gingrich for a lack of respect for the dead, it pulled the plug out of the whole thing. Jessie said, almost literally, that he would back Clinton because Clinton was good at funerals. The steam that had been carefully built up by the ladies to preserve affirmative action had disappeared. About that time I was thinking of heading out for dinner and had started sliding toward the sidelines so I wouldn't be noticed when everyone sat down again. Suddenly Jessie was asking for money.

"Hold up your money." People with garbage cans were coming through the crowd for contributions. I turned to look back and one person in this very large crowd was holding up a dollar. I only write checks for charity. Well, I can be talked out of cash by the Salvation Army which is right next to Mother Teresa in my book. Anyhow, very few were responding to the request for cash. In fact, as I reached the sidelines I was swept along by a parade of people headed out. The entire crowd, it seemed to me, had risen and instead of listening to Jessie, were headed for the exit! Needless to say, I missed the rest of Jessie's speech. Most of the audience was probably the usual college crowd and when Jessie turned the message from affirmative action to a lack of respect for a black leader, the crowd just got up and left. Makes you wonder if Jessie got the message when the audience which had waited patiently for hours to hear him speak, turned from a bunch of faces to the backs of heads of people leaving. He will probably accuse them of lack of respect. Research has proved that men will change the subject or ignore the subject that women, even the NOW ladies, bring up a huge percentage of the time. This is to establish power. Jessie did it one more time and the crowd answered the dinner bell instead of Jessie. Sometimes Jessie don't show no respect.

6.16.96 Sausaulito, CA Cute town. I decided not to go to the hostel because I went over on the ferry instead of the Golden Gate bridge because it was rainy and foggy. Once in Sausaulito the hostel was off course, not in the town, up a hill, wrong direction, etc. I would probably be there by now instead of in a restaurant trying to wait out a rain shower. Second lunch.

Later: Got lost once in Larkspur and pushed poor Green up a long hill but am now in Samuel P. Taylor State Park. It took an hour and 15 minutes to put up my new tent. It just doesn't look right. Too saggy and the directions that I found after I had put it up say I have to spray the seams to waterproof them. Me? Why don't they do it? They know what they are doing and I sure don't. And that waterproofing stuff is so ugly. It is forty-one miles to Bodega Bay tomorrow. I have passed up two hostels to get to this lonely campground. Me. Just me. One RV. Probably did about 25 miles today, 12:30 to 5:45. It was very cloudy, dark and rainy part of the day and brilliant sun for part. Feel like lying down to give my sore back as rest.

Redwood Mania

There are just lots and lots of redwood trees in California. I have looked at days of them. Mountains of them. Forests of them. Nevertheless the days I spent in the Redwoods State Forest on the Avenue of the Giants have to be a high point of my trip. I'm a devoted tree hugger. The towering mist shrouded, green and brown columns of each 1000 or 2000 year old tree is so individual and yet a grove of them is a religious experience.

Redwoods need the damp fogs and rain of this coast. They grow in an area 40 miles wide and from Carmel to the Oregon border, only in the coastal mountains. It is the Sequoia Gigantea that grow in the high Sierras. By the time, 1895, Californians realized that the old trees were almost all gone, 95% of the virgin growth had been cut. The Sempervirens group was organized and started buying up the old trees along the Eel River. The effort is on going and the park is now 38 miles long: downhill, out of the wind, sunshine, a perfect bicycle path.

Redwoods are the world's tallest trees and can be over 2000 years old. For age, consider the olive trees that may have been growing in the Holy Land at the time of Jesus are still producing olives, and there is a blueberry thing, bush or tree, in Pennsylvania that is supposed to be older than these, or the Banyan tree in Calcutta that covers an acre that is supposed to be the biggest around. None of these are as gracious as the redwood forest. Spots of sunlight turn gentle ferns to a brilliant yellow-green against the dark brown trunks of the massive trees. Delicate pink redwood myrtle makes carpets and sometimes throw rugs on the floor of deep soft, brown needles. The trees are shaggy or smooth, unmarred or incredibly battle scarred. Some of the survivors have most of their central wood gone but the cambium and bark live on and support a hundred feet of tree.

The indigenous people who make a living from this awesome forest are aware that tourists want to take back with them a souvenir. Mementos can come in a variety of sizes from the tables, chairs, benches, statues, or totem poles to redwood earrings or redwood key rings. Adorable little Hobbit houses are made from the hollow and living trees, with cunning little doors and windows and you are invited in to admire the intriguing collections of trinkets and picture frames and pictures of redwoods. Absolutely tree-hugable. I keep taking pictures of Green the bicycle emerging from a drive through trees. Live burl. For sale. Now I know a burl to be a disordered part of the tree where the tree has made a big effort to overcome a difficulty and the resulting lump has grain that swirls in lovely patterns of tangled grain. Burls make great wooden salad bowls and last because the grain is very dense. But a live burl?

There is this big twisty old stump and they call it LIVE burl. Even Burl Ives is dead.

In an area where lumbering is a big industry there are the logging trucks. Logging trucks and bicycles do not coexist well on narrow winding roads. The Avenue of the Giants was thankfully free of the loggers because the loggers use US 101 which is mostly 4 lane divided highway. At this time of year the RVs are minimal so that is good too.

A stop at the visitors center reassures the tree hugger that fire cannot destroy the forests. Sometimes the inner core of a tree will burn out but the life is in the cambium area just under the bark and will survive and the tree will go on even though partially burned. The core and bark have a lot of tannin which is a fire retardant. The bark is sometimes a foot thick, doesn't burn and is full of water which helps also. Fires actually help the redwoods by clearing out competing underbrush.

The forest's prime evil is, of course, man. One of the most amazing things to me is the acres and acres of cut trees that sit waiting for . . . . what ever. They have been cut and are just stacked and lying around. Getting old? Rotting away? There are piles and piles of aging cut wood, blackened to what seems to me to be an unusable point. Huge vans full of chips thunder by on their way to somewhere. Others rush back the other way. It all seems very wasteful. That which is to be sent to Japan is carefully wrapped in plastic. This all sits along the highways and harbors awaiting a call.

I met a guy who had just bought a couple of dozen acres of aged redwoods. His plan was to sell one a year for vacation money. He was a big, burly, aggressive fellow and I didn't get around to expressing my distress at his plan. Maybe he was just pulling my chain. I hope.

4.17.96 Marshall. Great night's sleep in the new tent. It took an hour to pack up the new tent. Only the fly was a bit damp where my breath collected on the underside and that only in one spot. So I plan to get to Bodega Bay, forty-two miles away, and rent a motel room and put the thing up in a motel room to seal the seams. The new visqueen ground cloth was about 700 times its original volume as it picked up redwood litter from the soggy forest floor. As I left the campground I turned right up the hill, reflecting that I had been going down and I figured that that had come to an end. The stream was pretty and I watched it until I came to a sign that said bike path. Cool. The connector to it was rough but Green and I struggled up. It was a muddy but OK surface and continued pleasantly until it ended abruptly at a fence. How annoying. The hometown Bradford Woods hatefulness at work. Worse, I was across the stream from the road. I skidded the heavy Green down the steep, gravely embankment to the stream where the object of my wrath became Adventure Cycling and their stupid maps. It would be fordable in the summer but was over my ankle high boots as I struggled across what turned out to be the first cold, wet creek. The second cold, wet creek dumped water down my boots and grabbed at the panniers. Then we had only the steep bank up to the road to deal with and it was the worst. Twice Green slipped out of my grasp slid back down. Finally we reached the road and I made the fourth mistake of the day. I continued up the hill. After a long while I arrived at the place where I bought last night's chicken breast. I, who have the greatest sense of direction, I, who always check things three times. I was climbing Mount Tamalpais a second time. So I turned around and went back down the hill. Susan Jeffers said I mustn't kick myself too much over mistakes but there wasn't anyone else to blame. The whole stupid waste . . . .

The rest of the day wasn't much better. I pushed Green up seven hills. When I reached Tamale it started to rain. After I had frittered away an hour in a restaurant, it continued raining. I took an expensive ($65) room in a restored Victorian hotel, slid into the tub, took a wonderful nap and now here I am after a steak dinner in the Saloon next door. The saloon continues the lace curtain and oak decor of the US Hotel but also has a lively bar and a roaring fire in a rough stone fireplace. It has rained steadily since I got here and the fire is heartening. How to live the good life while bicycling? Charge it on the husband's Master Card. I am still 15 miles from Bodega Bay.

At 7:30 PM the sun came out and presented Tamale with a fine double rainbow. The last one I saw was in Rotorura, North Island, NZ.

4.18.96 Really at Valley Ford. Took an hour to go seven miles, pushing two hills. It was a beautiful sparkly day with the sun reflected from last night's raindrops. The road was called Shoreline road but must have been named by some imaginative real estate developer because I never saw the sea. Even Bodega Bay which is still 8 miles away isn't on the water. It is famous for its dunes.

Conversations: 'Ifn yah don't understand the ocean, stay away from the son of a bitch.'

The previous conversation had been among local farmers who discussed engines and weather. The conversation concluded with a discussion of Word Perfect! Then the discussion turned to a lady who had crashed her car while driving drunk.

Pretty young thing behind the counter extolling how virtuous her youth had been. Must be all of 25. Guys at the bar wearing jeans and cowboy boots or the much cheaper high-top work boots. Sweatshirts or plaid wool shirt Jacks. Wool ball caps top off the attire. A row of stools which give a counter to lean on with the basic stainless steel napkin dispenser, stainless and glass sugar dispenser with the sugar hardened into an intractable lump. A plastic dispenser with the little packages of pink stuff and glass salt and pepper shakers with chrome tops. The counter girl is wearing flowered tights and a pink sweatshirt. Her blonde hair was bobbed at the shoulders.

Bodega Bay. Friendly except for the lady at the tourist info who, even from a sitting position, managed to look down her nose at me. The restaurant I picked is just great, on a dock with a large seal or three loafing around in the water, coming up to pose for pictures every now and then. The cheapest hotel is $48 which seems a bit over the budget. It is so pleasant today that I think I will camp. Can't move on because the next place with facilities is too far away. This is the place where Hitchcock shot 'the Birds.' Actually the town of Bodega, about 5 miles back still has the schoolhouse, house and church that were big in the film. This very restaurant where I am was the restaurant. Everyone here wants me to stay on for the festival but inertia is taking over and I know I will move on. Perhaps if I put the tent up and do the seams from the inside that will eliminate the wind problem. Maybe there won't be wind in the campground. I got the bonk as I entered the town. Waiting for it to go away.

Later picked a camper campground, $17, and worked on the tent. The top of the container with the sealer in it was not good and I wonder how good the sealing will be. Cheapest motel was way over $50.

4.19.96 Gualala, CA. So I bummed another ride in the rain. It is hard to feel guilty about bumming a ride down a mountain with 6 long switchbacks that I had pushed Green up. It had looked bad all day and when I was 15 miles out, at the top of the miserable mountain the skies opened up and it poured. I bummed a ride with Wally and Marilyn in a pickup that was too small for all of us. I paid for everyone's lunch, and then went to a hotel in a burst of budget breaking. The sun is out bright and cheerful now and perhaps I will go to a performance at the Gualala Art Center this evening. I feel pretty good after a long soak and a nap. Call Chas now to find out how his ankle is.

4.20.96 Gualala, CA feeling tired and shaky today. Waitress says it is going to rain. I should just stay here. But it is so pretty now. The hotels and motels are so expensive here. Some start at $75. It is Saturday and everything will be full. Anchor Bay is four miles and has all facilities but sometimes they are like the grouchy lady at Jenner who would see me drowned in the pouring rain before giving a bicycler a room. I must spend some quality time with Og. This is a terrific hotel and the body wants to stay here.

Later: Decided to stay. Went back to bed when the sun disappeared and it clouded up during breakfast. Breakfast was an orgy of huge steak etc which I paid $7.00 for in San Francisco and $13 here. It is so cozy. I'm very happy with the decision to stay. I am still very tired and my legs and knees are sore. I have decided to head into the interior after Crescent City because it is cheaper and the valley won't be as tough as these hills. I just need a break from this tough stuff.

Remembering the conversation yesterday with Wally and Marilyn. Wally said that old people talk for years about how they are going to fish when they retire but they have one bad day of fishing and they quit. They are going to travel and get discouraged when they have one bad motel room. They decide that it is too uncomfortable to travel and end up sitting in front of the TV with occasional trips to the refrigerator. Wally and Marilyn have been on safari to Africa and lots of other places. They come to Gaulala with a big group for abalone season. The younger ones go out with wetsuits and get the big clams from the ocean.

Bought cereal yesterday and fruit to carry with me. If I get to a big hill, I'll just eat it rather than push it up the hill.

Later. A T-Bird group arrived and parked their beautiful cars in a row beside this quaint old Hotel. The owners are, shall we say, seniors. They lit a fire in the pot bellied stove in the parlor and put out fixings for a cocktail party. The star of the cocktail party was a lady who as at least 75 and had managed to hang on to a pair of gold lame slacks and gold slippers with a white sweater trimmed in gold to match. Her very bouffant hairdo with the diamond edged glasses were straight out of the Far Side. Elderly gentlemen were falling all over her. Shrieks of high pitched feminine laughter shattered the dusty silence of the old building. They were having a great time and I wished I had been included. Hopefully their advanced age will set in and they will eat and then toddle off to bed at an hour proper for their age. The very pleasant restaurant across the street where I am having coffee and dessert has a super view of waves crashing on rugged brown cliffs, a sandy beach and then the river which wanders lazily across between our cliff and the ocean and then dumps into the sea. I am patiently awaiting the sunset at 7:35 and have a while to go. The trees on the cliff opposite are shaped by the winds and salt spray into tight triangles of tough dark green vegetation. In front of that a flattish field of salt grasses and scrub trees. The sky is pleasantly striped and blotched with clouds that are now turning a soft yellow. The budget is not doing at all well. Three over-budget days in a row. The sun is about a foot from the sea.

4.22.96 Elk. The day has been beautiful and sparkly after watching the TV which indicated rain. The coast is stunning here. Breathtaking. The towns are up on cliffs and small but nice. The cafe where I am now ensconced is just darling, wood, white enamel fire place which is lit. The best is that the big windows on three sides open out onto the most fabulous gardens. Next door is a garden shop which naturalizes its offerings as the nurseries here seem to do so I am surrounded by white clematis, magenta asters, baby blue baby's breath, something red. That's on the right. Straight ahead is the major garden with flat cushions of magenta Sweet William, spikes of pink and white Canterbury bells, Huge pink tulips, Blue delphinium, yellow roses, At the small but adorable white Victorian house, there is a mystery bush with yellow flowers, red geraniums, multi colored nasturtiums, with a back drop of rugged, green cliff and the Pacific Ocean. The left side has only Rose of Sharon and an unknown with huge purple cone shaped flowers and a palm tree. Breakfast was Tofu and veggies stir-fried with potatoes and a couple of very thick slices of toast. The room is very severely done in pink and blue-green with lots of plants. Goodness, but it is nice.

Today's ride started off with me bundled in my warmest rain gear and hiking boots. By 9:00 the sun was out and I was looking for a place to stop and shuck off the outer layers. There was a lookout point after an expensive development at Irish Beach and I was able to get into lighter garb for the severe down and up hills at Irish Beach and Elk Creek. It is only 10 miles to Albion and a campground. Be able to camp if is doesn't look any worse than it does now. Clouding up. Sun gone.

Later: just a tad short of Mendocino. It is my best day so far, most distance and least money. Third night of camping and I finally got all the ropes up on the tent in case it rains. Brings each night of camping to $63.00. At this rate the tent may pay for itself. Looked at the other way, the cheapest motel here is $65 .... oh let's not: too complicated, but in these circumstances it is so good to have the tent. State Park here, can't remember the name but it will let me get into expensive Mendocino and fool around then push off to less expensive Fort Bragg for tomorrow night.

4.23.96 Mendocino CA.

Met Margaret Mary O'Rourke as I was rolling into Mendocino.

She has such gorgeous, strawberry-blond hair, a huge, curly mass of it with just an orange comb stuck in for control. We chatted for a while and then she invited me to stay in her home and I gratefully accepted. She is the only 'Lady lawyer' in Mendocino. The town has an historic area that is reminiscent of a New England town and they shoot some of *Murder She Wrote* here. The cove here isn't Cabot Cove but it is the beautiful outlet of the Big River. This can have no connection with Big Mountain in Montana, of course, but there is an uncanny similarity of names, isn't there? You'd think with people coming from Russia, Norway, Ireland, Spain, and, that they could come up with something a little more special. Edmond Rostand's hero, Cyrano, was so upset with his nose being called merely, BIG, that it took an extra five minutes of poetry to slice and dice his tormentor.

At high tide the waves beat on the feet of rocky cliffs on the south side, across the river. Long rollers creep up the sandy beach as if they were a drowning man's crawling fingers. Tourists, all of whom have apparently gone to Harvard or Stanford, if you can judge by their sweatshirts, stroll slowly along the streets or along the walkways near the museum. The buildings are wood, painted an off white color, with the American flag accompanied by California Republic flag with the brown bear.

The park's museum is in a Victorian treasure which was the Sheriffs office in *Murder She Wrote*. Have yet to drop by Jessica's house. Not that I want to meet her since everyone she knows is either murderee or murderer. Four well-publicized episodes to go and then it is over. Darn. It was one show that I could stay awake for, being on at 8:00. Well, sometimes I fell asleep watching it. I never once guessed the murderer correctly. She never gave all the important clues until the wrap-up.

The hotel I lunched in was established in 1889 but lunch, lamb shank with red beans, was very French and reasonably priced. There was much meat still on the bone when I began to suffer pain from overeating. It was a big greasy hunk of stuff that I thought about doggy bagging. My dog at home in Pittsburgh would have given her canines for it. How would it be if I doggie bagged it a couple of thousand miles for her? There would probably be people fainting in post offices all across the country and there would be a want ad out for the 'Phantom Doggie Bagger'. I could make the FBI's most wanted and get on TV. Think of the punishment for such a crime: community garbage truck serving. How about like the Man without a Country, sent from place to place to clean up after the regular garbage guys have been on strike for three weeks? A Garbage Scab.

My dog would think it was worth it. She would roll in it until she was loathsome and then bury it for later, after some poor gagging person had cleaned her up.

Oh, look, a Yale sweatshirt.

Margaret Mary's house was just darling. It looked like an old shack on the outside and was pure California on the inside. The floors and walls were smooth old wood with a highly modern kitchen. The old tub with claw feet stood alone in a room with a big window that faced the woods and had no blinds. It was just gorgeous. She fixed me and her young daughter a nice dinner and we had a pleasant chat.

4.25.96 Ft. Bragg. Founded 1857 which probably has something to do with the US ripping off 1/3 0f Mexico. 'Mexicans' will be in the majority in the near future. Well, what goes round comes round. My philosophy on this immigration thing is that if they come to the US it is because we are great and they want to share the goodies and the good life. I have news for all new citizens: even if you are blessed with the right color, the right education, a super amount of enthusiasm for work and great skills, It is still tough to make a good living here. Movies aside, Americans work harder with longer hours and less vacation than most of the world. We are enormously productive. To join the famous rat race takes great effort, training, and skill. People who want to succeed must first learn the language. I taught Spanish. A lot of kids who came to me speaking Spanish were not literate in Spanish. Often they did not know how to read or write Spanish. And they were 12 years old. To me it seems pointless for the government to print up stuff in Spanish for them. That sort of thing only delays their assimilation into the mainstream (rat race.) Hey. If they want to keep on being poor and speaking Spanish, why did they come?

I really enjoyed the Spanish speaking students. They would tell me that they had never before really understood what their Spanish speaking relatives were saying. The misfortune comes when they don't want to put too big a wedge between themselves and their families by being really good in English, by being really successful in school. Happens in some emigrant families. I think it is very reactionary and backward to encourage people to use their ethnicity as an excuse for not assimilating into the US. I can't imagine, with such a big world out here, sitting on, say, an Indian reservation for the rest of my days. I can't picture being a little old Greek or Chinese grannie, cooking my ethnic goodies and viewing anyone who doesn't speak my language with suspicion, while living in the US. If travel is supposed to broaden me, I blew it. I can only have the deep desire to go back to the melting pot idea of America that was the ideal in the 40's. To me this is The Liberal Idea. Everybody marries everybody and lines blur and people blend. One of my kids married a part Arab, one married a part American-Indian. Both grand daughters are beautiful and super smart. We're all Americans. I just don't like the Jessies who make a living by dividing us. On the other hand, affirmative action does a lot of good. Will he vote Republican if the Republicans want a black man a heartbeat from the presidency? No. Jessie is his own kind of bigot. He would call a black conservative an Uncle Tom.

Later: Blew the budget bigtime today. $169 in repairs, new drive chain, new tires, new brakes. A worn back tire got me in the shop and one thing lead to another. Green had been very cranky since the day we forded the stream but the guy said the derailleur was OK probably the chain was stretched. It was and when you replace it you also replace the cluster. The new chain is supposed to be good quality if I can remember to grease it. it should last for the rest of the trip. My budget is down $100 and four days to go in April. With the weather turning better, I should be camping more. Perhaps that will save me. Could have eaten in the Safeway which is both good and cheap but I seem to forget these things and go on my spoiled way.

I have my ticket for the train to Willit tomorrow. The Skunk Train. Perhaps someone will let me know how it got its name. I have lots to do, writing out an article and working on the Alaska trip. I've covered about all I can and will send the Alaska book to Chas soon.

4,26. Skunk Train. 1200 ft. tunnel, leaves at 9:20. Had a pot bellied stove on it that people said they could smell a long time before they could see it. The smell was not great, hence the name, Skunk Train. Noyonn Valley. There was an elephant used in an episode of *Murder She Wrote*: the elephant pushed the Skunk Train. Jokes from the Engineer,

"Deer on the payroll. Does. They get a buck a day."

"The dogwood is in bloom. How do you know? You can see the bark."

As he neared a place where there was an establishment for which he had messages, he would throw the US MAIL bag at the area yelling, "Air Mail!"

4.26.96 Willet, CA. Took the Skunk Train over the cascades to Willet and then after lunch, found a campground on the edge of the town. Now ensconced in a Japanese restaurant. The campground is very pleasant for such a down at the heels town. The restaurant is also very nice. Tomorrow forty-six miles just to get to Leggett and then the campground is beyond that. Nothing in Leggett said a local. Not much between but, one hopes, snack and lunch stuff.

As I was getting off my bike in the campground, my foot hit the crossbar and it was as if I had kicked off against a wall. I went flying. Green went flying in the opposite direction. I landed flat on my back in deep grass. I still had on helmet and gloves and stuff and the soft grass felt great. I just laid there and laughed like a nut. After that, I noticed that my legs have lost a lot of flexibility. I started lifting the right foot over the crossbar with my right hand to make sure I don't get into a fight with the bicycle someplace where there is concrete to land on instead of grass.

4.28.96 Hartsook, CA This is a small resort with cabins that are redwood, in the redwood forest. Across the street is a redwood mania place with totems and bear, mountain lions, and even a Viking boat. Jewelry, rustic tables, chairs, picture frames, unbelievable amounts and variety of stuff, all made of redwood that has been lovingly cut and polished or not polished, varnished and lacquered and polymered. I don't buy anything because there is no way of carrying it and besides the budget doesn't allow. I am sorely tempted by postcards that are about a foot high to show the tallness of the worlds tallest trees that grow hereabouts. There were logging trucks out today even though it was Sunday but relatively little traffic on Rt. 101. Everyone tells me, I am here for the right season because later the RVs are very thick. RVs are such road hogs. The average RV is driven by Grandpa who KNOWS that those #$$%^ bicycles have no right to be on the road and he doesn't slow down nor does he give an inch of road clearance. Sometimes trailers are skewed and bite off a foot more to one side or the other more road space than the vehicle pulling them. This seems quite deadly. The logging trucks are so long that there is a problem if they pass while the bike is on the inside curve. They need to swing wider than they do.

The biking today on Rt. 101 was arduous as it was yesterday. Lots of big, big hills. It is hard to believe that Rt. 1 could have been any tougher. There were strong headwinds in the afternoon. I went through an area where they said you had better have chains so I guess I was up there altitude wise. Another area warned trucks and trailers of strong, gusty winds but I found them just strong. I should be on the down hill of a tributary of the Eel River but it ignores the reasonableness of being just a nice slope along the river and there are lots of ups and downs over steep mountains.

Later: I am sitting in the lobby of the resort listening to a guy play the huge grand piano that is here. There is a huge fireplace. Gershwin and Friml.

4.29.96 Humbolt Redwood Park. Sunny and finally warm. The redwoods are magnificent. They grow in a 40 mile wide stretch between Carmel and the Oregon border. They are the world's tallest trees and live to be 2000 years old. We really should cut them for the Japanese, shouldn't we? The road is the Avenue of the Giants. It is good because it does not appeal to the logging trucks and the RVs get bored with the winding. Not so many RVs yet. Too early. They are still resting comfortably in millions of back yards.

This has to be one of the world's bike days. Sunshine. Not too warm. Downhill through 38 miles of redwood forest parkland. The shade was so deep that many cars kept their lights on. I debated using my flasher quite a few times but put it off knowing I will need it more on a busier highway in the fog or rain.

04.30.96 Redcrest CA. I was trying to do everything right. I studied positive thinking. I reviewed my budget. Oops. Those motels are beginning to mount up. I did close to 50 miles. I was good. Redcrest in the Redwoods sounds like the top of a mountain and that's right, but it has been days and days since I have had to push Green up a hill. Getting stronger. So I was a proper good person and signed up for a campsite at a place that offered $44 cabins or $14 campsites. I explored Redcrest, a town with four places of business. The two eating places were closed already at five o'clock. The grocery had a couple of benches in front and a couple of locals loitering on them. As people came and went and I surveyed the mostly empty shelves, I became aware of the pretty young girl at the counter and the loud character on the porch. I bought my granola bars and Gatorade and wandered back to the porch for local color. The loudmouth offered a seat and I fell into it. We did all the usual 'Where ya been . . .', 'Where ya goin' . . . .' stuff.

"Here get me a beer," Loud says to a teenage boy with smooth face and large Adams apple.

The kid goes for the beer and the girl has to go back in to wait on him. "You all alone? How come your all alone?"

"Just too grouchy for company," I answer.

The loud one, blond, overweight, red-faced says something about the 'Freemen' being a danger. I say I don't think so with every Freeman being followed by two FBI guys. The "No I don't carry a gun." discussion ends with the kid coming back out and Loud telling him to drink the beer. The kid pops the can and sits down with the beer but jumps up again when a white truck arrives. The kid lets out an expletive or two and ducks away around the corner. The guy from the white truck glares at Loud hard enough to break rocks. and goes on in to the store. A flashy Transam drives up and Loud screams at it while muttering under his breath,

"What am I going to tell him about you? I'll tell him your my new girl."

"Tell him I'm your grandmother."

His head whipped around and he stared at me.

"Yuh." Then he screamed a conversation at the Trans Am guy while I stuck my fingers in my ears. I decided that not only was this enough local color but that I didn't want to put my tent up behind the row of trailers, on the dark side of the Laundromat. The motel people were happy to change me to a cabin with a lock on the door and I went there. Stayed there with the blinds pulled.

This whole area seems like the land where burn-outs go to die. Many trucks and vans have decayed to a mottled rust and have such tired springs that they barely clear the street. Tattoos, pony tails and personal grunge are at a high level. The town I had breakfast in, Garberville, made Playboy magazine as the marijuana growing capital of California, with the guesstimate that even with all the acres of grapes, oranges. strawberries, that marijuana is the biggest money crop in California. After breakfast were some little towns of trailer camps so full of junk and junk yard dogs, such a disaster of collected crud that no self-respecting tornado would bother it. If these guys are growing weed for profit, they've botched things again.

Indigo Aura

There was a book on auras, second—hand, $1.00. Whoever had it first hand must have fallen asleep with it on page two and never got back to it again because it had not been used. It had lots of swell lists of stuff to answer and I diligently plowed through all that, writing in the book my most intimate responses. Well, after that there was another list and then another list. At the conclusion of all this was the exciting compiling of the statistics. Now I am just dying to let the world that cannot see auras know that I have a really great aura. I am a super sensitive, new age person. I am so far out that most people don't understand me, think I am off my rocker. Hey. Wait. Maybe there is something to this.

Here's a clue to my great aura: 'You aint Ben Blue. No, no, no. You ain't Ben Blue til you've had that mood . . . .' That's it. My aura is new age indigo!

I'm getting the feeling that you have dropped off to sleep. Are you mumbling 'Bunk'. More California bird-brained . . . Never should have been turned loose in California . . . (snore.)'

It's lonely at the top. Probably it's lonely at the bottom, too. And most places in between.

If I am all that sensitive, I should be reading up on other people's auras and be ready to give them the benefit of my wonderfulness. Let's see' I left off at page . . . reading something about hopelessly incompetent, worthless . . . .

05.01.96 Eureka, CA I did the sights today. The two wonderful Victorian castles built by the man named Carson who made lots of money cutting down the Redwoods. By 1895 95% of the redwoods were gone and it was then that efforts started to preserve what was left. The harbor here is a good one but it is hard to see and it wasn't until California had been around a while that it was colonized. The guy that probably shouted Eureka, laid out building lots, and started selling off the land.

I ate my first sample of Dungeness crab at a picnic bench down by the dock. Just great. The crab was unaccompanied by anything at all and was the best meal I have had in a long time. The "Old Town" goes on for blocks with large Victorian buildings. Restorations have been careful and fun. The streets were fairly empty when I cruised them but if the very large selection of multi motels ever fills up with tourists, there should be lots of happy tourists here. The harbor is very attractive, on a spit that shelters yet once again the sheltered bay. A US Army Corps of Engineers dredge made a pinpoint turn while I smashed the crab shell with a handy hammer provided by the amiable owner of the crab shack. I spent a lot of the afternoon in the library going over details of the Alaska portion of the trip and then mailed my guidebook with suggestions to Chas.

5.2.96 Still in Eureka. Went to a clinic and got new stuff on the rash on my neck. It was looking particularly obnoxious today so, hopefully, it is worth a day or two to get it straightened out.

The clinic accepted Medicare so that was a help. (Actually, I kept getting bills at home for a long while. One would say that they had been paid, one would say that I still owed. I wrote and accused them of double billing and the bills stopped.) The medicine was only $11 this time, not $21 like the neck stuff I got at home that didn't work. Wash the area and apply three times a day. Wash the neck three times a day while traveling on a bicycle? Steroid. Should do the trick. I asked about having an x-ray and they said that they didn't think I needed to bother. Feeling tired. I'll find the tourist agency that can get me a ticket to San Francisco. Going home to be with Chas when he solos with the Williamsport Symphony.

5.4.96 San Francisco again. Actually passed under the city on BART which is their Metro. Why can't they just call it Metro so that out of towners know what to expect? Bart takes bicycles and it goes just about everywhere except the airport. It does go to Oakland's airport. Almost.

The ride from Eureka was made very pleasant by a Spanish speaking only lady who grew up in Santo Domingo. She met her husband in a Laundromat in Santo Domingo. He had come there to learn Spanish. They have two children who stay with the grandparents because the parents think that the kids are safer in Santo Domingo. This is the island that has the chaos of Haiti on the other end. She has been going to school to learn English but is too shy to give it a try at this point. She says that in Santo Domingo they have only four hours a day of electricity and 4 hours of water. Few people are rich. Most are poor. (Sounds like Nepal.) But she loves it and is very proud of her culture and wants her children to have that culture, not that of the US. She stays with her husband but is on her way to visit the children.

The second person that I chatted with was a young man from Massachusetts who welds stuff for an artist. He thinks he will stay in San Francisco.

The third was a black guy who spent a long time on Johnson Island in the Pacific as a civilian, destroying stuff for the Atomic Energy people. He also taught Junior High for a couple of years before he decided that that was a dead end. Now he is an electrical engineer and working on a PhD. in Physics. His company does the software for things like fighter planes that can fly themselves. He was as befuddled by the bus system as I was and we hung together for a while. He met a fellow Mississippian in the bus driver and they held a big reunion right there.

"Oprah is from my town."

"Tupelo? Alright, man"

Speaking of daytime TV, Phil Donahue is retiring. I thought he had some interesting people sometimes but hated the way he manipulated the audience into approving just any sort of weirdo stuff.

I am in San Francisco so I can be with M'love when he solos with the Williamsport Symphony on Tuesday. I can't wait to be with him. Getting erotic feelings in these old glands just sitting on the bus thinking of him. No fool like and old . . . .

05.11 San Francisco, CA. Back after a delicious trip home. Chas is so wonderful and supportive of my silly trip, I just didn't want to miss the concert with the symphony. I left Eureka on the 4th and bussed to Martinez then trained to Richmond, BARTed to Daly City and bussed to San Francisco Airport. This all costs $33 per round trip. Then I Delta Aired to Pittsburgh with my senior citizen coupon. It wasn't too bad a trip, changed planes in Atlanta. 26 hour trip. I was so glad to see my guy. Went home and grabbed some dressy clothes and we drove to Lock Haven where I spent my first year of college. On to Williamsport, Pa. where Chas soloed on the carousel projector. The orchestra, under Robin Fountain, did very well and it was such a pleasure to be there. I was suffering a lot from unsocial feelings. (This happens when you spend so much time alone. You get squirrelly.) I just wanted to hide in the hotel room but Chas dragged me out to the dress rehearsal. It was fun to be there with all the musicians. Such a different world from the redwood forest. The performance, Respigi's *Pines of Rome*, went very well. The audience was fairly restrained but the performance was fine. 1500 people.

Spent a day at home fussing with the Zaurus with no luck then visited with Bill and toted Don VK to the garage and then back to his home. Continue working with Chas on the Alaska Itinerary. Visited with Mac and his family. Next day firmed up plans for Alaska, Chas bought a 4 ticket senior citizen book of tickets and used only three of them to go to Anchorage and come back from Vancouver. Good deal. We will camp to help expenses there. Every little expedition in Alaska is a fortune. We plan to do a lot of hiking and walking and rent a bike for Chas when we need one. I will bike to Anchorage. Chas will arrive in Anchorage by the 1st of August.

5.12.96 Trinidad. At least I'm camping. My problem with food is that I just love restaurants. It is so pleasant. Trinidad is on a cliff overlooking Humbolt Bay. The bay has many strange rocks that float on the water. At least they seem to be floating until stared at, then they settle down to merely ducking under the waves, pretending to be whales. It is awesomely, handsomely rugged. A high dock sticks way out into the water. It has cranes for bringing stuff up to the dock and big barrels with water rushing through them. All sorts of incomprehensible activity. The Seascape Restaurant looks out on this lovely scene and is itself just so apppealing. People park a couple of hundred feet away at the state park and walk the beach on the other side of the headland. Windblown, sand-blasted, they wander into this delightful spot to cap off their enjoyment with a seafood dinner.

5.12.96 Trinidad, CA. Seemed like a tough day today with three really tough mountains to climb. The early part from Trinidad was great. Heard a sound like a lot of dogs or gulls barking and that turned out to be sea lions, herds of them, loafing on the rocks way below or diving and fishing nearby. Shortly after that there was a herd of elk. They were resting in the back of a restaurant that offered elk steaks. The wild elk in the next park were hiding. I opted for a crummy motel in Klamath. Klamath had been entirely washed away in the flood of '64 and what has been built since looks like the kind of stuff you do when you can't get insurance. The cafe, which hands out food through a slot in a window, closed early and the loafers mover from there to the grocery where I bought my dinner and breakfast.

I called the kids and left messages on two machines and talked to Tom. He is a good Libertarian and even knew the author of the book, *The Law That Never Was*. That was my Mother's Day, which according to the crossword puzzle I worked out was formerly known as Mothering Sunday. I usually try to remember to send cards to the daughter and daughters-in-law. They are on the front lines of motherhood and I am just an emeritus.

5.13.96 Crescent City CA I am 66 today. I'm in Northern California and it is raining. I was lucky in the weather today. It was raining when I got up and I waited for it to quit. Things were dried up by 9:00 and I cruised down through Redwood Forest Park, breakfasted at the Trees Restaurant, overlooking huge statues of Paul Bunyan and the Baby Blue Ox. After that it was about 100 miles of up hill. I think this is the biggest hill I have done in California, Every time the road would lose a lane and go back to one lane I would think I was at the top, but no. It kept going up and up and up. And up. The then down and then up. Finally it dumped me down into Crescent City. I got a $28 motel and the skies opened up and the rains they have come again. The road was just terrible, narrow and lots of traffic. I guess I will let the weather decide what I do. If it is raining tomorrow, I will take a day off. Wouldn't hurt to do so anyhow because I am very tired and beginning to get sore.

From my vantage spot here in the restaurant, I can see bikers going by. Two women just tooling along. If they are going to stop at the Wilkins Creek hostel, they have that awful hill to do. I thought the hostel seemed hostile and moved on. There was an unfriendly looking barrier to keep even a bicycle from going up the driveway. It is closed until 5:00 as many hostels are, those girls could spend a very miserable time in the rain.

A family went by on bikes with a small child in a child's seat trying to hide from the rain. Not my idea of a way to get a child to like bicycling. Into Alpha waves. Going to wade back to my motel and nap before my big pigout dinner.

5.13.96 Crescent City CA. If it ever stops raining long enough, I will try to find an ATM to refresh my wilted wallet. I'm holed up in a nice new 24 hr restaurant next to the aquarium which I will visit just as soon as I get some money. Rain stopped. Better run.

Later: Went to the library again and read and dozed through a lot more of Michner's *Alaska*. It was drizzling when I went looking for lunch, picked up and as I started for my room was raining earnestly. When I spotted a movie theater, I decided that I had found my shelter. Nothing like seeing some really bad weather to make you happy with what you've got. So I'm in McDonalds waiting a half hour for the theater to open. Another old lady here is reading USA TODAY. I have not yet located the bus station that I will need if it keeps raining like this. Thinking more and more of the Wilamet Valley rather than the Coast Highway.

5.15.96 The fog comes on little cat feet.

It sits, looking over harbor and town

And then, moves on.

Wasn't that Carl Sandburg? I have these bits of poetry rattling around in my head and sometimes they pop out. Well, the little cat feet happened here the last day in California. It rained a bit but it is spring.

"Hate California, it's cold and it's damp:

That's why the lady is a tramp."

Chapter XXXIV

OREGON

The days come and go like muffled and veiled figures sent out from a distant friendly party, but they say nothing, and if we do not use the gifts they bring, they carry them silently away.

Ralph Waldo Emerson

Now wouldn't my English teacher have called that a run-on sentence?

5.18.96 Gold Beach, OR. I started early from Brookings. McD's and then off to see the world. Two miles down the road it started to rain and after a while rained really hard then slacked off. Three of these and about four big hills and it was noon and I was in Gold Beach. Had the wind behind me. The road is really good with nice wide shoulder. The weather is supposed to be the same for tomorrow. I was totally soaked. I turned on CNN and crawled into bed and slept for hours. So, since I skipped lunch, I splurged on dinner at the restaurant across the street from the motel. It is a week into the salmon season and they had fresh salmon. Too much to pass up. I still feel very tired. I could sleep very well all night. Clarence Thomas was giving a speech on CNN. My man. He's no Jessie Jackson. Talked about his job as judge and how he didn't feel obligated to is race or sex or that stuff, just to how he thought the founding fathers and the Constitution read. Jessie always has a chorus of people in the audience saying, "Oh, yes." "Amen." Nobody seems to argue with him. Clarence gets a lot of very public disagreement. Interesting. Clarence mentions the confirmation

431

hearing as a burden and gets a laugh. He is a very serious man. If he did talk dirty to that pretty young thing, so what? Justice Douglas was married to such a young thing and who cared? His business. I don't think Clarence talked like that. Guys who talk like that do it with everybody. They were after him because he is a conservative. I watch the confirmation hearings on TV because I was recovering from my hysterectomy. The pretty black gal was lying. Black women hate black guys who marry white women. Motive enough to try to bring the man down. He is fairly safe now and contemplating 30 years as a judge.

5.19.96 Port Orford. Tough biking today even though it was only twenty-nine miles. There were more big hills. I met two guy bikers who were disgusted and annoyed by the weather. They had been holed up in Port Orford for two days. They were from Minneapolis. Then I met a fellow woman biker, traveling alone. She had been very discouraged by the weather. She has been camping. The two guys were enjoying motels. Big difference when it rains and rains. And rains. I chatted with the gal for a while and then we decided to do lunch and broke out all the stuff we had been carrying. It was great. We talked and talked. She is the editor of the Earth First Magazine. She and her fellows plot up media-enticing scenarios to attract attention and make the public aware of the most recent attacks on public land and trees. And so I told her about my writing and read "Bicycle Safety". She liked it. As we were about to part, she was headed south. She told me that she had been in jail last week! For trying to stop logging trucks. She is the only person I have met anywhere who bragged about being in jail. I got her address in Eugene and thought about protesting. Might be an interesting thing to do. I love the big trees. I was all packed to go to Selma to walk with Martin Luther King when some northern housewife got shot. Chas put his foot down. I wasn't to risk life and limb and possibly leave him with three small children to raise alone. So I didn't go. So when I protested against his racing sports cars, for the sake of three small children, he listened.

Port Orford is one of the nicest towns on the coast. Beautiful little cove with huge rocks scattered around the long roller surf. People walking the beach. Miraculously the sun is still shining.

Touring Bicycle Safety

For years and years I drove a car the way Caspar Milktoast did. Does anyone remember Caspar? He was tall, skinny cartoon character, funny, droopy mustash, long skinny neck with a big adam's apple. He was always dressed in a three piece suit and carrying an umbrella. Had thick glasses and was nervous about everything. I am Caspar Milktoast, come leaping . . . no, coming cautiously, a toe at a time, from the cartoon pages. I always have a problem of identifying with the wrong person. Nobody is supposed to be like Caspar. He was not 'cool'. Caspar was a nerd. Then I was Nurse Ratchet in *One Flew Over The Cookoo's Nest*. Hey, the guy was in there in the first place because he attacked authority figures like teachers . . . like me! Anyway, Caspar Milktoast was my wimp hero. I drove like Caspar and one day the authorities identified us wimps as 'Defensive Drivers.' Which means you drive as if every other car was driven by a vicious, illiterate, vacant-brained, nincompoop on drugs. Believing this about drivers does, occasionally, reduce me to hysterical fear, but in the main it has kept me reasonably safe. The other part of 'defensive driving' is to drive as if you, yourself, were a terrified-of-being-late, fuddled-headed, have-to-go-back-for-the-briefcase, nincompoop. With no gas. So what I have to preach is big time wimpy, cowardice bicycling.

Three big things advocated by Bikecentennial (now Adventure Cycling) for the trip across the US in 1976 were: 1) Never leave the pavement when you are in the desert, and 2) Wear a helmet. 3) Don't shoot the bird at obnoxious drivers

1) You don't leave the pavement because everything in the desert has been waiting all its life to puncture a tire. Won't even mention the kind of rattlesnake that hangs in the bushes on

hot days and strikes at anything going by. When we camped in the desert with Ole, there were rattlesnakes there! And jumping cactus!

2) As for the helmets, the first serious research on helmets was done by the Bike Centennial people in '76 and the results: The two deaths were people who did not have helmets. No one who crashed wearing a helmet had super serious injuries. A self-imposed goal when I return to Pittsburgh is to get the news people, when giving news of a bicycle accident to ask, automatically, as bicyclers do, 'Was he wearing a helmet?' We have a helmet law for kids now in Pennsylvania but the moms and dads should be wearing them also.

3) Shouting obscenities at obnoxious drivers will only get the guy who comes down the road next in trouble.

Now, I consider a dog bite serious when it happens to me but probably the statistic people wouldn't. I am living proof that a helmet does not prevent dog bite.

The best dog prevention is to be able to say, 'Your dog, Dear.' Dear, (Himself) has made friends with an amazing collection of dogs around the world. If he can, he outsprints them. One guy I know but will not name is deadly accurate with karate kicks. The other son, Tom, rides right at the dog and it turns and runs. I carry a whistle (donated by my Phys. Ed. Teacher daughter-in-law so I think that tells you what kind of whistle.) When I remember it, I use it and it works retty well. The dog stops and looks at the whistle and says, "Duh. What is this annoyance?"

I also carry pepper spray for the dogs that come along when Himself isn't there. I hate using the pepper spray in a dog's eyes but if it is me against a Doberman or Rotweiler, I need all the help I can get. Most owners are aware of leash laws and are good about keeping the dogs restrained but, be in a depressed area, there are sure to be the 'junk yard' dogs around to defend the rusting eyesores from . . . what? Other junk collectors? But I love them. Three times a day I work on how much I love them. Og Mandino would be proud of how much I love them.

My way of handling dogs on an up-hill is to look wimpy. I get off the bicycle and keep the bike between me and the dog while ordering it back in its yard with my best Junior High teacher bellow.

"Get back in that yard! Now! Do you have a street pass?"

If you have been able to stop fifty Junior High kids who are running insanely on their way to the afternoon bus, dead in their tracks, you can sometimes discourage a dog.

I started writing this because I was in Oregon. Oregon, is spelled R A I N. So what does that have to do with safety? I do not like to ride in the rain. Bicycle slip, fall down, go pain. Rain and temperatures between 32 and 50 degrees are an invitation to hypothermia. Did I mention wind-chill? When uncontrollable shivering starts, you are four hours from death. Best to make a move for shelter before getting into the 'clouded judgment' stage of irrational behavior.

If I find myself beginning to shiver and a long way from shelter, I stop, put out my thumb, and bum a ride to the next dry place. There are lots of empty pick-up trucks out there whose owners get such a feeling of superiority from being able to help a suffering bicycler. Go ahead. Make their day. $1.00 per mile is appreciated.

I am avoiding all that by sitting out rainstorms, two days in Crescent City CA and one day in Brookings O, one day in Coos Bay, O. As I read about other travelers, I become aware of how much time is spent just waiting. Patience, patience. Oregon is not too far from the home of the lady who wrote 'Miles From Nowhere,' Barbara Savage. Which I have never read. It was written by a gal about her bicycle trip around the world, and recommended by a lot of people.

"She is dead, you know."

I didn't know. Don't want to know. Don't tell me . . . .

"Killed by a hit and run murderer."

"I told you to not tell me!"

She biked all the way around the world, published her book, was run down by a despicable killer, in her home town of Santa Barbara, CA.

How to protect from that kind of aimless, drunken viciousness? A public that is aware of the right of bicycles on the road. The pamphlet that people study for the license test should state the rights of the bicycle. It should be a test question. Flunk that question and no license.

A bicycle lane is really good if it doesn't disappear at every intersection or bridge. The freedom that is the romance of bicycling is not inhibited. Caspar Milktoast and Green the Magic Bike and I feel very comfortable even with logging trucks if there is a decent shoulder. A wide shoulder to ride is my personal preference.

Little country roads are nice with company. Alone, I am always nervous about dogs, inside corners, lack of people and facilities. Inside corners? Cars always cut inside corners and cannot see around them in hilly areas. Inside corners receive the landslides. I am so wimpy that I will cross over and ride the outside of the curve (when no traffic is coming.) This is illegal because bikes are supposed to obey the rules as cars except to be as far to the right as is practical. But survival is survival.

In cities I do whatever the locals do. If they ride the sidewalks, I ride the sidewalks. I walk the bike if the sidewalk is crowded. I think people who ride bikes through people crowds should be arrested. Usually people crowds last only a couple of blocks and it interesting to get off the bike to see why the crowd has gathered.

It is debatable whether "bike" trails are the safest because many walkers and joggers are oblivious of bicycles. If you are going to be on a "bike" trail like Pittsburgh's North Park anytime or Ohio Pyle on the weekends, you will need tranquilizers and long periods of meditation. If you really must do this, I could lend out my large collection of self help or even the Og Mendino book. Look at it this way, on a crowded bike trail, a loaded bike is a logging truck. Nevertheless, a network of bicycle trails throughout the US is THE GOAL. The dog walkers and baby carriages are only around the towns and this leaves long stretches of peace and quiet.

Talking with bicycle tourers, I find myself promoting a tour in Eastern US. These are Brits and West Coast bicyclers who cannot imagine bicycling on the East Coast of the US. (It is so crowded, bad roads, muggers, etc.) They have never heard of Pittsburgh and never been to D.C. They camp.

I have them fly to Pittsburgh International. They assemble the bike at the airport and get to the Raddison that is where the Montour trail connects with Rt. 60. A stay at the relatively expensive hotel would give a chance to day-tour the city which is flat-out beautiful and has great trails. (Call me, I'll personally give you're the tour.)

Take the Montour west and south around the city to the McKeesport Bridge then up Youghiogheny River on the GAP Trail that takes you through the Alleghenies to Cumberland Maryland. The Great Allegheny Passage Companion guide to the GAP Trail is by our pal Bill Metzger. This is the Bill who was in Ocracoke with us. Buy it. It is good and fun to read and will give you the real skinny on how to navigate Pittsburgh.

The C&O canal became a National Park quite a few years back and its 175 mile trail takes you right into the center of D.C. The National Capitol itself has great trails. Along the way are the Civil War venues of Harpers Ferry, Antietam, and Gettysburg.

Tourism is the second biggest money maker in Pennsylvania (after agriculture). With our rails to trails opportunities, we should be able to excite people like the Japanese, Germans, Dutch, and English to come here and do their part to help replace the outflow of money with some inflow. And it is safe.

Restaurant

It is so hard to pass up a cutsey restaurant. Not that I am opposed to the fast food type. I flat out love McDonalds. In places where you have to pay to sit at a table (Italy), you can sit at McDonalds. In places where you can't afford to eat (France, Switzerland, Germany, Austria) McDonalds can give you the strength to enjoy the tourist trek without devastating the budget. In places where the toilet is, at best, a hole in the floor, McDonalds has a clean throne.

I've got Corvallis and Eugene out of order. Do you care?

I'm in a busy Mickey D's in Eugene, Oregon when I look up from the Zaurus when a couple of Mexicans who appeared to be laborers of some sort caused a bit of a stir. The youngest was carrying a full tray of fries and stuff. One of the fries packages fell and the poor guy that had been carrying it went into a quickie tailspin of "Oh I'm so clumsy," depression. He got the rest of the tray to the table and started "Ay, de mi: Ay de mi." A teenager, $4.00 an hour kid, hustled over to the fries and loaded another carton for the dismayed customer, and gave it to him then he recaptured his broom and swept up the mess before the Mexican's pal could really start to get on his case. It was all so smooth and so sweet. One of those small acts of decency. Kids today!

But I have weakness for restaurants with lace curtains that have all antique oak furniture and 100 year old photos on the wall. Or anyplace that puts bean sprouts in their sandwiches or serves bean soup. This is beginning to sound much purer than I am. A day that doesn't start with steak and eggs is one in which I expect to have an energy crash. Given a big bolt of greasy protein, I can last until evening. Breakfast places tend to be populated by newspaper readers and drowsy waitresses, have a thick odor of grease, and are not so cutesy.

Corvallis, Oregon has a couple of coffee house restaurants and everyone seems to like these best here. I order a huge glass of skim milk and a scone. They have gone to the edge with the scone. It is a lemon, poppy seed, ginger scone. Yum. Oregon State University is here and I can't tell whether the group lining up to see Tom Cruise at the movie theater is college or high school. Only one of them is wearing his baseball cap backward. Lots of bicycles here. More than that. Lots and lots. The coffee smells so great that I can enjoy the atmosphere as much as if it were a cup of coffee. Oh, oh. A girl with Chinese red hair. I don't think it is natural, but it does attract attention.

5.20.96 Coos Bay, Oregon. Been a busy day. About 20 miles into the ride, the front tire went flat. Even though I know I can't deal with tires, I tried and found once more that I can't deal with tires. The bead is so tight that my weak little hands can't even get the tire off the rim. I have all the repair stuff but just can't do it. I must have Spot for Alaska because I have to be able to make repairs there. Sigh. Have to tell Charles. Have to think about it some more. Two ladies picked me up and transported me in their van to Coos Bay, skipping a stop. I could have pushed on because it is such nice weather but my bottom is a bit sore and I want to take some pictures here and see why all those logs are floating in the river.

5.21.96 Coos Bay, OR So far held up again. Since it is only 13 miles to the next town, if it clears up before checkout time at noon, I'll start. Ironic that I didn't start yesterday when I had lots of time. I thought an early start over the double bridge would be safer. It appears to be a really long bridge on the map. I could see it yesterday. It is one of the last bow bridges. Today it fogged in. Staying at the Motel 6 which has a weight room, spa, and sauna. And a laundromat where you meet people. A young athlete from Youngstown O. is working on installing fiber optics for MCI in Brandon. I should have asked if it had anything to do with Brandon being the most westerly region of the lower 48. He says they are installing 4 gizmos that cost $4 M each. This town is out of the reach of USA TODAY at any price. I would love to figure out how to tour this interesting area in the rain but am stymied. Guess I'll try the library. Probably a nice long, wet walk from here. So far every library has had *Alaska* and none have had the much recommended Barbara Savage's *Miles From Nowhere*. Watched, on TV, people in Calaveras County training their frogs for the famous race. Pretty gross. Miss Piggy's taste is obviously in her mouth.

Chas says that John Olnes called. He says to be sure to be in touch when we get to Anchorage. I can't wait to hear their stories and see their pictures. He says he will try to locate Liz who is back in Salt Lake City. I should tell Chas to get her phone number so he can give her a call when he goes through Salt Lake City as one does on Delta.

Chas has been offered a spot on the Bradford woods Conservancy. I told him to grab it. To talk to George and Marian.

05.22.96 Coos bay. Again. Started sunny this morning but that didn't last long. It is pouring again but at least I'm not in the town where the twister went through and destroyed the drive-in theater that was playing "Twister." The weather report offers sun for the rest of the week and over the Memorial Day weekend. In

'76 when we biked the Bikecentennial, we didn't get any rain in Oregon. 50 degrees here.

5.26.96 Willsonville Or. Cloudy and chilly today. And they promised sunshine. I am on the outskirts of Portland. Actually Portland is still fifteen miles away. But I just can't see how to get there. I rode 99 E for about 38 miles and then it worked off to the left because the Wilamette River swings that way. Then I headed back to I-5 and have been riding it for a couple of miles, promising myself to stop at the first motel. I'll try the cheapie next door and see if it is cheap enough. The bicycle map of Portland shows trails that wander around and suddenly quit. It may be that there are some really bad areas that no one wants to bike in. I'll work my way over to Beaverton and try to get on Rt. 30 which should connect me up with the Adventure Cycling map in a couple of days.

5.27.96 Portland O. Can't believe I am in Portland. It is the largest city in Oregon, and, for me, the least bike friendly. I wandered around a bit on mall roads, then I-5 then I-205, then got off at a quiet road that went by the falls of the Wilamette River. The falls was a pretty impressive, horseshoe form like Niagara but nothing like as high and even though this one has volume, nothing like Niagara. It was surrounded by a lot of factories that towered over it. Then there was a short but lovely bike path. After that was the town of Oswego where I stopped to await the next street car. For $3.00 it took me and Green to the downtown area.

The trolley ride was fun and I unloaded in the downtown park section. I heard someone yell,

"Sally, is that you?"

The caller turned out to be a girl that I met in Calcutta at Mother Teresa's. Mary was a nurse from Seattle, visiting friends in Portland. I was into being squirrelly and non-communicative because I hadn't talked to anyone for a long time. It was sunny and nice and there was friendly Mary and lots of friendly people and I wanted to go hide somewhere. I found the hostel in a not great area.

Chapter XXXV

WASHINGTON

5.28.96 St. Helens. WA. Pulled a clever one today. I was staying at the Portland Hostel (disgusting place) where I made arrangements to be toured to Mount St. Helens. Mount St Helens is in Washington, north of the Columbia River which is pretty scary here. I am acrophobic and bridges are the worst for me. So the tour bus takes me over the bridge. Great tour. Fascinating. One of the best I can remember. No, the best. I had talked the tour guy into taking Green along and after a bit of a struggle got Green loaded into the 7 passenger van. After the tour, Green and I were dumped off in Washington State, across the fearsome Columbia River. I do hate bridges.

On my own again, I had to dodge the rain drops on my way to a nearby shopping mall with a movie theater. Now I'm in a Mexican restaurant like ChiChis, I am so horridly depressed because I couldn't make them understand that I can't eat spicy stuff. I now await, Tagamet in hand, the pain which will probably assault me. The news says that viruses cause ulcers? Wait until next year. They will find that the virus is nourished by spicy food. So it is a gall bladder instead of an ulcer? I had an attack of something this afternoon, that horrid pain that clamps down in the chest area. I took a tagamet then. I should have gone to Dennys. I would have been happy there. From dinner I feel like bed because I am very drowsy. I recorded notes from Mt. St. Helens and will try to transcribe them when I get back to the motel room. Right now I have a ticket to a movie about boxers. I hope a new bunch of movies comes out soon because I've seen most of the ones out now. Finished my book. What is left except reruns on TV? I must confess that I have dipped into home box office and been fascinated. However, as soon as an ad comes on I switch stations. I need to write cards and figure out my schedule again. I am now three days behind my schedule to Seattle. There is Amtrak here. I really want to see Mt. Rainier. If it is raining tomorrow, I will check into Amtrack. It would be nice to have some extra days in Seattle.

5.29.96 Seattle WA. It was such a dumb day and there was the sign pointing to Amtrack and so here I am in Seattle. Nice town.

So I am signing into the hostel, and the guy at the desk says that Louise of Ole and World Wander is there and also someone that was on the bike trip. Turns out to be Jodi Staunton from Warren, PA.

Jodi claims to have put in more miles than anyone. She heard about me from some of my fellow hearts players in Jomson, Nepal. She biked Morocco, Spain, France and England and flew from France to India. She says she biked India. She, the whitewater guide, white watered in Nepal. The rivers I saw there were pretty scary. She biked many miles in Australia. Meeting with her tomorrow evening. Ole and Regina were just here in Seattle for a week and have left, heading north. They plan to ferry to Skagway, etc. Helen, nobody knows. Michelle and John are together. Ric and Kevin are planning to start again in the fall. Liz was seen by Jody in Kathmandu. Charles and Lisa are in Canada and rolling on their tandem.

5.30.96 Seattle, WA. I seem to like Seattle better than San Francisco. It is really fun here. All sorts of loony stuff. I tape recorded stuff. Must get some film for the trip to the Boeing plant. The two tours are costing $44 but worth it. The tour director had been a native but flew in the Marine Air Corps. He is a real character. I'm lunching in a snack shop near the convention center where Grey Line nests. Madrona trees have a waxy leaf like a rhodendron but funny little white flowers. Lots of really rich people here. A very positive town. Pacific Rim. Waited for Jody but she never showed up.

5.31.96 Seattle. Met with Mary for breakfast and called Franz. Mary is a nurse in the neo-natal at a local hospital Because she wanted to know how Linda Schaefer was doing, I called Linda. Linda is due to have a baby September seven. She married George Snyder. She is working on a book about Calcutta or Mother Teresa or both. She said the bit that she did on me was on CNN (media darling) and she will send me a copy. Mary is a bit of a bicycler. She is a really nice person. She insisted I read through my articles. She loved them. Wants me to write a book.

After breakfast with Mary I went to the library where there wasn't *Alaska* so I worked on the route.

Franz met me at McDonalds and he drove way out of the city to the University area where he lives with his sister. I was very nervous in a car driven by an 88 year-old.

Franz had a pretty aggressive driving style and was really
very good at it.

443

I asked him if it wasn't sort of tough being the last one around. He said yes his friends did keep dying off, but, he added with a sly smile, he got to console the widows.

We dined in a Chinese restaurant and had dessert in a Dennys and then went to look at his canoe which was stashed in a really nice area with expensive houseboats. He showed me his garage workshop where he frames the beautiful stuff he brings back from his worldwide trips. It was stuffed full. He says it sells well at flea markets. He is thinking about spending most of the winter in China next year. We parted then, he showed me how to catch a bus for down town and went home to sleep since he had been up since 5 AM working on a neighbor's roof. The neighbor is 91 and a bit too old to be doing roofs so Franz, 88, is doing the roof. If it is a nice day tomorrow he will be back up on the roof with his screwdriver, working on the moss which is on the shingles. It's a different world.

06.01.96 Port Townsend. Tough day today. Biked 50 miles from Seattle. Left Seattle with a pleasant group of bikers, led by Louise, on a weekend tour to the islands. It was very pretty but hilly. I was very tired and sore, especially my back. Actually I didn't do too badly in the group. Kept up fairly well considering my load and advanced age. It was a beautiful ride and I finally saw Mt Rainer from the ferry. Gorgeous. The majestic Olympic Mountains were in view also. Port Townsend was an attractive Victorian town. The fort turned State Park was nice, too.

I had made a deal with a guy who was looking for a ride to share to Anchorage and we were supposed to meet here in Keystone but he hasn't turned up yet. If he doesn't show, I will head north with Mike. Mike is going to take the ferry from Bellingham. He plans to go to Ketchikan to Prince Rupert to Prince George, to . . . Denver?

None of that worked out. Waiting around for nothing. Probably safer if I just depend on myself.

6.04.96 Bellingham. Great day of bicycling. Taking a short day yesterday was good. Back pain and fatigue are gone. Staying at the sad little hostel. Cheap. Bellingham is a pleasant town. Haven't got stuff on the ferries but I had better do that. Couldn't find *Alaska* at the library so I read another Michener called *The Journey* which is about going to Alaska by way of Edmonton. I really should start eating more in groceries than restaurants if I am going to save money for ferry fees. Wean myself from lush comforts. The biggest hardship in Alaska will probably be money.

Chapter XXXVI

OH CANADA

Build thee more stately mansions, oh my Soul, as the swift sea-
sons roll. Let each new chamber, nobler than the last, seal me
from heaven with a dome more vast til thou at last are free;
leaving thine outgrown shell by life's unresting sea.

The above, a dedication to the incredible
Vancouver Library that is shaped in a spiral,
like the Chambered Nautilus.

6.6.96 Vancouver BC. Well, it was raining when I got up and I had already planned to take the nearby train if it rained and so here I am in Vancouver. Nice city. Great train ride. Saw two eagles. It took all afternoon to bike around town until I found the hostel. It is in a big park, on a bike path, on the water.

6.8.96 Vancouver, BC Yesterday's walking toured the downtown. The Art Gallery was yuk except for an enchanting room about mountains that featured idiosyncratic pianist, Glenn Gould, talking about the challenge of mountains and the north. Went to the Omnimax and saw a terrific movie about mountains shot in BC. Was supposed to be the Andes. This was at Canada Place.

Then I found the headquarters of a bicycle touring group, Company of Adventurers, that has some interesting tours. After much discussion, I decided to do the tour to Inuvik in the way far north, budget permitting. Chas has changed his plane reservation to SeaTac so it is upon me to make the ferry reservations from Ketchikan to Seattle and also the shuttle reservation to SeaTac. Seattle-Tacoma Airport.

Back to square one in the planning

6.19.96 Vancouver, BC, Beautiful, sunny Vancouver. It seems more "Pacific Rim" than Canadian. Like Singapore, like Hong Kong. First thing I saw were a couple of Oriental kids throwing rocks at my train. Then there were the two who got into a shocking fist fight in my downtown McDonalds. The very large manager threw himself between them and dragged them out the door. The angriest guy called the other guy a "Bitch". I stuffed down my burger hoping that he wouldn't go home and get his uzi and come back to gun us all down.

Why is it that in Vancouver where people look at you with big round eyes and say, "Vancouver is so safe," (like as compared to the US?) I keep running into hoodlums? I find it hard to forget the face of an Asian girl, about eight years old, that had been battered until it was swollen and purple everywhere. I had just a glance as she was being pushed up a street by an adult. It was the dead, vacant stare from those puffed eyes that seared my brain. From the USA TODAY: There were two women killed on my beloved Appalachian Trail, in Virginia.

I returned to the headquarters of the "Company of Adventurers", who do bicycle tours here in Vancouver, Northwest Territories, and Cuba. The president is a lady who looks Chinese. The computer guy I talked to had an accent that turned out to be Ecuadorian. Another Oriental was a Nepalese guy. The huge fellow who leads my tour and another "wide load" tour leader were white males from Canada, I guess. Very Pacific Rim.

Vancouver is such an incredible mix of people. I stopped at a tourist agency and was helped by a lady from Persia. Does she think no one knows that that it is Iran? Two other guys there were Pakistani and Texan. The guy who dishes up the daily special at the Jerico Hostel is Kurd from Kurdistan. Wait, isn't that Iraq? All of these seem to be the same as the dollar driven sorts in the USA. Vancouver has the feel of prosperity, there are 1.3 million people and growing. Los Angeles seemed laid back. San Francisco was moving a bit quicker but nothing to compare with Seattle, and even with Bill Gates, Boeing, and Starbucks, Seattle seems to run second to Vancouver.

I had picked up a Company of Adventurers brochure and had really come to inquire about the Kettle Valley Railway Tour. I had hoped that the 325 mile 'rail to trail' path would be going somewhere I was going. It wasn't. It winds around the mountains of South Central B.C. Been there, done that in 1983.

They have a 14 day tour of Cuba. How do you get to Cuba? The plane leaves from Toronto. It would be interesting but as a US citizen, I'd better not even think about it.

Ever hear of the Dempster Highway? This is an eleven day bike excursion up a gravel road to the Artic Circle. The target is a modern town of 3500 that governs the arctic part of Canada, Inuvik, Northwest Territories. It is almost four hundred miles north of Dawson Creek. From Inuvik, because there are no roads north, we will fly to Tuktoyaktuk, this on the Kugmallit Bay on the Arctic Ocean. We will be having a meal with the locals. Chewing the fat with the Eskimos.

We will hotel when possible and camp when we have to. The mosquitoes are bad in June but we will be there in July. There will be a sag wagon. This will be a bit of a budget breaker but the only way I could consider doing such a thing is with a group so I will abandon my independence for a vacation from my vacation. The tour ends in Whitehorse the day before I am to meet himself in Anchorage for a three week tour of Alaska. Can I do it all? Why not.

My biggest problem right now is getting from Vancouver to Vancouver Island to Port Hardy to catch a ferry to Prince Rupert where I will leave Canada to ferry to Ketchikan, Alaska. Vancouver Island has very few facilities in the northern part. Camping with bears!!!!!!!

6.15.96 Vancouver, BC. When did I plan to be in Vancouver until the 15th? Never. But here I am, stuck because I accepted a ride to Port Hardy which is at the north end of Vancouver Island. I keep telling myself I could survive for three days with no facilities on the way if I bike but the sensible, cautious part of me says,

"Yah. Right. When was the last time?"

So I'm at the wonderful library again, an architectural wonder that is made like a chambered nautilus.

In this library, I am luxuriating in excellent lighting, lots of room, desks, other people with no life who hang out here. Ole, the World Wander non-leader predicted that we would all spend much time in libraries. True. Every time I was held up by bad weather or waiting for a ticket to ripen, I was in a library. So I found the Libraryon Robinson Street in Vancouver. Approached from Robinson, you think you are coming up to the Coliseum in Rome. High, vacant, curving walls of pink concrete imitate the highest walls of the arena. You wander around in amazement and into the door which permits you to enter its coiling spiral. A study carrel next to one of the airy shafts can give an acrophobic like me some wiggly feelings.

6.14 I tried keeping a budget. It made no sense to me, but I tried. I did so admire Thomas Jefferson keeping such detailed expenses. He ended up in terrible debt in spite of being painstaking. Later presidents all seemed to make money????

6.16.96. Blackstone? B.C. On a road by the Fraser River, headed for Prince George. How I get into these things is how I get into these things. Impulsively saying, "Me, too. I want to do that." And then sticking by a stupid decision.

"I gave my word."

So instead of biking up Vancouver Island, heading for the ferry at Port Hardy, I am headed for Port George. The locals, Heidi and Andre, are from the Queen Charlottes Islands and they don't pay the $400 ferry fee. They drive around. So, therefore, we are headed toward Prince Rupert by B.C. roads through the desert. Forget Vancouver Island. My locals are Heidi and Andre whom I am not adding to the Christmas address list. Heidi and I discussed that I wanted to be on the ferry from Port Hardy to Prince Rupert. We did. I know we did. Heidi is one of those people who only hears what she wants to hear. She wanted me to share expenses. So here I am in the desert in British Columbia. Actually, it is pretty nice for a change from the lush greens of the coast. They picked me up at the hostel, only an hour late. No, actually they were an hour and 4 days late. And drove until 1:00 AM in spite of their having been up at 4:00 AM the previous day. I am stuffed in the back of a Toyota pickup where they had planed for one more passenger in addition to me. One more cat or canary? My knees are swelling with edema and they ache.

6.17.96 Terrace, B.C. Heidi is taking a driver's test and I am here in the Denny's. She passed the driver's test and then Andre took it and flunked it, just as Heidi had spent hours telling him he would flunk it. Hey, wait! If no person had passed the test before, shouldn't I have been doing the driving?

Six hours in a motel last night. It is one heck of a distance to drive, over a thousand miles. Lots of Ks. The countryside is beautiful and very bikeable. I should have biked it but how could I know? Good shoulder and lots of facilities. There are some areas of swamp, ergo mosquitoes, but in general it is very nice, green, farms and ranches, with snow-capped peaks for a back drop. The traffic hasn't been bad. Heidi remains an enormous pain is the neck. Someone told her she would have more fun if she dropped out of school and acted like a goof for a lot of years, so she has done that. Any subject that comes up gets turned to Heidi and her wonderful life and we are subjected to an hour long lecture on how Heidi, yada, yada, yada. I grunt every now and then and then she and Andre get into long, childish, bickering. They are good people, just incredibly humorless and boring. Heidi bought a tape of humorous stories and right in the middle of a story, Andre will break in with, 'Well. Je don unnerstan pourquois vous . . . .' and the tape gets turned off while they bicker some more. Is this a way to live? They are very disrespectful of each other. Respect begins at home. Heidi says she is Croatian. I respond,

"Born in Victoria, B.C.? Eh? Canadian.'"

She has some dopey idea of going to Croatia to help maintain peace. She can't even keep the peace with Andre. Why does she remind me of all the marriage counselor types who are divorced? I've gone back to serious reading of Og Mendino. Five times a day. Meditating. I LOVE you.

She complains that she doesn't get jobs to work with ind . . . .
Native people because they give those jobs to Natives. Feels she
has been discriminated against. How can a dedicated Croatian not
be a role model for a native girl?

Frankly, my Dear . . . .

And anyhow I would discriminate also. Heidi is an uncertified
substitute teacher. How can she be earning almost $100 per day?
Subs in Pittsburgh get about $50. You have to pay your dues to
join the club, Heidi. You have to sit through, live through, and
pass those teachers' education courses so you know how bad it is to
be in a classroom you detest. No way you can waltz through college
taking interesting courses that will be worthless when you get out.
Then when YOUR student's eyes begin to glass over and snores
fill the room, you've been there. Done that. Time to go back to
those memories of terminal boredom and make a huge effort to
keep it alive and interesting in the classroom. (With Heidi's stories
about Heidi, an interesting classroom can never happen.)

6.18.96 Prince Rupert, BC Canada Prince Rupert got its
name from a nationwide contest. Was the contest to determine
who could come up with the name most likely to confuse
tourists? It was a planned city. Rupert was the planner and was
not a prince. It was planned to be the terminus of the Grand
Trunk rail line that would come all the way across Canada and
be a better port than Vancouver which had come into being as
the terminus of the Canadian Pacific twenty years earlier. So it
had grand and ambitious plans which fizzled down to the 17,000
that now enjoy the handsome site next to the world's second
deepest port. It is not the Pacific Rim hummer that Vancouver
is. Nothing like that but instead a lovely, laid-back spot waiting
to be turned into a tourist Mecca.

The ferry for Ketchikan leaves Canada tonight and gets into
Ketchikan, Alaska at 3 AM. Not good, so I will put that off for ten
hours, take the 7:30 AM and get there at noon. The not-budget
travelers here have a couple of big hotels but not the gigantic one
designed for it by the same guy who did the wonderful hotels at

Victoria, Banff, and Lake Louise. That dream died when the chief promoter went down in the Titanic. It was said that he was last seen conducting the band.

I took the archaeological tour from the museum. We went to the site of a religious group on an island which had built a church that held 1000 people. Accompanying this were rows of very European houses. The whole thing burnt down after the group moved on up the islands to Alaska.

The sun is shining again today and it is cool and pleasant. I got a good rest last night but might enjoy a nap. Finished reading a book: *Where Lawyers Tread* by Lia Matera. Hilarious for a murder mystery.

Chapter XXXVII

ALASKA (South-East)

6.15.96 Michener's ALASKA—the MUST READ

In today's paper, I read that one of the campaign promises of Russian candidate for President, Vladmir Zhirinovsky, is that he will annex Alaska!

To read James Michener's ALASKA is to understand this piece of campaign pipedream. In great detail, Michener leads you through the story of Russian colonization, the sale, how the sale was engineered, and possible Russian claims of fraudulent sale. Must be that Vladmir read Michener's ALASKA so it is the least YOU can do.

Well, anyhow, caveat emptor. Backwards. Let the seller beware. Possession has always been nine points of the law. The Russian colonization was brutal and decimated the natives, the sea otters and other wild life. Fat chance they'd have of getting it back. Really. Then the other thing is that the Japanese wouldn't give up their pieces of it that they have acquired while we were sleeping.

Michener's book was finished a couple of years ago and then that dear man died so he can't go into what happened when the native people were free to sell the lands that had been granted to them. Some of the native corporations that were set up by lawyer-friendly laws were deeply in debt and avaricious lawyer types were circling like ravenous wolves, waiting for the land to go on the market.

Hey, wait! I had ancestral lands! I had ancestors who came to Western Pennsylvania because they fought in the Revolutionary

War. The grant of one square mile was their pay. Downtown Vandergrift, Pa should be mine, mine! Would you believe that my ignorant, naive, probably illiterate ancestors sold that land???? I was robbed! They didn't save a square inch for me. I've had to work and crimp and save to buy land just as if I were a Johnny-come-lately German or Italian or Irish!

Where was I? Oh, yes. Michener is one of my favorite authors. I had finally purchased a paperback but heavy copy of ALASKA in a secondhand bookstore and read it eagerly on rainy days. He spoons out history, geography, socioeconomics in fascinating yarns, spinning the truth and his cliffhanger fiction in thin threads. Characters emerge and then disappear. Their children or grandchildren go on to reveal another era. The original manuscript for ALASKA was an overweight 1100+ pages and was liposucked back to only 900+. The out-takes became another, more manageable book called THE JOURNEY which tells about a fictionalized group of gold seekers headed for the Klondike by way of the Mackenzie River and the Arctic Ocean. So if you read up to the gold rush of 1898 in ALASKA then read THE JOURNEY then go back to ALASKA you have the entire epic as the author planned it. I felt fortunate to have found THE JOURNEY in a library in rainy Bellingham, Washington. The locale of THE JOURNEY is the area that I plan to bicycle in July. I will be going the more usual way: Skagway, Alaska to Whitehorse, Yukon, Canada and then from Dawson City in the Yukon to Inuvik in the Northwest Territories, Canada.

One vignette in ALASKA tells about a prospector who was stuck for the winter in Dawson Creek when there was a new gold find in Nome. This fellow bought a bicycle, learned to ride, and biked the 1400 miles of the frozen Yukon River in the dead of the Alaskan winter. Only one of the many things that I would rather read about than do.

6.19.96 Ketchikan. On the ferry. No eagles, no whales. Going up through the islands of the Inside Passage. Strangely, there are snow covered peaks to the west. People have been very friendly starting off on this adventure. The ferry was not at all crowded. I recovered from my early 'mal de mare' by taking a snooze, (don't fight it.)

Two biking girls from New Zealand said that they had a wheel stolen from a bike in a campground in Prince Rupert. Am I glad I roomed it instead of camping??? Poor, dear Green could have been the victim. They had their bikes locked together but the cable wasn't long enough to go through the front tires.

The snow fields on the West are Misty Fiords National Park that one of our local AYH guys, Glenn, might not have seen. A retired accountant, he has a list of national parks and is checking them off, one by one as he visits them. Narrow here. While workingon the ferry schedule, I find that if I take in a festival in Juneau, I'll misss Petersburg. Can't do it all. The present schedule leaves plenty of time to do the Chillkoot, a trail leading north from Skagway that still has the remnants of the Gold Rush.

6.20.96 Ketchikan AK. Breakfasting at Annabella's. It is part of an old hotel and has high ceilings of embossed tin. There are large paintings on the dark mahogany walls of prostitutes and their patrons down on Creek Street, to which the ladies were banished when law and order came to Ketchikan. Ketchikan advertises itself as the "Salmon Capital of the World" and I have already been to a salmon viewing spot without laying eyes on one. The patrons here are a motley collection, a couple of girls with butch "non" hair-doos. Their faces are hard and hawk-like.

Fairly grubby men come in and out and I guess that they must belong to the fishing fleet that speckles the bays and harbors. There is a lot of work to fishing.

A man in his fifties with a beard like an Amisher has a young boy with him. The child is handsome and has a very intelligent look that contrasts with the wearied look of the man. More people with actually dirty clothes come in to relax on this plush spot with its old long bar with the large mirrors, brass rail and neon Coors sign. The TVs go on and on with no one paying any attention and a different program playing on the two different TVs.

A sign says that Ketchikan is Bob Dole country. Hopefully Dole will save this wild land from being annexed by Russia. The nut case in Russia is claiming Alaska as part of his campaign for presidency rhetoric.

The traffic is terrible when you consider that Ketchikan is all there is. No roads connect it to Canada or the lower 48 or the rest of South East Alaska. There are only 14,000 people in the area. Huge trucks thunder by. Busses, cars, everything. Where are they going? The town is skinny and strung along the water with impassable mountains to the East. I will get my act together soon and take the mapped walking tour.

Meanwhile, back at the hostel, a couple from New York are taking a float plane to Misty Fiords National Monument. The plane will carry their kayak and leave them for a couple of days and then pick them up again after they have kayaked and tented a couple of nights. The girl's white silk long johns and sock liners and glove liners were the envy of all who saw them drying in the hostel bathroom.

6.21.96 Ketchikan. I started up Deer Mountain full of ambition. The top could be reached in three to five hours. I counted the five hours from the 8:30 when I was starting and figured it would be getting pretty warm and late in the day with the downhill to go. Since it is the downhills and my knees that I worry about, I adjusted my time on the mountain to the energy suppliers. I had left my gear in the hostel and was carrying, a bottle of Snapple and a Snickers bar. I missed the last sign before the wilderness and ended up at the garbage dump, apparently a very popular spot because there was unending traffic going by. Signs warned not to tease or annoy the bears. A 'First Nations People' lady offered to take me to the real start of the trail and I accepted but was a bit edgy. I never saw any bears, perhaps because I kept on singing, whistling and yelling, 'Here I come, Bears.' This is supposed to be powerful anti-bear stuff and it worked!

When I told the lady at the hostel that I was going up the mountain, She responded that the day before there had been a fellow who was fussing about what to take up the mountain to eat. She suggested a sandwich. She told him there was some bread and peanut butter that someone had left behind. When he looked totally blank, she said,

"Well, all you have to do is spread the peanut butter on the bread to make a sandwich."

"Oh, I couldn't do that," the guy answered. "I don't cook."

So, anyhow, after a couple of hours of straight up climbing, I sat down to rest in a spot with a view that stretched all the way to the ocean. Suddenly there was a bear coming at me up the trail.

"Yeow," I yelled, but the yell fizzled out when the bear got closer and magically turned into a friendly dog. The owners said it was a German hunting dog. Its friendliness made up for its homeliness but really, with occasionally white hairs sticking out of its fur, it could have passed for a shrunk down grizzly. The girls with it are here for the summer to work in the cannery. One girl said she had worked there last year and made $2000 in three weeks. As we sat chatting and enjoying the view, an eagle drifted by. I was frantically trying to get to my camera while the bird disappeared and then circled back several times. It will probably show up as just a smear in the sky but really it was only about 20 feet away. It was all brown because it was young. My total supply of liquid was gone in three glugs and an empty Snickers wrapper meant that I had also demolished the candy bar. So I went back down. I made bear sounds whenever I met people coming up but they weren't too scared.

Back down, I toured Creek Street that had been the red light district. Dolly's house has all of Dolly's stuff still in it. She was the lone whore in the house, charged $3.00 per and didn't quit until she had $75 for the day. In spite of this she lived into her eighties. Prostitution was legal in Alaska until 1972 and when it was declared illegal, Dolly retired.

I have given up on the idea of kayaking here. Too expensive and the kayaks are right next to the enormous cruise ships that tower over the town. The kayaks come right up the cute creek that has the cute old whore houses on it. But no salmon.

Ketchikan, AK.
The Salmon Boy.

The local First Nation's People, the Tlingits, did not believe in punishing their children. Their way to get proper respect was by scaring the children into proper behavior with horrifying stories of weird and terrible fates for the unruly. The group that acted out the story of the Salmon Boy didn't look very First Nations People to me. First Nation's People is what is becoming Politically Correct for what were known as Indians when I was studying them in fifth grade. Back in 1906. Actually I like First Nation's People a lot better than "Native American". I'm native American. I was born here. Scotch-Irish, German, English: Native American. A mutt, a Native American. As for the indigenous people that where in Western Pennsylvania when my Scotch-Irish ancestors came toiling over the mountains, shortly after the Revolution, I would be happy to refer to them as First Nations People. Not that they were any more pure then than the tribes here because after all, the Scotch-Irish had been proceeded by the French. Fort Duquesne, right? And, well, you know what the French are like.

Except for one or two of them, these actors who claimed to be Haida, Tlingit and Tsaimsim didn't look any more First Nation's People than I do. Does this thing of trying to pass as Indian (oops), Native American (oops), First Nation's People have anything to do with the government dumping great pots of money into Alaska's Native Americans (First Nation's People) pockets? (I refer you to Michener's ALASKA.) How does a person get to be as suspicious as I am? Living such a long time? Anyhow, since I can't get the Indian names right and since the local tribespersons all have 'Christian' names, let the hero, or anti hero of our story be an obnoxious child called Boy. His mother is Jane and his father, Tarz. Tarz dresses up as a horrible monster and scares Boy half out of his mind from time to time. Tarz tries to scare Jane also but she is not so dumb. However, she isn't doing her proper duty of turning Boy over to Aunt Clara to be educated in the ways of the tribe. Mother Jane spoils Boy and, boy, is he a brat. Nobody can stand him. He goes out on the beach one day and has a tantrum, throwing himself down on the sand and screaming until he is tired and falls asleep. This is not too smart in a place with a twenty foot tide. As he is washing out to sea, the salmon king comes along and adopts the boy, turning him into a salmon. He leads the perilous life of a salmon for a few years, learning the ways of a salmon. Just as he is finally becoming a good and proper fish, he is speared by one of his human relatives. When they gut the poor thing they find the talisman he always wore and they realize that they have killed the young prince. Through some magic that I seemed to have missed, he comes back to life as a boy and they all live happily ever after with a kid who knows how to respect people, trees, salmon, and relatives. A real success story.

Do you get the feeling that perhaps the original story ended with the spearing and gutting which should be enough to terrorize the worst of kids? Modern kids can certainly be grateful that they only have to deal with Hell fire and brimstone.

6.22.96 Wrangell, AK. Had a nice chat with a young philosophy major at the hostel this morning. He was a fellow stoic. I am stoic and since stoa is Greek for porch, if you are an unchurched stoic you are really unporched, right? Even the philosophy major thought I was a bit dippy.

We are ferry cruising the islands and it is lovely.

6.23.96 Wrangel, AK was not great but the people were. It was a very lovely setting with unlovely human fish canning activities. I walked to the top of Mt. Dewey. The trail was well tended but being through muskeg and rock, it was still challenging. The muskeg is like the peaty soil of Maine and England. The muskeg dissolves under foot traffic and leaves just rock. The view from the top was nice and I stopped there for a while before rushing to the Presbyterian Church for services. The hostel is in the church and it seemed only right to slide in the door and sit in the back.

In the church service, there was a lot of folksy stuff that was part of the regular operation. They expressed concern and dismay over the churches that have been burnt in the Lower 48. A big item on the agenda was a group coming from Florida to help build an addition to the church. This church is actually the oldest Presbyterian church in Alaska. As they were organizing places for the guests to stay and food for them to eat, the chairman made an appeal for a couple of fish and, something Floridians really need, moose.

It was a very dramatic session. How can I do it justice? The things that annoyed me most about Presbyterian churches when I was young were how stuffy everyone was and how competitive to display personal wealth. Everyone was always dolled up in their Sunday best, reeking of perfume and furs and jewels. None of that in Wrangell. The minister was dressed in a short-sleeved, dark-green sport shirt. He talked to the children about the kind of love that says, I will like/love you if you do . . . something . . . for me. He identified this as Conditional Love.

During the sermon, he got all choked up talking about a bunch of verses from Matt. (14?) that told about Simon denying Jesus and he got so hung up on it that he couldn't read it without sniffling. Terrific. A fellow emotional idiot who weeps big tears. I sniffled right along with him. Then my nose ran. Neither he nor I had a hanky. It got worse. He said there were three things we should remember and held up four fingers. The congregation laughed through its tears. When the session was over I bee lined for the door because I didn't want to shake hands with him if his hands were in the same condition as mine, no hanky and all.

The trip through the Wrangell Narrows has been exciting. The forest service provides a commentator and we learn about the Naval navigational aids. A large flock of bald eagles was extra entertainment. Now we can see Petersburg down the channel. I am still in doubt as to whether I should get off or go on to Sitka and arrive there at 1:00 A.M. The church hostels have been good for the budget and I can afford a hotel for one night. I think. Saw a flock of eagles roosting in the spruce and on the beach and in the air in Wrangell narrows and later in Frederick Sound, a few humpback whales. One baby humpback cavorted for as long as we could see it and at one point leaped clear of the water, gave a twist and dove back in again.

6.24.96 Sitka AK. Was this place called New Archangel when I was young??? Getting so old that I can't remember. So far it looks a lot like a regular Southeast Alaska village. I didn't get much sleep last night with the ferry getting in at 1:30 AM. There was a shuttle waiting to take us to the hostel.

This morning, I tramped around town visiting the Russian Church and graveyard and the spot where the Russians turned the place over to the US. I was really impressed by the art in the Church and felt, for the first time, an urge to see Russia, particularly St. Petersburg, the Hermitage. There will be a performance in museum tomorrow and I will go to that before I catch the ferry to Juneau.

As I was wandering by the museum, I met up with a kayak group and elected to do that for a couple of hours. It was most enjoyable. I was in a two person kayak with a retired RCMP from Calgary. We saw leaping fish, eagles, baby loons, but no sea otters. In the shallow areas, the sea weed was beautiful. The leaves were large and not the bright green stringy stuff I usually see but a watery garden of great beauty. The ex-Mountie in the back of the canoe called it Sargasso. I had sailed through the Sargasso Sea which is in the Atlantic Ocean on Semester at Sea and admired the seaweed and flying fish. So, what does he know? He is from Calgary. I am trying to not be a know it all. What do I know? It was two hours of excellent paddling.

6.25.96 Sitka AK. McDonalds is where everything hangs out. This may be the world's greatest Mickey D's. The two dozen eagles that patrol the beach about 20 feet from the burger building are impressive. The eagles are fishing. Since the tide is high now, perhaps they are waiting for the things that are exposed as the water goes down, i.e. starfish. Some of them are wading the shallower places. There are large ravens hanging out here also. They are ravens, not crows. No crows here. The young eagles are all brown. They get their white head and tail at three years of age. Large birds aloft that soar magnificently are young eagles, not vultures. No vultures here. Perhaps the eagles await the arrival of the next run of salmon. The salmon run several times a year and the bears and birds know when and arrive at the proper time even if the salmon don't.

My ferry gets in and then hangs out for several hours because it can only go through the Wrangell Narrows when the tide is either full or out. An eagle just caught a fish. Swooped down and grabbed it with his claws. The rest are just sitting on the rocks near the water.

The men who hang out here are mostly short and powerfully built. Low gear guys. In most of them the Tlingit skin color is being overcome by white, and even blue eyes, but they remain short stocky body build and the slow rumble of the Tlingit speech It doesn't have the range of American. A question ends up about a half note low and one of our downer negatives is just a bit too high. The result is an accent that sounds very flat to my ear. The two nearest me are talking about going camping!

6.26.96 Juneau AK. A lady got mad at me just now because I said that I thought Internet was a big waste of time and money. She is connected with some institution that pays the bills. I have to pay $10 per month for AOL and that is just the begining. The telephone bills were horrendous because AOL is long distance. My son, the insomniac, loves internet and gets into long political debates which ended up with his running for congress. Why not? Maybe he can campaign by internet and his $600 budget will mean something.

Meanwhile, there was a sighting of a half-dozen whales. Everyone rushes to the rails to see. There is the rain left over from yesterday. I slept fairly well on the floor, no, deck, in the forward lounge but only about five hours. I would probably been happier in the solarium which is on the upper deck open air. There is a hostel in Juneau but Juneau is 20 miles from the ferry. Looks like I will be plenty wet by the time I get to the hostel. The hills are shrouded in wet clouds, and the islands further away than the closest are completely obscured by rain.

Later. I skipped the Mendenhall Glacier trying to make the quickest trip to the town. I arrived in Juneau soaked and grubby but reasonably comfortable. There was a bike path most of the way from the Ferry slip. It wasn't well marked and once a huge semi truck stopped and the driver got down from his truck and came back to point out where the bike path was! There were toilets and even a phone on the bike path. The hostel doesn't open until five o'clock but now that I am in the state capitol's tiny downtown, I can pick a time when it is not raining to push the bike up the very steep hill to the hostel. There are huge cruise ships in today but still it doesn't seem crowded. Perhaps the tourists all went somewhere in a tour bus. I think, after looking at the guide book that I will wait for the hostel to see if they have any suggestions. Often there are special deals for people staying at hostels. Time for me to leave McDonalds but I will be really cold when I go outside because I am so sweaty. Think I'll head for the library. Why McDonalds? Other eateries had stuff over the windows or no windows and I couldn't watch the bike.

The library was a dead loss. It was on the upper floor of a parking garage and I couldn't find a secure place to leave the loaded bicycle.

6.28.96 Juneau, AK. What joy! What despair! I went to see Dr. Cook, a dentist recommended to me by a local Juneauan. He took one x-ray and a bit of poking around and made me regret that I had not been able to go to the dentist in May when I was home. In April I had the dentist scheduled but had to cancel. So now my dentist is on vacation and the substitute has scheduled me for Monday afternoon. Dr. Cooks diagnosis was four possible crowns and two possible root canals!!! He said to go home. It will take a while and I will need tea and sympathy. So, a mixed blessing. I must interrupt the trip but I get to see my mate and my family.

Downtown Juneau is snuggled up tight against very high cliffs that still have snow fields on them. As I strolled the back and up a bunch streets near the Governor's mansion, I saw areas where these mountains had given up a bit of rocky, gravely material which had slid down to pretty close to the homes. Indeed the downtown area was built on the talus from the mines. There are enough hundred year old buildings in the down town areas to make it charming for the people from the huge cruise ships that pull in every day.

What with biking back down to the airport in the rain with my bicycle in order to store it in a bike shop, and the bus ride back, I didn't get to see all the tourist attractions. The one I wanted to see most was the Raptor Hospital where they bandage up the wounded eagles. I did take in a couple of excellent shows at the Forest Service Building. The best was one on the Aurora Borealis. Juneau is the wildest of the Southeast towns that I have been in. Sitka Spruce, towering cliffs and the Mendenhall Glacier in the suburbs are very exotic.

In the Juneau Airport people arrived from somewhere wearing cotton, sneakers, flowered shorts. Weird. Those of us waiting to leave in our gortex, hiking boots and long warm pants gazed at them with pity and the hope that their enormous bags held garments for cold and rainy. One guy thought I was a native. My polar fleece jacket, polypro shirt, nylon hiking slacks and light-weight, gortex boots do qualify for Alaska's best dressed. Some South East Alaskans get annoyed at the cruise boat types because they come in on the Dutch ship, eat at the Westmark Hotel and ride the Dutch tour bus and don't spend the big bucks on the local stuff.

Alaska again

The hiatus at home was so very unpleasant. My dear dentist was on vacation. Vacation? How could he? His substitute insisted on pulling my two upper front teeth! These bad guys had been loose for ever so long and I had developed a multitude of ways to avoid biting or chewing on them. The X-rays showed them to be broken! My regular dentist had inquired once if I had suffered a blow to the face and that confused me. Well, I was thinking in terms of something hitting me, not me taking my face and using it as a pile-driver. On a hiking tour across England, I was just standing talking to Alma, my hiking companion, and suddenly fell flat on my face. My nose was skinned, my chin was skinned, I had to get new glasses because they were badly scratched. I never thought about my teeth, but they were broken and caused nothing but trouble until now, three years later, they have been yanked out. From that time on my nightmares changed and became the day I could not find the two false front teeth. Nightmare this: I am standing in front of my seventh grade class and I speak and smile and my two front teeth are missing. A nightmare.

I arrived in the Juneau airport and retrieved Green from the nice guys at the bike shop near the airport. I had carefully planned my arrival and went north to the Mendenhall Glacier and then on to the ferry terminal. The Mendenhall was a thrill. There were a couple of little icebergs floating on the blue lake and lots of pines and snow-capped mountains to frame pictures that have to be calendar shots. I had also wrung a promise from Chas to meet me in Anchorage. So everything was going very well.

It must have been a "dark and stormy night" coming into Skagway. I guess. I was sound asleep on a deck chair in the solarium, the area on the top deck of the ferry that is fresh air. The ferry unloaded I slept on. The ferry loaded up again and prepared to leave and sounded its horn and I woke up. I saw Skagway and, instantly alert, dashed for Green, four decks down, chained to a railing on the auto deck. I found Green and unchained her and remembering that my backpack with all my money etc. was under the deck chair, dashed back up the four decks again, found the backpack under my chair and dashed down again. They were holding the ferry for me and as soon as I frantically pushed the bike up the ramp to the dock, it left for parts south. So now I'm in Skagway and it is the middle of the night.

I had studied my guidebook and remembered the location of the hostel. Good. I wouldn't have to put my tent up in the public park. As I approached the hostel, I saw a light go out and someone leave. I assumed that someone had met the ferry for the hostel. I knocked lightly on the door, not wanting to disturb sleepers. No one answered but the door slid open so I went in and spent the rest of the night on a couch in the living room. I was up at my usual early hour and slid out the door and went off to find breakfast. When I went back later I made the mistake of trying to pay the dragon who owned the place for the night's lodging. She made loud and frequent complaints about me and my bad character to the other hostellers who were there to wolf down their breakfasts. The cowed and craven hostellers were obligated to consider me a horrible example. It was a different sort of welcome than I had found in the church basements hostels on the Inward Waterway.

I rode out with a group of hikers that were bound for the Chillkoot Trail. The dragon's weird brother was the driver. The trailhead was unimpressive but I was sorry that I had no time to hike. He took up the cause and browbeat me all the way back to the hostel. I guess that was my Skagway city tour.

I didn't even have time to bike to Whitehorse. I got passage on an eleven passenger bus up over the mountain to Whitehorse in the Yukon. There I stashed Green in the hotel basement, met the Company of Adventurers group, and started off for the Artic Ocean.

Chapter XXXVIII

CANADA

(again) The Yukon

The trip as I wrote it up for the magazine:

The Dempster Highway

First of all, what kind of name is Dempster? Nothing to do with dumpster. This Yukon is an humungeous piece of real estate. And it isn't as though the area is loaded with TRUE stories of daring do. Really. But, after you are entertained by The Cremation of Sam Magee and the Shooting of Dan Magrew, after Jack London, how can mere truth hold up?

Dempster is the name of Corporal Dempster, who later shows up in one of those terribly stiff photo portraits as Sergeant Dempster of the North West Mounted Police. The present highway takes the route that Corporal Dempster took north from Dawson City, Yukon when he went looking for four RCMPs who had gone on patrol three months earlier. The 'Lost Patrol' had succumbed to scurvy, starvation and just general bad weather. Had they taken a native guide with them they would probably have lived. As it was, they made it almost to Ft. McPherson. We saw a small, simple marker for the four who died in the grave yard of the Ft. McPherson Anglican Cemetery. Old photos of the Mounties and dogsleds decorate the walls of the Eagle Plains Motel, an oasis in the taiga. The Dempster Highway was started in the 50's but not completed until the 70's. There have been bicycle touring types here, in fact an American stopped to tell us that he had helped an Israeli biker who had broken a chain. The Israeli had flown to New York City and biked to Inuvik, North West Territories. Did I mention somewhere that Israelis are tough?

We bicycle tourers have speculated on how you could do the Dempster on a solo bicycle and it seems to me that you could fend off starvation, scurvy, and general bad weather by mailing supplies to places like the Eagle Plains Motel. That is how people handle hiking the Appalachian Trail, which is also short on supplies in a lot of places. For the A-T, hikers set up a carefully planned series of mail drops ahead of time. Sometimes the hikers have more than they can carry and end up giving away pounds of supplies to the ambling goofs like I was who didn't plan ahead and therefore can carry the extra pounds of goodies. I made out pretty well on the A-T just scrounging stuff when people couldn't manage to carry what they mailed to themselves. The Dempster is different. You don't look out from your high point and see the lights of towns or cities. You don't see anything. There are no people at all.

The highway is gravel. This keeps it from being very big on most lists of tourist attractions. It isn't like a gravel road in Pennsylvania that would wind along a stream and have occasional areas of puddles and mud holes. The Dempster Highway is a huge effort of material and time that starts with a base of crushed rock to insulate the permafrost, then mounds of fill piled on top of that. The permafrost is hundreds of feet deep in some places and if you start it melting, things just start sinking and keep on going. So the highway is one long causeway with the surface of the road being at least six feet higher than the surrounding area. There are some spots of hard packed clay that are nice and smooth but most of the time there is some or a lot of loose gravel and big clouds of dust. I never got used to the gravel and braked on every downhill. This put me far behind the Canadian bicyclers. They tackled the problems with enormous verve and enthusiasm. Alaskan roads are very similar to Yukon roads and lead to the saying, *'Alaska has two seasons, winter and road repair.'* The way to get around the shredded tires and chipped windshield problem is to use a rental car. Rentals can handle these things a lot better than your own beloved car.

Like most commercial bicycle groups that I have been acquainted with, the bikers are not young. Five of the nine were over 60, most were women. I suppose that is because women are more cautious about venturing into the unknown alone than are men.

This tour is probably the first commercial tour to tackle the far north. We were treated like visiting royalty by the Company of Adventurers tour people. The three young folks who were in charge were very attentive, knowledgeable and good cooks. We all gained weight. Some of us puffed up a good bit.

The real star of the tour was the trailer. It had four compartments: two refrigerators, a toilet, and a baggage storage area. Bikes were carried in two racks both front and rear, and tired bikers could share a 15 passenger van. The toilet was never used.

There was only one accident. The youngest of the bikers would go flying down hills with her feet off the pedals yelling 'Whoopee!'.

Ever tactful, I tried to explain how bikers should keep the butt off the seat when there are downhills, bumps, gravel, or potholes. Stand on the pedals and push finger tips to finger tips to keep from having the hands clenched to the handlebars like vice grips. This allows the bike to bounce around under you and the mass (your chubby body) goes calmly on its way. If you lock your body to the seat you will be thrown around by every bump or pothole.

Of course she didn't listen to the drops of wisdom falling from my lips. She landed on her elbow and had an area as big as a half dollar with gravel ground in, accompanied by sprays of gravel tattooing her thighs. The guide kid who will enter medical school next month did a nice job with the bandage but didn't scrub out the gravel. When I was a track coach, I scrubbed gravel but they turned me down when I offered this time, thank goodness. With this generation paying to have tattoos, I guess a free one is considered a bonus.

The worst was, as predicted, the mosquitoes and flies. I won the award for being the biggest mosquito whiner. Canadians may have blood that is not tasty to bugs. Bugs love me. Only one evening did we feel brave enough to face the mosquitoes at the edge of the stream and bathe in the icy water. It was delightful to splash around in the stream and then sit down to an elegant meal from the miraculous trailer. Steak and huge British Columbia prawns.

The four hundred plus miles were accomplished in the allotted time.

We celebrated our arrival at the Arctic Circle with champagne and photos

The quaint town of Ft. McPherson was very small. Inuvik was larger and had interesting shops and museums. The most surprising structure was a dome shaped church that had been presented to the Inuits by Bing Crosby.

After cruising the town, we looked forward to the flight to Tuktoyaktuk.

We had to take two planes because they were fairly small. I asked the pilot of our plane if he was a bush pilot and he said not, that he needed a field to land on. We wore our warmest clothes. And got pictures taken with a large, handsome, stuffed polar bear. We were assured that we would see welfare bears that hang out at the garbage dump in Tuk but the stuffed one was it for this trip.

When we landed (everyone else could see white whales as we flew over the mouth of the McKenzie River.) we immediately took off by van for the much touted garbage dump but, no bears. The houses of the Inuits looked pretty much like wood houses in more southerly areas. Pretty much the same inside, too.

We were entertained by an Inuit family who seemed pretty regular. The lady of the house did show us her native dresses and a hood lined with wolverine fur. We had some soup and hard tack. It was fun. When we went strolling, we ended up in the only restaurant talking to the new principal of the school. We remarked about the large number of young people and children in the cemetery. She got started on the problems of the locals and could not stop. The problems in Tuk center around alcohol and depression. The winters are long and dull and dark. Alcohol fetal syndrome, she said, is when you spend Twenty minutes teaching a child to hang up his jacket, and the next time he can't remember how. One of our group is a high court judge. He wears a wig and gown to work. When I would sneak a peak at him, he was hanging his head and very solemn. Americans aren't considered to be too bright up north so my suggestion was passed off as, well, silly. So I'll make it here. These folks are all on welfare so why not give them a trailer and pickup, and send them south. They could spend the winter camping along the Colorado and fishing in its muddy waters along with the folks from Vancouver. Then if they are still depressed and suicidal in paradise, well, then you could give up on them.

We cruised to the beach and the kids jumped in. I thought I was brave to get ankle deep in the Arctic. We tried the dump again without success.

The rest of the tour group flew to civilization from Inuvik but I stayed with the crew to Whitehorse where I rented a pickup truck and set out for Anchorage. I just made it to the airport in time to meet Chas.

Chapter XXXIX

Alaska

8.4.96 We made contact with John and Cynthia Olnes and had breakfast with them. They were great. Told us all the good stuff to see. What really turned out was stopping at milepost 107 on the road to the Kenai Peninsula. There we could see the Dahl sheep and Chas climber way up the cliff and got some great pictures when the sheep came to about six feet away.

We couldn't decide which glacier tour to take so we took both of them. They were both so good. Incredibly beautiful. We were thrilled to the core with Alaska.

8.5.96 Homer AK It was drizzling when we got up and we had a really nice breakfast at the restaurant next to the hotel. We decided to see the Portage Glacier and it took most of the day just to drive up the peninsula to Portage and catch the ferry. The glacier was magnificent. It even calved a bit as we were leaving. It is a mile across and 250 feet high and very deep into the fiord. It was so strange, we were sitting next to people who turned out to be Trish Wilson who roomed across the hall from me at Lock Haven State Teachers College in 1948.

8.6.96 Anchorage, AK It took most of the day for me to type up the second part of the stuff to send off to Health and Fitness. I begged for the use of the computer at Olneses and we were there so long they fed us lunch and a wonderful dinner of halibut that John had caught and frozen. They have a really nice computer with Works '95. John and Chas toured the zoo. I had a second nap because I fell asleep while writing out the article. It was stimulating, however. After the ending which takes on the drug and alcohol

472

problems of the First Nations people there was long period of sharing landlords war stories. John drove us up a mountain for the view of the city and behold, we could see McKinley!! It is huge and white and beautiful.

8.7.96 Denali,AK. It is so exciting to be traveling north out of Anchorage on such a sunny day. We drove the top of a mountain outside of Anchorage and could see, not only the city, but the top of Mt. McKinley, 150 miles away. So as we drove north the mountain peeked out at us from behind the trees to be greeted with ohs and awes, and oh my goodness each time. Someone had called McKinley 'The weather maker' which seems much better than merely, Denali which means 'The big one, or 'the Great One.' Let's go with 'The Great One.' The snowy eminence of the Mountain above the others of the Alaska Range is what makes it so outstanding as mountains go. It rises to 20,320 from a base of 1700 ft.

Now we are waiting at Hudson Aviation in Talkeetna for a flight to the mountain. This is pretty exciting. We are in little planesville, Alaska. There is 1 licensed pilot for every 55 Alaskans. It is a way of life here. We saw a movie at the aircraft museum in Anchorage. We saw a lot of film footage of the Japanese invasion of the US at Attu. It took Over 12,000 American troops to get rid of the 800 Japanese troops. Fascinating film. It had Japanese generals and strategists talking about the attack on the US.

It seems we are both going up in the small plane because the price is a reasonable $59 each. I'm acrophobic and don't have much love for small planes. Besides, I'm cheap.

However, the flight was so very beautiful and thrilling. One of the high spots, and, well, yes. Chas got great pictures.

8.9.96 Denali,AK. All sorts of warnings are given about bears here:

"You'll get a lot of bear stories when you hit Denali."

"So what is yours?"

"It wasn't mine, really but I was there. When you go into the park, you go on busses the first day. Like really old school busses. They take you in and you get to see everything. The middle is the

473

best part. But there are so many bears. The bears are everywhere. There is no chance of not seeing bears. The next day you take your gear and tell them where to let you off. There aren't any campgrounds. No trails. It is all just rough. It is tundra. Knee high. And you have to go out far enough that they can't see your tent from the road. Then you put the tent up and use it for a base camp. You have to have your food in bear-proof cans. The cans are all covered with scratches and claw marks from the bears trying to get in them. You understand these bears can be ten feet tall."

I try to picture ten feet of bear.

"The bear attack that I saw was in the campground, by the entrance. There are those big iron boxes for keeping bears away from the food. The iron is all scratched from the bears.

Well, there was this woman walking through the camp and out of nowhere comes this bear, on all fours, charging right at her. She just stopped and faced it and started yelling at it."

He stopped and stared at me to see my reaction. I have no doubt that it was horror.

"That's what you have to do."

"Did it work?"

"Yes, the bear veered just ten feet from her and ran on by. They don't kill people, just scalp them or mess them up a lot."

However, Denali for most visitors is like one of those zoos where the people are incarcerated and the animals run free. Bears and other animals are never fed or otherwise coddled. If things are tough and they die, they die. This is a wilderness where very few humans are permitted to wander at will. Joe Average comes to the gate and buys a ticket for the creaky old/new busses. At the allotted hour he climbs on the bus for a day-long, fascinating tour of the sub artic. Forget the mountain, The Biggie's prima dona cameo appearances are a very small part of the tour. If viewing the mountain does not happen because it is shrouded in clouds, who notices? We have been here three days and two were rainy but still very rewarding tours. The third day was a repetition of the second because we had planned to get off the bus and hike around but elected to ride rather than wander around in a downpour. This was Chas most successful experience as a wild animal photographer. Hyperactive people are not great fishermen or wild animal photographers. He got some terrific shots of bear, moose, golden eagles, caribou, fox, ptarmagan, marmots, and merlin from the safety of the bumpy old school bus. He used a 300 mm lens for the stills and the video camera was just amazing. The bus guys don't let you out of the bus to frighten the critters. Moose and bear just walk around the bus if it is in their way.

The bus is a microcosm of touring. People semisnooze, bored, while the bus drones on and on. No snacks or food are sold in the park and lest crumbs feed the animals so people eat their stuff in the bus. Suddenly, a sighting! Everyone is crowding the windows, cameras or binoculars to the eyes. No matter how good the sighting, they are soon bored again and settle back in their seats for more riding. The drivers are entertaining at best and don't interrupt the dozing at worse. Even small children nod off.

The hunger that drives the animals here is the dominating force. They must eat enough to keep them through the terrible winter to come. The bears semi-hibernate in shallow dens that they dig in the snow. The moose and caribou forage for the bits of green they can find. The adorable marmots will totally hibernate by the end of August. Snows come in September and winter sets in. Meantime, the bears walk along sucking up berries into their mouths like vacuum sweepers.

Locals who climb The Biggie take the time to go up the back side. They take one trip up with dog sleds for about 35 miles, cache 200 pounds of food and go back down. Then they start walking from the park entrance and walk to the top, by way of the cache, and back. This takes a month. The people who get flown half way up climb the south side and it takes them only 2 weeks. It is dangerous from either direction.

8.10.96 Fairbanks, AK The Alaska Range lies between us and the south now. There are many glaciers on this side, some as long as 30 miles but we haven't seen anything but the terminals. Stopped to visit with a kid from Bradford Woods, her husband teaches at the university. They have a husky that pulls a sled in the winter.

Now they are growing huge veggies because the sun shines for so many hours a day. The biggest garden pest is a moose.

8.11.96 Chicken AK. So named because the founders, a bunch of gold seekers were going to call it ptarmigan. Then they realized that they didn't know how to spell ptarmigan and settled on the less lexological bird. It has a couple of dozen population but its own post office and strip mall. And outdoor toilet. The owner of the strip mall was up and about when we came looking for breakfast. She was busy making pies and didn't want to stop to fix breakfast for us but did give us free left over coffee and chatted happily. She and her husband have three airplanes. And, yes, the road (Top of the World Highway) is closed in the winter and, no, they don't spend the winter in Chicken. When winter comes, they take one of the planes to the Carribean.

8.12.96 Dawson City, Yk Canada Went to see a stage show in Dawson. Fun. Chas loved the old buildings that are sliding into the perma frost.

8.13.96 Whitehorse,YK. Driving from Dawson City. Of major concern today will be turning in the truck. The drive has been pleasant while we read to each other the tale of the 'Lost Patrol' by Dick North. The story goes into the rugged life of the leader of the patrol, Frank Richardson. This tale plainly describes the terrible difficulties faced by the Mounties in the far north. As we reach rivers and streams mentioned in the narrative they gain in personality. We were waiting on the Klondike Highway for one of the endless road repair trucks to do its thing and mentioned the book to the girl who was directing traffic. She was from Mayo, a nearby village. She had never heard of the Mountie named Dempster or the 'lost Patrol', much less North's book.

8.14.96 Skagway AK USA I am so cheap that I would return to the hostile hostel? Yep. We survived.

8.15.96 Juneau,AK. The ferry leaves from Skagway at 11:15 AM so we have accomplished our chores at the Hostel and are trying to figure if we have time and stuff for a small hike up the mountain beside Skagway. The mountains behind we will leave to some other time or life. The hostel itself is lovely, but it is overcrowded with two tiny bathrooms for 24 beds and the overflow which was sent to a nearby church.

In the early morning' I finished reading about the 'Lost Patrol' by Dick North, from whom we bought the book in Dawson. The 'Lost Patrol' went the same area as we biked on the Dempster Hwy. Or rather, we biked the same trail that Dempster took when looking for the lost patrol. The patrol actually got lost in the Wind River area, looking for Foster Creek, which they never found and they turned back to try to get back to Ft McPherson. Their bodies showed starvation and scurvy when found. They suffered a lot before they died. In the description of their swollen and cracked lips and the black spots on their cheeks, I saw again the faces of the people in Nepal who had come over the pass after the killing snowfall. Trekking in Nepal is not supposed to be all that dangerous but when the weather turned bad when I was almost to Jomson, some 60 people died.

I was the beneficiary of prior experience. Some people were for charging ahead in spite of hard rain and the creeks rising. The deep, rushing water reminded me of the time I was hiking on the Pacific Crest Trail and the hikers with me, much more experienced than I, decided to go through a stream swollen with spring melt off and nearly lost a hiker in the torrent. As it was the girl lost her boots. They were just ripped off her feet and hurtled over a cliff. If her husband hadn't grabbed her, she would have gone, too.

The Jomson Trail is part of a loop that goes around the Annapurnas called, strangely enough, the Anapurna Circuit. People like I was, people who just wandered into Nepal and decided to trek could rent gear and walk either the circuit or just go to Jomson. Jomson was at 9000 feet but the highest part of the Circuit was 16,000 feet and chancy if you are prone to altitude sickness. Altitude sickness was supposed to be the most dangerous part of the Circuit trek. I didn't have the three weeks that the circuit requires and figured I would walk to Jomson and fly back to Pokhara easily in the 16 days of my permit. I wasn't too sure my knees would hold up for the longer trek, especially with no preparation. I got to Jomson just as the weather closed in. I got a ticket for the plane but that was a laugh. No planes for days. Field too wet. The helicopter was freighting the survivors. And the bodies.

8.19.96 Wrangell Narrows. We are getting a lot more free time on the ferry Taku because of fog. We sat for three hours last night and are sitting again because the narrows are very narrow and the fog makes it very treacherous. The ship actually turned around while we were having breakfast. While we were turning the Matanuska went zipping by us but now it is just sitting up there in the channel.

When we were approaching Rake, we saw three bears in a creek. Then as we left and started up the narrows there was another black bear poking around on the beach. I'm in the land of my four bears. Chuck made me write that.

Chapter XXXX

WASHINGTON

(again)

We didn't make very many stops on the way back down the Inland Waterway because Chas had a plane to catch at SeaTac.

We parted in Bellington, he to fly home and I to start biking over the Cascades on the Adventure Cycling map course. The first day out of Spokane was spent with flat tires. The first one was repaired by a helpful biker. When the second one popped, I scrounged a ride to a bike shop and they did the repairs. The third one was a very short distance from the bike shop when a brand new tire went flat.

The next few days were spent grinding up some very nice hills and then some very nice mountains. When I finally got to Spokane I called Chas said to come home! I was to receive an award for my writing from the Golden Quill. Fantastic. By this time I could see from the weather map, it was snowing in the Rockies. The road through Glacier Park (Highway to the Sun) would be closed when I got back so I didn't plan to go back.

I got an honorable mention but still that was good. The Golden Quill awards media types, professionals. We went with the Health and Fitness folks and met some of the local TV stars. It was great fun.

Chapter XLI

CALIFORNIA

yet again

"Always be sincere. Even when you don't mean it"
Grip-it can cooler

Later, Helen called from California and said that there would be a final reunion of all who could make it at San Diego. So I went and there was John Olnes, Helen, the other John, Regina, and Ole. Six of the original 20 some. Not bad. Ole sprang for a small party with the money that he was still carrying from the sale of the tee shirts and we shared our best stories. The far and away winner was John Olnes.

John and Cynthia Olnes wanted to bike through Poland. They became nervous about biking there and rode a train into Warsaw. Warsaw like most European cities started out as a destination for a bunch of different rail lines. Rail lines terminate all over and are not necessarily connected. It can be very confusing to get around. Especially when you don't know the language. As they neared the city, they decided to detrain in the suburbs. Cynthia jumped down to be with the bike and gear. The train started to move so John went off in the train with the two bikes and Cynthia s left at Station A. At the next station, B, John gets one bike down and chains it to a fence and just in time jumps back on the train to be with the second bike as it goes off with the train. At station C, John and the second bike get off the train. He takes the bike down the steps and through the underground passage to the other, outgoing, side. He is at station C on the outgoing side. He gets on the first outgoing train with the bike and gets off at station B, chains that bike to the fence and goes under the tracks again to unchain the other bike and bring it under the tracks to the outgoing bike. He now has two bikes, at station B (outgoing). and no Cynthia. At station B, he enlists the help of a non-English speaking railroad fellow for the next outgoing train. The two of them get the two bikes and John on the train at Station B. At station A, John throws the wretched bikes off the train, locks them to a fence and goes off in search of Cynthia who has left the station. After a while he finds her calmly eating at a restaurant. Her comment would be a suitable ending to the entire World Wander tour:

"I knew you could manage," she said.